The New
IRIS SYRETT
Cookery Book

The New
IRIS SYRETT
Cookery Book

Herbert Lees & Mary Lovell

FABER & FABER
3 Queen Square
London

First published in 1973
by Faber & Faber Limited
3 Queen Square London WC1
Printed in Great Britain by
Western Printing Services Ltd, Bristol

ISBN 0 571 09613 1

Contents

List of Plates

(Between pages 208 and 209)

INTRODUCTION

The writers make no apology for the title of this book. From the time of the completion of the first book, Iris Syrett was working on the second, with our close collaboration. Most of the recipes which appear here were prepared by her. On her death in 1964 she left the uncompleted manuscript, and this we have tried to complete as she would have wished.

We had hoped to be able to produce the book much earlier but many things have made this impossible. Not least the necessity to move the Tante Marie School of Cookery, which Iris Syrett founded, from its original premises over a shop to its present home in a delightful Victorian 'residence' in Carlton Road, Woking. Moving the school made any other work impossible for almost two years. By this time metrication reared its ugly head. It is unlikely that anyone who is already a housewife will bother to use metric weights in her kitchen, but the rising generation is already being taught metric weights and measures. For this reason we have included them in this volume. This meant rewriting and testing the whole book when it was almost finished, and another eighteen months passed. Fortunately the delay has brought some advantages, for the recipes have been well tried and tested in the school. Some other recipes have been added.

The reader will find that the quantities of ingredients are set out with the metric on the left and the avoirdupois on the right. These must be used independently and no attempt made to mix them. Supposing some time in the future we have butter in 250 gramme packs, this must not be used instead of the present ½ pound pack.

Some basic mixtures and methods have been taken without alteration from The Iris Syrett Cookery Book. This is because we do not feel able to improve on the original version. We thought it essential that this book be complete in its own right so that anyone buying it would be able to use it without reference to any other volume.

In writing this introduction, it is impossible not to come back again and again to the fact that the Tante Marie School of Cookery was able to withstand the blow of the death of Iris Syrett. This was really due to the faith and single mindedness of Wendy Majerowicz who worked with Iris for seven years and succeeded her as Principal. She has carried on the spirit of the school to such effect that it has not only survived, but increased and prospered.

INTRODUCTION

We hope that anyone who uses this book will find enjoyment in it. There is no art that we can think of which enables one to achieve something in so little time, with such a small effort and which brings pleasure alike to the giver and the receiver.

METRIC EQUIVALENTS

The equivalent for 1 oz. is given below as 30 g. It is, in fact 28.35 g. By multiplying 30 g. one multiplies the error which is probably insignificant up to about 6 oz., but could throw the recipes out of proportion above that. The conversions I have used are:

½ oz.	15 g.	6 oz.	170–180 g. (depending on the recipe)
1 oz.	30 g.	8 oz.	240–250 g. ,, ,, ,, ,,
2 oz.	60 g.	¾ lb.	350–360 g. ,, ,, ,, ,,
4 oz.	120 g.	1 lb.	460 g.–½ kg. ,, ,, ,, ,,
		1½ lb.	700–750 g. ,, ,, ,, ,,

In some cases it is more convenient to round off to the nearest kilo or half kilo, but this has been done only if it will not upset the proportions of the rest of the ingredients. (1 oz. is to 1 pint as 50 g. is to 1 l.). For this reason use **either** the metric **or** the imperial measures given in each recipe—do not mix the two.

LIQUID MEASURES

¼ pint	(1 gill)	1½ dl.	1 pint	6 dl.	
½ pint	(2 gills)	3 dl.	1½ pints	9 dl.	
¾ pint	(3 gills)	4½ dl.	1¾ pints	1 l.	
			2 pints	1 l. 1½ dl.	

The same applies here to rounding off to the nearest ½ dl.

TABLE OF COMPARATIVE OVEN TEMPERATURES

Fahrenheit	Celsius	Gas mark	Description of the oven
250	120	½	Very cool
275	135	1	Very cool
300	150	2	Very cool
325	165	3	Cool
350	180	4	Moderate
375	190	5	Fairly hot
400	200	6	Fairly hot
425	220	7	Hot
450	230	8	Very hot
475	245	9	Very hot

(The Celsius temperature has been approximated to the nearest 10°.) Oven temperatures are never 100% accurate!

STARS

* A simple and often quick recipe suitable for a beginner.

** A dish for the average cook with a good basic knowledge of cookery.

*** A more complicated dish requiring skill and probably taking some time to prepare.

Culinary Terms

ABATS   Offal, i.e. heart, liver, kidneys, brains, sweetbreads, tripe, etc.

AU GRATIN   A dish covered in sauce or breadcrumbs and sometimes a mixture of the former with cheese, browned in the top of a hot oven or under a red hot grill.

AU MAIGRE   Lenten or Fast dishes in France which are prepared without meat or meat stock.

BAIN-MARIE   A large pan usually square or oblong, but sometimes round, like a large saucepan, containing about 4–5 inches of boiling water into which sauces etc. can be placed in pans to keep hot. For dishes to be cooked in the oven in a bain-marie a meat roasting dish is commonly employed.

TO BARD OR BARDER   To tie fat bacon round the breast of poultry or game.

BASTE   To spoon over gravy or liquid.

BEIGNETS   Fritters.

BEURRE MANIÉ   Butter and flour worked to a smooth paste on a plate or board, used for thickening sauces and gravies.

BEURRE NOISETTE   Butter which has been cooked to a nutty brown colour.

BISQUE   A thickened soup made from shell fish.

BLANCH   (1) To place in boiling water.

(2) To place in cold water and bring to the boil.

(3) To place in boiling water to remove skins, e.g. almonds.

BOUCHÉES   Small cases made from puff pastry and filled with a savoury mixture, e.g. chicken, lobster, mushroom, etc.

BOUILLON   Stock.

BOUQUET GARNI   A sprig of parsley, thyme and a bayleaf tied together and used to flavour sauces, stews, fish dishes, etc. It must always be removed before serving. Some dishes call for additional herbs such as tarragon, fennel, etc.

BRAISE   A means of cooking meat, poultry, fish and some vegetables on a mirepoix with a little stock in a covered pan.

CANAPÉ   A small round or other shaped slice of bread either fresh, fried or toasted, used as a base for a savoury mixture and served as a savoury or an aperitif accompaniment.

COURT BOUILLON   Liquor for poaching fish made with vinegar and water to which has been added a bouquet garni and a slice of carrot, onion and seasoning.

CRÊPES   Pancakes.

CROQUETTES   Minced meat, poultry, fish or eggs, etc. coated in egg and breadcrumbs and fried in deep fat.

CROÛTE   Pastry. Alternatively a slice of bread toasted on which small game is roasted.

CROÛTONS   Small dice or other shapes of bread fried in butter and served as a garnish for soup, or in the latter case, as a garnish for savoury dishes.

DARIOLE   A small mould, as is used for castle puddings. Also used for risotto, etc. as garnishes for large dishes.

DÉGLACE   To emulsify the fat and the cooking liquor at the bottom of a pan by adding wine or brandy and sometimes stock.

DÉGRAISSE   To remove fat from the top of gravy or cooking liquor.

DUXELLE   A savoury mushroom mixture used as a farce.

ENTRÉE   A dish usually served before the main course but which is a complete dish in itself.

ENTREMETS   Dishes served as sweets.

ÉSCALOPE   A thin slice of meat or fish.

FARCE   Forcemeat, or stuffing for meat, fish, vegetables, crêpes, etc.

FÉCULE   Arrowroot.

FÉCULE DE BLÉ   Cornflour.

FÉCULE DE POMMES DE TERRE   Potato flour.

FLAME   (1) To pour in spirit to a dish and set alight to it.

(2) To singe – as in poultry.

FLAN   An open pastry tart cooked in a flan ring.

FLEURONS   Crescents of puff pastry used as a garnish.

FRAPPÉ   Iced.

FUMET   Liquor in which fish is poached and which has been reduced.

GALETTE   A round flat cake.

GARNISH OR GARNITURE   Additional vegetables, croûtons, etc. used to give extra colour and flavour to savoury dishes.

GLACE DE VIANDE   Stock very much reduced, used for coating meat and game, etc. Sometimes for flavouring and colouring sauces.

TO GLAZE   To brush with syrup, melted jam or glace de viande.

GRATINER   To brown the top of a dish in the top of a hot oven or under the grill. See Au Gratin.

HACHIS   A minced meat mixture.

HACHOIR   A curved chopper, usually with a handle at each end.

HORS D'ŒUVRE   Sometimes a single dish served at the beginning of a meal, more often a variety of small dishes composed of vegetables, fish, egg, fruit, etc.

JULIENNE   Vegetables cut into match-like sticks.
JUS   Gravy.
JUS LIÉ   Thickened gravy.

TO LARD   To thread pieces of bacon fat through meat, poultry and game deficient in fat.
LARDON   A small strip of bacon.
LIAISON   A binding or thickening used for sauces, gravies, etc. added at the end of the cooking. Can be egg yolks, cream, beurre manié, fécule or blood.

MACÉDOINE   A mixture of various vegetables cut into dice. Sometimes fruit similarly cut.
MACERATE   To soak fruits, etc., in wine, spirit, liqueur or syrup.
MARINADE   A type of pickling mixture made with wine, wine vinegar, vinegar, spices, etc., in which meat, venison and fish are steeped before cooking to give a good flavour and render more tender. The marinade is usually used in the finished dish.
MARMITE   A French earthenware stock pot or small individual soup cup.
MÉDAILLONS   (1) Slices of ham or tongue cut to an oval or round shape. (2) Small biscuits or thin chocolate rounds.
MIREPOIX   The foundation of diced vegetables for a braised dish.

NAPPER   To coat with a sauce or aspic or glaze.
NOISETTES   Pieces of lamb or mutton cut from the best end, shaped as a cutlet without a bone.

PANACHÉ   A mixture of colours, flavours.
PANADA   A thick mixture of butter, flour and liquid used in the making of soufflés, croquettes, etc.
PAPILLOTES   Paper cases in which individual portions of meat or fish are cooked and served.
PAPRIKA   A blend of Hungarian peppers used in goulash, etc. and for decoration.
PASS   (1) To strain through a strainer.
(2) To warm through in butter.
(3) To dip in seasoned flour.
PÂTE   A basic mixture used in pastries, cakes, batters, meringues, etc.
PÂTÉ   A fine savoury mixture made from liver, pork, game, etc.
PÂTISSERIE   Sweet pastries and cakes as sold in French bakeries and cake shops.
PAUPIETTES   Fish or meat, spread with a farce, rolled up and tied with fine string which is removed after cooking.
POT-AU-FEU   Famous French broth.
PRALINE   A toffee-like mixture made with sugar and nuts, powdered and used in flavouring.
PURÉE   Any meat, fish, vegetable or fruit mixture sieved.

QUENELLES A very finely minced and sieved mixture made from fish or white meat to which is added white of egg and a panada. Poached and served with a sauce, or as a garnish.

RAGOÛT A stew.

RAVIOLI A thin noodle paste filled with a savoury mixture, cut into squares. Poached and served with a sauce.

RECHAUFFÉ A re-heated dish.

REDUCE To place a liquid over a good heat and reduce by evaporation, thereby intensifying the flavour.

REFRESH To pour cold water over vegetables after they are cooked or blanched, to preserve the colour. They must be warmed through again, if they are to be served hot.

REPÈRE A flour and water paste used to seal lids of pans to ensure long and slow cooking.

RISSOLE A mixture of minced meat, etc. enclosed in thin pastry and fried in deep fat.

RISSOLER To toss in hot butter until brown.

ROUX Melted butter to which has been added flour – the basis of a sauce.

SALAMANDER An iron used red hot to brown the surface of dishes. The modern equivalent is a grill.

SALPICON Dice or strips of meat or fish or poultry with mushrooms, truffles, etc. liaised with a sauce.

SAUTER To cook in hot butter or oil in a sauté pan.

SLAKE To mix flour or arrowroot with cold water to form a thin paste to add to soups, sauces, gravies, etc.

TAMMY A cloth through which sauces, etc. are pressed.

TIMBALE A dish which is either cooked in a special moud or is served piled up.

TOMBER DES LEGUMES Vegetables cooked in water and butter until all the water has evaporated and the vegetables are covered in a buttery glaze. See Carottes Vichy, etc.

TOURNEDOS A slice of fillet of beef.

TO TURN (1) To roll and fold as in pastry.

(2) To shape vegetables to olive shapes.

(3) To peel an olive in a spiral fashion, leaving the stone and allowing the olive to spring back into shape.

(4) To cut a decorative design on mushrooms.

VOL-AU-VENT A case made of puff pastry similar to a bouchée but much larger.

ZEST (1) The grated rind of an orange or lemon.

(2) Strips of the above, peeled without any of the white pith.

Useful Information

BEURRE MANIÉ

Butter and flour worked on a plate to a smooth paste using a fork or the blade of a small knife. The proportion of butter should be slightly in excess of that of flour to facilitate easy mixing, e.g. 20 g. (¾ oz.) flour to 30 g. (1 oz.) butter. This paste can then be added to the liquid which requires thickening (i.e. sauces, soups, gravies, fish liquors, etc.).

When it is only a liquid it can be whisked with a sauce whisk. Where there are meats or vegetables in the liquid it is better to stir gently with a wooden spoon. In all cases the liquid must be brought to the boil again to allow the flour to cook.

CARAMEL

Ingredients:

120 g. sugar (4 oz.)   1½ dl. water (1 gill)

Method: Use a small strong pan. Put in the sugar with the water and stir gently with a wooden spoon over a low heat until the sugar has dissolved. Stop stirring, remove the spoon, and raise the heat. Allow it to boil rapidly. During this time brush down the inside of the pan to the level of the syrup with a pastry brush dipped in cold water. This will dissolve the crystals formed as the syrup splutters. Continue to boil until the syrup reaches the required colour. 380–400° F. (193–204° C.).

CARAMEL FOR COLOURING

Proceed with the quantities and method as for Caramel. Continue to cook until the syrup reaches a dark mahogany colour. Remove from the heat and carefully pour in 1½ dl. (1 gill) boiling water. Return to the heat to allow the caramel to dissolve. Cool and store in bottles.

This caramel is useful for adding colour to meat dishes, sauces, gravies, etc.

CHICKEN STOCK

To make a well flavoured stock in which to cook a chicken, put the chicken into a large pan, cover with cold water and add 2 carrots cut into four, an onion stuck with a clove, a bouquet garni, 4–5 peppercorns, a little coarse salt and, if liked, a strip of lemon peel. If available a leek cut up and a stick of celery can be included.

This stock can then be used as the basis of a sauce as in Poulet à la Vigneronne (see page 180) or to cook rice as in Poulet à la Hongroise (see page 179).

CLARIFICATION OF ASPIC FOR MEAT

Ingredients:

250 g. shin of beef (½ lb.)
1 l. veal stock (2 pints)
1 medium sized leek
1 medium sized carrot
1 branch of celery, or celery salt
1 tomato or peel and pips of
   tomato or 1 tablespoon of
   tinned tomatoes

1½ dl. water (1 gill)
4 whites of egg
30 g. leaf gelatine (1 oz.)
wine or sherry to flavour
caramel to colour
seasoning

Method: Put the gelatine to soak in cold water. Slice the beef thinly. Place it with the stock in a saucepan and deepen the colour with caramel if necessary. Put the whites in a basin with the water and whisk them lightly. Dice the vegetables very finely indeed and add them to the whites together with the tomato, plenty of seasoning and the softened gelatine. Put all the ingredients in the saucepan and bring slowly to the boil, stirring gently until the liquid begins to cloud. Stop stirring and allow it to boil very gently for 5–10 minutes. Strain it carefully through a clean damp cloth into a perfectly clean dry bowl. Allow it to cool, and finally add the wine or sherry to taste. Use as required.

CLARIFICATION OF ASPIC FOR FISH

Ingredients:

1 l. court bouillon (2 pints) (see
   page 18)
30 g. leaf gelatine (1 oz.)
1½ dl. dry white wine (¼ pint)

1 onion
4 whites of egg
fresh herbs
seasoning

Method: Make exactly as for meat aspic, but use fennel and tarragon if possible for flavouring the court bouillon.

GENERAL COMMENTS ON THE PREPARATION OF ASPIC

A well flavoured and seasoned stock is important, otherwise the jelly is uninteresting in flavour. It should be sufficiently dark to be appetising. Meat aspic is generally darker than fish aspic. The gelatine should be thoroughly softened before mixing with the stock, so that it dissolves almost immediately. The vegetables should be finely and evenly diced, so as to expose the maximum surface thus giving more flavour. It is not necessary to whisk the whites of egg more than a little. The water simply breaks the whites up, so that they become effective throughout the whole mixture. Overwhisked whites do not clarify.

GENERAL COMMENTS ON THE METHODS FOR ASPIC

It is important to stir continuously, moving the spoon over the bottom of the pan, so as to prevent the whites and gelatine from sticking.

The slower the heating process, the better, so as to ensure thorough clarification.

Once the egg white has started to coagulate and the liquid as a result looks cloudy, stirring should stop. It can then be boiled gently for 5–10 minutes, until the liquid below the scum is clear. It is important to boil for a sufficiently long time to cook the egg white.

Place a clean damp cloth over a scrupulously clean bowl. Ladle the scum off the top on to the cloth. This will act as an additional filter. Spoon or pour the liquid very gently, allowing it to drip through the cloth. At no time must the cloth be squeezed, as this will at once make the aspic cloudy.

When all the liquid has been strained, lift the cloth very carefully from the top of the bowl. Taste, and add the wine or sherry when the liquid is cool. It is advisable not to season after the straining, as pepper will show and salt will tend to diminish the brilliancy.

Aspic for coating is used when just on the point of setting. Chopped aspic is sometimes used as a garnish. In this case it must be completely set before being chopped.

Aspic jelly should be used within 12 hours of making, as it deteriorates very rapidly.

COURT BOUILLON

This is a stock used for cooking fish, usually when it is poached, either on the top of the stove or, as in many of the recipes, in the oven. The usual form when cooking large pieces or whole fish is to make up a liquid of roughly these proportions:

to 3 l. (6 pints) water allow 1½ dl. (1 gill) vinegar (this can be wine or tarragon vinegar) and to give a more delicate flavour add:
125 g. (4 oz.) onion 250 g. (8 oz.) carrots, sliced thinly, 2 finely chopped shallots, a good bouquet garni (containing parsley, thyme, tarragon and a bayleaf) and sometimes 1–2 cloves and plenty of salt and black peppercorns for seasoning.

When cooking whole fish, this stock is made first, allowing it to simmer for 45 minutes. Then it is left to get cold. The fish is then placed in the cold liquid and brought to barely simmering point. It must not boil or cook too rapidly. When the fish is to be served cold, it should be allowed to cool in the court bouillon. This will keep it moist and it will retain the maximum amount of flavour.

For small fillets of fish to be poached in the oven, dry white wine or wine and water or sometimes dry cider, are used in place of the water and vinegar. It is advisable to pour the wine over the fish first, and then according to the depth of the dish add sufficient cold water just to cover it. Sliced carrots, onion and shallot are added as well as a bouquet garni. This is then well seasoned with salt and black pepper. After the fish is cooked the liquor can be strained off and used as a basis for a sauce to serve with the fish. Should it not be possible to use wine or cider, vinegar can be substituted, but should only be added in the proportion of 3 tablespoons vinegar to every litre (2 pints) of water.

COOKING OF HARICOT BEANS

Beans should be put to soak in lukewarm water and left overnight. As far as possible they should be stirred from time to time so as to allow the water to circulate round them. The next day the water should be drained off. A pan should be filled with plenty of warm water to which is added a bouquet garni, a carrot, an onion cut in half and salt. Add the beans. Bring it slowly to simmering point and simmer for $1-1\frac{1}{2}$ hours, filling up with more boiling water as required. Test by tasting – that is actually biting into the bean to see if it is sufficiently cooked. Escoffier recommends that the beans should only be put into cold water, brought slowly to the boil, drained and the process repeated. Then the beans should be allowed to simmer for 2–3 hours. Some readers may find this a more convenient way. One thing is certain: the beans should be cooked very, very slowly.

TO STONE OLIVES

Green olives are easier to stone than black ones which are more spongy. Hold the olive in one hand and using a small sharp knife begin to pare the olive in a spiral fashion from the top to the bottom (as one would peel an apple). Keep the blade of the knife firmly on the stone. When the olive is completely pared and the stone removed the olive should spring back again into shape.

TO TURN VEGETABLES

This means that root vegetables are peeled and then trimmed to neat shapes, actually 'turned' with a small sharp knife. The usual size is that of a large olive. Carrots are sometimes 'turned' to resemble small young ones. The trimmings need not be wasted but can be used for making soups.

CROÛTONS

Croûtons of bread are used as a garnish for soups or savoury dishes. When they are to be used for soups they must be very small indeed. Croûtons as a garnish for dishes such as Bœuf Marius (see page 120) can be cut into triangles, crescents or heart shapes using a heart shaped cutter. The bread in all cases should be stale. The larger croûtons can be fried in deep fat, but a better flavour is obtained by frying them in butter, or if possible clarified butter. Heat the butter and put in only a few croûtons at a time. Allow the underside to brown before turning them to brown on the other side. Always drain them on plain kitchen or tissue paper before using.

Croûtons for soup should be served on a paper doyley. The croûtons should be a pale gold and not a dark brown colour.

FISH STOCK

Ingredients:

½ kg. sole bones (1 lb.)
1 sliced onion
1 sliced carrot

bouquet garni
1½ l. water (3 pints)
1½ dl. dry white wine (1 gill)
seasoning

Method: Wash the bones thoroughly. Put them into a deep pan with all the other ingredients. Bring them up to the boil slowly, then lower the heat and simmer, uncovered, for 30 minutes. Strain and use as required.

FRIED PARSLEY

It is important to see that the parsley is absolutely dry. If it has to be washed, it must be thoroughly dried before frying, otherwise it will cause the fat to splutter, which is dangerous.

Select good sized sprigs and using a frying basket, lower them carefully into very hot, deep fat. It will make a sizzling noise for the first few seconds. As soon as this stops, remove the basket and drain the parsley on white kitchen paper. If the parsley is fried for too long, it will lose its colour.

FRITTER BATTER

Ingredients:

60 g. plain flour (2 oz.)
1 dl. tepid water (½ gill)

1 white of egg
1 dessertspoon olive oil
pinch of salt

Method: Sieve the flour and salt into a basin. Make a well in the centre. Add the oil and water gradually, stirring the flour in from the sides of the bowl. Mix it smoothly. Beat well and put it aside in a cool place for ½ hour. Just before using, whisk the white very lightly and fold in gently.

Comment: This batter must be light and thick enough to coat the food without running off. It should be crisp when fried. Oil helps to make it crisp and the whisked white of an egg gives lightness to the mixture.

GARLIC

It is said about garlic that the further north you go, the stronger the flavour. Garlic, although frequently chopped in France, is almost always crushed in England, using a little coarse salt to help to reduce it to a pulp. Having first been skinned, it should be roughly chopped, then mixed with the salt and crushed under the blade of a large kitchen knife. It is inadvisable to fry it as it tends to become very bitter.

On many occasions one will find whole cloves of garlic used as a garnish for roast, or an integral part of a ragoût, when large numbers of cloves of garlic are added.

GLACE DE VIANDE

This is made from brown stock. Remove all trace of fat from the stock, then place it in a large, perfectly clean, pan and boil rapidly without a lid. Skim it from time to time. When it begins to form a thin, syrupy consistency, start to stir it with a clean metal spoon and continue stirring until it is of the consistency of treacle. This can be poured into a small jar, well covered, and kept in the refrigerator for two or three weeks.

MARMELADE DE POMMES OR APPLE MARMALADE

Select sound apples. Wipe them with a clean cloth. Cut them into quarters, but do not peel or core them. Put them in a preserving pan with sufficient water to cover. Cook slowly over a low heat, stirring frequently, until they are reduced to a thick purée. Pass this purée through a sieve or vegetable mill.

Wash the pan they were cooked in. Measure the pulp and to each pint of pulp allow one pound of sugar. Put the pulp and sugar into the clean pan and cook, stirring continuously, until it is of a jam-like consistency. It should be so thick that when a wooden spoon is drawn across the base of the pan, it leaves a 'channel' which does not close up again.

This marmelade de pommes can be potted and kept in the same way as jams and jellies.

It is advisable to wear long sleeves during the stirring after the sugar has been added, as the pulp tends to splutter and can be painful.

When a small quantity of marmelade de pommes is required for a particular recipe, it is useful to remember that 1 kg. (2 lbs.) apples makes approximately 500 g. (1 pint) pulp. If half a kg. (1 lb.) of sugar is added to this quantity of pulp, a half a kg. (1 lb.) of marmelade will result.

MUSHROOM LIQUOR

Ingredients:

125 g. mushrooms (4 oz.)

30 g. butter (1 oz.)

juice of ½ lemon

a little water

seasoning

Method: Wipe the mushrooms well on a clean cloth. Cut them into quarters. Melt the butter in a pan over a gentle heat, then add the mushrooms, lemon juice, water and seasoning. Cover the pan with greaseproof paper and the lid and stew them gently for 5–7 minutes. Drain off the liquor and use as required.

Comment: Mushroom liquor is frequently used in flavouring sauces. The mushrooms can often be used as a garnish.

NOTES ON STOCK

Much has been written, and still is written, about stock in any general cookery book, so much so that I feel I should include some general observations in this book.

Many households feel that keeping a stock pot these days is rather too much of a good thing, and this is a point of view which I perfectly understand. There are extremely good bouillon cubes on the market which make excellent substitutes for stock and for those who have not the time, these are the answer. However, for others who may wish to make their own stock, the following points may be helpful.

Ideally a stock pot with a tap is the best, but few readers will possess this type of stock pot in small households, so that failing that, a deep heavy pan should be used. In France it is frequently made of earthenware, which is good on the solid fuel type of stove but not so good on a gas or electric cooker. Copper, lined with tin, is also useful, but failing both these, cast iron or enamel can be used quite well.

To prevent the stock from being over greasy, bones without marrow should be used. These should be blanched in boiling water before being used and should previously have been sawn or broken into convenient sized pieces for the pot in which they are to be used. Should a brown stock be required, to use as a basis for a brown sauce, the bones should be placed in a roasting pan and put fairly high up in a hot oven, gas mark 8 or 450° F. (230° C.) to get properly brown before being boiled. A carrot and an onion, roughly sliced, can be added to the roasting pan and these browned also to give extra colour.

Vegetables are used in a stock pot to give extra flavour and a bouquet garni should be included. The following vegetables can be included to advantage – carrots, onions, leeks and celery. Strong flavoured vegetables, such as turnips, swedes, parsnips, should not be used, as their flavour is apt to predominate. Green vegetables, cabbages, cauliflowers, lettuces, spinach, etc. should never be included, nor should potatoes, which break up easily and produce a cloudy and unpleasant stock. Cooked bones should not be mixed with raw bones and it is deplorable to add the remains of sauces, etc.

Place the bones in the stock pot, cover with cold water and bring slowly up to simmering point. This must be done carefully and should take about half an hour. Remove the scum which forms on the surface. Add the vegetables, cut into quarters and bring again to simmering point. Then add the bouquet garni tied with a piece of thin kitchen string. Cover with the lid and cook at simmering point for 4–5 hours. Strain off the liquid and use as needed. A richer stock can be made by adding a piece of shin of beef; sometimes this is left whole and sometimes it is shredded as for Consommé. If the latter practice is adopted, the stock should not be simmered for too long as this tends to make it cloudy. It is important only to remove the white scum from the stock pot and not the brown – this is coagulated protein and will act as a filter when the stock is strained.

If the stock is not to be used the day it has been made, it can stay in the stock pot, but should be brought to boiling point the next day. Vegetables should not be left in the stock pot as these tend to go sour very quickly.

Those who are fortunate in having a freezer can preserve stock in convenient sized containers for future use. Less space is occupied if the stock is well reduced in volume prior to freezing.

PASTRY FLEURONS

These are used as a garnish for fish and meat dishes and can be made from the trimmings of puff or flaky pastry.

Roll out the pastry to about $\frac{1}{2}$ cm. ($\frac{1}{4}$–$\frac{1}{3}$ inch) thick. Stamp into half moons using a 5–7 cm. (2–2$\frac{1}{2}$ inch) round, fluted cutter. Place them on a baking sheet and cook as usual.

REPÈRE PASTE

A stiff paste of flour and water which is used to seal the lid to the pan when braising foods, thereby reducing loss of liquid by evaporation. Repère paste is also used to cover hams, small game birds etc. in roasting.

SUGAR SYRUP

Used for poaching fruit, softening fondant, etc.

The proportion of sugar to water is usually 200 g. to $\frac{1}{2}$ l. ($\frac{1}{2}$ lb to 1 pint) water, unless otherwise stated. Very often a vanilla pod is added to the pan whilst the syrup is being prepared. If the syrup is to be flavoured with liqueur or rum, this should be added after the syrup has been made. For poaching fruit, the sugar is dissolved in the pan with the water and the fruit is then added.

THE PREPARATION OF SOUFFLÉ DISHES AND THE COOKING OF SOUFFLÉS

Most soufflés are baked in white china special soufflé dishes or fireproof glass ones. In all cases the dish should be well greased with *butter*. When making savoury soufflés, the dish is dusted out after buttering, with white breadcrumbs or a mixture of breadcrumbs and finely grated cheese, such as Parmesan. Sweet soufflés are baked in dishes dusted out with sugar. Although some cooks advocate tying a piece of greaseproof paper in a band round round the outside of the soufflé dish, this should not really be necessary provided the whites have been thoroughly folded in and the mixture is of an even consistency. If the whites are not sufficiently folded in, pockets of egg white will remain and this will cause the soufflé to rise unevenly.

The prepared dish should be filled two-thirds full, then using the thumb, run round the inside edge of the soufflé dish making a small indenture all round. Smooth off the top evenly. Place it a little below the middle of a fairly hot oven, gas mark 5–6 or 375–400° F. (190–200° C.). Allow approximately half an hour for cooking. If the surface tends to become too brown in the last 10 minutes, lay a piece of buttered grease-proof paper on the top. No soufflé should be allowed to stand after it has been cooked – it must be eaten at once.

In estimating the quantity required for a dinner party, it should be borne in mind that after two or three people have been served from the dish, the soufflé will have shrunk visibly and is often unappetising in appearance, so that it is probably better to make two smaller ones, rather than one large one.

TO BOIL RICE

Wash the rice well under the cold tap, until the water is quite clear. This will remove the starchy covering on the outside of the rice grains. Rice which is cooked without being previously rinsed tends to become sticky and to clog together.

Always use a very large pan for boiling rice, bearing in mind that the rice will swell considerably during cooking. Allow approximately 60 g. (2 oz.) rice per person, depending on the nature of the dish, and place it in boiling water, allowing approximately ½ l. (1 pint) for 30 g. (1 oz.) rice. Add salt as required. As the rice is added the water will reduce in temperature. Bring it to the boil again and allow it to boil rapidly for 12–15 minutes. The actual cooking time depends on the quality of the rice, but after 12 minutes cooking, it is a wise plan to bite a grain of rice to see if it is tender. This is the best test.

Once the rice is cooked, remove it from the pan and place it in a colander. Allow the hot tap to run over it. Shake the colander well to dispose of the excess moisture. Place the rice in a large, flat, buttered dish. Cover with a piece of thickly buttered greaseproof paper or buttered aluminium foil and put it in a fairly cool oven, gas mark 1–2 or 275–300° F. (135–150° C.) until it is required. In this way the rice will keep moist and the grains separate.

Comment: Savoury and curry dishes are usually made with Patna rice, whilst sweet dishes are usually made with Carolina rice.

TO BONE A SHOULDER OF LAMB OR MUTTON

Most butchers will bone a shoulder for you if they are asked, but should this not be possible, the following instructions may prove helpful.

Take a small, sharp kitchen knife and beginning at the shank bone end, slit the meat at the side of the bone and then continue to work, in short strokes, until the knuckle is felt. Now ease the meat over the knuckle and loosen the meat all round as far as possible. Then starting at the opposite end of the meat, keeping the knife on the blade bone, scrape the meat away from the bone and continue in this way until the ball and socket joint is reached in the centre of the meat, cut round this carefully. Work with the fingers, loosening this bone until it will be found that it can be pulled out quite easily. The meat is now like a large, flat pocket without any bone. Spread the farce or stuffing in this, fold together carefully and sew up with a trussing needle and thick thread.

TO BROWN NUTS

Almonds should be blanched in boiling water to remove their skins before being browned. Hazel nuts can be browned first and then rubbed in a clean cloth to remove the skins.

Put the nuts on a clean baking sheet in the top of a fairly hot oven, gas mark 6 or 400° F. (200° C.) and look at them every few minutes – they burn quickly.

TO POACH EGGS

Only perfectly fresh eggs should be used.

Fill a shallow pan with boiling water and add a little vinegar. Break the eggs on to a saucer or in a cup if preferred. Take a whisk and make a whirlpool in the water. Slide the egg into this, let the water barely reach boiling point. Draw the pan aside from the heat and spoon the water over the egg all the time, thus preserving an oval shape and so that the yolk is completely enclosed in the white. Allow approximately 3 minutes for poaching. Lift the eggs out of the pan with a draining spoon and place them in hot water if they are to be served hot, or in cold water if they are required cold. Trim to shape.

DEEP FAT FOR FRYING

The fat used for deep frying is variable – many people use pure lard, or clarified dripping, although there is a modern tendency to use oil now – this being unsaturated.

After each use, the fat or oil should be carefully strained when cool to remove small particles of food and coatings. If these are allowed to remain they eventually burn and form an unpleasant speckled finish to food being fried.

To test for frying temperature, a small cube of bread lowered into the fat will sizzle and brown in a few seconds. A more reliable method is to use a thermometer; it should be borne in mind that rechauffé foods such at Œufs en Côtelettes would need a higher temperature for heating them through than Pommes de Terre Pont Neuf, which require a slightly lower temperature to cook the raw food thoroughly.

The normal frying temperature ranges from 350° F. (175° C.) to 380° F. (193° C.).

There are a number of thermostatically controlled deep frying pans available which make the process more foolproof and safe.

It is wise to have available a baking sheet large enough to cover the pan completely should the fat become over heated and catch alight. Turn off the heat. If necessary cover with a thick rug or fire blanket.

TO RENDER DOWN FAT

Remove the skin and gristle from the fat. Cut it into small cubes and place them in an uncovered roasting tin. Allow them to melt slowly in a cool oven. Strain and clarify before using.

TO CLARIFY FAT

Put the fat into a large strong pan, cover with cold water and bring slowly to the boil, keeping the pan uncovered. Allow to simmer for 20–30 minutes. Cool and pour it into a large bowl. Put it aside for 24 hours in a cold place.

It will then be seen that the fat is set on the top of the water. Lift the fat off carefully and scrape off the impurities which will be found adhering to the under side. Put the fat back again into a clean pan and heat it through gently until it is free from moisture and does not splutter any more. Fat from deep fat pans and dripping from the bottom of roasting tins should be treated in this manner.

TO CLARIFY BUTTER

Salt butter can be clarified to remove the salt. Put the butter into a small pan and heat it gently. As soon as the scum rises to the top, remove it with a spoon. Strain the butter off through a muslin, leaving as much of the sediment behind as possible. Cool slightly, when any remaining sediment will be found to rest in the hollow of the bottom of the bowl. Pour carefully into a clean bowl.

TO TURN MUSHROOMS

Some recipes call for 'turned' mushrooms. This is done by holding the mushroom securely in one hand and with the point of a knife held in the other hand, make a series of curved 'spokes' radiating from the centre of the mushroom towards the edge. This takes practice to give a neat effect, but the finished appearance to the mushrooms, for a garnish, is greatly improved.

VANILLA SUGAR

By using a blender or liquidiser, perfectly satisfactory vanilla sugar can be made. One vanilla pod will perfume 500 g. (1 lb.) granulated sugar. Chop the vanilla pod roughly before putting it in the blender with the sugar. Blend until it is well pulverised. Pass the mixture through a sieve. Store it in an airtight container.

VANILLA PODS

These are usually sold in glass tubes and are used for flavouring liquids. After use they should be washed and put to dry out thoroughly before being put back in their cases. They can be used several times in this way. If they are not perfectly dry, they will rapidly go mouldy. A vanilla pod kept in a sugar jar will give a good flavour of vanilla, although it is not as strong as vanilla sugar.

VANILLA ESSENCE

Most vanilla essence obtained in Britain is an artificial substitute and is not recommended. Small packets of vanilla sugar are often flavoured with this artificial essence (vanillin) and are not recommended either.

Sauces

The tendency in Britain has too often been to think of a sauce as an afterthought; something which can either be prepared time permitting, or else served in a bottle at the table, regardless as to whether it is complementary to the food or not.

A sauce should be considered an essential part of a dish and can very often transform something ordinary into something quite delicious. It can be quite simple, such as lemon juice added to the butter in which fish has been fried. Alternatively, the sauce may be elaborate in preparation, more so in fact than the food which it is to accompany, e.g. Poached Turbot with Sauce Hollandaise.

A sauce enhances the dish with which it is served either as a contrast of flavour, colour and texture (e.g. Sauce Béarnaise or Beurre Maître d'Hôtel with a fillet steak), or as a complement in flavour (Sauce Nantua with Filets de Sole or Quenelles de Poisson). By stimulating the appetite, a sauce aids digestion as well as increasing the nutritive value of the meal.

SAVOURY SAUCES

SWEET SAUCES

ROUX SAUCES

These are basic sauces made from fat, flour, and liquid. There are three kinds of roux – brown for sauces such as demi-glace, pale roux which can be used in a veloutée sauce and a white roux for white sauces such as Sauce Béchamel (sometimes spelt Béchamelle). The colour of the roux depends on the length of time it is cooked. In all cases the fat must first be melted over a low heat, then the pan should be removed from the heat and the flour mixed in perfectly. The pan is now returned to the heat and the roux (i.e. the fat and flour) is cooked, stirring all the time, for 2–3 minutes in the case of a white roux and longer for a fawn or brown roux. When making a white roux, it will be noted that at the end of 2–3 minutes cooking, the mixture of flour and fat will haved change texture and taken on a honeycomb aspect. Whereas butter is used in white and frequently pale or blond roux, good dripping is usually used in making a brown roux. The length of time taken in making a brown roux is not easy to gauge and it depends on the heat. It is advisable to cook it extremely slowly, whilst keeping it stirred all the time. If it is cooked too quickly the flour will become scorched and the fat will separate out from the flour – thus making the sauce greasy. A bitter flavour results also, which no seasoning will correct. A pale roux should not be cooked longer than will just faintly colour it. Liquid in the form of milk for white sauces, stock for veloutée and brown stock for demi-glace sauces, etc., should be added gradually, stirring meanwhile. The liquid can be cold or hot, but it is not advisable to add boiling liquid, as this tends to thicken too quickly and is difficult to mix smoothly. After the liquid is added to a white or veloutée sauce, it must be brought slowly to boiling point and boiled for *AT LEAST* five minutes to cook the flour. In some cases it may be found necessary to cook it for a longer period, say 7–10 minutes, depending on how thoroughly the original roux was cooked. It is better to taste the sauce, rather than judge by the actual time. This is an important point which must be adhered to when preparing a sauce. In the case of brown sauces, the length of cooking is considerably longer.

Should the sauce become lumpy during cooking, whisk lightly with a sauce whisk and the lumps will disappear. Do not whisk a white sauce for a prolonged time if it is being cooked in an aluminium pan – the whisk is liable to take the surface off the aluminium, thereby resulting in a grey sauce – a few brisk whisks should be sufficient. The whisking of sauces is better than sieving to dispel lumps. In the latter case the proportions of fat to flour are distorted and the fact of pressing the flour lumps through a sieve merely gives you a sauce with finer lumps, but does not correct the consistency.

Sauces with a roux base are made with different proportions of fat, flour and liquid according to their purpose. In most recipes the fat and flour are of equal quantities, but in some cases where a richer sauce is required, the proportion of fat to flour is increased. Below are the generally recognised quantities for the various sauces:

Pouring	*Coating or 'Napping'*	*Panada or Binding*
20 g. (¾ oz.) fat	30 g. (1 oz.) fat	60 g. (2 oz.) fat
20 g. (¾ oz.) flour	30 g. (1 oz.) flour	60 g. (2 oz.) flour
3 dl. (½ pint) liquid	3 dl. (½ pint) liquid	3 dl. (½ pint) liquid

Sauce Béchamel as made in France is made with milk and seasoned only with pepper, salt and a pinch of nutmeg. In England it is sometimes made with milk, in which have been infused sliced vegetables, such as carrot, onion and bouquet garni.

LIAISONS

Liaisons are thickening agents added to sauces. To enrich them beaten yolks or whole eggs and cream or creamy milk are employed. In these instances the eggs are whisked in a bowl, with or without the cream as the case may be. A little of the hot sauce is then added and the whole whisked again and strained into the main sauce, which is then thickened over a low heat – keeping stirred all the time and not allowing it to boil or the sauce will become too hot and curdle. Other thickening methods are the addition of Beurre Manié (see page 16) or arrowroot, which has been slaked, or mixed to a smooth paste, with a little water and then added to the sauce. In both the last examples the sauce must be boiled to cook the thickening agent.

REDUCTION SAUCES OR SAUCES AU BEURRE

Sauces such as Béarnaise, Hollandaise and Bercy, etc., are made by reducing a liquid – in the case of Béarnaise, vinegar; Bercy, white wine;

Hollandaise, court bouillon; then adding the reduction to egg yolks which are whisked over a gentle heat until they thicken or partially cook. In all cases they should be whisked over hot water and not over direct heat. The temperatute of the water should not approach boiling point and the eggs should be whisked over tepid water to begin with. The heat is then increased to about 175° F. (75° C.). Since it is not easy to test the temperature whilst preparing the sauce, it may be as well for the amateur cook to heat some water and test for temperature with a thermometer, then test again with the finger to assess the heat before making the sauce. The softened butter is then whisked in, in small knobs. All reduction sauces are served hot or warm and never cold.

COLD SAUCES

SAUCE MAYONNAISE

This type of sauce is the basis for several varieties, i.e. Tartare, Rémoulade, etc. When making these sauces, which have an oil and yolk basis, great care must be exercised in adding the oil. The yolk or yolks and seasonings are placed in the bottom of a pudding basin. (This should be large enough to whisk in, but not as large as a mixing bowl.) The oil must be added very gradually (one yolk will blend evenly with up to 3 dl. or half a pint of oil). A convenient way to proceed is to have the oil in a jug or measure at the side of the bowl and to dip the blade of a small knife into the oil and then let it drip into the bowl with the yolk, stirring all the time. Some cooks prefer to use a sauce whisk for this and others prefer to use a small wooden spoon, but it is a matter of individual taste. As the yolk and oil thicken, the oil can be added more quickly and in slightly larger quantities. Should it become very thick indeed, a small quantity, say a teaspoon, of vinegar can be stirred in to slacken the mixture slightly before adding more oil. A curdle will be noticed by the thinness of the mixture – the oil floating on the top of the yolk. In practically all cases the curdle is caused by adding the oil too quickly and by insufficient stirring between each addition of oil. Should this happen, it is useless to continue to add the oil – it is better to break a second yolk or yolks into a clean basin and add the curdled mayonnaise drip by drip to the fresh yolk. It must be borne in mind that a greater proportion of oil will now be needed to give a thick mayonnaise. Olive oil, though frequently advocated in mayonnaise recipes, is exceedingly rich in flavour and many tastes prefer other vegetable oils which have a less pronounced flavour and are not so expensive. In some recipes the vinegar, added finally, is boiling. This gives a whiter mayonnaise which will keep better. However, any covered mayonnaise will keep in a refrigerator for several days.

SAUCES CHAUDFROID

These can be white or blond and brown. To Béchamel, Veloutée or demi-glace sauces, add aspic jelly, allowing one-third of the latter to two-thirds of the sauce. These sauces are then used for coating cold dishes of fish, meat, poultry, etc. In all cases after the coating has set, the food should be re-coated with a thin layer of setting aspic jelly.

Such sauces as Tomate are not classified under the preceding headings and are purée sauces.

BEURRE MAÎTRE D'HÔTEL *

Ingredients:
125 g. butter (4 oz.)
juice of ½ lemon

2 tablespoons finely chopped
  parsley
salt and pepper

Method: Beat the butter well until it is of a creamy consistency. Work in the lemon juice little by little with the finely chopped parsley. Season well to taste. Put aside in a cool place to harden.

Comment: Serve a pat with grilled sole, chops, cutlets, steaks, etc.

BEURRE NOISETTE *

Ingredients:
60 g. butter (2 oz.)

a squeeze of lemon juice
seasoning

Method: Heat the butter in a pan until it turns a nutty brown colour. Add the lemon juice and seasoning. Stir round well. Use as required.

SAUCE BÉARNAISE **

Ingredients:
125 g. butter (4 oz.)
2 yolks of egg
2 tablespoons tarragon vinegar
1 chopped shallot
6 peppercorns

1 tablespoon white stock
salt
To finish:
1 tablespoon finely chopped
  tarragon

Method: Put the peppercorns, shallot and vinegar into a pan, reduce by half over a good heat. Strain into a clean bowl, add the stock and the beaten yolks. Stand the bowl in a bain-marie or over a double boiler.

Whisk continuously. When it becomes a thick custard, remove from the heat.

Beat in the butter bit by bit. Lastly add the chopped tarragon. Add salt to taste.

Comment: Serve this sauce with grilled meat, fish, eggs and some white meats.

SAUCE BÉCHAMEL OR BÉCHAMELLE *

Ingredients:
30 g. plain flour (1 oz.)
30 g. butter (1 oz.)

3 dl. milk (½ pint)
pepper and salt
a pinch of nutmeg (optional)

Method: Melt the butter in a saucepan, draw aside from the heat and add the flour – mix carefully. Return to a gentle heat to cook the roux for 2–3 minutes, stirring constantly. When the roux begins to bubble gently add the cold milk slowly, continuing to stir. Bring slowly to simmering point and simmer for 5 minutes. Season, adding a pinch of nutmeg.

This is the basic recipe. The sauce can be used as a foundation for other sauces, for example – Sauce Mornay (see page 36) made with grated cheese.

SAUCE DEMI-GLACE **

Ingredients:
2 shallots
50 g. bacon (2 oz.)
1 small onion
1 small carrot
125 g. mushroom stalks and/or
  peelings (4 oz.)

1 dessertspoon tomato purée
2 tablespoons plain flour
45–60 g. dripping (1½–2 oz.)
1 dl. sherry (½ gill)
¼ l. stock (¾ pint)
seasoning

Method: Cut the bacon into strips and fry it in the dripping. Take out the bacon and add the vegetables cut into very small dice. Cook these slowly, stirring well, until they are just beginning to turn a golden brown. This process cannot be hurried or the vegetables will become scorched. Sprinkle in the flour, continue to stir over a low heat until it browns. Half an hour should be allowed for this operation. Then add the stock, bacon and mushroom trimmings. Keep the mixture stirred. Bring to the boil. Skim carefully and simmer uncovered for half an hour. Stir in the tomato purée and sherry. Taste and adjust seasoning. Cook again for 15–20 minutes. Pass through a fine metal strainer or if preferred through a tammy cloth.

SAUCE HOLLANDAISE **

Ingredients:

2 tablespoons court bouillon (see page 18)
2 yolks of egg
125 g. butter (4 oz.)
1 tablespoon lemon juice
pepper to season

Method: Boil the court bouillon to reduce it by half. Strain on to the beaten yolks. Return to heat, either in a double boiler or in a bowl standing over hot water. Whisk continuously until a thick creamy custard consistency is obtained. When it has thickened remove at once from the heat and whisk in the butter bit by bit. Finish by adding lemon juice and pepper to taste. Serve tepid.

Comment: Use this sauce for serving with boiled or steamed fish. If it is to be served with eggs or vegetables substitute white stock for court bouillon.

JUS LIÉ *

Ingredients:

3 dl. veal stock (½ pint)
2 teaspoons arrowroot

Method: Slake the arrowroot with a little of the stock. Add to the whole amount and cook until it thickens. Season.

SAUCE MADÈRE **

Ingredients:

1½ dl. Madeira (1 gill)
1½ dl. Sauce Demi-glace (see page 34) (1 gill)
15 g. butter (½ oz.)
1 tablespoon Glace de Viande (see page 21)
seasoning

Method: Put the Madeira in a pan with the glace de viande. Place over a good heat and boil it quickly to reduce it by half. Add the sauce demi-glace which must be quite free from grease. Cook 1–2 minutes. Remove from the heat and whisk in the butter. Adjust seasoning.

Comment: This sauce should be served with meat, game, ham, etc.

SAUCE MALTAISE **

Ingredients:

As for Sauce Hollandaise (see above) with the addition of
the juice and the blanched grated rind of 1 orange.

Method: Make exactly as for sauce Hollandaise. After all the butter has been added, stir in the strained orange juice, little by little. Finish by adding the grated rind. Taste and season as required.

SAUCE MAYONNAISE **

Ingredients:
1 yolk of egg
3 dl. olive oil (½ pint)

½ teaspoon French mustard
2–3 tablespoons wine vinegar
seasoning and white pepper

Method: Put the mustard in the bottom of a bowl. Add the yolks and whisk lightly. Pour on the oil, drop by drop. Do this *very* slowly, whisking or stirring without ceasing. The Mayonnaise will thicken until it is almost solid by the time that all the oil has been added. Taste and season with salt and white pepper. Stir in the vinegar at the end, using sufficient to give the required consistency.

Comment: Vegetable oil is largely used in place of olive oil and many people prefer it to the rather rich taste of olive oil.
If the mixture curdles, it is because the oil has been added too rapidly. In such a case, break another egg yolk into a clean bowl and add the curdled Mayonnaise drop by drop. It must be remembered that by using 2 yolks, more oil must be added to achieve the correct ultimate result. If the mixture becomes too stiff during the making, it can be thinned down with a little vinegar. If the Mayonnaise is to be kept for some time before using, hot vinegar is sometimes added. This will give a smoother and whiter finish.

SAUCE MORNAY *

Ingredients:
Sauce Béchamel (see page 34)   60 g. grated cheese (2 oz.)

Method: Make the sauce Béchamel as usual, seeing that it is well seasoned. Remove from the heat, whisk in the cheese. The heat of the sauce will melt the cheese. If it is cooked again after the cheese has been added, the cheese will harden and form stringy lumps.

Comment: A well-flavoured cheese should be used for this whenever available. Gruyère and Parmesan are both excellent.

SAUCE NANTUA **

Ingredients:

Sauce Béchamel made with 60 g. (2 oz.) plain flour, 60 g. (2 oz.) butter, and ¼ l. (¾ pint) milk (see page 34)

1 dl. thick cream (½ gill)

Beurre d'Écrevisses made with 60 g. (2 oz.) butter, approx. 125 g. (4 oz.) crayfish

cayenne pepper

carmine colouring

seasoning

Method: Make the sauce Béchamel in the usual way. Add the cream and mix well. Allow to simmer gently for a few minutes.

Make the Beurre d'Écrevisses. Remove the shells and heads from the crayfish. Reserve the tail flesh. Pound the shells and heads using a pestle and mortar. Add an equal quantity of butter by bulk and pound again, so that the colour is transferred from the shells to the butter. Pass through a wire sieve.

Remove the sauce Béchamel from the heat and gradually whisk in the Beurre d'Écrevisses. Taste and adjust the seasoning, add a little cayenne. Adjust the colour as necessary, using a drop of carmine. Finally add the tail flesh of the crayfish. Serve hot.

SAUCE ROBERT **

Ingredients:

1 onion

30–40 g. butter (1–1½ oz.)

1½ dl. dry white wine (1 gill)

1 tablespoon wine vinegar

freshly ground pepper

3 dl. Sauce Demi-glace (½ pint) (see page 34)

1 dessertspoon Dijon mustard

pinch of sugar

seasoning

Method: Chop the onion finely. Melt the butter in a pan, 'sweat' the onion in this until it is completely soft. Do not allow it to brown. Add the wine, vinegar and pepper. Raise the heat, and reduce quickly until it is half the original quantity. Add the sauce Demi-glace, simmer for ten minutes. Stir in the mustard, pepper and sugar. Taste, and rectify the seasoning.

Comment: This sauce is excellent with roast pork, or pork chops.

SAUCE RÉMOULADE **

Ingredients:

3 dl. Sauce Mayonnaise (½ pint) (see page 36)

1 level teaspoon Dijon mustard

1 tablespoon finely chopped capers

1 tablespoon finely chopped gherkins

1 tablespoon finely chopped tarragon

1 teaspoon anchovy essence

seasoning

37

Method: Blanch the tarragon leaves and chop finely. Make the Mayonnaise as usual, adding the mustard (more can be added if an especially hot sauce is required). Stir in the anchovy essence and chopped tarragon, capers and gherkins. Taste and re-season if necessary.

SAUCE SOUBISE *

Ingredients:

½ kg. medium onions (1 lb.)
Sauce Béchamel (see page 34)

60 g. butter (2 oz.)
2 tablespoons cream (optional)
seasoning

Method: Chop the onions, put them into cold water, and bring to the boil. Boil for five minutes. Drain and dry them. Melt the butter in a pan, add the onions, and stir over a low heat until they are completely soft. Pass them through a sieve or vegetable mill.

Mix them with the sauce Béchamel, adding the butter as well. Stir in the cream, and season to taste.

Comment: This sauce can be used with egg and vegetable dishes, cutlets, etc.

SAUCE TARTARE **

Ingredients:

1 hardboiled egg yolk (sieved)
1 raw egg yolk
3 dl. oil (½ pint)
1 tablespoon wine vinegar
1 dessertspoon chopped capers

1 dessertspoon finely chopped chives
1 tablespoon finely chopped tarragon
salt, pepper, mustard

Method: Place the sieved egg yolk in a bowl with the raw yolk and proceed as for Sauce Mayonnaise (see page 36). Finish with the blanched chopped tarragon and the finely chopped chives and capers.

Comment: Serve with fried fish, etc.

SAUCE TOMATE (Method I) *

Ingredients:

¾–1 kg. ripe tomatoes (1½–2 lb.)
1 tablespoon castor sugar
1 clove garlic

3 rashers bacon
1 onion
bouquet garni
black pepper and salt

Method: Roughly chop the tomatoes. Put them into a strong pan together with the finely sliced onion, the bacon cut into strips, the garlic crushed with a little salt and the seasoning and sugar. Tie the bouquet garni with a piece of string and add to the pan. Cook over a gentle heat until the tomatoes are soft and mushy. Put the mixture through a fine sieve or a vegetable mill. Re-heat in a clean pan. Adjust the seasoning.

Comment: If the sauce is too thin it may be thickened with a little beurre manié (see page 16).

This sauce may be made with tinned tomatoes.

SAUCE TOMATE (Method II) *

Ingredients:
¾–1 kg. ripe tomatoes or 1 equiva-
    lent size tin tomatoes (1½–2 lb.)
1 onion
1 clove garlic
bouquet garni – composed of
    bayleaf, parsley, thyme, and
    tarragon

1 teaspoon sugar
1 teaspoon tomato purée
½ teaspoon salt
1 shallot
1 gill water
seasoning
To finish:
30 g. butter (1 oz.)

Method: Chop the shallot very finely and cut the onion into thin rings. Skin and pip the tomatoes and cut into shreds. Crush the garlic with a little salt.

Put all the ingredients into a strong pan and simmer very gently until a thick purée is obtained. Remove from the heat, take out the bouquet garni and adjust the seasoning. Whisk in the butter bit by bit.

Comment: This sauce should be served unsieved.

SAUCE VELOUTÉE **

Ingredients:
75 g. butter (2½ oz.)
60 g. plain flour (2 oz.)

¾ l. veal stock (1¼ pints)
seasoning

Method: Melt the butter in a fairly large pan, draw aside from the heat and stir in the flour. Return to a very low heat to cook the roux allowing about 5 minutes. Stir all the time. Do not allow it to brown. Pour on the stock. Taste and season. Stir with a sauce whisk just until it comes up to boiling point. Lower the heat. Simmer very, very gently over a low heat for 45 minutes to 1 hour. Strain into a clean pan. Remove all grease. Rectify the seasoning.

Comment: Many sauces are derived from this basic sauce – examples: Suprême and Poulette.

SAUCE VINAIGRETTE *

Ingredients:

to three parts of olive oil use one part wine vinegar, salt, pinch of sugar, made mustard and pepper

Method: Mix the seasonings with the vinegar. Add the oil little by little, whisking well with a sauce whisk or fork.

Comment: This sauce is used as a salad dressing. Finely chopped fresh herbs can be added in some cases.

CRÈME ANGLAISE **

Ingredients:

4 yolks of egg
75 g. castor sugar (2½ oz.)
3 dl. milk (½ pint)

1–2 teaspoons vanilla sugar
a pinch of arrowroot or fécule de pommes de terre

Method: Put the yolks, sugar, vanilla sugar and arrowroot into a bowl and work well with a wooden spoon or spatula. Heat the milk and pour on to the mixture gradually, keeping well stirred. Return to the pan, which has been rinsed out, and stir over a low heat until it thickens, without boiling. Remove at once and strain into a bowl.

Comment: A less rich sauce may be made by only using 3 yolks, 90 g. (3 oz.) castor sugar to 3 dl. (½ pint) milk.

CRÈME ANGLAISE AU CAFÉ **

As above, but use half milk and half strong black coffee.

CRÈME ANGLAISE AU CHOCOLAT **

As before, but add 125 g. (4 oz.) softened plain chocolate to the yolks and sugar mixture, or if preferred, add to the milk whilst it is heating.

SAUCE CARAMEL **

Ingredients:

90 g. castor sugar (3 oz.)
1½ dl. water (1 gill)

juice of ½ lemon
¼ l. extra water (1–1½ gills)

Method: Melt the sugar with 1½ dl. (1 gill) water. When dissolved, raise the heat and cook until it is a deep brown colour. Remove from the heat and add the second amount of water by degrees, together with the lemon juice. Take great care not to splash your hand. Reheat slowly and use as required.

SAUCE CHOCOLAT *

Ingredients:
125 g. plain chocolate (¼ lb.)
2 tablespoons castor sugar

1½ dl. hot water (1 gill)
60 g. butter (2 oz.)
pinch of salt

Method: Break the chocolate and place it with the sugar, hot water, and salt in a pan over a low heat. Allow to melt, stirring all the time. Raise the heat and continue cooking until it is of a syrupy consistency. Just before serving beat in the butter, bit by bit.

SAUCE SABAYON **

Ingredients:
2 yolks of egg
3 dessertspoons castor sugar

3 tablespoons white wine
2 tablespoons kirsch

Method: Whisk the yolks, sugar and white wine in a bowl over very hot water until thick and fluffy. Remove and whisk until cool. Add the kirsch. Serve with sweets.

Comment: This sauce served in small glasses with biscuits such as Tuiles (see page 362) can be used as a sweet. It is important to serve it immediately it is made. Other liqueurs can be substituted if kirsch is not available.

SAUCE ABRICOT *

To sieved apricot jam, add sufficient sugar syrup (see page 24) to moisten. Heat through gently, keeping well stirred. Remove from the heat and, still keeping well stirred, thin down to the required consistency with rum, kirsch or lemon juice.

Hors d'Œuvres

In travelling in France and eating with French families one meets an imaginative variety of hors d'œuvres or light entrées. These are basically small portions of simple foods or mixtures which are designed to tempt and to stimulate the flow of gastric juices and, of course, to complement the following larger dishes.

In France hors d'œuvres are usually served at luncheon, but this general practice has been abandoned elsewhere. From the hostess's view, they make a pleasant beginning for a dinner and in many cases the dishes can be prepared and ready well in advance of the guests' arriving.

In this figure conscious age, it may be found practical to utilise some of the dishes suggested as hors d'œuvres for light luncheon or supper dishes.

Imagination should be allowed full rein. Individual taste and combination of flavours make for interesting eating. A simple selection of young, daintily prepared vegetables accompanied by a spicy dressing is nourishing and health giving (Crudités Naturiste).

Some of the classical hors d'œuvres such as oysters, prawn cocktail, Charentais or Cantaloupe melon, smoked salmon, foie gras, scampis, caviare, pâté maison and terrine are acceptable when the occasion is right, but they are expensive. The hostess however can practise economy, while at the same time giving an individual touch to her menu, by serving one or a selection of the following:

Artichauts à la Grecque
Oeufs Mêlés
Céleri-Rave aux Moules
Choufleur à la Mirabeau
Salade Beaucaire

Accompanied by good bread or rolls and butter, what could be better?

It may be helpful to realise that a collection of this sort in greater variety could form an excellent buffet lunch or supper with perhaps a selection of cold meats (Assiette Anglaise).

Some dishes contain only vegetables, Ratatouille à la Niçoise, Céleris à la Grecque, Pointes d'Asperges à la Crème, Tomates aux Olives, which are also useful for vegetarian and maigre days.

Very often shell fish is used. Crabe à l'Indienne, Crabe Farci Chaude, Barquettes aux Huitres, Barquettes Normande, as well as a multitude of mussel recipes. 'In Brittany they serve what is called a Plateau des Fruits de Mer. This is a *tray* full of delicious crustaceans and molluscs. The centre piece is usually a spider crab and it is surrounded by oysters, prawns, shrimps, mussels and some very active cockles. Like Alice, I have never been able to bring myself to eat someone who has stood up on my plate and bowed. [H.L.]

There are also some very acceptable savoury flans including Tarte du Saumon, Tartlettes de Morue, Quiche Bourguignonne, Karolys aux Crevettes. These can be served as hors d'œuvres, as cocktail canapés, or as savouries at the end of the meal, depending on their size. Equally pleasant are a variety of canapés cut *slightly* larger than as for cocktails.

Egg dishes are easily digested and vary in their cooking, Œufs à la Russe, Œufs Argenteuil, Œufs en Côtelettes, Œufs Farcis, Œufs Chimay and the renowned Piperade Basquaise. Using eggs as a basis for a soufflé forms an ambitious, but praiseworthy, entrée. Soufflé d'Endives à la Pompadour is delicately flavoured and the accompanying sauce is colourful.

Salads are nourishing and attractive, including, in some cases, meat, e.g. Salade de Langue, Salade de Poulet. Other unusual salads are Salade de Mais, Salade Egyptienne, Salade Impératrice and Salade Orloff.

Some pasta are pleasant, though they can be bulky.

Never give so much that there is no room for what is to follow. In each case only small quantities should be served, so that full justice can be done to the following courses.

No recipes have been given here as the variety of dishes is grouped into chapters, according to the main ingredient.

Now more than at any other time, the cook-hostess can serve a highly individual menu. What is still important is the quality, variety, texture and flavour as well as the colour. At all times neatness of service and simple but imaginative decoration tempt the guest to the hors d'œuvres and so stimulate the appetite for the rest of the meal.

HORS D'ŒUVRES

HORS D'ŒUVRES

Soups

It is the normal custom in France to serve hors d'œuvres at lunch and soup at dinner. This is an excellent habit, and could well be followed in ordinary English households.

Although there are many commercially prepared soups both in packets and tins which are excellent in their way, these all cost something. It is quite possible to prepare an excellent soup in one's own kitchen from trimmings.

Care should be taken that the soup is in contrast to the main course.

Electric blenders and vegetable mills have taken much of the hard work out of the preparation of purées. It is now really easy to produce a soup in seconds.

SOUPS

BISQUE DE CREVETTES **   (for 3–4 persons)

Ingredients:

125 g. shrimps (4 oz.)
1 onion
1 medium carrot
1 stick celery
1 small leek
60 g. butter (2 oz.)
250 g. tomatoes ($\frac{1}{2}$ lb.)
bouquet garni
1 small glass brandy

1 glass dry white wine
$\frac{1}{2}$ l. fish stock (1 pint)
1 teaspoon concentrated tomato
   purée
seasoning

To finish:

2 tablespoons thick cream
60 g. shelled shrimps (2 oz.)
1 small glass Champagne (optional)

Method: Chop the vegetables finely. Heat 45 g. (1$\frac{1}{2}$ oz.) butter and cook the vegetables in this until they are soft, but not browned. Toss the shrimps in the butter. Add the brandy and flame it. Pour in the wine and stock, add the tomatoes cut into quarters, and tomato purée, seasoning and bouquet garni. Bring to the boil and simmer gently for 30 minutes. Remove the bouquet garni. Strain off the liquor and reserve it. Pound the shrimps and vegetables in a mortar, then mix them with the liquor and pass it through a fine wire sieve. Add the cream, adjust the seasoning, reheat and add the shelled shrimps. If possible add 1 small glass Champagne at the last moment.

CONSOMMÉ **   (for 6–8 persons)

Ingredients:

250–350 g. shin of beef ($\frac{1}{2}$–$\frac{3}{4}$ lb.)
1 l. bone stock (2 pints)
1 dl. sherry ($\frac{1}{2}$ gill)
Materials for Clarification:
1 medium sized leek
1 medium sized carrot

1 stick celery or celery salt
1 tomato or peel or pips
$\frac{1}{2}$ glass water
3–4 egg whites
fresh herbs
seasoning

Method: First remove the fat, then cut the meat into shreds. Put the egg whites in a basin with the water and lightly whisk them. Chop the vegetables very finely. Put the meat and cold stock into a pan, season well, add the vegetables, the herbs tied in a bunch, the tomato and the egg whites. (Cut the tomato into quarters if it is a whole one.) Bring slowly to simmering point, stirring all the time. When it begins to cloud, stop stirring. Continue to boil very gently for 10–15 minutes until the egg has hardened and the liquid is clear and brilliant. (Test with a clean metal spoon.) Place a perfectly clean, wet cloth over a clean bowl and ladle the soup into this, taking care to keep the cloth in place. Remove the cloth carefully. Do not press or squeeze. Taste, re-season and add the sherry.

Comment: A small spoonful of caramel will give a slightly better colour. Some authorities add the shells of the eggs as well as the whites and there is no reason why this should not be done.

CONSOMMÉ À LA CELESTINE **   (for 6–8 persons)

Ingredients:
1 l. chicken stock (2 pints)
materials for clarification (see
   consommé, page 48)
½ glass sherry
seasoning

For the Garnish:
Pâte à Crêpes (see page 255)
oil for frying
1 tablespoon mixed fresh herbs
seasoning

Method: Remove all the fat from the surface of the stock, which should be cold. Clarify the stock in the usual way (see page 48). Add the sherry and reheat carefully.

Meanwhile chop the herbs very finely and stir them into the pâte à crêpes. Season well. Make several small, very thin crêpes. Roll them up and cut into julienne strips.

To Serve: Pour the consommé into a hot tureen and just before serving add the julienne of crêpes.

Comment: Finely chopped debris of truffle may be used instead of the herbs if available and preferred.

CONSOMMÉ AUX CHEVEUX D'ANGES **
(for 6–8 persons)

Ingredients:
1 l. chicken consommé made as
   for Consommé Celestine (2 pints)
   (see page 49)

For the Garnish:
90 g. very fine vermicelli (3 oz.)
1½–2 l. chicken stock (3–4 pints)
seasoning

Method: Make the consommé.

Meanwhile cook the vermicelli in the well seasoned boiling chicken stock. When it is just cooked, drain the vermicelli well and refresh it in hot water, drain well.

To Serve: Pour the consommé into a hot tureen and just before serving, add the vermicelli.

CONSOMMÉ À LA PAYSANNE ** (for 6–8 persons)

Ingredients:
1 l. beef stock (2 pints)
materials for clarification (see
    Consommé, page 48)
½ glass sherry
seasoning

For the Paysanne Garnish:
60 g. each carrots, turnips, peas
and French beans (2 oz.)
30 g. butter (1 oz.)
seasoning

Method: Make the consommé (see page 48).
Prepare the paysanne garnish, cutting the carrots and turnips as for Soupe à la Paysanne (see page 62). Cut the French beans to small lozenges and cook all the vegetables separately in boiling salted water until just tender. Drain, refresh and drain them again. Toss the vegetables in the hot butter.

To Serve: Pour the consommé into a hot tureen, drain the excess butter from the vegetables and stir them into the consommé. Serve at once.

CONSOMMÉ À LA ROYALE ** (for 6–8 persons)

Ingredients:
1 l. chicken consommé (2 pints),
    made as for Consommé Celestine
    (see page 49)

For the Royale Garnish:
2 yolks of egg
1 dl. dry white wine or 1 dl. white
    stock (½ gill)
seasoning

Method: Make the consommé.
Meanwhile make the royale garnish. Butter three or four dariole moulds. Beat the egg yolks with the white wine or stock and season well. Strain it into the prepared moulds. Stand them in a bain-marie or roasting tin containing boiling water and cook on the top of the stove or in a moderate oven, gas mark 4 or 350° F. (180° C.) until they are firmly set, approximately 10–15 minutes. Remove from the oven and allow them to become quite cold.
Tap the moulds gently and turn out the custards carefully on a board.

Using a sharp knife cut the custards into slices ⅓ cm. (⅛ inch) thick. Cut small round, square or triangular shapes from the slices.

To Serve: Pour the consommé into a hot tureen and just before serving add the garnish.

CRÈME FLORENTINE ** (for 4 persons)

Ingredients:

2 small leeks	2 yolks of egg
90 g. butter (3 oz.)	2 tablespoons thick cream
500 g. spinach (1 lb.)	1½ l. white stock (3 pints)
¾ kg. potatoes (1½ lb.)	seasoning

Method: Wash and prepare the leeks and chop them finely. Wash and pick the spinach leaves. Peel the potatoes and cut them into even sized pieces. Heat 60 g. (2 oz.) butter in a large pan. Stir the leeks and potatoes in the hot fat until they start to turn colour. Add the spinach and the white stock. Season well. Bring it to the boil and cook slowly in an uncovered pan for 35 minutes. At the end of this time, remove from the heat, pass it through a vegetable mill or fine sieve. Heat again. Beat the yolks with the cream in a bowl, pour on a little of the hot soup, stir well, then pour it into the pan with the rest of the soup. Taste and adjust the seasoning. Heat until it thickens, stirring all the time. Do not let it reach boiling point. Whisk in the rest of the butter bit by bit. Serve at once in a hot tureen.

CRÈME DE LÉGUMES RUE L'ARCADE *

(for 6 persons)

Ingredients:

250 g. new carrots (½ lb.)	1 onion
500 g. new peas, unshelled (1 lb.)	60 g. butter (2 oz.)
2 new turnips	1½ l. chicken or veal stock (3 pints)
1 heart of celery	2–3 tablespoons thick cream
3 medium sized potatoes	bouquet garni
	seasoning

Method: Wash and peel the root vegetables and wash the celery. Cut them into even sized pieces. Chop the onion.

Shell the peas. Put all the vegetables and the bouquet garni into a large saucepan and the hot stock. Season well. Cook them for 40–45 minutes or until the vegetables are just soft. Pass the soup through a vegetable mill or wire sieve. Re-heat it in a clean pan and adjust the seasoning. Stir in the cream.

Remove the soup from the heat and 'mount' it by whisking in the butter little by little. Pour the soup into a hot tureen and serve at once.

CRÈME VICHYSSOISE * (for 6–8 persons)

Ingredients:
8–10 small leeks
500 g. potatoes (1 lb.)
1 l. chicken stock (2 pints)
3 dl. thin cream (½ pint)

60–90 g. butter (2–3 oz.)
seasoning
To finish:
3–4 tablespoons finely chopped
chives

Method: Wash and clean the leeks thoroughly. Remove the green part and slice the white part thinly. Heat the butter in a fairly large pan and add the leeks. Season lightly. Cover with greaseproof paper and the lid and 'sweat' them over a low heat, shaking the pan frequently, so that they do not stick. They must not be allowed to brown in any way.

Peel the potatoes. Slice them thinly and add them to the pan, adding more butter if necessary. Turn quickly in the hot butter. Pour in the chicken stock, bring it to the boil and simmer for 20 minutes or until the vegetables are soft.

Remove from the heat and pass the soup through a fine sieve or vegetable mill. Just before serving stir in the cream and reheat. Adjust the seasoning. Pour into a hot tureen and sprinkle with finely chopped chives.

CRÈME DE VOLAILLE ** (for 3–4 persons)

Ingredients:
¾ l. well flavoured chicken stock
  (1½ pints)
90 g. butter (3 oz.)
30 g. crème de riz (1 oz.)
2 yolks of egg

2–3 tablespoons thick cream
seasoning
To finish:
a little cooked white chicken meat,
  shredded. Finely chopped parsley

Method: Heat 30 g. (1 oz.) of butter in a large stewpan, draw aside and stir in the crème de riz. Cook for one minute, keeping well stirred. Stir in the chicken stock and bring to the boil, stirring all the time. Season as required. Simmer for 10 minutes. Draw the pan aside. Beat the egg yolks with the cream and add a little of the chicken soup and whisk well, then return it to the pan. Place on a low heat and add the shredded chicken. Keeping stirred all the time heat it gently until it thickens slightly. It must not boil. Adjust the seasoning. Remove from the heat and whisk in the remaining butter bit by bit. Serve at once in a hot tureen with a sprinkling of finely chopped parsley.

POTAGE À L'ANDALOUSE * (for 4–5 persons)

Ingredients:

1 kg. tomatoes (2 lb.)
60 g. butter (2 oz.)
2 green peppers
½ l. beef stock (1 pint)
bouquet garni
pinch of sugar
1 dessertspoon fine tapioca
seasoning

Method: Cut the tomatoes into quarters. Heat the butter in a stewpan. Add the tomatoes, together with the bouquet garni, seasoning and a pinch of sugar. Cook slowly for 10 minutes, stirring occasionally, then add the stock. Continue to simmer gently for a further 15 minutes.

Whilst it is cooking, halve the peppers and remove the pith and seeds. Cut them into fine strips and blanch them in boiling salted water for 10 minutes. Drain and refresh in cold water. Pass the tomato soup through a sieve or vegetable mill. Return to the heat and add the tapioca. Cook for 15 minutes. Add the peppers. Taste and re-season if necessary. Serve in a hot tureen.

POTAGE BELLE DE MAI * (for 6 persons)

Ingredients:

¾ kg. carrots (1½ lb.)
60 g. bacon (2 oz.)
30 g. butter (1 oz.)
2 firm lettuce hearts
60 g. vermicelli (2 oz.)
seasoning
To finish:
30 g. butter (1 oz.)
1 yolk of egg
1 dl. stock (½ gill)

Method: Wash, scrape and slice the carrots. Cook them in 1½ l. (3 pints) of boiling, lightly salted water for 20 minutes. At the end of this time pass them through a coarse sieve or vegetable mill, together with the water they were cooked in.

Meanwhile cut the bacon into lardons. Cook it in the butter without browning. Add the lettuce hearts cut into shreds. Stir all together in the hot butter until the lettuce is well coated, then add the carrot soup. Reheat, add the vermicelli and cook quickly for a further 7–8 minutes. Taste and rectify the seasoning. Just before serving remove the soup from the heat and beat in the butter and the yolk, which has been whisked with the stock. Serve at once.

POTAGE BONNE VIEILLE * (for 6 persons)

Ingredients:

1 kg. shelled peas (2 lb.)
3–4 leeks
90 g. butter (3 oz.)
½ l. milk (1 pint)
1 tablespoon finely chopped
    chervil
seasoning
To finish:
tiny croûtons fried in butter

Method: Cook the peas in about 1 l. (2 pints) of boiling, lightly salted water. When they are tender pass them, and the cooking liquor, through a fine sieve or vegetable mill.

Wash the leeks and slice the white part finely. Heat 60 g. (2 oz.) butter in a large strong pan. Add the leeks and cook them in the butter over a low heat, keeping them well stirred. When they are soft, but not brown, put in the pea purée. Season and simmer for 10 minutes, stirring well. Heat the milk and add this to the soup. Draw the pan aside from the heat and whisk in the remaining butter. Lastly stir in the chervil. Taste and adjust the seasoning. Pour the soup into a hot soup tureen, and serve with tiny croûtons handed separately.

POTAGE CHAMPENOIS *   (for 4–5 persons)

Ingredients:
30 g. butter (1 oz.)
200 g. white part of leeks (6 oz.)
¾ kg. potatoes (1½ lb.)
1 l. of water (2 pints)
bouquet garni composed of
 parsley and chervil

30 g. macaroni (1 oz.)
seasoning
To finish:
60 g. grated cheese (2 oz.)
4–5 slices French bread

Method: Melt the butter in a large saucepan. Cut the leeks into 1 cm. (½ inch) lengths and put them to soften in the butter, stirring frequently so that they do not colour.

Peel the potatoes and cut them into small dice, add to the leeks and stir well. Pour on the water and add the bouquet garni and seasoning. Bring to the boil and cook over a moderate heat for 45 minutes. Now add the macaroni in short lengths and continue to cook for another 15 minutes. Remove the bouquet garni.

Spread the slices of bread with the grated cheese and brown under a hot grill. Place them in a layer at the bottom of a soup tureen. Taste the soup and adjust the seasoning. Pour it over the top of the bread. Serve very hot.

POTAGE CLAIR DE LUNE **   (for 4 persons)

Ingredients:
300 g. finely chopped onions (10
 oz.)
75–90 g. butter (2½–3 oz.)
3 large tomatoes

2 yolks of egg
75 g. grated Gruyère cheese
 (2½ oz.)
seasoning

very good

Method: Heat 60 g. (2 oz.) butter in a thick saucepan and cook the finely chopped onions in this without allowing them to colour, stirring frequently. Add ¾ l. (1½ pints) boiling salted water. Simmer for 25 minutes.

Whilst this is taking place, skin the tomatoes and cut them into strips. Heat the rest of the butter in a small pan and soften the tomatoes in this.

Pass the onions together with the cooking liquor through a fine sieve or vegetable mill. Add the tomatoes and the butter in which they have been cooked. Season. Simmer gently for 10 minutes. Adjust the seasoning.

Whisk the yolks lightly. Stir in a little of the hot soup, then add to the pan and heat through until the soup thickens slightly, stirring all the time. Do not allow it to boil. Remove from the heat. Lastly stir in the grated Gruyère cheese and serve at once in a hot tureen.

POTAGE COMBES *   (for 6–7 persons)

Ingredients:
300 g. split peas (10 oz.)
1 large onion
4 tablespoons Patna rice

seasoning
To finish:
60 g. butter (2 oz.)

Method: Soak the peas overnight. Drain the peas and place them in a large pan with 2 l. (4 pints) of water and the onion cut into slices. Bring to the boil. Cook slowly until the peas are tender. Pass them, with the liquor, through a fine sieve or vegetable mill. Season well. Return the soup to the heat and bring to the boil. Add the rice and cook for another 20 minutes, stirring occasionally. Place the butter in the bottom of a soup tureen, pour in the soup and stir round quickly. Serve at once.

POTAGE DAME MARIE *   (for 6 persons)

Ingredients:
60 g. butter (2 oz.)
170 g. mushrooms (6 oz.)
2 cooked fonds d'artichauts
150 g. white breadcrumbs (5 oz.)

1½ dl. thick cream (1 gill)
1½ l. well seasoned white stock
(3 pints)
seasoning and a tiny pinch of
nutmeg

Method: Heat the butter in a pan. Add the roughly chopped mushrooms. Stir for 2–3 minutes over a low heat. Add the artichokes, roughly chopped. Pour in the hot stock and bring to simmering point, then stir in the breadcrumbs. Taste and season, adding the nutmeg. Allow it to cook for a moment or two longer. Remove from the heat and stir in the cream. Serve at once.

POTAGE FRÉNEUSE À LA TOMATE *   (for 6 persons)

Ingredients:

½ kg. potatoes (1 lb.)

½ kg. turnips (1 lb.)

1 kg. tomatoes (2 lb.)

1 large onion

45–60 g. butter (1½–2 oz.)

bouquet garni

seasoning

To finish:

fried croûtons (see page 20)

1 tablespoon finely chopped
  chervil

Method: Skin the tomatoes and cut them into quarters. Peel the onion, potatoes and turnips and chop them roughly. Put all together in a large pan and cover with cold water, using about 1½ l. (3 pints). Season very well and add the bouquet garni.

Cook gently for about 45 minutes or until the vegetables are soft. Remove the bouquet garni. Pass the vegetables and their liquor through a sieve or vegetable mill into a clean pan. Reheat. Remove from the heat and whisk in the butter bit by bit and adjust the seasoning.

Put the fried croûtons in the bottom of a hot tureen. Pour over the soup. Sprinkle with the finely chopped chervil. Serve at once.

POTAGE GARBURE *   (for 6–8 persons)

Ingredients:

2–3 carrots

2 turnips

3 large potatoes

2–3 ripe tomatoes

1½ l. stock (3 pints)

½ firm white cabbage

2–4 tablespoons haricot beans,
  (soaked for 12 hours and cooked
  see page 19)

3 dl. of the liquor the beans were
  cooked in (½ pint)

120 g. butter (4 oz.)

seasoning

To finish:

slices of French bread

grated cheese

Method: Melt half of the butter in a deep stewpan. Cut the carrots, turnips, potatoes and cabbage into julienne strips. Move them round quickly in the hot butter. Cover with greaseproof paper and the lid and cook over a very gentle heat. The pan must be shaken from time to time, so that the vegetables do not stick to the bottom. When they are soft enough, pass them through a sieve or vegetable mill, together with the haricot beans, and the raw tomatoes.

Return the vegetable purée to the pan, which has been rinsed out, and stir in the stock and the liquor from the beans. Bring slowly to boiling point. Season. Remove from the heat and whisk in the remaining butter bit by bit. Cut slices of French bread, sprinkle them thickly with grated cheese and brown it under a hot grill. Lay them in the bottom of a hot tureen and pour over the soup. Serve at once.

POTAGE GENTILHOMME *   (for 4 persons)

Ingredients:

3–4 medium sized potatoes
1 medium sized onion
45 g. butter (1½ oz.)
3 dl. milk (½ pint)
½ l. white stock or water (¾ pint)
a good pinch celery salt

seasoning
For the Garnish:
4 medium sized carrots
4 leeks
1 firm lettuce
30–45 g. butter (1–1½ oz.)

Method: Peel and slice the onion and the potatoes thinly. Heat the butter in a fairly large saucepan. Add the potatoes and onion and cook them gently for 5 minutes, stirring all the time to prevent them from sticking to the bottom of the pan. Add the stock and seasoning and simmer gently until all is reduced to a pulp.

Whilst this is taking place prepare the garnish: cut the carrots into thin julienne strips and slice the leeks thinly. Wash the lettuce leaves and dry them thoroughly. Roll them up and cut them into a 'chiffonade'. Heat the butter in a strong pan, add the carrots and leeks and cook them in the butter, keeping them covered with greaseproof paper and the lid. Shake the pan from time to time to prevent their sticking. As soon as they are tender, add the lettuce and stir this in the hot butter for 1–2 minutes. Keep hot.

Pass the soup through a sieve or vegetable mill, then return to the pan, which has been rinsed out. Stir in the milk, reheat and taste for seasoning, adding the celery salt. When the soup is hot, add the garnish and serve at once.

POTAGE JUANITA *   (for 6–8 persons)

Ingredients:

2 onions
90 g. butter (3 oz.)
½ kg. tomatoes (1 lb.)
2 medium sized potatoes
2 peppers

1½ l. stock (3 pints)
60 g. mushrooms (2 oz.)
seasoning
To finish:
1 tablespoon chopped chervil
30 g. butter (1 oz.)

Method: Chop the onions finely. Heat 60 g. (2 oz.) butter in a deep pan, add the onions and soften them gently without colouration.

Meanwhile skin and pip the tomatoes and cut them into shreds. Peel and slice the potatoes. When the onions are soft stir in the potatoes and tomatoes. Pour on the stock and bring it to boiling point. Season. Cook gently for 20 minutes. Pass the vegetables and their liquor through a sieve or vegetable mill.

Cut the peppers in half and discard the seeds and pith. Cut the peppers into strips. Blanch them for 2–3 minutes in boiling water. Drain. Heat the rest of the butter and cook the peppers and the finely chopped mushrooms slowly in this until they are soft. Stir them in to the soup. Reheat. Rectify the seasoning. Remove from the heat and whisk in the butter and the chopped chervil. Serve at once.

POTAGE DE LAITUES *   (for 6 persons)

Ingredients:

4 good sized lettuces
100 g. butter (3½ oz.)
1 l. Sauce Béchamel (2 pints) (see
   page 34)

1½ dl. thick cream (1 gill)
½ l. milk (1 pint)
3–4 tablespoons finely chopped
   chervil
seasoning

Method: Wash the lettuces and plunge them into boiling salted water for 2–3 minutes. Remove them and refresh them in cold water. Press them with the hands to expel all the moisture. Put them on a board and using a sharp knife chop them finely. Put them in a large pan over a gentle heat, stirring them with a wooden spoon allow all the water to evaporate. Add the butter and cover the lettuce with a piece of greaseproof paper and the lid of the pan, stew it gently for 10 minutes. At the end of this time add the hot sauce Béchamel, taste and season. Pass the soup through a fine sieve and add the boiling milk, return to the heat to heat through thoroughly. Just before serving whisk in the cream and add the chervil. Rectify the seasoning.

POTAGE AU MACARONI *   (for 6–7 persons)

Ingredients:

120 g. macaroni (4 oz.)
350 g. sorrel (¾ lb.)
250 g. spinach (½ lb.)
1½ l. white stock (3 pints)

½ l. creamy milk (¾ pint)
60 g. butter (2 oz.)
2 tablespoons finely chopped
   chervil
seasoning

Method: Break the macaroni into 2–3 cm. (1 inch) lengths and cook it in boiling salted water for 15 minutes. Drain well. Refresh in cold water. Wash and strip the spinach and sorrel and shred it finely. Heat one ounce of the butter in a deep pan, add the spinach and sorrel and stir them in the butter over a low heat for 2–3 minutes. Pour in the stock and the milk.

Bring to the boil and boil for 2–3 minutes. Season. Remove from the heat and stir in the remainder of the butter bit by bit. Place the macaroni in the bottom of a hot tureen, pour in the soup and stir in the chopped chervil. Serve very hot.

POTAGE AUX MARRONS *   (for 4 persons)

Ingredients:

¾ kg. chestnuts (1½ lb.)

90 g. butter (3 oz.)

1 large onion

1 or 2 carrots

¾ l. white stock (1½ pints)

1½ dl. thin cream (1 gill)

seasoning

Method: Put the chestnuts into cold water and bring them to the boil. Boil for 2 minutes, remove the saucepan from the heat and taking one chestnut at a time remove the skins. If the water cools off too quickly and the chestnuts become difficult to peel, bring them to boiling point again.

Meanwhile, slice the onion and the carrots thinly. Heat the butter in a thick saucepan, add the onion and carrots and stir over a low heat until they have softened, but not browned. Add the stock, together with the chestnuts. Season. Cover the pan and simmer until the chestnuts are quite soft. Rub all through a fine sieve or put through a vegetable mill. Rinse out the pan and return the soup to heat through, stirring all the time. Lastly stir in the cream and adjust the seasoning. Serve very hot.

POTAGE MENESTREL *   (for 4–6 persons)

Ingredients:

4 large fillets whiting

3 tablespoons olive oil

1 l. fish stock (2 pints)

2 red peppers

1 large potato

a large pinch saffron

60 g. vermicelli (2 oz.)

bouquet garni

seasoning

To finish:

grated Parmesan cheese

Method: Cut the whiting into strips about 2½ cm. (1 inch) wide. Fry them very lightly in the hot oil, to which has been added the bouquet garni. When the fish is soft, crush it with a fork. Cover with the stock.

Cut the peppers in half, remove the pith and seeds. Chop the peppers and blanch them for 2–3 minutes in boiling water. Drain well and add them to the fish and stock, together with the potato peeled and cut into slices and the saffron and seasoning. Cover the pan and simmer gently for half an hour. Pass the soup through a vegetable mill or sieve. Rinse the pan, replace the soup, bring to the boil and add the vermicelli. Simmer for 5–7 minutes, or until the vermicelli is cooked. Serve in a hot tureen accompanied by grated Parmesan cheese.

POTAGE POULETTE * (for 5–6 persons)

Ingredients:

250 g. haricot beans (½ lb.)
1 large carrot
1 large onion
1 small bouquet garni
30 g. butter (1 oz.)
120 g. sorrel (4 oz).
120 g. lettuce leaves (4 oz.)

a few sprigs of chervil
seasoning
To finish:
1½ dl. creamy milk (1 gill)
60 g. butter (2 oz.)
1 dl. thick cream (½ gill)
1 tablespoon finely chopped
   chervil

Method: Soak the beans overnight. Rinse them and put them in a large saucepan containing about 1½ l. (3 pints) of cold water, add the carrot cut into slices and the onion finely chopped. Season and add the bouquet garni. Cover the pan and simmer for at least an hour, or until the beans are well cooked. At the end of this time pass the soup through a sieve or vegetable mill. Return it to the pan, which has been rinsed out, and reheat it.

Melt the 30 g. (1 oz.) butter in a pan, add the sorrel and lettuce leaves roughly chopped, together with the sprigs of chervil. Turn these for a few moments in the hot butter – add these to the soup, at the same time adding the milk and cream and the butter cut in small knobs. Reheat gently. Adjust the seasoning. Pour into a hot tureen. Dust over with the finely chopped chervil. Serve hot.

POTAGE DE VOLAILLE ** (for 6 persons)

Ingredients:

1 chicken carcase, cooked or raw.
30 g. butter (1 oz.)
125 g. mushrooms (4 oz.)
3 tablespoons crème de riz
For the stock:
1½ l. water (3 pints)
2 carrots

1 turnip
1 large onion
1 stick celery
bouquet garni
seasoning
To finish:
2 yolks of egg
30 g. butter (1 oz.)

Method: First make the stock. Peel the carrots, turnip and onion. Wash the stick of celery. Cut the carcase into three. Put all these with the bouquet garni and plenty of seasoning into a large stewpan. Pour over the water. Bring up to simmering point and simmer *very* gently for 45 minutes.

Whilst this is taking place wipe the mushrooms on a clean cloth and chop them finely. Melt the butter in a saucepan, add the mushrooms, season them and cover with greaseproof paper and the lid and cook them very gently for 5 minutes.

When the stock is ready, strain it into a clean pan, discard the bouquet garni. Cut the vegetables into small dice and reserve them.

Mix the crème de riz with a little cold water, add this and the mushrooms to the soup. Bring it quickly to the boil and simmer for 2–3 minutes. Draw the pan aside from the heat and add the beaten yolks of egg mixed with a little of the hot soup, stir well, then beat in the remaining ounce of butter, bit by bit. Taste and adjust the seasoning.

Just before serving, add the diced vegetables to the soup.

SOUPE MARINE *   (for 6 persons)

Ingredients:

700 g. cod (1½ lb.)
2 onions
2 cloves garlic
120 g. noodles (4 oz.)

120 g. prawns (4 oz.)
grated zest of 1 small orange
a good pinch saffron
1 tomato
seasoning

Method: Skin the cod and cut it into portions. Cut the tomato into quarters, crush the garlic with a little salt, and slice the onions thinly. Put them all into a large pan with the orange zest. Season and cover with about 2 l. (4 pints) of cold water. Bring to the boil, lower the heat and allow it to simmer for 15–20 minutes.

Whilst this is taking place, cook the noodles in plenty of boiling salted water for 10–15 minutes. Drain and rinse them in hot water. Pass the soup through a sieve or vegetable mill. Return it to a clean pan and make it hot, adding enough saffron to colour the soup. Add the noodles and continue to reheat until the noodles are hot. Adjust the seasoning.

Shell the prawns. Dish the soup in a hot tureen, sprinkle the surface with the prawns. Serve at once.

SOUPE AUX MOULES AU LARD **   (for 6 persons)

Ingredients:

2 l. mussels (2 quarts)
120 g. lean bacon (4 oz.)
1 medium sized onion
3 tomatoes
2 green peppers

1½ l. vegetable stock or water
(3 pints)
2 tablespoons tapioca
30 g. butter (1 oz.)
pinch of curry powder
seasoning

Method: Cut the bacon into strips and chop the onion very finely. Heat the butter in a large stewpan and cook the onion and bacon in this over a gentle heat until the onion is soft but not brown.

Meanwhile cut the peppers in half and remove the seeds and pith. Cut the peppers into lozenge shaped pieces. Cook them in boiling salted water for 5 minutes. Drain. Skin the tomatoes and cut them into slices. Stir the peppers and tomatoes gently in the hot butter until well coated. Pour on the stock or water, season well, adding a small pinch of curry powder. Bring to the boil and simmer gently for 20 minutes.

While the soup is cooking, wash and scrape the mussels, place them in a large pan with a knob of butter and shake them over a good heat for 5–6 minutes or until all are open (see notes on mussels, page 70). Strain the liquor through a muslin into the soup. Stir in the tapioca and cook for a further 10 minutes (or until the tapioca is cooked). Taste and season. Discard the shells and add the mussels to the soup. Serve at once.

SOUPE À LA PAYSANNE *　　　　　　　　　(for 4–6 persons)

Ingredients:
4–6 medium sized carrots
1 medium sized turnip
2 leeks or 2 medium sized onions
1 stick celery or a pinch celery salt
2 medium potatoes

1 l. white stock approx. (2 pints)
75 g. butter, approx. (2½ oz.)
seasoning
To finish:
slices of French bread and butter
finely chopped chervil

Method: Wash all the vegetables and cut them into paysanne shapes. (Put the prepared potatoes aside in a bowl of cold water.) Heat the butter in a large stewpan, add the carrots, leeks or onions, turnip and celery. Stir these over a low heat until they are slightly soft. Do not allow them to brown in any way. Draw aside from the heat and pour on the boiling stock. Season to taste. Return to the heat and simmer gently for 20 minutes. Add the potatoes and continue to cook for a further 15 minutes or until all the vegetables are soft.

Spread the slices of French bread with butter, allowing one slice per person. Lay these in the bottom of a hot tureen.

Taste and adjust the seasoning in the soup before ladling it over the bread and butter. Just before serving, sprinkle with finely chopped chervil.

Comment: Paysanne shapes are made by trimming square, round or triangular lengths of vegetable, about 1 cm. (½ inch) side or diameter, these are then sliced thinly and have a decorative effect. Vegetables in season should be used for this soup and green beans cut into lozenge shapes and/or peas may be added with advantage. These latter should be added at the same time as the potatoes, so that they will not be overcooked.

VELOUTÉ DE ROQUEFORT *　　　　　　　　(for 6 persons)

Ingredients:
2 medium sized onions
1 heart of celery
1 clove garlic
2 carrots
125 g. butter (4 oz.)
60 g. plain flour (2 oz.)
1½ dl. milk (1 gill)

1½ l. white stock, or water (3 pints)
1½ dl. thick cream (1 gill)
60 g. Roquefort cheese (2 oz.)
seasoning
To finish:
small slices of French bread,
　lightly toasted

Method: Wash and prepare the vegetables. Chop the onions, carrots, celery and garlic finely.

Heat three-quarters of the butter in a fairly large pan. Put in the vegetables and season them well. Cover with greaseproof paper and the lid, and sweat them over a gentle heat, shaking the pan from time to time. When all the vegetables are soft draw the pan aside from the heat and sprinkle in the flour, mix it in well. Return the pan to the heat and stir for a moment or two, then add the hot milk and stock or water. Simmer all together for 10 minutes. Meanwhile crush the cheese with a fork and work it in to the rest of the butter. Remove the soup from the heat and whisk in the cheese and butter together with the cream. Taste and adjust the seasoning.

Place a round of toasted bread in each soup cup or plate, pour the hot soup over and serve at once.

Fish

It would be pleasant to be able to report a startling improvement in the supply of varieties of fish since The Iris Syrett Cookery Book was written. It is possible sometimes in places where there is a large immigrant population to find the less usual fish. In fact, one independent fishmonger in WOKING found a ready sale for octopus!

It is now possible to buy quite good frozen trout and salmon. Much of the sea fish which can be bought frozen is, in fact, fresher than that which one would find in the local fish shop and sold as fresh.

THE PURCHASING OF FISH

Fish that appears to be stale or which has an unpleasant smell – which is easily recognised – should not be used. The following tests are well known and should be useful to the inexperienced:

1. Firm Flesh
2. Eyes Bright
3. Gills Red
4. Tail Stiff
5. Scales Plentiful

Although it is usually the practice to have fish cleaned and filleted by the fishmonger, there are times in everyone's life when one can be confronted by a present from an angler and then it may be necessary to carry out these preparations oneself.

To Clean Flat Fish (sole, plaice, etc.)   Cut out the gills, make a small incision in the stomach and pull out the gut, etc. Wash the fish well. If the head is to be removed, do this with a semi-circular cut. The stomach of the fish lies just behind the head.

To Clean Round Fish (herrings, whiting, etc.)   Slit the stomach of the fish from the head towards the tail. Remove all the entrails. Remove the head with a clean cut if desired.

To Fillet Flat Fish   Lay the fish on a board and, with a sharp pointed knife, make an incision on either side of the backbone, from head to tail, cutting through the flesh until the bone can be felt with the blade of a knife. Start with the left-hand top fillet, keeping the knife at an oblique angle and 'stroke' it through, allowing it to rest on the bone, in three or four strokes from head towards the tail. Pull off this fillet. Turn the fish round with the head nearest you and repeat – this time working from the tail towards the head. Turn the fish over and repeat the process on the other side. This will give you four fillets.

To Fillet Round Fish   Round fish should be placed on a board with the head away from you. With a sharp pointed knife, slit the fish down the backbone from head to tail. Then remove the top fillet, cutting it neatly at the head. Turn over and repeat on the other side. Round fish have two fillets to each fish.

To Split Round Fish   Slit the fish down the stomach from head to tail. Remove the gut and roe. Place it on a board with the cut side down. Then with the palm of the hand, press the fish firmly all down the back bone. Turn over and it will be found that the back bone and side bones come away quite easily.

To Skin Flat Fish (sole)   Wash the fish and dry thoroughly on a clean cloth. Remove the fins. Lay the fish on a board with the tail facing you and the black skin uppermost. Make an incision in the skin from left to right – just above the tail – and loosen the skin on both sides. Dip the fingers into salt to prevent them from slipping, then holding the tail down firmly with one hand, take hold of the skin with the other hand and draw it quickly and firmly towards the head. The white skin is sometimes left on, but if it is to be removed, repeat the method used for removing the black skin.

To Skin Plaice, Fresh Haddock Fillets, etc.   Plaice and fresh haddock are usually filleted first, in which case place the fillet, skin side downwards, on a board and with the tail facing you, make a small incision through the *flesh only,* just above the tail. Dip the fingers into salt and keeping the knife upright, work towards the head with a slightly sawing movement, whilst at the same time pulling the fillet gently towards you with the other hand.

METHODS OF COOKING FISH

Poaching   This method can either be carried out using a fish kettle and cooking it on the top of the stove, or in a fireproof dish in the oven. When cooking whole fish such as salmon, trout, etc., it is advisable to use a fish kettle which has a drainer in the shape of a perforated plate in the bottom. This plate has two handles to enable the fish to be lifted out of the pan without risk of damaging or breaking it. If such a utensil is not obtainable, a saucer may be placed upturned in the bottom of a stewpan and a clean wet cloth put on top, allowing the ends to hang over the sides of the pan. The fish is then cooked in this hammock and can be lifted out easily. The saucer prevents the fish from coming into direct contact with the hot metal base during the cooking process. For trout or salmon, a court bouillon is usually prepared first, allowed to cool and then the fish is put on the drainer and the liquor poured over it, allowing just enough to cover the fish. The kettle containing the fish should be placed over a low heat, covered, brought gradually up to simmering point and allowed to cook very, very gently – in fact only an occasional bubble should show on the surface of the liquid. Any suggestion of rapid cooking will cause the flesh to break up and disintegrate. In some cases the fish, if it is to be served cold, is cooled in the court bouillon.

Fish with coarse flesh, such as turbot, cod, bream, etc., should be placed in a hot court bouillon which has come to the boil. This has the effect of immediately sealing the juices, which otherwise would escape in the liquid, causing the fish to taste insipid. The times given for poaching fish appear to be different in every reference book and can be confusing to the amateur. Probably the best guide is to note that cooked fish becomes opaque looking, that a white creamy liquid will flow from the fish and that it comes away from the bone easily. For a large fish weighing from four to five pounds, twenty to thirty minutes should be allowed. For small fish from one and a half to two pounds, ten to twenty minutes should be allowed. These times are given for fish cooked in a fish kettle on the top of the stove. Fish poached in a fireproof dish in the oven will take slightly longer. In this case the fireproof dish should be buttered first and a piece of greaseproof paper or aluminium foil laid over the top, twisting the ends under the sides of the dish to enclose it completely. Fish that is poached in the oven with its carcase laid over the top will take longer to cook than that covered with paper. A fireproof dish which has its own lid can be used instead of paper, but again it will take longer for the heat to penetrate through. These methods of poaching can be employed where fish is to be 'boiled', since as already stated, boiling is not to be recommended.

The court bouillon which the fish is cooked in is frequently used as the basis of a sauce to serve with the fish. For that reason, when a court bouillon has half water and half wine, it is better to pour the wine over the fish first and then add the water as required, to cover the fish. In this way a more concentrated wine flavour will be obtained.

Cod, turbot or hake which are to be served plain and with a sauce handed separately, should be drained well of all liquid first and then laid on a folded linen napkin on a hot serving dish.

Frying Frying is classified as *deep or shallow*. For deep fat frying, a fish fryer and a wire basket should be used. Pure lard is the best medium, but vegetable fats may be used. Shallow frying can be carried out using butter or oil.

PREPARATION OF FISH FOR FRYING

Fish to be fried must have a protective coating, either:

1. Seasoned flour
2. Batter
3. Egg and oil and white breadcrumbs

First clean, wash and dry the fish thoroughly on a clean cloth. Secondly season the fish with salt and pepper and, if liked, a few drops of lemon juice. Thirdly dip in the coating preparation. When coating with egg and breadcrumbs, whisk the egg lightly up with a tablespoon of oil, season well and strain into a soup plate. Dip the fish in this and then into a pile of breadcrumbs, which have been made by passing stale bread through a fairly coarse sieve. The breadcrumbs must be dry. A better result is obtained by coating with egg and crumbs *twice* before frying. The fish should only be lightly dipped into the egg or brushed over with egg. It is a mistake to leave the fish in the egg for more than a moment, or the egg will soak into the fish and give a soggy result. It is a good idea to have a heap of white breadcrumbs at the side, lift the fish out of the egg, hold it up and allow it to drain, lay it in the breadcrumbs and press the crumbs on lightly, using the flat blade of a knife. Shake off any surplus crumbs before frying and if possible allow it to rest for a few moments before frying to enable the crumbs, etc. to set. It is inadvisable to use bought 'packet' crumbs, except in cases of dire emergency. These crumbs are usually a strong shade of yellow or orange and when fried they turn to a bright mahogany colour, which is unappetising in appearance as well as incorrect. The term 'golden' in relation to food fried in egg and breadcrumbs is explicit. The crumbs should never have a scorched appearance.

The fat in the pan should be about two-thirds of the way up the sides. The fat should be heated slowly to a temperature of approximately 370° F. (190° C.) depending on the food to be fried (i.e. food which has already been cooked such as croquettes, will require less heat than potatoes, thin fillets of fish less still). For many years the test of whether the fat was hot enough was to watch for a 'faint blue haze which will rise from the centre of the pan'. This test was perfectly sound when frying in lard, but it does not apply to vegetable fats. The best test is to put a small square of bread into the fat. If it immediately bubbles quickly and becomes crisp and golden in a matter of thirty seconds or so, then the fat is ready for frying. If on the other hand there is little or no bubbling, then the fat is not hot enough. Food fried in fat that is too cool will be greasy, sodden and indigestible. It is important not to fry too much food at once. If fillets of fish are fried, fry two at a time. Too much food in the pan will cause the fat to overflow, which is dangerous and it will have the effect of cooling off the fat. Lift the fish carefully with a draining spoon and place on a plate on which ordinary white kitchen or tissue paper has been placed. This will absorb the surplus grease. Do not stand this plate too near the deep fat pan – it is easy to set light to the draining paper, thus causing an accident. Some cooks advocate placing the draining paper in a roasting tin, the high sides of which give protection against contact with a naked flame. Food should always be lowered *carefully* into the pan, never thrown in, which causes it to splash and thereby causing burning. In many recipes, fried fish is served on a paper doyley to absorb the remaining fat. The time required for frying must be judged by the thickness of the fish. Always lift the fish from the pan a little before it reaches the correct colouring. It will continue to brown for half a minute or so after it has been removed from the hot fat.

Directly after frying, allow the fat to cool, then strain into a clean dry bowl. Fat which has been made too hot and which has thus become burnt should not be used again. Dripping can be used for frying, but it must be clarified first (see page 26).

Fried parsley is often served with fried fish. This must be perfectly dry or it will splutter and cause burning. It is better to fry it in a frying basket in a deep fat pan, as it is difficult to retrieve it from a pan by itself. Lower it carefully into the hot fat, it will at once make a sizzling noise. As soon as this ceases, remove the parsley and put it to drain on kitchen or tissue paper as for fish.

Shallow Frying Fish fried in shallow fat is usually only dipped in seasoned flour. Butter or oil are the best mediums for this type of frying.

Grilling Fish to be grilled should be cleaned and washed in the usual way and dried carefully on a clean dry cloth. It should be scraped to remove the scales. When thick fish is to be grilled, it should be 'scored' with a sharp knife on either side to hasten the cooking process. Sole should have the head removed with a diagonal cut and the black skin removed. The fins should be trimmed. Fish such as mackerel or herrings which are split open should be grilled on the open side first. As in the case of meat, the grill must be pre-heated before the grilling is started and both the grill rack and the fish should be brushed over with melted butter. It may be desirable to brush the fish again with more melted butter before the end of the grilling time.

SHELL FISH

In this chapter will be found recipes for lobsters, crabs, scallops, mussels, oysters, prawns and shrimps. Some recipes call for crayfish or écrevisses as a garnish. These are difficult to come by and most fishmongers would shake their heads sadly if asked for them. Small Dublin Bay prawns are often used in their place.

Most lobsters are bought already cooked by the fishmonger, but in some recipes it is desirable to use live lobsters. There are two accepted ways in which to kill lobsters. One is to plunge them into boiling court bouillon and cook them for ten to fifteen minutes per pound, and the second way is to place the lobster on a board and taking a really sharp knife, drive it through the centre of the cross which is plainly marked on the head. This has the effect of piercing the brain and death is instantaneous. Lobsters are at their best and cheapest between June and September, crabs from April to October. Oysters are in season in England when there is an 'R' in the month, but in France, where they are more plentiful, they are eaten practically all the year round. Scallops are in season from November until April.

Most shell fish have some part which is dangerous to eat: the gills, or dead man's fingers, in lobsters and crabs, the beards of mussels, oysters and scallops.

The medium sized lobsters and crabs are best in flavour. The female or hen lobster has spawn beneath her tail. This is usually cooked separately and is excellent for colouring. To test if a lobster is fresh when it is purchased already cooked by the fishmonger, pull the tail sharply and it should spring back at once. After the lobster has been split open, remove the sac in the head and the intestine which runs in a black line through the meat near the tail. The lobster coral is bright red when cooked. This can be removed and pounded with equal quantities of butter and then sieved. This is one manner of making Beurre de Homard. The second method is to dry the lobster shells very thoroughly, pound finely using a pestle and mortar, adding an equal quantity of butter. Warm very slightly and then pass through a fine sieve.

To Open a Cooked Crab Remove the claws with a twist. Lay the crab on its back, place the fingers between the shell and the body and using the thumbs, push away the lower part of the shell from the upper. Take out the poisonous fingers lying inside the shell, the sac and intestines.

Oysters Oysters can be opened with a small sharp pointed knife. Hold the oyster firmly in the palm of the hand, insert the knife at the hinge and retain the liquor. Remove the beard.

Mussels Mussels should never be used if they are damaged or open. Place them in a bowl of cold water, scrub the shells well and continue in this way, changing the water two or three times. (This is most important since the liquor from the mussels is frequently used in making the sauce to go with them.) Then with a sharp knife, scrape off the 'beard' which looks like a shaggy piece of fine seaweed.

Scallops Scallops are usually sold open and with the beard removed. They should be well washed before cooking. The deep shell is frequently used for serving the scallops in. It is advisable to ask for this shell when buying the scallops from the fishmonger.

In cooking all shell fish it is *very important not to overcook them*. They rapidly become tough and flavourless.

Prawns and Shrimps Prawns and shrimps are usually bought cooked. Both are often very salt and this should be borne in mind when adding them to a sauce or soup.

NOTES ON RED MULLET

This fish is often referred to as the 'woodcock of the sea' since it is frequently cooked uncleaned and with only the gills removed. However, if this practice is not liked, it may be better to clean and scale the fish and retain the liver.

FISH

ANGUILLES AU VERT ** (for 4 persons)

Ingredients:

4 eels of approx. ½ kg. each (1 lb.)
6 shallots (finely chopped)
1 sprig thyme
3 bayleaves
a good bunch parsley
3–4 sprigs tarragon
½ kg. sorrel, well washed (1 lb.)
½ teaspoon powdered aniseed
3 dl. court bouillon (see page 18) (½ pint)

¼ l. dry white wine (1½ gills)
15 g. fécule de pommes de terre or potato flour (½ oz.)
4 yolks of egg
1½ dl. thin cream (1 gill)
60 g. butter (2 oz.)
3–4 tablespoons oil
juice of 2 lemons
seasoning

Method: Have the eels cleaned and scaled. Cut them into 4 or 5 slices each. This can be done with a sharp knife or if preferred with kitchen scissors. Place the pieces in a shallow dish and season well.

Put the butter and oil into a sauté pan. Heat it, then add the eels and allow them just to brown lightly, keeping them moving in the pan by turning them with a wooden spoon. This is important, otherwise they will stick and burn. Add the shallots and continue to cook until they too have turned a light gold.

Chop the thyme and bayleaves roughly. Sprinkle them on the top. Season. Lower the heat. Cover with greaseproof paper and the lid and allow to cook very slowly for 5 minutes. At the end of this time, add the chopped sorrel, parsley and tarragon. Stir well for 2–3 minutes. Pour on the court bouillon, wine and lemon juice mixed with the aniseed. Cook gently for 10 minutes.

Whisk the yolks with the fécule de pommes de terre. Add the cream.

When the eels are cooked, lift them with a draining spoon on to a serving dish. Strain 3 dl. (½ pint) of the liquor they were cooked in on to the yolks and cream. Pour into a clean pan and stir the sauce over a gentle heat until it thickens, without boiling. Adjust the seasoning. Pour over the eels and serve hot or cold.

BROCHET À LA MANON ***   (for 8–9 persons)

Ingredients:

1 pike weighing from 1½–2 kg. (3–4 lb.)

For the Court Bouillon:

3 dessertspoons tarragon vinegar
1 medium onion, sliced
1 carrot, sliced
bouquet garni
3–4 parsley stalks
seasoning

For the Garnish:

10–12 tartlet cases made with Pâte Brisée (Method II using 240 g. (8 oz.) plain flour) (see page 338)

Sauce Béchamel made with 3 dl. (½ pint) milk, 45 g. (1½ oz.) plain flour, 45 g. (1½ oz.) butter, seasoning (see page 34), with 1 dl. (½ gill) thick cream
250 g. prawns (8 oz.)
60 g. butter, approx. (2 oz.)
1 dl. thick cream (½ gill)
Cayenne pepper
carmine colouring
seasoning

To finish:

9 whole prawns, approx.
parsley

Method: Make the court bouillon. Put the vinegar and ½ l. (¾ pint) water into a pan and add the bouquet garni, the parsley stalks tied together, the vegetables and the seasoning. Bring up to simmering point. Place the pike, already cleaned, in this, resting on its stomach. Cook *very gently* indeed for 15 minutes. Draw aside from the heat and allow the fish to cool completely in the court bouillon. Lift it out very gently on to a damp cloth to drain. Then lift it onto a long serving dish. Leaving the skin on the head and tail, remove the rest.

Make the pâte brisée tartlets.

Make up the sauce Béchamel and mix in the cream.

Take the heads and shells from the 250 g. (8 oz.) prawns. Chop the prawns roughly and mix them with the cream.

Make the beurre de crevettes rouges by pounding the heads and the shells of half the prawns using a pestle and mortar. Add an equal quantity by bulk of butter and pound again so that the colour is transferred from the shells to the butter. Pass it through a wire sieve.

Warm the sauce Béchamel a little, and gradually mix in the beurre de crevettes rouges. Mix in the prawn flesh and cream. Taste and adjust the seasoning and add a little Cayenne pepper and if needed a drop of carmine. Fill this mixture into the tartlet cases.

Make an incision down the back of the fish and insert the whole prawns in a line down the length of the fish.

Garnish the head with parsley and arrange the tartlets at each side of the dish. Serve cold.

FILETS DE CABILLAUD AUX CHAMPIGNONS *

(for 4 persons)

Ingredients:

750 g. cod fillet (1½ lb.)
250 g. mushrooms (½ lb.)
125 g. butter (4 oz.)
Sauce Béchamel made with 45 g.
(1½ oz.) butter, 45 g. (1½ oz.)

plain flour, ¼ l. (1½ gills) milk,
seasoning (see page 34 for
method)
¼ l. thick cream (1½ gills)
juice of 1 lemon
seasoning

Method: Cut the fish diagonally into 8 portions. Dry it with a clean cloth.

Make 90 g. (3 oz.) butter hot in a frying pan, put in the pieces of fish and fry them gently on both sides for approximately 3–4 minutes or until they begin to brown. Remove the pan from the heat and carefully lift out the fish. Arrange the pieces in a buttered fireproof dish, pour over the butter they have been cooking in together with the strained lemon juice. Season well. Cover the dish tightly with a piece of buttered greaseproof paper or aluminium foil. Put it in a moderate oven, gas mark 5 or 375° F. (190° C.) for approximately ¼ hour.

Wipe the mushrooms on a clean cloth. Chop them very finely. Make the rest of the butter hot in a small pan, put in the mushrooms, season them and cover with a piece of greaseproof paper and the lid. Cook them over a gentle heat for 5 minutes. Remove them and keep them hot.

Make the sauce Béchamel and when it is cooked, whisk in the cream. Season very well. Heat again and keep it hot.

When the fish is cooked, remove it from the oven. Wipe round the dish to remove unsightly browning marks. Scatter the mushrooms on top of the fish. Pour over the sauce Béchamel carefully. Serve at once.

CARPE À LA POLONAISE **

(for 4–6 persons)

Ingredients:

1½–2 kg. carp (3–4 lb.)
2 onions
2 carrots
1 leek
1 small parsnip
bouquet garni
peppercorns
salt
For the Sauce:
60 g. butter (2 oz.)
45 g. plain flour (1½ oz.)

1 tablespoon sugar
60 g. stoned raisins (2 oz.)⎤ soaked
3 prunes ⎦ overnight
30 g. chopped blanched almonds
(1 oz.)
1 small honey cake or ginger biscuit
1½ dl. red wine (1 gill)
1 tablespoon wine vinegar or
lemon juice
To Garnish:
1 sliced lemon

Method: Have the carp cleaned, remove all the scales and wash it well.

Clean all the vegetables, cut them into slices and put them into a large pan with the bouquet garni, salt, peppercorns and 1 l. (1½ pints) water.

Bring to the boil and simmer for 10 minutes. Add the fish, either whole or cut into steaks 3–4 cm. (1–1½ inches) thick. Simmer gently for 40–50 minutes if whole, or 15–20 minutes if in steaks.

Make the sauce. Heat the butter and add the flour and sugar. Cook the roux, stirring all the time until it is a pale golden colour. Add ½ l. (1 pint) of strained fish liquor and the wine and mix well (keep the fish hot in the remaining liquor). Add the raisins, the chopped stoned prunes, the biscuit and the almonds. Bring to the boil, stirring constantly and simmer over a low heat for 15 minutes. Then add the vinegar or lemon juice. Cook for a few minutes longer. Lift the fish carefully, drain it well and arrange it on a hot serving dish. Coat with the sauce and garnish with lemon slices.

CÉLERI-RAVE AUX MOULES ** (for 4 persons)

Ingredients:
3–4 l. mussels (3–4 quarts)
1 finely chopped shallot
15 g. butter (½ oz.)
1 dl. dry white wine (½ gill)
1 root of celeriac

3 dl. Sauce Mayonnaise (see page 36) (½ pint)
seasoning
To finish:
finely chopped parsley

Method: Discard any mussels which are damaged or open. Wash the remainder in several changes of water and remove their beards. Put them in a saucepan with the shallot, butter, wine and seasoning. Cover tightly and place the pan over a good heat, shaking it from time to time until the mussels are open. This will take approximately 5 minutes. Discard any which fail to open. Remove from the heat and allow to get quite cold.

Make up the sauce Mayonnaise in the usual way, seasoning it very well indeed. Wash and peel the celeriac and cut it into small dice of about ½ cm. (¼ inch).

Dry the mussels on a clean cloth. Reserve twelve or so for decoration. When they are quite cold remove the shells from the rest and mix the mussels with the celeriac and sauce Mayonnaise. Pile the mixture in a shallow dish. Sprinkle it with finely chopped parsley and arrange the mussel decoration at each side. Serve very cold.

COQUILLES SAINT-JACQUES À LA CRÈME **
(for 2 or 4 persons)

Ingredients:
4 scallops
1½ dl. dry white wine (1 gill)
90 g. cap mushrooms (3 oz.)
slice of onion
slice of carrot
½ bayleaf
2 peppercorns
45 g. butter (1½ oz.)

seasoning
For the Sauce:
30 g. butter (1 oz.)
30 g. plain flour (1 oz.)
¼ l. court bouillon (see page 18)
    (1½ gills)
1 yolk of egg
1 dl. thick cream (½ gill)
seasoning

Method: Remove the scallops from their shells. Reserve the deep shells and wash them well. Wash the scallops well and cut the white flesh into slices. Chop the red flesh roughly. Heat the wine with the vegetables, bayleaf and peppercorns and poach the scallops in this over a gentle heat for 4–5 minutes. When cooked remove scallops with a draining spoon and drain them on a clean dry cloth. Reduce the liquor they were cooked in to half its original quantity.

Slice the mushrooms neatly. Heat the butter in a small pan. Put in the mushrooms and seasoning. Cover with greaseproof paper and the lid and cook over a gentle heat until they are soft.

Make the sauce – melt the butter in a small pan, draw it aside from the heat and stir in the flour. Return to the heat and cook for 2–3 minutes, stirring continuously. Strain on the court bouillon and scallop liquor. Bring to the boil, continuing to stir. Simmer for 5 minutes. Beat the yolk with the cream and add a little sauce to this, whisking it well. Return it to the pan, stir over a low heat to thicken slightly, but do not allow it to boil. Taste and adjust the seasoning.

Arrange the scallops in the shells and arrange the sliced mushrooms round the edges. Coat all over with the sauce and brown under a hot grill or in the top of a hot oven, gas mark 7 or 425° F. (220° C.). Serve at once.

COQUILLES SAINT-JACQUES AU PORTO **

(for 2–3 persons)

Ingredients:
4–6 scallops
1½ dl. dry white wine (1 gill)
2 shallots
bouquet garni
seasoning
For the Sauce:
30 g. plain flour (1 oz.)

30 g. butter (1 oz.)
1½ dl. milk (1 gill)
1 teaspoon concentrated tomato
  purée
1 yolk of egg
1 dl. Ruby port (½ gill)
60 g. grated cheese (2 oz.)

Method: Wash the scallops and wash the deep shells. Make the wine hot in a pan with the chopped shallots, bouquet garni and seasoning. Put in the scallops and simmer them gently for 4–5 minutes. Remove them and cut each scallop into quarters.

Heat the butter in a pan, remove from the heat and stir in the flour. Return to the heat, stir in the milk and strain in the liquor in which the scallops were cooked. Bring to the boil and simmer for 5 minutes, stirring all the time. Stir in the tomato purée and seasoning. Beat the yolk with the port. Stir in a little sauce, return this to the pan. Keep stirring and allow to thicken slightly over a gentle heat, without allowing the sauce to boil. Mix the scallops with the sauce. Divide the mixture evenly into the shells and sprinkle with grated cheese. Brown under a hot grill or in the top of a hot oven, gas mark 7 or 425° F. (220° C.). Serve at once.

COQUILLES SAINT-JACQUES DIABLE *

(for 2 or 4 persons)

Ingredients:

4 scallops
1 heaped teaspoon flour
1 teaspoon made mustard
1 small onion
1 teaspoon Worcestershire sauce
2 tablespoons white breadcrumbs
a little milk
30 g. butter (1 oz.)
a pinch of Cayenne pepper

seasoning
Court Bouillon made with:
1½ dl. dry white wine (1 gill)
slice of onion
½ bayleaf
½ clove garlic
seasoning
To finish:
grated cheese
browned breadcrumbs

Method: Put the wine with 3 dl. (½ pint) water and all the other ingredients for the court bouillon into a pan and simmer for 20 minutes. Allow it to get cold. Remove the scallops from their shells and wash them well. Put them in the court bouillon and bring to simmering point. Simmer for 2–3 minutes. Remove and chop them rather roughly. Retain the court bouillon in which they were cooked.

Soak the breadcrumbs in a little milk, press with the hands until almost dry. Heat the butter in a pan, add the finely chopped onion and cook over a low heat without colouring, until it is soft. Remove the pan from the heat, stir in the flour, return to the heat and cook the roux for 1 or 2 minutes. Stir in the strained court bouillon, then add the breadcrumbs, mustard, Worcestershire sauce and a pinch of Cayenne pepper and plenty of seasoning. Cook for a further 2–3 minutes, stirring all the time. Add the scallops and warm through. Fill the shells with the mixture, sprinkle with grated cheese and browned crumbs and brown under a grill or in the top of a hot oven, gas mark 7 or 425° F. (220° C.). Serve very hot.

COQUILLES SAINT-JACQUES MASCARILLE **

(for 6 persons)

Ingredients:

12 scallops
1 dl. dry white wine (½ gill)
1 dl. water (½ gill)
12 rashers back bacon
90 g. butter (3 oz.)
juice ½ lemon
30 g. white breadcrumbs (1 oz.)
1 clove garlic
bouquet garni

1 tablespoon finely chopped
    parsley
seasoning
To finish:
Pommes de Terre Duchesse,
    Method II, made with 1 kg.
    (2 lb.) potatoes (see page 226)
1 tablespoon finely chopped
    parsley

Method: Wash the scallops well in several changes of water. Scrub six deep shells. Heat the wine and water with the bouquet garni and seasoning in a saucepan. Place the scallops in this and poach them over a very gentle heat for 4–5 minutes. At the end of this time lift the scallops out with a draining spoon and lay them on a clean dry cloth. Wrap each scallop in a rasher of bacon and secure each carefully with a wooden cocktail stick. Season them with a little freshly ground black pepper. Melt 15 g. ($\frac{1}{2}$ oz.) of the butter and brush them over evenly with this.

Make up the pommes de terre duchesse in the usual way adding the tablespoon of chopped parsley. Season well. Using a forcing bag and large rosette pipe, pipe a border of potato round each scallop shell.

Put the scallops on a baking sheet and place them in the top of a hot oven, gas mark 8 or 450° F. (230° C.). Turn them over from time to time until the bacon is cooked.

Place two scallops and the bacon in each shell. Melt 30 g. (1 oz.) of the butter in a pan, add the lemon juice and sprinkle this over the scallops. Keep them hot.

Heat the remainder of the butter in a pan, stir in the breadcrumbs. Cook them until they are gold, add the very finely chopped garlic, the parsley and a pinch of salt. Continue to cook all together for a moment or two. Place a portion of this mixture on each scallop and serve very hot.

TIMBALE DE COQUILLES SAINT-JACQUES **

(for 4–5 persons)

Ingredients:
Flaky pastry (see page 335)
For the filling:
4–5 scallops
125 g. mushrooms (4 oz.)
45 g. butter (1½ oz.)
1½ dl. dry white wine (1 gill)
1 or 2 slices of onion
2 yolks of egg

bouquet garni
1 tablespoon brandy
Sauce Béchamel made with $\frac{1}{4}$ l.
    (1 gill) milk and $\frac{1}{4}$ l. (1 gill) of
    the wine the scallops were
    poached in (see p. 34 for
    method)
seasoning
To finish:
a little finely chopped parsley

Method: Make up the flaky pastry in the usual way. Put it aside to relax for 20 minutes. Then roll out the pastry and line it into an 18 cm. (7 inch) flan ring. Prick the base very well indeed. Line with a piece of greaseproof paper, fill with beans and 'bake blind' in a hot oven, gas mark 6–7 or 400–425° F. (200–220° C.) for 20–25 minutes. Remove the paper and beans and return the case to a cooler oven, for a further 5–7 minutes to dry off the base.

Wash the scallops well. Cut each one into four. Place them in a pan with the slices of onion, bouquet garni, wine and seasoning. Bring them to simmering point and cook them over a gentle heat for 4–5 minutes. Remove them from the pan with a draining spoon. Put them on one side.

Make the sauce Béchamel in the usual way, straining in the liquor from the scallops. Remove it from the heat when it is cooked and whisk in the yolks of egg.

Wipe the mushrooms on a clean cloth. Cut them into $\frac{1}{2}$ cm. ($\frac{1}{4}$ inch) slices. Melt the butter in a saucepan, put in the mushrooms, season, cover with greaseproof paper and the lid. Cook them over a gentle heat, shaking the pan from time to time. At the end of 5 minutes, remove the paper and mix the scallops with the mushrooms. Heat them through gently. Heat the brandy in a separate pan, pour it over the hot scallop mixture and 'flame' it. Stir the scallops and the mushrooms carefully into the sauce. Adjust the seasoning. Pour this mixture into the flan case. Return it to the oven, gas mark 6 or 400° F. (200° C.) for a minute or two. Dust with finely chopped parsley and serve hot.

CRABES À L'INDIENNE *   (for 4 persons)

Ingredients:
2 medium sized cooked crabs
125 g. Patna rice (4 oz.)
2 shallots
2 tomatoes
125 g. mushrooms (4 oz.)

$\frac{1}{4}$ l. Sauce Béchamel (1 gill)
(see page 34 for method)
125 g. butter (4 oz.)
2 teaspoons curry powder
seasoning

Method: Clean the crabs as usual (see page 70). Remove the flesh from the body and claws and flake it. Wash the crab shells and dry them.

Cook the rice in plenty of boiling salted water. When tender drain and refresh it in cold water, then drain again. Heat the butter in a thick pan, add to it the finely chopped shallots and cook them gently until soft, but not coloured. Then add the finely chopped mushrooms, the tomatoes skinned, pipped and roughly chopped and the curry powder. Sauter lightly together. Thicken with the sauce Béchamel. Stir in the crab meat and the rice. Return to the heat and season well. When the mixture is hot, fill it into the crab shells and serve at once.

CRABES FARCIES CHAUDES *   (for 2 persons)

Ingredients:
2 cooked crabs
1 shallot
$\frac{1}{2}$ stale brioche or slice of milk loaf
a little butter
75–100 g. shelled prawns (2–3 oz.)
1 yolk of egg

1 tablespoon thick cream
1 tablespoon chopped parsley
a little hot milk
seasoning
To finish:
4 whole prawns

79

Method: Clean the crabs in the usual way (see page 70). Take out all the flesh from the body and claws. Place this in a bowl with the prawns and the finely chopped shallot. Soak the brioche in the hot milk, squeeze it out well and add it to the crab meat, etc. Beat all well with a fork. Stir in the yolk of egg, the cream and the parsley. Season well.

Wash the crab shells thoroughly and fill them with the mixture. Dot with knobs of butter and cook in a moderate oven, gas mark 5 or 375° F. (190° C.) for 15–20 minutes. Just before serving arrange 2 prawns on each. Serve very hot.

KAROLYS AUX CREVETTES ** (for 3–4 persons)

Ingredients:
Pâte à Choux (see page 336)
a little beaten egg
Sauce Béchamel made with half

milk and half thick cream (see page 34)
2 tablespoons brandy
250 g. unshelled prawns (½ lb.)

Method: Make up the pâte à choux in the usual way. Using a forcing bag and a 1 cm. (⅜ inch) plain tube, pipe the mixture out into fingers about 8 cm. (3 inches) long on a greased baking sheet. Brush them over with a little beaten egg and bake them in a hot oven, gas mark 7–8 or 425–450° F. 220–230° C.) for 10 minutes. After this time reduce the heat to gas mark 5 or 375° F. (190° C.) for a further 20 minutes.

Meanwhile, shell the prawns, retaining the heads. Make up the sauce Béchamel, seasoning it well. Add the prawns and brandy to the sauce and keep it hot.

When the karolys are well risen and crisp, remove them from the oven. Take a sharp knife and cut each lengthwise down one side, near the top, leaving a good depth for the filling. With a teaspoon fill the karolys with the prawn sauce and decorate the opening with 3–4 prawn heads. Serve at once whilst they are still very hot.

PILAF AUX CREVETTES * (for 2–4 persons

Ingredients:
1 cup Patna rice
1 red pepper
1 green pepper
125 g. shelled prawns (4 oz.)
60 g. butter (2 oz.)
2 cups fish stock or court bouillon
2–3 sticks celery, chopped finely

1 onion
pinch of nutmeg
pinch of Cayenne pepper
seasoning
To finish:
finely chopped parsley
coraline pepper

Method: Chop the onion finely. Heat the butter in a large thick pan and cook the onion in this until it is soft but not coloured.

Remove the pith and seeds and cut the peppers into strips. Blanch them in boiling salted water for 5 minutes.

Add the rice to the onion and turn it quickly in the butter until it is a white colour. Pour on the hot stock and mix in the peppers, celery and prawns. Season well, adding the nutmeg and Cayenne pepper. Cover with buttered greaseproof paper and the lid and cook in a moderate oven, gas mark 5 or 375° F. (190° C.) for 20–25 minutes. Do not disturb or stir during the cooking.

When the rice is cooked, heap the mixture in a hot serving dish and rough it up gently with a fork. Sprinkle with coraline pepper and parsley and serve at once.

DAURADE À LA BRETONNE **   (for 4–6 persons)

Ingredients:

¾–1 kg. sea bream fillets (1½–2 lb.)
½kg. new potatoes (1 lb.)
a little butter
For the Farce:
125 g. mushrooms (4 oz.)
2 shallots
¼ l. dry white wine (1¼ gills)
1 tablespoon finely chopped parsley

2 or 3 rosemary leaves
60 g. white breadcrumbs (2 oz.)
½ beaten egg
30 g. butter (1 oz.)
seasoning
For the Garnish:
60 g. butter (2 oz.)
½ kg. peas (1 lb.)
½ kg. new carrots (1 lb.)
chopped parsley

Method: Make the farce. Chop the mushrooms finely with the shallots. Heat the butter in a pan, put in the mushrooms and shallots. Season. Cover with greaseproof paper and the lid. Cook over a low heat, shaking the pan from time to time until the shallots are soft. Chop the rosemary leaves finely with the parsley, add to the mushroom mixture, pour on the white wine, reduce by half over a good heat. Remove the pan from the heat and stir in the breadcrumbs and the beaten egg. Cook very gently until the mixture leaves the sides of the pan. Adjust the seasoning.

Wash and skin the fish fillets and season them with salt and pepper. Spread the farce on each fillet, fold over and tie with fine string. Well butter a fireproof dish and lay the fillets in the centre.

Wash and peel the potatoes, cut them into fine julienne strips and cook them in boiling salted water until they are just cooked. Drain and toss them in hot butter. Lay them round the fish. Sprinkle the fish with water. Cover all over with buttered greaseproof paper and cook in a moderate oven, gas mark 5 or 375° F. (190° C.) for 20–25 minutes or until the fish is cooked.

Meanwhile, cut the carrots into dice and shell the peas. Cook separately in boiling salted water. Drain and toss one after the other in melted butter. Keep them hot.

To Serve: Remove the string and arrange the fish in the centre of a hot serving dish with the potatoes on each side and the carrots and peas at either end. Pour the butter from the vegetables over the fish and sprinkle with finely chopped parsley. Serve hot.

HOMARD À L'AMÉRICAINE *** (for 4 persons)

Ingredients:

2 live lobsters, about ½ kg. each (1 lb. each)
2–3 tablespoons olive oil
60 g. butter (2 oz.)
1 wineglass brandy
1 wineglass dry white wine
½ l. fish stock (see page 20.) ½–¾ pint)
250 g. tomatoes (½ lb.)

2 teaspoons concentrated tomato purée
1 tablespoon finely chopped fresh herbs
1 onion, 1 carrot ⎫
1 small leek ⎪
1 stick celery ⎬ finely chopped
2 shallots ⎭
30 g. plain flour (1 oz.)
seasoning

Method: Kill the lobsters (see page 69). Remove the claws and legs and crush the claws slightly. Cut off the tails. Cut the head portions in half lengthwise. Remove the sacs and discard them. Take out the coral, and creamy part from inside the head and keep it on one side. Slice the tails neatly across the joints. Season the flesh of the lobsters well.

Heat the oil in a sauté pan. Put in the lobster pieces and the claws and turn them all until the flesh is firm and the shell is a good red colour. Remove the pieces and drain off the oil.

Heat 45 g. (1½ oz.) butter in a pan and cook the carrot, onion, leek, shallots and celery. When they are soft, return the pieces of lobster to the pan, pour in the brandy and 'flame' it. Then add the white wine, stock, tomato purée and the tomatoes skinned, pipped and chopped. Season. Bring to simmering point and cook gently for 15 minutes.

Remove the lobster from the pan and keep it hot. Mix the rest of the butter, the flour and the coral to form a paste. Stir this into the cooking liquor. Boil for 2 minutes and strain it. Reheat the sauce. Stir in the herbs. Adjust the seasoning.

Remove the flesh from the claws and pile it, with the tail pieces, in the centre of a hot serving dish. Pour the sauce over the lobster. Serve hot.

Comment: Alternatively the flesh may be removed from the shell, re-heated in the sauce and served in a ring of plain boiled Patna rice.

HOMARD À LA CRÈME ** (for 2 or 3 persons)

Ingredients:

2 cooked lobsters, approx. ½ kg. each (1 lb.)
¼ l. thin cream (½ pint)
125 g. button mushrooms (4 oz.)

a little lemon juice
2 tablespoons brandy
90 g. butter (3 oz.)
beurre manié (see page 16)
seasoning

Method: Cut the lobster flesh into slices. Slice the mushrooms. Heat 30 g. (1 oz.) butter in a pan, add the mushrooms, a little lemon juice, 1 dl. (½ gill) water and seasoning. Cover with greaseproof paper and the lid and cook gently for 5 minutes.

Heat the lobster through in the rest of the butter with the brandy and strained mushroom liquor. Taste and season.

When the lobster is hot, remove it to a hot serving dish and keep it hot. Reduce the liquor the lobster was heated in until two tablespoons remain. stir in the cream, bring it to the boil and thicken with sufficient beurre manié to make a coating consistency. Boil for a further 3 minutes. Stir in the mushrooms. Adjust the seasoning. Pour over the lobster and serve very hot.

HOMARD À LA PALESTINE ***   (for 4 persons)

Ingredients:

1 live lobster, 1 kg. approx. (2–2½ lbs.)
1 large carrot, finely chopped
1 large onion, finely chopped
125 g. butter (4 oz.)
2 tablespoons oil
1½ dl. dry white wine (1 gill)
2 tablespoons brandy
1 shallot, finely chopped
fish stock (see page 20)
125 g. Patna rice (4 oz.)
1 stick celery, finely chopped
1 small leek, finely chopped
1 dessertspoon curry powder
1 teaspoon plain flour
seasoning

Method: Kill the lobster (see page 169). Remove the claws and legs and crush the claws slightly. Cut off the tail half. Cut the head portion in half lengthwise. Remove the sac and discard it. Take out the coral and creamy part from inside the head and keep it on one side. Slice the tail neatly across the joints. Season the flesh of the lobster well.

Heat the oil in a sauté pan, put in the lobster pieces and the claws and turn them all until the flesh is firm and the shell a good red colour. Remove the lobster pieces from the pan, and pour off the excess oil. Add 30 g. (1 oz.) butter to the sauté pan. Sauter the carrot, onion, celery and leek in the butter until they are lightly coloured. Pour in the brandy and 'flame' it. Return the lobster to the pan. Pour in the white wine and sufficient fish stock to cover the lobster, season well. Cover with a lid, bring to simmering point and cook over a low heat for 5–10 minutes.

Remove the flesh from the shell, including the claws, and keep it hot in a little melted butter. Pound the shell roughly in a mortar. Stir it into the cooking liquor and cook for a further 15 minutes. Strain the sauce through a wire sieve, allow to stand for a few minutes and remove all fat from the surface.

Heat 30 g. (1 oz.) butter in a pan, cook the shallot in this until it is soft but not coloured, stir in the curry powder and the flour and cook for a minute or two. Stir in the sauce and bring to the boil and allow it to boil for 2–3 minutes. Remove the sauce from the heat, strain and reheat it. Add the remaining butter bit by bit, together with the creamy part of the lobster and the coral. Adjust the seasoning.

Meanwhile, cook the rice in plenty of boiling salted water, drain, refresh with hot water, drain again. Put it to dry in a well buttered fireproof dish covered with buttered greaseproof paper in a cool oven.

To Serve: Make a ring of rice on a hot serving dish. Arrange the lobster flesh in the centre, coat with a little of the sauce. Serve the rest of the sauce separately.

BARQUETTES D'HUÎTRES À LA NORMANDE **

(for 6 persons)

Ingredients:

Half quantity Pâte Brisée (Method I, omitting the sugar) (see page 338)
60 g. shrimps (shelled) (2 oz.)
6 large mushrooms
2 scallops
slice of onion and slice of carrot
bouquet garni

1½ dl. dry white wine (1 gill)
1 dozen oysters
75 g. butter (2½ oz.)
1 yolk of egg
½ teaspoon lemon juice
Cayenne pepper
seasoning
To finish: 12 unshelled shrimps

Method: Make twelve boat shaped tartlet cases with the pâte brisée.

Chop the mushrooms. Heat 30 g. (1 oz.) butter in a small pan and cook the mushrooms, lemon juice and seasoning gently in this for 4–5 minutes.

Open the oysters and poach them in their own liquor for 2 minutes, then remove and drain them. Reduce their liquor by half over a good heat.

Poach the scallops in the white wine with the onion, carrot and bouquet garni for 3–4 minutes. Drain the scallops and chop them roughly. Mix them with the mushrooms and shrimps. Strain the scallop liquor into a clean pan, and add the liquor from the oysters and mushrooms. Reheat, then stir a little liquor with the yolk of egg. Return to the pan and heat without boiling, stirring all the time. Season, if necessary, adding a pinch of Cayenne pepper.

Place an oyster in each tartlet with a spoonful of the mushrooms, shrimps and scallops. Coat with a spoonful of sauce. Heat in a hot oven, gas mark 7 or 425° F. (218° C.) for a few minutes. Garnish each with a shrimp and serve at once.

CANAPÉS AUX HUÎTRES **   (for 6 persons)

Ingredients:

1 dozen oysters
a little dry white wine
12 slices bread 5 cm. square (2 inches)
1 small tin tunny fish, approx. 200 g. (7 oz.)
3 tablespoons olive oil

240 g. butter (8 oz.)
2 hardboiled yolks of egg
oil for frying the bread
a little lemon juice
1 tablespoon finely chopped fresh herbs
seasoning to include ½ teaspoon Dijon mustard

Method: Fry the slices of bread in the oil until golden brown and crisp. Drain them on white kitchen paper and put them on one side to get completely cold.

Open the oysters using an oyster knife, carefully preserving their liquor. Put them and their liquor into a pan with a little dry white wine if there is not sufficient liquor. Poach them for 1–2 minutes over a very gentle heat. Remove them and allow them to drain and become cold.

Cream the butter well, add the tunny fish, which has been well mashed with a fork. Beat it vigorously, adding the seasoning and the mustard. Using a forcing bag with a coarse rosette tube, pipe a border of tunny fish butter on each square of bread.

Sieve the egg yolks. Season with salt and pepper and mustard. Add the olive oil little by little. Lastly add the lemon juice and stir in the mixed herbs.

Take each oyster and coat it carefully with the egg yolk mixture. Arrange one in the centre of each canapé. Serve very cold.

LANGOUSTINES EN COQUILLES FROIDES **
                                       (for 4–5 persons)

Ingredients:

1 packet frozen scampi (approx. 460 g.) (1 lb.)
1½ dl. dry white wine (1 gill)
macedoine of mixed cooked vegetables, approx. 60 g. (2 oz.) each of peas, beans, carrots and new potatoes
1½ dl. Sauce Vinaigrette (see page 40) (1 gill) to which has been added 1 tablespoon chopped chervil

3 dl. thick Sauce Mayonnaise (see page 36) (½ pint)
handful of spinach leaves
1 lettuce
4–5 scallop shells
bouquet garni
seasoning
To finish:
1 chopped hardboiled egg

Method: Pour the white wine into a saucepan, add the scampi, bouquet garni and seasoning and poach gently for 6–7 minutes. Allow them to cool in the liquor.

Mix the macedoine of vegetables with the vinaigrette dressing.

Make the sauce mayonnaise. Wash the spinach well, blanch it in boiling water for 2–3 minutes, drain and refresh it with cold water. Drain again. Squeeze out with the hands. Pass it through a sieve and mix it with the sauce mayonnaise to give it a pale green colour.

Wash the lettuce, drain well and shred it finely. Arrange a bed of lettuce in each scallop shell, with a spoonful of the vegetables on top. Divide the scampi equally and arrange them on top of the vegetables. Coat all over with the sauce mayonnaise and decorate the edges with the chopped hardboiled egg. Serve ice cold.

MAQUEREAUX QUIMPER ** (for 4 persons)

Ingredients:
4 mackerel
Court Bouillon made with:
2 dl. dry white wine (1 gill)
1 stick celery
1 small onion, sliced
1 carrot, sliced
bouquet garni including bayleaf,
   thyme, tarragon and parsley
seasoning

For the Sauce:
2 yolks of egg
1 teaspoon wine vinegar, approx.
60 g. softened butter (2 oz.)
1 tablespoon Dijon mustard
3 tablespoons chopped fresh herbs
pinch of sugar
seasoning
To finish:
fresh parsley

Method: Clean the mackerel, wash them well and split them in two, removing the backbone.

Make the court bouillon. Pour the wine into a shallow pan with 3 dl. ($\frac{1}{2}$ pint) of water. Add the vegetables, the bouquet garni and seasoning. Bring gently to simmering point, lay the fish in this and allow them to poach over a very low heat until they are done, approximately 15–20 minutes. Draw away from the heat and allow the fish to cool completely in the liquor. When the fish are quite cold, remove them and drain them on a clean, slightly damp cloth.

Make the sauce. Put the yolks into a bowl with the mustard, seasoning, sugar and herbs. Work together well with a spatula. Continue stirring whilst adding the butter little by little. When all is smoothly mixed, thin down to the consistency of fairly thick sauce Mayonnaise with the vinegar.

To Serve: Arrange the fillets round the edge of a serving dish. Heap the sauce in the centre. Decorate in between each fillet with sprigs of fresh parsley. Serve very cold.

MERLANS À LA GRECQUE *   (for 2 persons)

Ingredients:

4 small whiting
2 tablespoons olive oil
350 g. ripe tomatoes (¾ lb.)
2 or 3 shallots, finely sliced

3–4 sprigs thyme
1 bayleaf
pinch saffron
3 dl. dry white wine (½ pint)
seasoning

Method: Clean and wash the fish. Score them well and lay them in a shallow fireproof dish, which has been well coated with the oil. Slice the tomatoes and lay them on the top of the fish with the shallots. Lay the sprigs of thyme and the bayleaf on the top. Sprinkle with the saffron. Season very well. Pour over the wine. Poach in a moderate oven, gas mark 4 or 350° F. (180° C.) for 20–25 minutes. Remove from the oven and allow to get quite cold before serving.

MORUE À L'ITALIENNE *   (for 4–5 persons)

Ingredients:

700 g. salt cod, previously soaked
for 24 hours (1½ lb.)
700 g. ripe tomatoes (1½ lb.)
2–3 tablespoons oil for frying
1 clove garlic
1 cup Patna rice
2 cups fish stock (see page 20)

60 g. butter (2 oz.)
1 small onion, finely chopped
bouquet garni
seasoning
For the Garnish:
slices of lemon
black olives
anchovy fillets

Method: Drain the fish, dry it on a clean cloth and cut it into pieces about 5–7 cm. (2–3 inches) square. Heat the oil in a sauté pan and fry the fish in this, turning it carefully to cook both sides. Add the tomatoes, cut into quarters, and the garlic crushed with a little salt. Season with pepper. Cover tightly and cook gently for 15–20 minutes.

Heat the butter in a deep pan and fry the onion in this without allowing it to brown. Stir in the rice and mix until it is well coated with the butter. Pour in the boiling stock. Season and add the bouquet garni. Cover with greaseproof paper and the lid and cook in a moderate oven, gas mark 5 or 375° F. (190° C.) for 20–25 minutes.

Remove the fish and arrange it down the centre of a hot serving dish. Adjust the seasoning. Strain the tomato sauce over the fish. Make a border with the rice. Decorate each piece of fish with a thin slice of lemon and fillets of anchovy arranged in a cross. Place a stoned black olive in the centre.

Comment: In measuring a cup of dry rice, the same sized cup must always be used for the liquid. If ripe tomatoes are not available, tinned tomatoes may be used. Smoked cod or haddock fillet can be used for this dish if salt cod is unobtainable.

MORUE À LA PAYSANNE * (for 4–5 persons)

Ingredients:

700 g. salt cod, if unobtainable use smoked cod, fillet or smoked haddock (1½ lb.)
1 kg. new potatoes (2 lb.)
1 onion
60 g. butter (2 oz.)

2 tablespoons mixed, finely chopped parsley, chervil, chives and tarragon
½ l. thin cream or creamy milk (¾ pint)
seasoning

Method: If using salt cod, first soak it for 24 hours. Wash smoked haddock or cod. Butter a shallow fireproof dish and lay the fish in this with the onion cut into slices. Season with pepper. Cover with water and poach in a very moderate oven, gas mark 4 or 350° F. (180° C.) for 20–25 minutes. When cooked, drain the fish and flake it, removing all skin and bones.

Meanwhile, cook the potatoes in their skins in boiling salted water. When they are just cooked, rub off their skins and cut the potatoes into slices.

Butter a clean fireproof dish, lay one-third of the potatoes in the bottom. Dot with knobs of butter. Spread half the fish on top, scatter half the herbs over the fish and season with pepper. Now put another layer of potatoes on top, more knobs of butter, then the rest of the fish and herbs. Pour over the cream and finally arrange the remainder of the potatoes neatly on the top. Dot with butter and put in the top of a hot oven, gas mark 7 or 425° F. (220° C.) for 20–25 minutes, or until the top is crusty and brown. Serve at once.

MORUE À LA SOISSONNAISE * (for 4 persons)

Ingredients:

700 g. filleted salt cod (previously soaked for 24 hours) (1½ lb.)
250 g. haricot beans (previously soaked for 24 hours) (½ lb.)
4 medium sized onions
2 cloves garlic
2 bouquets garnis each made with 1 bayleaf, 1 sprig thyme, tarragon and parsley

60 g. butter (2 oz.)
2 dessertspoons concentrated tomato purée
a little extra butter
2 tablespoons thick cream
seasoning
To finish:
finely chopped parsley

Method: Put the beans into a pan of tepid water with the two cloves of garlic crushed with a little salt, a bouquet garni, and one onion cut into thin slices. Season. Bring very slowly to simmering point – this should take about half an hour – cover with a lid and continue to cook for a further 1½ hours on a low heat.

Cut the cod into convenient sized pieces for serving and put it in a pan with sufficient water to cover. Add the second bouquet garni and season with pepper. Poach gently on a low heat for 30–40 minutes.

Chop the remaining onions finely. Heat the butter in a pan. Cook the onions in this until they are soft but not brown. Remove from the heat and stir in 3 dl. (½ pint) of the liquor the beans were cooked in and the tomato purée. Return to the heat and simmer for 2–3 minutes. Season with freshly ground black pepper. Remove again from the heat and whisk in a good knob of butter and the cream.

Lift the pieces of fish with a draining spoon and arrange them down the centre of a hot serving dish. Put the beans, also drained, down each side. Pour over the sauce and sprinkle thickly with finely chopped parsley. Serve very hot.

Comment: This dish can be equally well made with smoked haddock, which will not require soaking.

TARTE À LA MORUE ** (for 4 persons)

Ingredients:
Flaky pastry (see page 335)
For the Filling:
250 g. salt cod or smoked haddock fillet (½ lb.)
450 g. tomatoes (1 lb.)
2 medium onions
75–90 g. butter (2½–3 oz.)
2 tablespoons olive oil

1 clove garlic
bouquet garni
paprika
seasoning
To finish:
2 hardboiled eggs
60 g. stoned black olives (2 oz.)
30 g. grated Gruyère cheese (1 oz.)
2 tablespoons thick cream

Method: If using salt cod put it to soak for 24 hours, changing the water frequently.

Make up the pastry in the usual way and put it aside to relax. Roll it out on a lightly floured board and line it into an 18 cm. (7 inch) flan ring. Bake it blind in a hot oven, gas mark 7 or 425° F. (220° C.) for 25–30 minutes.

Make the filling. Remove the skin and cut the cod or haddock into strips, approximately 3 cm. (1 inch) wide by 6 cm. (2½ inches) long. Make the butter and oil hot in a sauté pan, put in the fish and sauter it gently until done. Remove it with a draining spoon. Dust with paprika. Put it aside and keep it hot.

Skin and pip the tomatoes and cut them into shreds. Chop the onions very finely. Crush the clove of garlic. Put all these with the bouquet garni into the pan with the oil and butter that the fish was cooked in. Cook until the onions are soft and the tomatoes are fairly dry looking. Return the fish to the pan and allow it to continue cooking for 2–3 minutes to enable the fish to take on the flavour of the tomatoes and herbs. Remove the bouquet garni. Taste and adjust the seasoning.

Fill the flan case with the fish mixture. Arrange the slices of hardboiled eggs on the top, with the olives in between. Just before serving, pour over the cream. Dust with the grated Gruyère cheese and brown in the top of a hot oven, gas mark 7 or 425° F. (220° C.) or under a hot grill. Serve at once.

MOULES À LA BOULONNAISE *   (for 3–4 persons)

Ingredients:
2 l. of mussels (2 quarts)
1 onion
bouquet garni made with parsley,
    thyme and bayleaf
60 g. fresh butter (2 oz.)

black pepper
1 finely chopped shallot
2–3 tablespoons finely chopped
    parsley
30 g. white breadcrumbs (1 oz.)
juice of ½ lemon

Method: Wash the mussels in several changes of water and remove their beards. Discard any which are open or which have broken shells. Place them in a thick pan with the sliced onion and bouquet garni, which should be rather a large one. Cover the pan and shake over a good heat until all the mussels are open. This will take approximately 5 minutes. Remove them from their shells. Reserve their liquor.

Meanwhile, heat the butter, add the finely chopped shallot and sauter for a moment. Then add the mussels and shake them in the hot butter. Strain in the liquor they were cooked in and make it hot. Season with pepper and add the lemon juice. Stir in the white breadcrumbs and the parsley. Pile up in a hot serving dish. Serve at once.

MOULES À LA MÉNAGÈRE *   (for 2 persons)

Ingredients:
1 l. mussels (1 quart)
1 large onion
sprig parsley, bayleaf
30 g. fresh butter (1 oz.)
120 g. streaky bacon (4 oz.)

1 tablespoon plain flour
pepper
To finish:
white breadcrumbs
knobs of butter

Method: Wash the mussels in several changes of water and remove their beards. Discard any which have opened. Chop the onion very finely. Put it in a large saucepan with the parsley and bayleaf and pepper. Add the mussels. Cover the pan. Shake over a good heat for 5 minutes or until all the mussels have opened. Strain the liquor through a piece of muslin.

Take the mussels out of their shells and lay them in a well buttered fire-proof dish. Keep them warm, but not hot as they will toughen.

Cut the bacon into strips. Heat the butter in a pan and cook the bacon in this over a low heat. Remove from the heat, sprinkle in the flour, return to the heat and stir well for 1–2 minutes, then stir in the liquor from the mussels. Simmer for 5 minutes. (If the sauce is too thick, add a little water. It should be the consistency of thin cream.) Taste and season. Pour the sauce over the mussels. Cover thickly with the breadcrumbs and dot with knobs of butter. Brown under a hot grill or in the top of a hot oven, gas mark 7 or 425° F. (220° C.). Serve at once.

MOULES AU FUMÉ LIMOUSIN * (for 1–2 persons)

Ingredients:

1 l. mussels (1 quart)
90 g. lean smoked bacon (3 oz.)
45 g. fresh butter (1½ oz.)

3 shallots
1 clove garlic
¼ l. dry white wine (1½ gills)
black pepper to season

Method: Wash the mussels thoroughly in several waters. Remove their beards. Discard any which are open or which have broken shells. Chop the garlic extremely finely and also chop the shallots. Cut the bacon into ½ cm. (¼ inch) dice. Heat the butter in a large strong pan, add the shallots, bacon and garlic and stir for 2 minutes over a good heat. Add the mussels. Cover the pan securely, and maintaining a good heat, shake the pan for 5 minutes, or until all the mussels are open. Then pour in the wine and bring it to the boil. Season with black pepper. Pour into a hot dish and serve at once.

RAGOÛT DES MOULES EN CROÛTE ** (for 4 persons)

Ingredients:

Flaky pastry (see page 335)
For the Filling:
2 l. mussels (2 quarts)
125 g. mushrooms (4 oz.)
1 small clove garlic
1 small onion
45 g. butter (1½ oz.)

30 g. plain flour (1 oz.)
¼ l. dry white wine (1½ gills)
2–3 sprigs parsley
pepper
To finish:
finely chopped parsley
4–5 slices lemon

Method: Make up the flaky pastry in the usual way and put it aside to relax. Roll it out and line it into an 18 cm. (7 inch) flan ring. Bake 'blind' in a hot oven, gas mark 7 or 425° F. (220° C.) for 20–25 minutes.

Meanwhile, wash the mussels in several changes of water and remove their beards. Reject any that are open or have shells that have been damaged. Place in a strong pan over a good heat and shake them from time to time for 5 minutes or until all the mussels are open. Remove their shells and place the mussels in a bowl over a pan of *warm* water. Reserve the liquor they have made.

Wipe the mushrooms on a clean cloth. Cut them into quarters. Peel the onion and cut it into wafer thin slices. Chop the parsley and crush the clove of garlic with a little salt. Heat the butter in a thick pan. Add the sliced onion and cook it over a gentle heat until it is soft and transparent. It is important not to brown the onion slices. Then add the mushrooms, parsley and garlic and continue to cook gently for a further 2 minutes or so. Sprinkle in the flour off the heat and stir well. Return to the heat and mix well, then add the wine, together with the cooking liquor from the mussels, which should make the quantity of liquid up to 3 dl. (½ pint). Bring up to boiling point and keeping well stirred, simmer for 5 minutes. Remove from the heat and pass the mixture through a fine sieve or vegetable mill into a clean pan. Taste and season as necessary. When the sauce is hot, stir in the mussels and pour the mixture into the prepared heated flan case. Arrange 4 or 5 slices of lemon down one side allowing them to overlap. Sprinkle over the chopped parsley. Serve at once.

Comment: If preferred a vol-au-vent case could be used.

TARTE AU SAUMON **   (for 4 persons)

Ingredients:
Pâte Sablée made with 240 g.
   (8 oz.) plain flour, 3 yolks of
   egg, 150 g. (5 oz.) butter
For the Filling:
250 g. poached fresh salmon (8 oz.)

1½ dl. thick cream (1 gill)
2 yolks of egg
beaten egg to brush over
seasoning
To finish:
5 anchovy fillets

Method: Make up the pâte sablée – sift the flour on to a board, make a well in the centre, put in the egg yolks and the butter and work them together with the fingertips as for pâte sucrée (see page 339). Form it into a ball and put it aside to relax in a cold place or refrigerator.

Make the filling. Remove the skin and bones from the salmon and chop it roughly. Whisk the egg yolks gently with the cream, adding a little milk if the mixture is rather thick. Mix this with the salmon and season well.

Cut the pastry in half, then roll out one half and line it into an 18 cm. (7 inch) flan ring. The pastry will be difficult to handle but if carefully manipulated it will line the flan ring easily. Pour the filling into the pastry case. Moisten the edge of the pastry. Roll out the remaining pastry to a circle to cover the flan, pressing the edges well together. Brush over with beaten egg. Bake in a fairly hot oven, gas mark 6 or 400° F. (200° C.) for 25–30 minutes. When the tart is cooked remove it from the oven and decorate the edge with rolled up fillets of anchovy. Serve hot or cold as desired.

Comment: This is a convenient recipe for using up remains of salmon. Alternatively tinned salmon may be used.

CASSEROLETTES DE FILETS DE SOLE ***

(for 4 persons)

Ingredients:

1 sole, approx. 500 g. (1 lb.)
2 shallots, finely chopped
1½ dl. dry white wine (1 gill)
3–4 mushroom stalks
seasoning
Flaky pastry made with 120 g.
   (4 oz.) plain flour (see page 335)
For the Duxelles:
90 g. mushrooms (3 oz.)
1 shallot, finely chopped
30 g. butter (1 oz.)

seasoning
Sauce Béchamel made with 30 g.
   (1 oz.) plain flour, 30 g. (1 oz.)
   butter, 1½ dl. (1 gill) creamy milk
   and 1½ dl. (1 gill) of the liquor
   the fish was cooked in (see page
   34 for method)
30 g. butter (1 oz.)
1 yolk of egg
16 cooked asparagus tips, warmed
   through in a little butter
seasoning

Method: Make up the flaky pastry in the usual way and put it aside to relax.

Skin and fillet the sole, retaining the skins and the bones. Cut each fillet into six equal portions. Lay them in a very lightly buttered fireproof dish. Put round the sides the chopped shallots and the mushroom stalks. Season well and pour over the wine. Lay the skin and bones on the top of the fish. Place the dish in a moderate oven, gas mark 5 or 375° F. (190° C.) for approximately 20 minutes, or until the fish is cooked.

Meanwhile roll out the pastry and line it into 4 deep tartlet tins, approximately 10 cm. (4 inches) in diameter by 2 cm. (¾ inch) deep. Prick the bases well with a fork, and line them with greaseproof paper and beans. Roll out the trimmings and make 4 strips to imitate the handle of a casserolette. In each handle make a small incision near one end. Put the tartlets and the 'handles' on a baking sheet, and cook them in a hot oven, gas mark 7 or 425° F. (220° C.) for about 15 minutes. (The 'handles' will take less time and must be removed earlier.)

When the sole is cooked, lift the pieces out carefully with a draining spoon. Cover them lightly with a piece of buttered greaseproof paper to prevent them from becoming dry and put them aside in a warm place. Retain the liquor they were cooked in.

When the tartlet cases are cooked, remove the paper and beans and return them to a cooler oven to dry off the bases. Then lift them carefully out of their tins and put them on a wire rack.

Make the duxelles. Chop the mushrooms finely, using the stalks as well as the caps. Squeeze them in a clean, dry cloth so that as much liquid as possible is extracted. Melt the butter in a saucepan, add the finely chopped shallot and keeping it well stirred, cook it over a low heat until it is soft, then stir in the mushrooms. Season, and continue to cook until all the moisture from the mushrooms has evaporated. Spread a quarter of the duxelles in the bottom of each tartlet case. On the top of the duxelles arrange 4 tips of asparagus in a neat row.

Make the sauce Béchamel, using half creamy milk and half liquor that the fish was cooked in, to give a correct quantity of liquid. Remove it from the heat and whisk in the 30 g. (1 oz.) butter, bit by bit, lastly add the yolk of egg and whisk again. Adjust the seasoning.

Put 6 portions of sole in each tartlet case, on top of the asparagus tips and carefully coat them with the sauce. Return the tartlets to a baking sheet and put them in the top of a hot oven, gas mark 7–8 or 425–450° F. (220–230° C.) for 2–3 minutes, so that the tops become a light brown. Arrange them on a dish paper on a hot serving dish. Just before serving place the 'handles' in position to complete the casserolettes. Serve hot. (*See Plate 2.*)

FILETS DE SOLE À L'ANDALOUSE *   (for 4–6 persons)

Ingredients:
8 fillets sole
6 tiny onions
3 red peppers

90 g. butter, approx. (3 oz.)
Sauce Tomate (Method 1) (see
    page 38)
seasoning

Method: Remove the pith and seeds from the peppers. Cut the peppers into strips and blanch them for 2–3 minutes in boiling water. Remove and drain them.

Make the sauce tomate.

Skin the fillets, wash and dry them. Fold them into three and place them in a very well buttered fireproof dish. Season well.

Make the butter hot in a pan and cook the onions until they are almost soft. Add the peppers to the pan and continue to cook until both are soft. Add the sauce tomate. Mix well and pour over the sole. Cover with buttered greaseproof paper and cook in a moderate oven, gas mark 5 or 375° F. (190° C.) for 20–25 minutes. Re-dish, if necessary, in a hot serving dish and serve at once.

FILETS DE SOLE À LA BEAUJOLAISE **

(for 4 or 8 persons)

Ingredients:
8 fillets sole
¼ l. Beaujolais (1½ gills)
a slice of carrot
a slice of onion
bayleaf

3–4 parsley stalks
beurre manié (see page 16)
170 g. button mushrooms (6 oz.)
45 g. butter (1½ oz.)
seasoning

Method: Wash and dry the fillets. Fold them in half and place in a lightly buttered fireproof dish. Lay the carrot, onion, parsley stalks and bayleaf down the sides. Season. Pour over the wine and sufficient water to cover the fish. Lay a piece of buttered greaseproof paper on the top. Poach in a moderate oven, gas mark 4–5 or 350–375° F. (190° C.) for 15–20 minutes, or until the fish is cooked.

Whilst the fish is cooking, slice the mushrooms. Heat the butter in a pan, add the mushrooms and season well. Cover with greaseproof paper and the lid and cook over a gentle heat for 5–7 minutes, shaking the pan from time to time.

Remove the fish from the oven. Arrange the fillets down the centre of a hot serving dish and keep them hot. Strain off the liquor into a clean pan. Bring it to the boil and whisk in sufficient beurre manié to give a coating sauce. Taste and adjust the seasoning. (If the sauce is a bad colour, add a little carmine.) Stir in the mushrooms, together with their liquor. Pour the sauce over the fish and serve at once.

FILETS DE SOLE À LA DUCHESSE *** (for 8 persons)

Ingredients:

8 fillets sole, and the bones and skins
1½ kg. Pommes de Terre Duchesse (see page 226) (3 lb. approx.)
melted butter
3 shallots
8 or 9 large mushroom caps
30 g. butter (1 oz.)
240 g. prawns (½ lb.)

8 mussels
¼ l. dry white wine (1½ gills)
Sauce Béchamel made with 30 g. (1 oz.) plain flour, 30 g. (1 oz.) butter, 1½ dl. (¼ pint) milk (see page 34)
bouquet garni
30 g. extra butter (1 oz.)
seasoning

Method: Make up the pommes de terre Duchesse in the usual way. Place in a forcing bag with a large rosette tube and pipe out into squares on to a greased baking sheet. Make little cases large enough to take a fillet which has been folded in half. Make 8 in all. Bake them in a hot oven, gas Mark 7–8 or 425–450° F. (220–230° C.) for 2–3 minutes, then brush them very gently with a little melted butter and return them to the oven for another 4 minutes or until they are golden brown.

Flatten the fillets under the blade of a knife. Fold them in half. Lay them in a sauté or shallow pan, together with 2 shallots, finely chopped. Pour over the wine. Lay the skin and bones over the fillets. Season and poach over a low heat for 10–15 minutes.

Whilst this is taking place, make the sauce Béchamel. When the fish is cooked, lift the fillets carefully with a draining spoon. Strain 1½ dl. (¼ pint) of the liquor they have been cooking in and add this to the sauce Béchamel. Taste and season as required. Remove from the heat and beat in the 30 g. (1 oz.) extra butter. Keep hot.

Heat the 30 g. (1 oz.) butter in a shallow pan and cook the mushroom caps carefully in this and keep them hot.

Shell the prawns and mix them with a little sauce.

Wash the mussels and remove their beards. Place them in a pan with the remaining shallot, finely chopped, and the bouquet garni. Cover and shake them over a good heat for 5 minutes. Remove the mussels from their shells.

To Serve: Take a large serving dish and arrange the potato cases on this. Put a fillet of sole in each. Coat carefully with the rest of the sauce. On the centre of each place a mussel. In between the cases arrange the mushroom caps, and fill them with the prawn mixture. Serve at once. (*See Plate 1.*)

FILETS DE SOLE À LA SAINT VALLIER ***

(for 4–8 persons)

Ingredients:
8 fillets sole
¼ l. dry white wine (1½ gills)
2 shallots
½ quantity Sauce Béchamel (see page 34) to which has been added 1 dessertspoon concentrated tomato purée
45 g. butter (1½ oz.)
seasoning
For the Farce:
240 g. raw minced whiting (8 oz.)

panada made with 3 dl. milk
  (½ pint)
60 g. butter (2 oz.)
75 g. plain flour (2½ oz.)
1 egg, lightly beaten
pinch of nutmeg
seasoning
For the Garnish:
8 whole pink shrimps
120 g. button mushrooms (4 oz.)
30 g. butter (1 oz.)

Method: Make the farce – put the milk on to boil with the butter. When it is boiling, draw aside and shoot all the flour in at once as for pâte à choux (see page 336). Return to the heat and stir all the time until the mixture leaves the sides of the pan and forms a ball. Remove from the heat and beat in the egg a little at a time. Mix this with the minced whiting. Pass all through a wire sieve. Season well, adding the nutmeg. Skin, wash and dry the fillets of sole and spread a layer of this farce on the skinned side of each fillet. Fold them in half to enclose the farce. Place them in a buttered fireproof dish with 1 large or 2 small shallots, finely chopped and the wine. Season. Cover with a piece of buttered greaseproof paper. Poach in a moderate oven, gas mark 5 or 375° F. (190° C.) for approximately 15–20 minutes.

Cut the mushrooms in quarters and sauter them in 30 g. (1 oz.) butter, seasoning them very well.

Make the sauce Béchamel. Season it very well, adding the tomato purée. When the fillets are cooked, drain them carefully and arrange them in a circle on a hot serving dish. Strain the liquor into a saucepan and reduce it over a good heat until only one tablespoonful remains. Beat this into the hot sauce Béchamel, then beat in the butter bit by bit. Taste and rectify the seasoning.

Pile the mushroom garnish in the centre of the dish. Carefully coat the fish and garnish with the sauce. Place a shrimp on each fillet. Serve at once.

FILETS DE SOLE ALSACIENNE * (for 4 or 8 persons)

Ingredients:

8 fillets sole
1½ dl. dry white wine (1 gill)
bouquet garni
1 carrot sliced
1 onion sliced
1 tin sauerkraut, about 340 g.
   (12 oz.)

30 g. butter (1 oz.)
1½ dl. Sauce Mornay made with
   1½ dl. (¼ pint) milk to 30 g.
   (1 oz.) plain flour and 30 g.
   (1 oz.) butter (see page 36)
a little extra grated cheese
seasoning

Method: Skin and wash the fillets and dry them well. Season them, fold them in three and lay them in a buttered fireproof dish with the sliced vegetables and the bouquet garni. Season. Pour on the wine and add sufficient water just to cover the fish. Cover with buttered greaseproof paper and poach in a moderate oven, gas mark 5 or 375° F. (190° C.) for about 15–20 minutes or until cooked.

Make up the sauce Mornay.

Heat the sauerkraut through in the butter and spread it in the bottom of a hot fireproof dish. When the fish is cooked drain it carefully and arrange it on the sauerkraut. Strain the liquor the fish was cooked in into the sauce Mornay. Whisk well, heat thoroughly and adjust the seasoning. Pour the sauce over the fish. Sprinkle with the rest of the grated cheese and brown quickly under a hot grill or in the top of a hot oven, gas mark 7 or 425° F. (220° C.). Serve at once.

FILETS DE SOLE CARMELITE *** (for 8–10 persons)

Ingredients:

8 fillets sole
500 g. tail of salmon (1 lb.)
For the Farce:
Sauce Béchamel made with ¼ l.
   (1½ gills) milk, 30 g. (1 oz.) plain
   flour, 30 g. (1 oz.) butter (see
   page 34 for method)
1 egg
3 yolks of egg
1½ dl. thick cream (¼ pint)

seasoning
For the Garnish:
Sauce Nantua (see page 37)
1 l. mussels (1 quart)
240 g. prawns (8 oz.)
120 g. button mushrooms (¼ lb.)
a little lemon juice
knob of butter
seasoning
1 small tin fonds d'artichauts
1 truffle

Method: Skin, wash and dry the fillets of sole. Flatten them lightly with a knife. Remove the skin from the salmon and using a very sharp knife slice the flesh lengthwise into even sized fillets. Remove the rest of the flesh from the bone. Butter a ring mould and line first with five strips of salmon radiating from the centre. Intersperse with the fillets of sole.

Pound the remaining salmon in a mortar. Make the sauce Béchamel and mix in the pounded salmon, the cream, the egg and the yolks and pass all through a wire sieve. Mix well. Taste and season thoroughly. Spoon this farce into the mould, taking care not to disturb the fillets. Fold the ends of the fillets over the farce. Bake in a bain-marie or roasting tin containing boiling water in a moderate oven, gas mark 5 or 375° F. (190° C.) for about half an hour.

Meanwhile prepare the garnish. Wash the mussels well and remove their beards. Put them in a covered saucepan and cook over a good heat for 5 minutes or until all the mussels are open. Remove them from their shells.

Make the sauce Nantua and keep it hot.

Wipe the mushrooms, place them whole in a saucepan with a squeeze of lemon juice, a knob of butter and a little water and seasoning. Cover with greaseproof paper and a lid. Bring to the boil and boil for one minute. Peel the prawns and mix them with the drained mushrooms, mussels and fonds d'artichauts. Mix with a little of the sauce Nantua.

To Serve: Carefully unmould the turban onto a hot serving dish. Fill the centre with the garnish and carefully coat it with the rest of the sauce, being careful not to drip any on the ring of fish.

Place a thin slice of truffle on the top of each section of sole.

Serve at once, with the rest of the sauce handed separately. (*See Plate 5.*)

FILETS DE SOLE CHAUCHAT ** (for 4 or 8 persons)

Ingredients:

8 fillets sole
1½ dl. dry white wine (1 gill)
1 carrot sliced
1 onion sliced
bouquet garni
juice of ½ lemon
60 g. grated cheese (2 oz.)

3 dl. thin cream or creamy milk (½ pint)
45 g. plain flour (1½ oz.)
60 g. butter (2 oz.)
seasoning
For the Garnish:
500–750 g. new potatoes (1–1½ lb.)
pastry fleurons (see page 23)

Method: Butter a fireproof dish, lay in it the sliced vegetables together with the bouquet garni. Wash the fillets, season them and fold them in half. Place them in the dish. Pour over the wine and lemon juice and add sufficient water to cover the fish. Cover with a piece of buttered grease-proof paper. Poach in a moderate oven, gas mark 4–5 or 350–375° F. (190° C.) for 15–20 minutes or until the fish is cooked.

Whilst it is cooking, select even sized potatoes, scrub them well without peeling and cook them in boiling salted water until just done.

When the fish is cooked, drain and reserve the liquor it was poached in, keep hot.

Melt 45 g. (1½ oz.) butter in a pan. Draw aside from the heat, stir in the flour, mix well, return to the heat. Cook for 2–3 minutes stirring all the time. Now add the cream or milk and 1½ dl. (¼ pint) of the liquor in which the fish was cooked. Bring the sauce to the boil, stirring all the time and simmer for 5 minutes. Draw it aside from the heat and whisk in three-quarters of the cheese. Taste and adjust seasoning.

To Serve: Spread a layer of this sauce in the bottom of a fireproof dish, lift the fillets with a draining spoon and arrange them on the sauce. Pour the rest of the sauce over the fish. Rub the skins from the potatoes and slice them thinly. Arrange the slices overlapping round the dish. Sprinkle the rest of the cheese over the fish. Use the remaining butter to dot over the top. Brown quickly under a hot grill or in the top of a hot oven, gas mark 7 or 425° F. (220° C.). Serve at once with pastry fleurons around the edge of the dish.

FILETS DE SOLE GRANDGOUSIER ** (for 4 or 8 persons)

Ingredients:
8 fillets sole
3 dl. dry white wine, approx. (½ pint)
240 g. button mushrooms (½ lb.)
60 g. butter (2 oz.)
1 tablespoon concentrated tomato
    purée
460 g. fresh tomatoes (1 lb.)

paprika
bouquet garni
seasoning
To finish:
2 globe artichokes
a little extra butter
8 prawns
pastry fleurons (see page 23)

Method: Skin, wash and dry the fillets of sole. Season well. Fold each in three. Put them in a buttered fireproof dish with the bouquet garni and just enough wine to cover. Chop the mushrooms finely and sprinkle them over the top of the fish. Season again. Lay a piece of buttered greaseproof paper on top and poach gently for 20 minutes in a moderate oven gas mark 4 or 350° F. (180° C.).

When it is cooked, remove the fish, drain and re-dish on a hot serving dish. Keep it hot. Remove the bouquet garni, and reduce the liquor the fish was poached in to three-quarters of the original quantity. Add to it the tomato purée and the tomatoes skinned, pipped and cut into shreds. Cook for 5 minutes. Take off the heat and whisk in the butter bit by bit. Adjust the seasoning, adding a little paprika. Pour over the fish.

Meanwhile, trim the artichokes and cook them in boiling salted water for 20 minutes. Remove and refresh them in cold water. Drain. Cut them in quarters and remove the chokes. Then toss the artichokes in a little hot butter. On each piece of artichoke place a prawn. Arrange the fleurons round the edge of the dish alternately with artichoke quarters and serve at once.

FILETS DE SOLE ÎLE DE FRANCE **   (for 4 or 8 persons)

Ingredients:
8 fillets sole
1½ dl. dry white wine (1 gill)
1 bayleaf
1 sliced carrot
1 sliced onion
3–4 peppercorns
salt
For the Sauce:
1 tablespoon finely chopped shallots
3 dl. dry white wine (½ pint)
1½ dl. of liquor the fish was poached in (1 gill)

15 g. butter (½ oz.)
beurre manié (see page 16)
1 tablespoon finely chopped parsley
1 teaspoon lemon juice
seasoning
For the Garnish:
240 g. tomatoes (½ lb.)
cooked asparagus tips (approx. 12–15)
90 g. butter (3 oz.)
60 g. sliced mushrooms (2 oz.)

Method: Skin, wash and dry the fillets. Put them in a shallow buttered fireproof dish with the carrot, onion, bayleaf and peppercorns round the sides. Pour over the wine and sufficient water to cover. Lay a piece of buttered greaseproof paper over the fish and poach it in a moderate oven, gas mark 5 or 375° F. (190° C.) for 15–20 minutes. Remove the fish, drain it, reserving the liquor. Keep the fish hot covered in a clean serving dish.

Prepare the sauce – soften the shallots, without browning, in the hot butter. Add the 3 dl. (½ pint) of white wine and reduce it quickly over a good heat until it is half its original quantity. Add the 1½ dl. (1 gill) of fish liquor, seasoning, parsley and lemon juice. Whisk sufficient beurre manié into the sauce over the heat until it thickens to a coating consistency. Simmer for 2–3 minutes. Pour the sauce over the fish. Keep hot.

Chop the tomatoes roughly, season and stew them in 30 g. (1 oz.) of butter. Cook the mushrooms in 30 g. (1 oz.) of butter. Season. Heat the asparagus tips in the remaining butter. Arrange the mushrooms at one end of the dish and the asparagus tips at the other, with the tomatoes on each side of the fish. Serve hot.

FILETS DE SOLE ORLY **   (for 4 or 8 persons)

Ingredients:
8 fillets sole
For the Marinade:
1½ dl. dry white wine (1 gill)
3–4 parsley stalks
1 small onion, finely chopped
seasoning

fritter batter (see page 20)
deep fat for frying (see page 26)
To finish:
Sauce Tomate (Method I) (see page 38)
lemon slices
fried parsley (see page 20)

Method: Skin, wash, dry and season the fillets. Pour the wine into a shallow dish. Lay the fish in this with the chopped onion, parsley stalks and seasoning. Leave for 2 hours turning the fish from time to time. Remove the fillets and allow them to drain on a clean cloth. Dip each into the batter and fry in deep fat until golden brown. Drain on kitchen paper.

To Serve: Arrange the fillets on a paper doyley on a hot dish, garnished with thin slices of lemon and fried parsley. Hand the sauce tomate separately.

FILETS DE SOLE SAINT GERMAIN **   (for 4 or 8 persons)

Ingredients:
8 fillets sole
90 g. butter (3 oz.)
fresh white breadcrumbs

Pommes de Terre Noisette made with 1 kg. (2 lb.) potatoes (see page 228)
Sauce Béarnaise (see page 33)

Method: Prepare the pommes de terre noisette.
Skin, wash and dry the fillets of sole. Season well on both sides. Melt the butter and dip the fillets first in the butter, then in the breadcrumbs. Sprinkle with melted butter.
Make the sauce Béarnaise in the usual way.
Heat the grill and cook the fillets until they are golden brown on each side, turning them carefully.

To Serve: Arrange the fillets of sole on a hot serving dish and the pommes de terre noisette around them. Hand the sauce Béarnaise separately.

FILETS DE SOLE VERONIQUE *   (for 4 or 8 persons)

Ingredients:
8 fillets sole and their backbones
75 g. butter (2½ oz.)
1 onion
3 dl. dry white wine (½ pint)
bouquet garni
a squeeze of lemon juice

30 g. flour (1 oz.)
1½ dl. milk (1 gill)
2 tablespoons thick cream
seasoning
For the Garnish:
250 g. white grapes, approx. (½ lb.)
finely chopped parsley

Method: Well butter a fireproof dish. Season the fillets, fold them into three and place them in the dish. Lay round the sides the onion sliced and the bouquet garni. Add the lemon juice. Wash the backbones of the fish, lay them on top and pour over the wine. Cover with a piece of buttered greaseproof paper and cook in a moderate oven, gas mark 5 or 375° F.

(190° C.) for about 25 minutes. (Fish cooked with the bones on top will necessarily take longer to cook.)

Pour boiling water over the grapes, skin and pip them. Put them in a pan with 15 g. (½ oz.) melted butter, season and sprinkle them with chopped parsley. Heat them through and keep them hot.

When the fish is cooked, strain off the liquor and reduce it quickly over a good heat until it is rather less than half its original quantity. Keep the fish hot.

Make the sauce – melt 30 g. (1 oz.) of butter in a pan, draw it aside from the heat, add the flour, stir well. Return to the heat and, keeping it well stirred, cook for 2–3 minutes. Stir in the fish reduction together with the milk. Bring the sauce to the boil and simmer it for 5 minutes, keeping it well stirred. Remove it from the heat, stir in the cream and the rest of the butter, bit by bit. Taste and season.

To Serve: Arrange the fish in a hot serving dish and coat it carefully with the sauce. Pile up the grapes at each end of the dish. Serve at once.

SOLE COLBERT *** (for 4 persons)

Ingredients:
4 small soles
a little milk
seasoned flour
2–3 beaten eggs
a little oil
white breadcrumbs

Beurre Maître d'Hôtel made with
  90 g. butter (3 oz.), etc. (see
  page 33)
deep fat for frying
To finish:
fried parsley (see page 20)

Method: Cut off the fins from each sole using a pair of scissors. Leave the head on. Remove both the dark and white skins. Wash the soles and dry them on a cloth. With the dark skinned side uppermost, run the filleting knife down the backbone and raise the fillets at each side, cutting almost to the edge. Turn them back but do not remove. Using the scissors sever the backbone at each exposed end and in the centre, to facilitate removal after cooking.

Leave the fillets folded back. Dip each sole into milk, then in seasoned flour, beaten egg and breadcrumbs. See that the fillets are pressed back.

Deep fry the fish in hot fat and when they are a golden brown drain them on kitchen paper. Remove the backbone from the soles. Place the fish on a dish paper on a hot serving dish. Fill the cavity with overlapping slices of beurre maître d'hôtel just before serving. Scatter fried parsley over. (*See Plate 3.*)

Comment: This is a modern interpretation. Beurre Colbert was formerly used, which is made by adding a tablespoon of good meat glaze to the beurre maître d'hôtel.

SOLE BRAISÉE CHAMPENOIS **   (for 4 persons)

Ingredients:
8 fillets sole
1 wine glass Blanc des Blancs or dry white wine
bouquet garni
1½ dl. thick cream (1 gill)
20 heads cooked asparagus or 1 small tin asparagus tips

beurre manié (see page 16)
seasoning
For the Garnish:
4 lemons
250 g. cooked spinach (½ lb.)
8 button mushrooms
a little butter
a squeeze of lemon juice

Method: Butter a fireproof dish. Season the fillets, fold them in three and lay them in the dish. Pour over the Blanc des Blancs. Place the bouquet garni at the side. Cover with a piece of buttered greaseproof paper and poach in a moderate oven, gas mark 4 or 350° F. (180° C.) for 15–20 minutes.

Meanwhile 'turn' the mushrooms and cook them slowly in a little butter with the lemon juice and seasoning.

Wash the spinach in several waters. Cook it in a little boiling salted water. Drain well. Refresh it in cold water and drain again. Chop the spinach roughly and toss in a little melted butter. Season well. Keep it hot.

Cut the lemons into baskets, removing the flesh. Put them aside. Just before the sauce is ready, fill the lemon baskets with the hot spinach.

When the fish is cooked, drain it well and arrange the fillets on a hot serving dish. Keep them hot. Strain the fish liquor into a clean pan. Stir in the cream and bring it to the boil. Whisk in sufficient beurre manié to thicken the sauce to a pouring consistency. Add the asparagus tips. Adjust the seasoning. Place a mushroom on the top of each fillet. Coat all over with the sauce. Arrange the lemon baskets at each end of the dish. Serve at once. (*See Plate 4.*)

TRUITES À LA HUSSARDE **   (for 4 persons)

Ingredients:
4 river trout
3 good sized onions
60 g. butter (2 oz.)
¼ l. dry white wine (1½ gills)
For the Farce:
1 small onion, chopped
30 g. butter (1 oz.)

2 tablespoons white breadcrumbs soaked in a little milk
1 tablespoon chopped parsley
1 yolk of egg
paprika
seasoning
To finish:
beurre manié (see page 16)
30 g. butter (1 oz.)

Method: Have the trout cleaned and the backbones removed. Make the farce. Chop the onion finely. Heat the butter in a small pan and cook the onion in this until it is soft but not coloured. Remove it from the heat and stir in all the other ingredients for the farce. Divide it into four equal portions and fill each trout.

Slice the 3 onions thinly. Make the butter hot, and cook them until they are soft and transparent looking. Spread them in the bottom of a fireproof dish. Lay the trout on the top, pour over the wine and season well. Poach in a moderate oven, gas mark 4–5 or 350–375° F. (190° C.) until both fish and onions are cooked, approximately 20–25 minutes.

Re-dish the trout in a hot dish. Keep them hot. Pass the onions together with the liquor the fish has been poached in through a fine sieve or vegetable mill into a pan and reduce it by half over a good heat, stirring occasionally. Whisk in sufficient beurre manié to make a coating sauce. Allow it to boil and simmer for 2–3 minutes. Adjust the seasoning and then remove from the heat and beat in the butter bit by bit. Pour the sauce over the fish. Brown quickly in the top of a hot oven, gas mark 7 or 425° F. (220° C.) or under a hot grill. Serve at once.

TRUITES AU PULIGNY ET À LA CRÈME **

(for 4 persons)

Ingredients:
4 river trout
½ bottle of Puligny or dry white Burgundy
1½ dl. thick cream (1 gill)
2 teaspoons concentrated tomato purée

beurre manié (see page 16)
seasoning
For the Garnish:
triangular fleurons of puff or flaky pastry (see pages 23)

Method: Have the trout cleaned. Scale, wash, dry and season them. Bring the wine to simmering point in a shallow pan and poach the trout gently for 5–7 minutes, depending on their size. Lift them carefully with a draining spoon on to a hot serving dish and keep them hot.

Raise the heat under the pan in which the trout were cooked and reduce the liquor to about half the original volume. Whisk in sufficient beurre manié to give a thick coating consistency, pour in the cream and stir in the concentrated tomato purée. Cook for 2–3 minutes, keeping well stirred. Season to taste. Coat the fish carefully with this sauce. Arrange the pastry fleurons round the edge of the dish. Serve at once.

Comment: This is a speciality of the Hôtel du Terminus at Arnay le Duc, Côte d'Or.

TRUITES AU VAL DE LOIRE **   (for 4 persons)

Ingredients:

4 trout
60 g. button mushrooms (2 oz.)
2 tablespoons finely chopped
  blanched almonds
chopped parsley
30 g. plain flour (1 oz.)
30 g. butter (1 oz.)

3 dl. dry white wine (½ pint)
bouquet garni
1 dl. thick cream (½ gill)
2 yolks of egg
1 teaspoon lemon juice
fleurons of flaky pastry (see page
  23)

Method: Clean the trout, split them down the stomach and remove the backbones. Wash and dry on a clean cloth. Soften 30 g. (1 oz.) of the butter with a fork and mix with the almonds and 1 teaspoon of chopped parsley. Season well. Fill this into the trout. Lay them in a buttered fireproof dish, season, add the bouquet garni and pour over the white wine. Cover with buttered greaseproof paper and poach in a moderate oven, gas mark 4–5 or 350–375° F. (190° C.) for 20 minutes or until cooked.

Meanwhile 'turn' the mushrooms. Then place them in a small pan with the lemon juice, 15 g. (½ oz.) butter and 1 dl. (½ gill) water. Season and cover with greaseproof paper and the lid and cook gently for 4–5 minutes.

When the trout are cooked lift them carefully into the serving dish. Keep them hot. Melt the remaining butter in a pan, draw it aside from the heat and add the flour. Return to the heat and cook the roux for 2–3 minutes, stirring well. Strain the fish liquor and mushroom liquor and add to the roux away from the heat. Bring to the boil, stirring well, and boil for 5 minutes. Beat the egg yolks with the cream. Stir in a little of the sauce, return to the pan and cook over a low heat until it thickens without allowing it to boil, stirring all the time. Taste and season. Pour the sauce over the fish. Garnish with the mushrooms and fleurons. Serve hot.

TRUITES DE RIVIÈRE AU CHABLIS *   (for 4 persons)

Ingredients:

4 river trout
2–3 tablespoons finely chopped
  fresh herbs
1 teaspoon grated lemon rind

1½ dl. Chablis (or White Burgundy) (1 gill)
30 g. butter, approx. (1 oz.)
2 tablespoons thick cream
seasoning

Method: Have the trout cleaned. Wash and dry them. Season the inside of the fish. Place them in a buttered fireproof dish. Sprinkle over the finely chopped fresh herbs and the lemon rind. Pour over the wine and dot with knobs of butter. Cover with a piece of buttered greaseproof paper and cook in a moderate oven, gas mark 5 or 375° F. (190° C.) for 15–20 minutes. At the end of this time remove the trout. Drain them and arrange them on a hot serving dish. Keep them hot.

Pour the liquor the fish were cooked in into a small pan. Whisk in the cream and simmer for a few moments. Adjust the seasoning and pour over the trout. Serve at once.

PAIN DE POISSON GITAN **   (for 4 persons)

Ingredients:
450 g. (1 lb.) cooked white fish
3 dl. (½ pint) thick Sauce Béchamel made with 45 g. (1½ oz.) plain flour 45 g., (1½ oz.) butter, 3 dl. (½ pint) milk, seasoning. (see page 34 for method)
3 eggs
seasoning to include nutmeg and a pinch of cayenne pepper

For the sauce:
700 g. tomatoes (1½ lb.)
5 shallots
2 cloves garlic
sprig thyme, rosemary and a bayleaf tied with string
1 clove
1 dl. oil (¾ gill)
seasoning
For the Garnish:
3 red peppers
3 green peppers

Method: Make the sauce Béchamel using the increased quantities of butter and flour. Remove from the heat. Separate the eggs and beat the yolks into the sauce.

Remove all the bones from the fish and flake it carefully with a fork. Mix it with the sauce Béchamel, seasoning it well and using a pinch of grated nutmeg and the Cayenne pepper. Whisk the whites very stiffly indeed and fold them lightly into the fish mixture. Pour this into a buttered 15 cm. (6 inch) charlotte mould and stand it in a bain-marie or roasting tin containing boiling water. Cook in a moderate oven, gas mark 5 or 375° F. (190° C.) for 45 minutes.

Meanwhile make the sauce. Peel and slice the shallots thinly. Heat about half the oil in a saucepan, add the shallots and cook them gently until they are transparent. Stir in the tomatoes skinned and pipped and roughly chopped. Crush the garlic with a little salt, add this with the herbs and the clove. Season well and simmer gently for ½ hour.

Prepare the garnish. Cut the peppers in half and discard the pith and seeds. Cut them into strips and plunge them into boiling salted water. Cook them for 3–4 minutes. Drain them and dry them on a clean cloth. Heat the rest of the oil in a small pan, put the peppers in this, season them and cook them gently for 2–3 minutes.

To Serve: Remove the herbs and the clove from the sauce. Taste and adjust the seasoning. Turn out the pain de possion on a hot dish. Pour the sauce over the top and arrange the peppers round it. Serve very hot.

TIMBALE AUX FRUITS DE MER *** (for 4–5 persons)

Ingredients:

700 g. fresh haddock fillets (1½ lb.)
5 eggs
1½ dl. thick cream (1 gill)
1 shallot
3 scallops
1½ dl. dry white wine (1 gill)
240 g. prawns (8 oz.)
3 dl. mussels (½ pint)
¼ l. milk (1½ gills)

bouquet garni
seasoning
Sauce Joinville made with:
Sauce Béchamel (see page 34)
a handful of prawn heads and shells
60 g. butter (2 oz.)
pinch of Cayenne pepper
carmine
seasoning

Method: Skin the fish and cut it into small pieces. Pound it in a mortar with the chopped shallot adding 2 beaten eggs little by little. (Alternatively use an electric mixer.) When the fish is pulped, pass it through a nylon sieve. Stir in the cream carefully and season well.

Remove the scallops from their shells and poach them gently in the white wine with a bouquet garni and seasoning. When they are cooked, drain them and cut each into four pieces. Shell the prawns and reserve the heads and shells for the sauce. Wash the mussels well and remove their beards. Shake them in a covered pan over a good heat for 5 minutes or until all the mussels are open. Remove the shells.

Butter a 15 cm. (6 inch) charlotte mould or cake tin and line the base and sides with a 1 cm. (½ inch) layer of the haddock mixture. Carefully fill the centre with the mixed mussels, scallops and prawns. Beat 3 eggs with the milk, season lightly and strain carefully into the charlotte mould. Cover with buttered greaseproof paper. Place the mould in a bain-marie or roasting tin containing boiling water and cook in a moderate oven, gas mark 5 or 375° F. (190° C.) for ½–¾ hour or until the mixture is set.

Meanwhile make the sauce Joinville. Pound the prawn debris with the butter using a pestle and mortar. Pass this through a fine wire sieve. Make a well seasoned sauce Béchamel and stir in the prawn butter. Taste and adjust the seasoning, adding the Cayenne pepper and a little carmine to colour slightly.

When the timbale is cooked, unmould it carefully on a hot serving dish. Pour over some of the hot sauce and serve at once, with the rest of the sauce handed separately.

Meat

The vast growth of supermarkets and chain butchers has made it more difficult to find the high quality of meat and service provided by the family butcher. Prepacked cuts and refrigeration have caused a further deterioration. If one is lucky enough to have a self-employed butcher who is interested to hang meat sufficiently long, the resulting quality in texture and flavour is well worth the slightly higher price. Unfortunately the average housewife is not able to pay extra for service and quality.

OFFAL

Many recipes included in this chapter deal with offal, or abats, as it is called in France. These are useful additions to any menu, but require to be cooked when quite fresh, as they very soon deteriorate.

BRAINS OR CERVELLES

The best brains are from calves. Before cooking, they should be soaked in cold water for not less than 1½ hours. This water should be changed from time to time. The fine skin or membrane which covers the brains must be removed. This can be achieved by holding the brain so that it is submerged in a bowl of cold water. The skin should pull off fairly easily. All traces of blood should be removed before cooking.

HEART OR CŒUR

The hearts of sheep, lamb and ox are all used in cookery. Sheep hearts seldom weigh more than half a pound. Ox heart is much larger and will weigh up to four pounds. They are usually stuffed or braised.

KIDNEYS OR ROGNONS

Kidneys are obtained from sheep, lamb, veal and ox. The veal kidneys weigh approximately half a pound, whereas those of sheep weigh about 60–120 g. (2–4 oz.). Ox kidneys are not used whole as a rule. Sheep or lamb's kidneys are frequently used sauté. Before cooking, remove the fat from the kidney and with the point of a sharp knife, make a small incision in the skin of the kidney and pull it off on both sides. Some of the 'core' or hard centre piece will come away with the skin. Using the point of the knife again, work round the hard core and remove it. Cut the kidney almost, but not quite, in half. Care must be taken not to over cook them as this will produce a hard tough meat. Veal kidneys differ considerably in appearance and are more delicate in flavour. The skin and core must again be removed before cooking.

LIVER OR FOIE

Calves' liver is by far the best liver, being more tender and more delicate in flavour, although frequently pig and ox liver is sold in place of calf. This will be stronger in flavour and less tender and will require prolonged slow cooking.

SWEETBREADS OR RIS DE VEAU AND RIS D'AGNEAU

There are two kinds of sweetbreads, the heart and the throat. The heart is the better buy of the two. It is larger and more compact and can be served whole. Frequently it is larded (see notes on larding, page 13). Veal sweetbreads are more delicate than sheep's sweetbreads. Both should be soaked in cold water before cooking and all traces of blood removed. The sweetbreads are then blanched and the skin and membrane removed.

OX TAIL OR QUEUE DE BŒUF

Ox tail is excellent for an inexpensive stew. It requires long, slow cooking. Remove the excess fat before cooking.

TONGUE OR LANGUE

Ox and lambs' tongue both make delicious dishes. Ox tongues are usually purchased when they have been salted and this must be borne in mind when seasoning the dish. For dishes where the tongue should be unsalted and served with a piquant sauce, if the butcher is given due notice it is usually possible to buy an unsalted tongue but failing this, the tongue must be soaked for twenty-four hours before cooking. The tongue should be skinned before serving. Lambs' or sheeps' tongues are not salted, but they should be well rinsed in cold water before cooking. These also must be skinned before serving.

MEAT

BLANQUETTE D'AGNEAU DES BORDS DU RHÔNE ***

(for 4 persons)

Ingredients:
1 shoulder of lamb 1½ kg. approx.
  (3 lb.)
60–90 g. good dripping
  (2–3 oz.)
2 carrots cut into rounds
2 medium onions, finely chopped
bouquet garni
beurre manié (see page 16)
1½ dl. Sauce Mayonnaise (see
  page 36) (1 gill)

juice of 1 lemon
seasoning
For the Garnish:
250 g. French beans ⎫
  (½ lb.)   Cooked
250 g. young carrots ⎬ separately
  (½ lb.)   and tossed
1 cauliflower cut into ⎪ in butter
  flowerets ⎭
finely chopped parsley

Method: Remove the fat and bone from the meat. Cut the meat into 5 cm. (2 inch) squares. Make the dripping hot in a pan, add the finely chopped onions and the carrots and turn them in the hot fat until they begin to shrink. They must not brown. Add the meat. Turn this also in the fat, but do not let it get too brown. Just cover with hot water. Season well and add the bouquet garni. Place the lid on the pan and simmer gently for 1 hour. After three-quarters of the cooking time, beat in sufficient beurre manié to make a fairly thin sauce. (The amount of beurre manié will depend on the quantity of liquor in the pan, but probably about 75 g. (2½ oz.) butter and 60 g. (2 oz.) flour.) Cook it for a further ¼ hour. Then dish the meat in a large hot dish. Mix a little of the liquor with the sauce Mayonnaise. Return to the pan. Whisk all together off the heat. Adjust the seasoning and add the lemon juice. Strain over the meat and group the vegetable garnish round the sides of the dish. Sprinkle them with finely chopped parsley. Serve at once.

CÔTELETTES AUX AMANDES *   (for 4 persons)

Ingredients:
8 lamb cutlets
75 g. butter (2½ oz.)
1 glass Madeira (approx. 1 dl.)
    (¾ gill)

125 g. blanched almonds (4 oz.)
2 hardboiled eggs
seasoning

Method: Trim the cutlets and remove the excess fat.

Select 8 good shaped almonds and put them on one side.

Heat the butter in a frying or sauté pan. Put in the cutlets. Season them. Fry them until they are brown, allowing about 3–4 minutes on each side. Remove them from the pan and keep them hot. Put the main quantity of almonds into the pan the cutlets were cooked in. Turn them in the hot butter until they are golden brown, but do not let them burn. Pour off the excess fat, leaving about two tablespoons. Add the Madeira, stir round well. Adjust the seasoning, pour this sauce and the almonds over the cutlets.

Serve with a slice of hardboiled egg on each cutlet and an unbrowned almond on each slice of egg.

CÔTELETTES D'AGNEAU VILLEROI **

(for 4 persons)

Ingredients:
4 lamb cutlets
2 tablespoons olive oil
white breadcrumbs
1 egg
45 g. butter (1½ oz.)

Sauce Béchamel made with 45 g.
    (1½ oz.) plain flour, 45 g. (1½ oz.)
    butter and 3 dl. (½ pint) milk
    (see page 34)
deep fat for frying
seasoning
a little extra milk

Method: Trim the cutlets, removing all fat. Beat them with the blade of a knife, season with pepper and salt. Melt the oil and butter in a shallow frying pan. When it is hot put in the cutlets and fry them quickly for 1–2 minutes on each side. Remove and drain them.

Make up the sauce Béchamel in the usual way – it will be a good deal thicker than an ordinary coating sauce. Remove it from the heat. Separate the egg and beat the yolk in to the sauce. Season well. Take each cutlet, one by one, and dip it into the sauce. Turn each round carefully to allow all sides to be coated. Grease a plate with a little butter or oil, place the coated cutlets on this and stand it in a cold place for the sauce to harden. At the end of ½ hour or so, make the deep fat hot. Dip the cutlets quickly into the white of egg which has been beaten to a froth in a deep plate, then coat them in the breadcrumbs. When the fat is hot, fry the cutlets for 5 minutes. Drain them on kitchen paper and serve them very hot on a dish. Heat the remainder of the sauce gently, add a little extra milk to give a pouring consistency and serve separately.

Comment: Garnish with peas or other suitable green vegetables in season.

CÔTELETTES D'AGNEAU AUX POINTES D'ASPERGES ** (for 4 persons)

Ingredients:
4 lamb cutlets or chops
1 clove garlic
2 yolks of egg
beurre manié (see page 16)
60 g. butter (2 oz.)
2 shallots
1½ dl. dry white wine (1 gill)
3 dl. chicken or veal stock (½ pint)
2 tablespoons thick cream

2 tablespoons finely chopped parsley
seasoning
For the Garnish:
1 bundle asparagus
shell macaroni
a little extra butter
croûtons 1 cm. (½ inch) (see page 20)

Method: Melt the butter in a sauté pan. When it is hot, put in the cutlets and brown them quickly and well on each side. Remove the cutlets and pour in the wine to déglace the pan. Stir round quickly then add the stock. Put the cutlets back into the pan, and bring it to simmering point. Add the crushed clove of garlic, together with the shallots, which have been finely chopped, and the parsley. Season well. Cover and put into a moderate oven, gas mark 5 or 375° F. (190° C.) for 40 minutes.

Whilst the cutlets are cooking, scrape the asparagus and cook it for 20 minutes in boiling salted water. Drain and keep it hot in a little melted butter. Cook the macaroni also in plenty of boiling salted water. Drain and keep it hot also. Fry the croûtons, drain them and mix them with the macaroni.

To Serve: Place the cutlets in the middle of a serving dish and keep them hot. Stir a teaspoonful of beurre manié into the sauce and cook it over a good heat until it thickens. Whisk the egg yolks with the cream, stir in a little of the hot sauce, then return the egg mixture to the sauce in the pan and cook over a gentle heat until it thickens slightly. Pour carefully over the cutlets. Arrange small bunches of asparagus and the macaroni and croûtons round the edge of the dish. Serve hot.

Comment: If shell macaroni is not obtainable short lengths of large macaroni may be used.

GIGOT À LA BRETONNE * (for 6–8 persons)

Ingredients:

1 leg lamb, approx. 2 kg. (4 lb.)
250 g. haricot beans (½ lb.)
2 carrots
2 onions stuck with 3 or 4 cloves
1½ dl. thin cream (1 gill)

120–150 g. butter (4–5 oz.)
250 g. lean bacon (½ lb.)
a little good dripping
a little good stock
bouquet garni
seasoning

Method: Soak the beans overnight. Then cook them with the bouquet garni, the sliced carrots and the onions stuck with cloves. (See page 19 for method.) When they are cooked, rinse them and drain well.

Cut the bacon into lardons and brown them carefully in a little dripping in the bottom of a roasting pan. Remove the bacon with a draining spoon and mix it with the haricot beans, together with the cream and three-quarters of the butter. Season well. Pour this mixture in the bottom of a large fireproof dish and dot it with the rest of the butter.

Spread the lamb with the dripping, season it and place it in the roasting pan. Cook it in a hot oven, gas mark 7 or 425° F. (220° C.) for 20 minutes, then lower the heat and continue cooking at gas mark 5 or 375° F. (190° C.) for a further 70 minutes. Baste from time to time with a little hot stock. About 15 minutes before the joint is cooked, place the haricot mixture on the top shelf in the oven.

To Serve: Place the joint on the top of the haricot mixture. Pour the excess fat from the roasting pan. Add a little extra stock, bring quickly to the boil, stirring well from the bottom of the pan. Season, strain the gravy into a sauce boat and serve separately.

GIGOT DES CHASSEURS * (for 6–8 persons)

Ingredients:

1 leg lamb, approx. 2 kg. (4 lb.)
1 l. dry white wine (1½ pints)
2 tablespoons oil
2 tablespoons wine vinegar
2 carrots
2 shallots
6–8 peppercorns

3 cloves
bouquet garni composed of rose-
    mary, thyme and bayleaf
90 g. butter (3 oz.)
larding bacon
125 g. redcurrant jelly (¼ lb.)
seasoning

Method: Lard the meat (see page 13 for notes on larding). Put into a large bowl the wine, oil, vinegar, cloves, bouquet garni, peppercorns, the carrots sliced and the shallots finely chopped. Marinate the lamb in this for 3–4 days in winter or 2 days in hot weather. Turn it twice a day. Keep it covered with a muslin. At the end of this time remove the joint and wipe it with a clean cloth. Spread it with the butter. Cook it in a roasting tin in a hot oven, gas mark 7 or 425° F. (220° C.) for 1½ hours. Baste frequently with the marinade.

To Serve: Place the meat on a hot serving dish. Pour off the excess fat from the pan. Reduce the liquor by half over a good heat. Mix in the red-currant jelly and heat through until it is melted, stirring well. Adjust the seasoning. Pour a little gravy over the meat. Serve the rest separately.

Comment: In winter months this dish can be served with a purée de marrons.

MOUSSAKA **   (for 4–6 persons)

Ingredients:

¾ kg. shoulder of lamb (1½ lb.)
4 aubergines
125 g. mushrooms (4 oz.)
1 onion
4 eggs
2–3 tablespoons of finely chopped
   fresh herbs

90–120 g. butter (3–4 oz.)
1½ dl. olive oil (1 gill)
1 teaspoon paprika
seasoning
To finish:
Sauce Tomate (Method I see
   page 38)

Method: Cut the aubergines in half lengthwise. Run a thin bladed knife in between the flesh and the skin all round each one. Make cross incisions in the flesh. Dust well with salt and place them upside down on a wire rack to drain. At the end of 20–30 minutes remove them and dry them completely with a clean cloth. Make the oil hot in a large frying pan and fry the aubergines gently in this on both sides. Remove and drain them.

Cut the lamb into convenient sized pieces, removing all the bone and fat. Sauter them in 60 g. (2 oz.) of the butter until they are well browned on all sides, cool slightly and then pass them through a fine mincer.

Chop the onion finely and chop the mushrooms. Melt the remaining butter in a pan, add the mushrooms and seasoning and cook them gently for 5 minutes. Lift them with a draining spoon, put aside. Cook the onion in the same butter until it is tender but not brown.

Remove the flesh from the aubergines without damaging the skins. Mix it with the mushrooms, onions, herbs and 2 beaten eggs. Add the paprika, taste and adjust the seasoning.

Take a well oiled 15 cm. (6 inch) charlotte mould and line it with the skins of the aubergines, allowing the dark side of the skin to remain against the inside of the tin.

Beat the remaining eggs and stir them into the minced lamb. Season well. Fill the mould with a layer of minced meat, a layer of the aubergine mixture, a layer of minced meat and finally the rest of the aubergine mixture. Fold over the aubergine skins so that they cover the top of the mould. Bake it in a moderate oven, gas mark 5 or 375° F. (190° C.) for 45 minutes.

To Serve: Unmould on to a hot serving dish and pour over a well flavoured sauce tomate.

NOISETTES D'AGNEAU DE PRE-SALÉ À LA BERGERETTE *** (for 3 persons)

Ingredients:
6 noisettes of lamb
60 g. butter (2 oz.)
For the Garnish:
Pommes de Terre à la Parisienne
  (see page 221)
6 even sized, small ripe tomatoes

6 artichoke hearts, tinned or fresh
30 g. butter (1 oz.)
a good bunch of parsley
18 tarragon leaves
lemon juice
a little oil
seasoning

Method: Prepare the garnish. If using fresh artichokes, break off the stalk at the bottom of each artichoke. Using a stainless knife and working round from the stalk end, cut off the leaves at their bases, thus exposing the heart. Rub over with lemon juice. Having removed the leaves, cut out the choke and rub over the rest of the heart with lemon juice. Cook the hearts in boiling salted water to which has been added a tablespoon of lemon juice or vinegar. Allow 20–30 minutes according to size. Drain them and toss them in 30 g. (1 oz.) hot butter. Season and keep them hot. If tinned ones are to be used, drain them well and heat them in butter in the same manner.

Make the pommes de terre à la Parisienne.

Take the tomatoes and brush them over with a little oil. Season and place them on a baking sheet in a moderate oven, gas mark 5 or 375° F. (190° C.) for about 10 minutes. Keep them hot.

Trim the noisettes as needed and tie them round with thin string. Season. Heat the butter in a sauté pan. Fry the noisettes carefully in this, allowing approximately 3–4 minutes on each side. Remove the string.

To Serve: Pile pommes de terre à la Parisienne in the centre of the dish. Place the noisettes round them. Arrange 3 blanched tarragon leaves on each. Round the edge of the dish arrange the tomatoes, each one on the top of an artichoke heart. Dust the tomatoes copiously with finely chopped parsley. In between them arrange the rest of the pommes de terre à la Parisienne in small clusters. Serve very hot.

Comment: To prepare 6 noisettes of lamb bone out a six rib piece of best end. Roll it up and tie evenly with six strings. Slice between each string.

BIFTECKS À LA HONGROISE * (for 4 persons)

Ingredients:

4 pieces rump steak, approx. 120–
  170 g. (4–6 oz.) each
½ kg. onions (1 lb.)
60 g. butter or dripping (2 oz.)
1½ dl. thick cream (1 gill)
2 teaspoons paprika

1 teaspoon plain flour
seasoning

For the Garnish:
½ kg. even sized new potatoes
  (1 lb.)
a little extra butter

Method: Make the butter hot in a strong pan. Cut the onions into thin slices and fry them in the butter until they are lightly browned. Remove them and keep them hot.

Put the meat in the pan and turn it carefully in the hot fat to seal the juices. Sprinkle in the flour and brown it carefully. Return the onions to the pan, pour over the cream and add the paprika. Taste and season. Cover with greaseproof paper and the lid of the pan and cook in a moderate oven, gas mark 4 or 350° F. (180° C.) for approximately ½ hour.

Prepare the potatoes. Cook them in boiling salted water until they are done, but still firm. Drain them well and toss them in a little melted butter.

Arrange the meat in a hot dish. Place the onions at each end and the potatoes at each side of the dish. Dust the potatoes lightly with paprika. Stir the sauce, adjust the seasoning, and pour it over the meat. Serve at once.

BŒUF EN GELÉE *** (for 6 persons)

Ingredients:

1 piece of topside of beef, approx.
  1½ kg. (3 lb.)
1 calves foot
3 carrots
1 clove garlic
4 onions
bouquet garni
30 g. butter (1 oz.)
1–1½ l. beef stock (2–3 pints)
1 tablespoon oil
1 dessertspoon concentrated tomato purée
seasoning

Materials for clarification:
4 whites of egg
5 leaves of gelatine
1½ dl. water (1 gill)
sherry to flavour
caramel to colour (see page 16)
seasoning

For the Garnish:
12 tiny onions boiled and drained
3 cooked carrots cut into barrel
  shapes
2 cooked turnips diced
cooked peas and beans as available

Method: Have the calves foot split in two. Put it into cold water, bring it to the boil, drain and rinse it in cold water. Dry it on a clean cloth.

Make the butter and oil hot in a thick pan. Place the beef in this and turn it quickly in the hot fat until it is well browned on all sides. Remove it from the pan. Cut the onions and carrots in quarters. Add them to the pan and sauter them well until they are dark brown in colour. Return the meat to the pan, add the garlic which has been crushed with a little salt, the bouquet garni, calves foot, tomato purée and seasoning. Pour on just sufficient stock to cover. Bring slowly to boiling point. Cover with the lid. Lower the heat and simmer gently for 2 hours. At the end of this time, remove the pan from the heat and allow the meat to cool completely in the liquid. When it is cold, remove the fat from the top of the stock. Strain the stock through a clean wet cloth.

Take 1 l. (2 pints) of the stock and put it into a clean saucepan. Using the materials for clarification, clarify the stock as for making aspic (see page 17). Allow it to get completely cold, but not set.

When it is on the point of setting, pour a little of the jelly in the bottom of a large serving dish. Allow it to set completely. Carve the meat into slices and lay them slightly overlapping down the centre of the dish. Arrange the vegetables in a decorative pattern round the edge. Coat the meat and vegetables with aspic jelly, using it when it is just on the point of setting. Leave to set completely in a cold place.

Serve cold.

BŒUF EN MATELOTE * (for 4–5 persons)

Ingredients:

¾ kg. stewing steak (1½ lb.)
6 shallots
3–4 medium sized onions
2 cloves garlic
bouquet garni
60 g. butter (2 oz.)

½ l. red wine (¾ pint)
seasoned flour
seasoning
For the Garnish:
plain boiled potatoes
chopped parsley

Method: Remove all the fat and gristle and cut the meat into 5 cm. (2 inch) cubes. Roll them in seasoned flour. Peel the onions and slice them very thinly. Peel the shallots and chop them finely. Heat the butter in a thick stewpan, put in the meat and brown it well on all sides. When the meat is browned, remove it. Put in the onions, shallots and garlic, which has been crushed with a little salt. Cook them all together slowly for 4–5 minutes or until the onions are tender but not browned. Pour in the wine. Season well. Return the meat and add the bouquet garni. Cover with greaseproof paper and the lid and cook in a slow oven, gas mark 2–3 or 300–325° F. (150–160° C.) for approximately 2 hours. When the meat is tender, remove the bouquet garni and adjust the seasoning. Serve on a large dish with a border of potatoes. Sprinkle with finely chopped parsley.

BŒUF GRATINÉ *   (for 3 persons)

Ingredients:

6 slices cold beef, roast or boiled
3 aubergines
2 green peppers
¾ kg. ripe tomatoes (1½ lb.)
2 cloves garlic
Pommes de Terre Mousseline
    (see page 228)
1 teaspoon chopped chives

1 tablespoon finely chopped
    parsley
2 tablespoons grated cheese,
    Parmesan or Gruyère for
    preference
3–4 tablespoons oil
a little butter
a little flour
seasoning

Method: Cut the peppers in half. Remove the seeds and pith. Blanch them for 5 minutes in boiling salted water. Drain and dry them.

Peel the aubergines and cut them lengthwise into ½ cm. (¼ inch) slices. Sprinkle them over with salt and place them on a wire rack to drain for 20 minutes. Then dry them on a clean cloth and dust them with a little flour. Make the oil hot in a sauté pan and fry the aubergines in this, together with the peppers. Season. Place this mixture in the bottom of a well buttered fireproof dish.

Skin the tomatoes and cut them into rounds. Add them to the oil in the sauté pan with the cloves of garlic which have been crushed with a little salt, the chives and parsley. Season well. Stir quickly for 2–3 minutes. Spread half this on the aubergine mixture. Arrange the slices of cold meat overlapping on the top. Cover with the rest of the tomatoes, etc. Finally spread the potato mixture on the top and cover with the cheese. Dot with knobs of butter and place in the top of a hot oven, gas mark 7 or 425° F. (220° C.) for 15–20 minutes to heat through and brown the top. Serve at once.

BŒUF MARIUS **   (for 4–6 persons)

Ingredients:

½ kg. cold cooked beef (1 lb.)
250 g. boiled bacon (½ lb.)
1 kg. courgettes (2 lb.)
30 g. butter (1 oz.)
½ l. Sauce Tomate (Method I) (¾ pint)
    (see page 38)

oil for frying
seasoned flour
paprika and Cayenne pepper
seasoning
To finish:
fried croûtons of bread

Method: Cut the beef and bacon into 2 cm. (1 inch) cubes. Peel the courgettes and cut them into cubes the same size as the meat. Roll the courgette cubes in seasoned flour, so as to absorb the moisture. Fry them quickly in hot oil, browning them on all sides. Drain and keep them hot.

Make the sauce tomate as usual and season it very well with Cayenne pepper and a good pinch of paprika.

Heat the butter in a thick pan. Add the bacon and fry it gently. Then lower the heat and add the meat. Heat through. Lastly add the courgettes, stirring carefully with a wooden spoon, being careful not to damage them.

To Serve: Pile on a hot dish and coat completely with the sauce tomate. Surround with a garnish of fried croûtons.

Comment: If courgettes are unobtainable, small vegetable marrows may be used.

ENTRECÔTE À LA MIRABEAU *   (for 2–4 persons)

Ingredients:

1 piece of entrecôte steak, ½–¾ kg.
  (1–1½ lb.)
60 g. butter (2 oz.)
1 tablespoon anchovy essence

6–8 anchovy fillets
12 green olives, stoned
a little oil
seasoning

Method: Rub the steak over with a little oil and season it with salt and pepper. Work the butter to a paste and add the anchovy essence. Toss the olives in a little hot oil and keep them hot. Grill the steak according to thickness and preference. When it is cooked spread the anchovy butter on the top. Arrange the anchovy fillets in a lattice design with stoned olives in between. Serve at once. (*See Plate 7.*)

Comment: Alternatively the steak can be lightly fried in a little butter. It can be garnished with plain new potatoes and a bunch of watercress.

FRICADELLES DE BŒUF **   (for 4–5 persons)

Ingredients:

¾ kg. cold beef (preferably from
  pot-au-feu) (1½ lb.)
¾ kg. potatoes, boiled and sieved
  (1½ lb.)
3 yolks of egg
1 onion
30–60 g. butter (1–2 oz.)
seasoning with a little sugar
Sauce Tomate:
3 large tomatoes
1 stick celery
45 g. butter (1½ oz.)

45 g. plain flour (1½ oz.)
½ l. well flavoured stock (¾ pint)
2 onions
2 cloves garlic, roughly chopped
bouquet garni
1 dessertspoon concentrated
  tomato purée
For Frying:
120 g. butter (4 oz.)
2–3 tablespoons oil
To finish:
very finely chopped parsley

Method: Make the sauce. Chop the onions very finely. Heat the butter in a saucepan and fry the onions carefully in this until they are just beginning to colour. Add the flour and continue to cook. This process cannot be hurried or the flour will be scorched. When the onions and flour are a light brown, stir in the stock. Add the bouquet garni, the celery roughly chopped, the tomatoes quartered and the garlic. Stir in the tomato purée and simmer uncovered for 45 minutes to 1 hour, stirring from time to time.

Chop the meat very finely. Do not mince it. Chop the onion very well. Heat the butter in a good sized saucepan and cook the onion in this until it is quite tender. It must not brown. Beat in the potatoes and the yolks. Warm together over heat, keep beating until it is light and fluffy. Season. Mix the meat and potato mixture together. Turn it on to a floured board and shape it into flat cakes about 5 cm. (2 inch) in diameter. Make the butter and oil hot in a sauté pan and fry the cakes in this, turning them carefully.

Pass the sauce through a sieve or vegetable mill. Adjust the seasoning, adding sugar to taste. Arrange the fricadelles in a hot dish. Sprinkle with the parsley. Serve the sauce separately.

GRILLADE DE BŒUF À LA RHODANIENNE **

(for 3–4 persons)

Ingredients:

1 piece of rump steak, about ¾ kg. (1½ lb.)
60 g. butter (2 oz.)
For the Sauce:
1 finely chopped onion
2 tablespoons oil, approx.
4 fillets of anchovy
1 dl. wine vinegar (¾ gill)
2 cloves garlic

1 bayleaf
sprig of thyme
2–3 cloves
¼ teaspoon paprika
1 tablespoon plain flour
3 dl. stock (½ pint)
2 gherkins
1 tablespoon capers
seasoning

Method: First make the sauce – heat the oil in the pan, add the finely chopped onion and cook it until it is soft. Wash the anchovy fillets to remove the salt, dry and chop them. Add them to the pan, together with the vinegar, garlic (uncrushed), bayleaf, thyme, cloves, paprika and seasoning. Allow to cook until the vinegar is reduced by half and then stir in the flour. Lower the heat and cook the flour, keeping well stirred until it is just turning colour. Pour in the stock and bring it to the boil, stirring all the time, then leave it over a low heat to simmer for ½ hour. At the end of this time, pass the sauce through a strainer. Adjust the seasoning and lastly stir in the chopped gherkins and capers. Keep hot. Make the butter very hot in a strong pan and fry the steak quickly on both sides. Serve on a hot dish. Pour over the sauce and serve at once.

'OISEAUX' SANS TÊTES ** (for 6 persons)

Ingredients:

6 slices rump steak cut very thinly
6 slices lean ham
1 onion, sliced
1 carrot, sliced

60 g. butter or good dripping (2 oz.)
¼ l. dry white wine (1½ gills)
bouquet garni
½ kg. tomatoes (1 lb.)
seasoning

Method: Season the slices of steak and lay a piece of ham on each slice. Roll them up and tie them neatly with a piece of thin string.

Make the butter or dripping hot in a pan, put in the steaks and brown them well on all sides. Add the carrot and onion and turn them in the hot fat. Pour in the wine and add the tomatoes, roughly chopped. Add the bouquet garni and season very well. Cover with greaseproof paper and the lid. Place in a moderate oven, gas mark 5 or 375° F. (190° C.) for 1½–2 hours. At the end of this time, remove the string and arrange the steaks on a hot serving dish. Remove the bouquet garni and excess grease from the sauce. Adjust the seasoning, strain it over the steaks. Serve very hot.

RAGOÛT DE BŒUF AU RIZ ** (for 3–4 persons)

Ingredients:

¾–1 kg. chuck steak (1½–2 lb.)
3 rashers lean bacon
6 shallots
125 g. mushrooms (4 oz.)
180 g. Patna rice (6 oz.)
3 tomatoes
1 clove garlic

3 teaspoons concentrated tomato
  purée
90 g. butter (3 oz.)
15 g. plain flour (½ oz.)
½ l. beef stock approx. (¾ pint)
bouquet garni
1½ dl. red wine (1 gill)
seasoning

Method: Remove all the fat and gristle and cut the meat into 5 cm. (2 inch) squares. Make 60 g. (2 oz.) butter hot in a thick pan and sauter the meat well in this. When the meat is browned well on all sides, remove it from the pan. Meanwhile chop the shallots finely, crush the garlic with a little salt, cut the bacon into strips and chop the mushroom stalks. Add all these to the pan and season well. Cook them slowly over a low heat for 10 minutes, stirring occasionally to prevent their sticking. After this time, sprinkle in the flour and allow it to brown lightly, stirring continuously. Remove from the heat, then mix in the tomato purée. Replace the meat and pour in the red wine and sufficient stock to cover. Add the bouquet garni and season well. Bring very slowly to the boil, keeping it well stirred. Then cover it with greaseproof paper and a tightly fitting lid and cook in a moderately hot oven, gas mark 5 or 375° F. (190° C.) for 2 hours, or until the meat is tender.

Whilst the meat is cooking, cook the rice in a large saucepan of fast boiling salted water. When it is done, strain, then rinse in hot water and drain again. Put it in a hot buttered fireproof dish, cover with a piece of buttered greaseproof paper and allow to dry in a cool oven.

Slice the mushroom caps, skin and pip the tomatoes and cut them into strips. Make the rest of the butter hot in a sauté pan, put in the mushrooms and tomatoes, season well and cook for 2–3 minutes. Add the rice to this mixture and stir with a fork. Adjust the seasoning and keep it hot.

To Serve: Remove the meat from the oven, adjust the seasoning and take out the bouquet garni. Pour the ragoût into a hot serving dish, pile the rice mixture at each end. Serve very hot.

TOURNEDOS À LA PIÉMONTAISE *** (for 5 persons)

Ingredients:

5 tournedos barded with larding bacon (see Tournedos Andalouse, page 125)
5 rounds of bread cut the same size as the tournedos
250 g. Patna rice (8 oz.)
1 onion
2 shallots
1 small clove garlic

4 small tomatoes
beef stock
120–150 g. butter, approximately (4–5 oz.)
150 g. tongue, cut into julienne strips (5 oz.)
150 g. cooked ham, cut into julienne strips (5 oz.)
1 small glass brandy
seasoning

Method: Melt 30 g. (1 oz.) of the butter in a small saucepan, add the onion, finely chopped and allow it to soften and then brown slightly. Measure the volume of the rice before adding it to the pan. Turn it quickly in the hot butter. Add twice the volume of the rice in stock, together with the clove of garlic crushed with a little salt and the tomatoes, which have been skinned and pipped and roughly chopped. Season well. Bring the mixture to simmering point. Cover with a piece of greaseproof paper and the lid. Put to cook in a moderate oven, gas mark 5 or 375° F. (190° C.) for 20 minutes.

Meanwhile sauter the rounds of bread in hot butter: about 60 g. (2 oz.). When they are fried put them to drain, add a little more butter to the pan and make it hot. Fry the tournedos quickly in this allowing 1–2 minutes on each side, according to their thickness. Place one on each croûton on a serving dish. Keep hot.

To the hot butter add the finely chopped shallots. Cook gently until they are soft. Déglace the pan with brandy, reduce this a little, then add about 1 dl. ($\frac{1}{2}$ gill) stock. Lastly add the tongue and ham. Season. Remove the sauce from the heat and stir in 30 g. (1 oz.) butter, bit by bit.

When the rice is cooked stir it gently with a fork. Adjust the seasoning. Arrange it in small mounds in between the tournedos, coat with a little sauce. Hand the rest of the sauce separately. Serve at once.

TOURNEDOS ANDALOUSE ***   (for 4 persons)

Ingredients:

4 tournedos	1 aubergine
2 slices ham	2 green peppers
350 g. tomatoes (¾ lb.)	4 slices bread
125 g. Patna rice (4 oz.)	chopped fresh herbs
180 g. butter (6 oz.)	larding bacon
2 tablespoons oil	a little extra butter
250 g. Chipolata sausages (½ lb.)	seasoning

Method: Halve the peppers, remove the seeds and pith. Blanch the peppers in boiling salted water for 5 minutes. Drain and refresh them.

Cook the rice in boiling salted water for 12–15 minutes. Refresh this also with cold water. Drain well and dry it on a clean cloth.

Cut the aubergine into four diagonal slices. Sprinkle them with a little salt and leave them to drain for 10–15 minutes.

Cut a strip of larding bacon the same depth as the steaks and tie with string round each. Cut a round of bread the same size as each of the steaks. Skin and pip the tomatoes. Chop the ham and the tomatoes, add a table-spoonful of tomato and half the chopped ham to the rice with the chopped herbs and seasoning and put this mixture into the peppers. Dot with butter, cover with buttered foil or greaseproof paper and bake them in a moderate oven, gas mark 5 or 375° F. (190° C.) for 20 minutes.

Meanwhile, wipe the aubergine slices and fry them slowly in 60 g. (2 oz.) of hot butter until they are tender. Season, remove and drain them. Keep them hot. Heat the rest of the ham and tomatoes in the same butter. Season. Remove and keep hot also.

In a separate pan heat 30 g. (1 oz.) butter. Slowly fry the chipolatas in this, and when they are cooked drain them and keep them hot.

Fry the croûtons in the oil with 30 g. (1 oz.) butter until they are crisp and golden brown. Drain them on kitchen paper and keep hot.

Finally, heat the remaining butter in a clean pan and when it is hot, put in the steaks. Cook them quickly for 1–2 minutes on each side according to their thickness.

To Serve: Arrange the croûtons on a hot dish. Place the tournedos on top. Surround with stuffed peppers and the chipolata sausages. Place a slice of aubergine on top of each steak, and then a spoonful of the tomato mixture. Sprinkle with finely chopped herbs. Serve immediately.

JAMBON À LA CRÈME *   (for 4 persons)

Ingredients:

8 slices cooked ham	125 g. button mushrooms (4 oz.)
75 g. unsalted butter (2½ oz.)	6 tablespoons French vermouth
3 dl. thick cream (½ pint)	seasoning

Method: Wipe the mushrooms. Heat 30 g. (1 oz.) butter in a small pan, put in the mushrooms, season, cover with greaseproof paper and the lid. Cook over a low heat for 3–5 minutes. Shake the pan frequently.

Meanwhile heat the remaining 45 g. (1½ oz.) butter in a sauté pan and warm the ham through over a *very* gentle heat. It is important not to shrivel the slices of ham. Remove them, place them on a hot plate and cover with a second hot plate to keep hot.

Strain the liquor from the mushrooms into the sauté pan. Pour in the vermouth and the cream. Stir over a low heat and allow the cream to thicken. This will take 3–4 minutes. Taste and season.

To Serve: Stir the mushrooms into the sauce. Arrange the ham slices, folded in half, down the centre of a hot dish. Pour over the cream and mushroom sauce. Serve at once.

Comment: This dish is a speciality of Savoie, although variations of it are found in all departments of France. In the Savoie district the Chambéry vermouth is used.

JAMBON AU VIN ROUGE ** (for 6–8 persons)

Ingredients:

1 piece of gammon hock, 1½–2 kg. (3–4 lb.)
1 onion
6 cloves
bouquet garni
3–4 peppercorns
1 bottle red wine

½ l. white stock (1 pint)
1 tablespoon arrowroot

For the Braise:
60 g. carrots (2 oz.)
60 g. onions (2 oz.)
60 g. leeks (2 oz.)
45–60 g. butter (1½–2 oz.)

Method: Soak the gammon for 24 hours. Put it into a large pan containing sufficient boiling water to cover it. Add the onion stuck with cloves, a large bouquet garni and the peppercorns. Simmer for 1 hour. After this time, lift out the gammon and remove the skin.

Heat the butter in the bottom of a 'braisière' or roasting pan with a lid. Toss the coarsely chopped vegetables in this, then lay the gammon on top. Pour over the red wine and the stock, which have been heated. Cover with the lid and seal with a repère paste (see page 23). Cook in a moderate oven, gas mark 5 or 375° F. (190° C.) for a further hour. At the end of this time, lift out the gammon, cut it into slices and arrange them overlapping down the centre of a hot serving dish. Skim off the excess fat from the pan. Slake the arrowroot with a little cold water. Stir it into the pan, adjust the seasoning and continue to cook for a further 5 minutes. Strain it over the gammon. Serve with Pommes de Terre Mousseline or Pommes de Terre à l'Anglaise (see pages 219 and 228).

JAMBON SURPRISE ** (for 6 persons)

Ingredients:
Flaky pastry made with 240 g. (8 oz.) plain flour etc. (see page 335)
6 slices cooked ham
For the Filling:
30 g. butter (1 oz.)
1 tablespoon oil
120 g. mushrooms (4 oz.)
2 shallots
1 small onion
1 tablespoon brandy

3 tablespoons thick cream
3 tablespoons thick Sauce Béchamel (made with 20 g. (¾ oz.) butter, 20 g. (¾ oz.) plain flour, to 1½ dl. (¼ pint) milk) (see page 34)
seasoning
To finish:
beaten egg to brush over
Sauce Tomate, Method I (see page 38)

Method: Make up the pastry in the normal way and put it aside to relax.

Make the filling – wipe and chop the mushrooms finely using stalks and trimmings. Chop the shallots and onion finely. Put the mushrooms into a clean cloth and squeeze them to expel the moisture. Heat the butter and oil together in a small saucepan, add the onions and shallots and cook without allowing them to brown. They must be stirred all the time. Now add the mushrooms and continue to cook until all the moisture has evaporated. Remove from the heat, stir in the sauce Béchamel, the cream and the brandy. Season well. Put it aside to cool.

Roll out the pastry thinly and divide into six oblong portions.

Spread a layer of filling on each of the slices of ham and roll them up. Put each roll on a piece of pastry and join the edges of the pastry neatly, using a little beaten egg to make them adhere. The ham should be completely enclosed in the pastry. Place them on a baking sheet, with the joined side underneath. Using a 1 cm. (½ inch) plain cutter, remove a circle of pastry from the centre of each one. With any trimmings left from the pastry, make leaves and arrange them round the circles. Brush them over with beaten egg. Place them in a hot oven, gas mark 6–7 or 400–425° F. (200–220° C.) for 15–20 minutes until golden brown. Serve hot with a well flavoured sauce tomate.

MÉDAILLONS DE JAMBON AU RIZ ** (for 6 persons)

Ingredients:
6 slices cooked ham
170 g. liver pâté or pâté de foie (6 oz.)
60 g. butter (2 oz.)
1 tablespoon thick cream
120 g. Patna rice (4 oz.)
60 g. cooked diced carrots (2 oz.)

60 g. cooked diced turnips (2 oz.)
60 g. cooked diced peas (2 oz.)
1 red pepper or ½ tin red peppers
1½ dl. Sauce Vinaigrette (¼ pint) (see page 40)
finely chopped parsley
paprika
seasoning

Method: Cook the rice in boiling salted water until tender. Drain, rinse in cold water and drain again. Allow to cool. Cut the pepper in half and remove the seeds and pith. Cut it into dice. Blanch it in boiling salted water for 5 minutes. Remove and drain. If using tinned pepper, cut it into dice. Mix the rice, the vegetables and the pepper together.

Prepare the sauce vinaigrette. Mix it with the rice and vegetables. Arrange in a mound on a serving dish.

Meanwhile cut the ham into an even number of rounds. Pass the liver pâté through a sieve, beat in the butter, and cream and a little paprika. Season well. Put this mixture into a forcing bag with a rosette nozzle and pipe generous rosettes of pâté all over half the rounds of ham. Cover with the remainder of the rounds. Arrange them at the base of the rice and vegetable mixture. Sprinkle the rice with paprika and chopped parsley. Serve cold.

Comment: This dish can be further garnished if desired with a decoration of piped sauce mayonnaise (see page 36). The trimmings from the ham make an excellent omelette filling.

MÉDAILLONS DE JAMBON CHAUD ** (for 8 persons)

Ingredients:

8 large slices cooked ham
90–120 g. white breadcrumbs
  (3–4 oz.)
a little milk
30 g. butter (1 oz.)
3 tablespoons thick Sauce Béchamel (see page 34)

2 tablespoons thin cream
2 yolks of egg
1 dl. dry white wine ($\frac{1}{2}$ gill)
2 tablespoons finely chopped fresh
  herbs
seasoning
To finish:
finely chopped herbs

Method: Using a sharp pastry cutter, cut the ham into rounds. Chop the trimmings finely. Soak the breadcrumbs in a little milk. Squeeze out with the hands. Mix them with the ham trimmings and herbs. Beat together the yolks, cream, melted butter and the sauce Béchamel. Stir in the ham trimmings, the herbs and the breadcrumbs. Season very well. Place a portion of this mixture on half of the rounds of ham. Cover with a second round. Arrange the médaillons in a buttered fireproof dish. Moisten with the wine. Cover with a piece of buttered greaseproof paper and place in a moderate oven, gas mark 5 or 375° F. (190° C.) for 10–15 minutes. Serve hot, dusted with finely chopped herbs.

PAUPIETTES PANACHÉES ** (for 6 persons)

Ingredients:
240 g. underdone lean roast beef, minced (8 oz.)
6 large slices cooked ham
2 shallots, finely chopped
30 g. butter (1 oz.)
1 teaspoon paprika
1 tablespoon finely chopped parsley
seasoning

For the Garnish:
460 g. new carrots, boiled, drained and tossed in a little melted butter (1 lb.)
Pommes de Terre Duchesse, Method II, (see page 226)
To finish:
90 g. butter (3 oz.)
90 g. grated Gruyère cheese (3 oz.)

Method: Heat 30 g. (1 oz.) butter in a small pan, put in the shallots and stir them gently over a low heat until they are soft. They should not brown. Add the beef, seasoning, paprika and the parsley. Heat through for 2–3 minutes, keeping the mixture well stirred. (If the beef is not underdone it may be necessary to add a spoonful of stock or dry white wine to moisten it.)

Heat the slices of ham, by placing them in between two buttered plates over a pan of boiling water. When they are hot, lift them carefully on to a board or large dish, divide the beef mixture equally into six portions. Spread one portion on each slice of ham. Roll them up and place them down the centre of a hot fireproof dish.

To finish, melt the butter in a small saucepan, remove it from the heat and stir in the grated cheese. Spread or pour this mixture down the centre of the paupiettes.

Put the pommes de terre duchesse in a forcing bag with a large rosette tube and pipe a border in a shell design down each side of the dish. Place the dish under a hot grill or in the top of a hot oven, gas mark 7 or 425° F. (220° C.) to set the potatoes and to melt the cheese and butter mixture. When the latter is golden brown, remove the dish and place the carrots at each end. Serve hot.

BROCHETTES DE MOUTON À L'INDIENNE **

(for 4 persons)

Ingredients:
250 g. fillet of mutton ($\frac{1}{2}$ lb.)
250 g. calves' liver ($\frac{1}{2}$ lb.)
120 g. streaky bacon in a piece (4 oz.)
2 large tomatoes
1 green or red pepper
60 g. butter (2 oz.)
seasoning
Riz à l'Indienne:
120 g. Patna rice (4 oz.)

30 g. butter (1 oz.)
1 small onion
1 teaspoon curry powder
3 dl. white stock ($\frac{1}{2}$ pint)
bouquet garni
seasoning
For the Garnish:
slices of lemon
parsley

Method: Begin by making the Riz à l'Indienne. Cook the rice in plenty of boiling, salted water for 15 minutes or until it is done. Rinse it in hot water and drain it. Place it in a buttered dish. Cover with greaseproof paper which has been thickly buttered and put it in a cool oven to dry.

Whilst the rice is cooking, make the sauce. Heat 30 g. (1 oz.) butter in a saucepan. Add the onion finely chopped and soften it over a low heat. As soon as it is tender, sprinkle in the curry powder. Stir well, then pour in the stock. Season, add the bouquet garni. Bring up to simmering point and simmer for 30 minutes. Remove the bouquet garni.

Cut the mutton, liver and bacon into cubes, making 4 cubes of each. Cut the pepper into halves, remove the pith and seeds and cut into twelve pieces. Cut the tomatoes in halves.

Now arrange on four skewers as follows. First half a tomato, then a cube of mutton, then a piece of pepper, a cube of liver, a piece of pepper and then a piece of bacon. Finally finish with a piece of pepper. Melt the 60 g. (2 oz.) butter and dip each brochette into it, turning well to allow all the meat, etc., to be well covered. Grill under a moderately hot grill, turning from time to time. When the blood shows from the meat, season well.

Heap the rice in the centre of a hot serving dish. Pour over the sauce. Lay the brochettes on the top. Decorate the edges of the dish with thin slices of lemon and sprigs of parsley. Serve at once.

CÔTELETTES DE MOUTON EN PAPILLOTE **

(for 4 persons)

Ingredients:

4 mutton cutlets	30 g. butter (1 oz.)
2 slices ham	120 g. mushrooms (4 oz.)
30 g. butter (1 oz.)	2 shallots
seasoning	pinch of nutmeg
For the duxelle:	seasoning
1 tablespoon oil	
1 small onion	Sauce Tomate, Method I (see page 38)

Method: Make the duxelle – chop the mushrooms finely using the stalks and the trimmings. Squeeze them in a cloth by twisting it so that as much of their moisture is extracted as possible. Heat the oil and the butter in a pan and brown the finely chopped onion lightly. Then add the finely chopped shallots and the mushrooms together with the seasoning and a pinch of nutmeg. Stir over a good heat until all the remaining moisture from the mushrooms has evaporated. Put the duxelle on a plate to cool and divide it into eight.

Cook the cutlets. Heat the butter in a frying pan and sauter the cutlets in this very lightly. Season well, drain.

Cut each slice of ham into four. Prepare some heart shaped pieces of greaseproof paper. On one half of each put a portion of duxelle, cover with a piece of ham, then the cutlet, a second piece of ham, and finally a second portion of duxelle.

Fold the papers in half and fold the edges tightly together so as to seal the cutlets inside. Brush all over the paper with oil or melted butter.

Bake in a moderately hot oven, gas mark 6 or 400° F. (200° C.) for 10–15 minutes. Serve immediately in their paper cases with the sauce tomate handed separately.

CÔTELETTES DE MOUTON À LA BRETONNE **

(for 4 persons)

Ingredients:

4 mutton cutlets
1 egg
olive oil
seasoned flour
white breadcrumbs
60–90 g. butter for frying (2–3 oz.)
For the Garnish:
250 g. haricot beans, cooked (see page 19) (½ lb.)

1 small onion or 2 shallots
250 g. tomatoes (½ lb.)
105 g. butter (3½ oz.)
1 teaspoon concentrated tomato purée
1 clove garlic
1½ dl. dry white wine (1 gill)
To finish:
chopped parsley

Method: Make the sauce. Chop the onion or shallots finely. Melt 30 g. (1 oz.) butter in a small pan and soften them in this. Add the tomatoes, which have been skinned, pipped and roughly chopped, together with the garlic, crushed with a little salt, and the tomato purée. Cook until they form a pulp. Add the white wine. Strain into a clean pan. Reduce by half over a good heat. Remove from the heat and whisk in the remaining 75 g. (2½ oz.) butter, bit by bit. Mix in the beans carefully.

Meanwhile trim and flatten the cutlets. Dip them into seasoned flour, then into the egg, which has been lightly beaten with the olive oil, finally into the breadcrumbs.

Heat the butter in a frying pan and fry the cutlets quickly, approximately 5–7 minutes on each side.

Heat the beans in the sauce and pile them in the centre of a hot serving dish. Arrange the cutlets round the sides and dust them with finely chopped parsley. Serve hot.

CÔTELETTES DE MOUTON CHASSERESSE **

(for 4 persons)

Ingredients:

4 mutton cutlets
90 g. butter (3 oz.)
1 tablespoon finely chopped
  shallots
6 large mushrooms, chopped
¼ l. dry white wine (1½ gills)
1 tablespoon tomato purée
12–15 stoned green olives
1 tablespoon finely chopped chervil

1 tablespoon finely chopped tarragon
Rice pilaf made with:
1 teacupful Patna rice
3 teacupfuls white stock
1 medium sized onion
60 g. butter (2 oz.)
2 tablespoons sultanas
1 pinch quatre épices or mixed spice
seasoning

Method: Begin by making the pilaf. Chop the onion finely. Heat the butter in a fairly large pan. Add the onion and soften it over a low heat without colouration. Put in the rice and stir this until it is well coated in the butter. Then add the sultanas and the stock, which has been heated with the quatre épices. Season well and bring slowly up to simmering point. Cover with greaseproof paper and the lid. Put in a moderate oven, gas mark 5 or 375° F. (190° C.) for approximately half an hour. Do not stir or disturb the rice whilst it is cooking.

Meanwhile prepare the cutlets. Trim off excess fat. Heat the butter in a sauté pan. Fry the cutlets in this for 2–3 minutes on each side according to preference. Remove them from the pan and keep them hot. Into the butter in which the cutlets were cooked, put the shallots and mushrooms. Cook gently for 2–3 minutes. Pour in the wine, stir in the tomato purée. Cook for a further 2 minutes then add the olives and the chopped herbs.

When the rice is cooked, arrange it in a border in a hot serving dish. Place the cutlets overlapping down the centre. Pour over the sauce and serve at once.

ÉPAULE DE MOUTON BRAISÉE MÉNAGÈRE **

(for 6 persons)

Ingredients:

1 shoulder of mutton, approx.
  1½–2 kg. (3–3½ lb.)
For the Farce:
360 g. pork sausage meat (¾ lb.)
2 medium sized onions finely
  chopped
2 heaped tablespoons chopped
  parsley
1 heaped tablespoon mixed fresh
  herbs, finely chopped (tarragon
  chervil, sweet basil)

4 tablespoons white breadcrumbs
¾ l. white stock (1½ pints)
2 cloves garlic
120–180 g. butter or good dripping, approx. (4–6 oz.)
seasoning
For the Garnish:
12–15 young carrots
12–15 small onions
½ kg. small, even sized new potatoes (1 lb.)

Method: Bone the shoulder (see page 25). Heat about 45–60 g. (1½–2 oz.) butter or dripping in a pan and cook the onions in this until they are soft but not coloured. Remove from the heat and pour off the excess fat. Mix the onions with the sausage meat and breadcrumbs. Add one clove of garlic crushed with a little salt, the parsley and the herbs. Season well. Fill the cavity left by the bone with the farce. Roll up and fasten with thin string or sew up with a trussing needle.

Put 60 g. (2 oz.) butter or dripping into a deep roasting pan with a lid. Make it very hot and turn the meat in it on all sides to brown it well. Add the carrots cut into quarters lengthwise and the small onions left whole with the second clove of garlic, also crushed with a little salt. Pour in sufficient boiling stock to come half-way up the side of the meat. Cover with buttered paper tucking it well down the sides. Put on the lid and braise in a moderate oven, gas mark 5 or 375° F. (190° C.) for 2–2½ hours. Half an hour before it has finished cooking, place the potatoes in a pan of boiling salted water. Boil for 2–3 minutes and remove. Dry them well. Melt the remaining butter or dripping in a small pan. Add the potatoes and rissoler them until cooked. Shake the pan frequently to prevent them sticking.

Remove the meat from the pan, take off the fat from the gravy and adjust the seasoning.

To Serve: Put the mutton on a hot dish. Remove the string. Arrange the carrots and onions at each side and pile up the potatoes at one end. Pour a little gravy over the meat. Serve the remainder in a sauceboat.

GIGOT DE MOUTON À LA BOULANGÈRE *

(for 6–7 persons)

Ingredients:
1 small leg of mutton, approx.
  3 kg. (6 lb.)
4–6 medium onions

6–8 medium sized potatoes
2 tablespoons mutton dripping or
  butter
seasoning

Method: Slice the potatoes and onions very thinly. Butter a large deep roasting pan, place a layer of potatoes in the bottom and then some onions on the top. Season very well. Continue in this way until the pan is three-quarters full, making the top layer potatoes. Dot with knobs of dripping or butter. Add sufficient water to come to the level of the potatoes. Place in a moderate oven, gas mark 5 or 375° F. (190° C.) or on the top of the stove over a low heat until it comes to the boil.

Season the meat well. As soon as the water is boiling, put the meat on the top of the vegetables. Roast in a moderate oven, gas mark 6–7 or 400–425° F. (200–220° C.) for about 2½ hours. Serve hot.

RAGOÛT DE MOUTON À L'ITALIENNE **

(for 4–5 persons)

Ingredients:
¾–1 kg. best end neck of mutton
  (1½–2 lb.)
75 g. butter (2½ oz.)
2–3 carrots
1 turnip
1 clove garlic
250 g. haricot beans soaked
  overnight (½ lb.)
1 bouquet garni

1 teaspoon arrowroot, slaked with
  a little cold water
Sauce Tomate (Method I) (see
  page 38)
seasoning
To finish:
3 tomatoes
30 g. butter (1 oz.)
2 medium sized potatoes

Method: Have the meat chined and cut into cutlets. Cut the carrots and turnip into slices. Make the butter hot in a deep pan, add the meat and vegetables and brown them all gently. Season and add the clove of garlic crushed with a little salt and the bouquet garni. Pour in 3 dl. (½ pint) boiling water. Cover with greaseproof paper and the lid and place in a moderate oven, gas mark 5 or 375° F. (190°C.) for 1–1½ hours.

Whilst it is cooking, place the haricot beans first in cold salted water and bring to the boil. Refresh and return them to a clean pan of boiling salted water and cook until tender, approximately 1 hour. Make the sauce tomate. Boil the potatoes in salted water. When the meat is cooked, pour in the arrowroot, stir well and add 2–3 tablespoons of the sauce tomate. Cook for 4–5 minutes. Cut the tomatoes into slices and heat them through in the remaining butter.

Place the haricot beans in the bottom of a large hot serving dish. Cover with the rest of the sauce tomate. Arrange the meat down one side of the dish and the rounds of tomatoes down the other. Pile the carrots, turnips and cooked potatoes cut into slices in the middle. Pour the gravy over the top. Serve very hot.

Comment: French beans, when in season, can be substituted for haricot beans.

CÔTELETTES DE PORC À L'ITALIENNE **

(for 4 persons)

Ingredients:
4 pork cutlets
120 g. grated cheese (4 oz.)
120 g. butter (4 oz.)
4 tomatoes
120–170 g. long macaroni (4–6 oz.)
1 clove garlic
1 dessertspoon tomato purée
60–90 g. salami sausage (2–3 oz.)

120 g. white breadcrumbs (4 oz.)
2 eggs lightly beaten with a little
  oil and seasoning
3 tablespoons oil
seasoning
For the Garnish:
4 small tomatoes
a little extra butter
8 green and 8 black olives

134

Method: Cook the macaroni in boiling salted water. Drain, rinse and drain again. Melt 30 g. (1 oz.) butter with 2 tablespoons oil in a sauté pan. Add the tomatoes skinned, pipped and cut into shreds and the salami cut into strips. Toss lightly and then add the garlic crushed with a little salt, the purée and the macaroni. Stir quickly in the pan and keep it hot.

Trim the cutlets. Dip them into the beaten eggs and then into a mixture of white breadcrumbs and 60 g. (2 oz.) grated cheese. Make about 90 g. (3 oz.) butter hot in a shallow pan, add the remaining tablespoon of oil and fry the cutlets allowing about 7 minutes on each side.

Whilst they are cooking, cut the tomatoes for the garnish in half. Scoop out the centres and put a nut of butter in each. Brush over with oil. Stone the olives and fill them into the tomatoes. Cover with buttered paper and place in a roasting tin in a moderately hot oven to heat through, gas mark 5–6 or 375–400° F. (190–200° C.) for 5–10 minutes.

To Serve: Place the cutlets in the centre of a large serving dish. Stir the remaining cheese into the macaroni. Taste and season. Arrange it in a ring around the cutlets with the tomatoes round the sides. Serve hot.

CÔTES DE PORC À L'ORANGE **   (for 4 persons)

Ingredients:
4 pork chops
30 g. butter (1 oz.)
2 oranges
a little finely chopped thyme

3 lumps sugar
2 tablespoons wine vinegar
seasoning
For the Garnish:
1 orange

Method: Trim the pork of excess fat. Season. Heat the butter in a thick pan and fry the chops in this, making sure that they are well cooked on both sides, at least 15 minutes in all, depending on the thickness of the chops.

In a small pan dissolve the sugar in the vinegar. Allow it to turn to a caramel, then pour in the juice of the 2 oranges and the juice from the pan the chops were cooked in, together with the thyme. Swill round well. Arrange the chops in a hot serving dish, pour the sauce over the top and decorate with thin slices of orange.

CÔTES DE PORC AU CÉLERI **   (for 4 persons)

Ingredients:
4 pork chops
4 shallots
1½ dl. dry white wine (1 gill)
1 medium root celeriac
3 dl. white stock (½ pint)
60 g. butter, approx. (2 oz.)

1 tablespoon finely chopped
   tarragon
bouquet garni
1 tablespoon wine vinegar
seasoning
To finish:
finely chopped parsley

Method: Heat about half the butter in a sauté pan. Add the chops, which have been trimmed of excess fat. Cook them until well browned on both sides, approximately 5–7 minutes each side. Now add the finely chopped shallots, the bouquet garni and the wine. Season well. Cover with grease-proof paper and a tightly fitting lid. Cook gently for half an hour.

Meanwhile, peel and cut the celeriac into ½ cm. (¼ inch) finger lengths. Place them in a pan of cold salted water, bring them to the boil and boil for 2–3 minutes. Drain and dry them on a clean cloth. Return them to the pan. Add the hot stock, chopped tarragon and seasoning. Simmer for 15 minutes or until just tender.

When the chops are cooked, dish them in a hot serving dish. Arrange the celeriac at each side. Pour the stock it was cooked in into the meat pan. Swill round and add the vinegar. Remove from the heat. Beat in the remaining butter. Taste and season. Pour over the chops. Sprinkle with the chopped parsley. Serve at once.

CÔTES DE PORC AUX PRUNEAUX, SAUCE ROBERT **

(for 4 persons)

Ingredients:
4 pork chops
Sauce Robert (see page 37)
60 g. butter (2 oz.)
1 tablespoon oil

To finish:
3–4 sliced gherkins
12 prunes, soaked and cooked in
demi-sec Vouvray or white wine

Method: Make the Sauce Robert.

Trim the chops and remove the excess fat. Heat the butter and the oil together in a sauté pan. Put in the chops and cook them slowly and thoroughly. They will take about 20 minutes and must be turned frequently. When they are cooked, remove them from the pan, place them on a hot serving dish, pour over the hot sauce Robert, scatter over the sliced gherkins and arrange the prunes round the sides of the dish. Serve very hot.

CÔTES DE PORC GRAND CHEF *

(for 4 persons)

Ingredients:
4 pork chops
seasoning
Purée Soubise made with ½ kg.
(1 lb.) onions
60 g. butter (2 oz.)

2 tablespoons thin cream
2 tablespoons dry white wine
2–3 tablespoons white breadcrumbs
2 tablespoons grated cheese
seasoning

Method: Make the purée soubise – peel and chop the onions. Put them into a pan of cold water and bring them to the boil. Boil for 5 minutes. Drain them thoroughly. Heat the butter in a pan, add the onions and cook them over a low heat until they are completely soft, then pass them through a sieve or vegetable mill. Reheat the purée in a clean pan. Stir in the cream and adjust the seasoning.

Mix about a third of the soubise purée with the white wine and pour it into the bottom of a buttered fireproof dish. Season the chops and place them on top of the purée. Coat them with the rest of the purée. Sprinkle the top with the breadcrumbs and the grated cheese. Place the dish in a moderate oven, gas mark 5 or 375° F. (190° C.) and cook for 50–55 minutes. Serve at once.

SAUTÉ DE PORC MIREILLE ** (for 4–5 persons)

Ingredients:

¾–1 kg. lean breast of pork or lean pie pork (1½–2 lb.)
1½ dl. oil, approx. (1 gill)
1 clove garlic
1 small onion
2 aubergines
1½ dl. white stock (1 gill)
460 g. small ripe tomatoes (1 lb.)

1 teaspoon paprika
¼ teaspoon saffron dissolved in a little boiling water
1 green, 1 yellow, 1 red pepper
seasoned flour
seasoning
To finish:
120 g. boiled Patna rice (see page 24) (4 oz.)

Method: Peel the aubergines. Cut them into convenient mouthfuls, sprinkle with salt. Put them on a wire rack to drain. Turn them from time to time. Dry them on a clean cloth.

Cut the meat into convenient sized pieces. Remove all excess fat. Melt two tablespoons of the oil in a sauté pan. Put in the meat and turn it quickly in the hot oil until it is well browned on all sides.

Chop the onion finely and crush the garlic with a little salt – add to the meat.

Take all the tomatoes, except three, and cut them into quarters. Add them to the meat, together with the hot stock. Season and add the saffron and paprika. Cover the pan with greaseproof paper and the lid. Cook over a gentle heat. Shake the pan from time to time to prevent the meat from sticking to the bottom.

Cut the peppers into strips about 1 cm. (½ inch) wide, discarding the pith and seeds. Cook them in boiling salted water for 10 minutes and then drain.

Roll the aubergines in seasoned flour and fry them in hot oil. Keep them hot. Cut the rest of the tomatoes in half. Heat them through, cut side down in the hot oil, then cook them through on the other side, when it will be found easy to remove the skins.

Heat the peppers through in the hot oil. Mix the tomatoes, aubergines and peppers with the meat. Season.

Arrange a border of plain boiled rice in a hot serving dish. Place the pork, and vegetables in the middle. Serve at once.

CÔTES DE VEAU PERSILLÉES *   (for 6 persons)

Ingredients:
6 veal chops
3 tablespoons olive oil
1 liqueur glass kirsch

1½ dl. thin cream (1 gill)
2 tablespoons finely chopped
  parsley
seasoning

Method: Heat the oil in a sauté pan. When it is hot, put in the chops. Cook them for approximately 15 minutes, turning them after the first 7 minutes. At the end of the cooking time pour off the excess oil. Season well and pour the kirsch into the pan and 'flame' it.

Arrange the chops neatly on a hot serving dish and keep them hot. Quickly stir the parsley and the cream in the pan in which the chops were cooked. Heat them through without allowing them to boil. Season to taste. Pour this sauce over the chops and serve very hot.

CÔTES DE VEAU À LA CUSSY ***   (for 4 persons)

Ingredients:
4 veal chops
seasoned flour
white breadcrumbs
1 egg
1 dessertspoon oil
120 g. butter (4 oz.)
juice of ½ lemon
For the Filling:
60 g. finely chopped ham (2 oz.)
60 g. mushrooms (2 oz.)
1 small carrot, diced
1 shallot, chopped
45 g. butter (1½ oz.)

15 g. plain flour (½ oz.)
1½ dl. milk (1 gill)
seasoning
For the Risotto:
2 onions, finely chopped
1 teacup Patna rice
2 teacups veal stock
60 g. butter (2 oz.)
45 g. grated Parmesan cheese
  (1½ oz.)
1 truffle (optional) or
  120 g. mushrooms (4 oz.)
seasoning

Method: First prepare the filling for the cutlets. Cook the carrot in sufficient water to cover with 15 g. (½ oz.) butter and a pinch of sugar and salt. Boil until the liquid is almost all evaporated and the carrot tender. Heat the rest of the butter in a small pan, cook the shallot over a low heat until it is soft but not browned. Add the finely chopped mushrooms and cook for a further 3–4 minutes. Remove from the heat and sprinkle in the flour. Stir in the milk. Bring to the boil and simmer for a few minutes, stirring all the time. Add the ham and the carrot and season well. Allow to cool.

Next make the risotto. Heat 30 g. (1 oz.) of the butter in a large pan, add the onions and cook them slowly until they are transparent. Then stir in the rice until it has absorbed all the butter. Pour on the stock, bring it to the boil and cover with a lid. Then cook in a moderate oven, gas mark 5 or 375° F. (190° C.) for 25–30 minutes. When the rice is tender and the liquid absorbed, stir in the rest of the butter and the cheese and the finely chopped truffle (or the mushrooms cooked in extra butter).

Meanwhile, make a slit in the flesh of each chop and fill each with ham mixture. Season the cutlets, then dip them into seasoned flour, then the egg, beaten with the oil and lastly the breadcrumbs. Heat 90 g. (3 oz.) butter in a frying pan and fry the chops in this for 10–15 minutes.

To Serve: Pile the risotto in a border on the hot serving dish. Arrange the chops in the centre. Heat 30 g. (1 oz.) butter in a clean pan and when it is browned, pour in the lemon juice. Stir round and pour over the chops.

CÔTES DE VEAU AU RIZ *   (for 4 persons)

Ingredients:
4 veal chops
1 onion
1 shallot
60 g. butter (2 oz.)
1 dessertspoon oil
1½ dl. dry white wine (1 gill)
1 teaspoon concentrated tomato
    purée
seasoning

For the Risotto:
4 rashers bacon
1 teacup Patna rice
3 teacups stock
30 g. butter (1 oz.)
1 onion, finely chopped
seasoning
To Finish:
2 rashers bacon
chopped parsley
sliced lemon
grated cheese

Method: First make the risotto. Heat the butter in a pan. Cook the chopped onion slowly in this without allowing it to brown. Stir in the rice until it is well coated all over with the butter. Then pour in the stock. Cut the 4 bacon rashers into 'lardons' and add these to the pan. Bring to the boil and season well, bearing in mind the bacon may be salt. Cover with greaseproof paper and a lid and cook in a moderate oven, gas mark 5 or 375° F. (190° C.) for 25–30 minutes. Do not disturb during the cooking.

Chop the onion and shallot finely. Heat 30 g. (1 oz.) butter and the oil in a large pan. Cook the onion and shallot in this until they are beginning to turn golden. Then place the chops in the pan with extra butter if needed. Brown them well on both sides. Season well. Tuck a piece of greaseproof paper over the top. Cover with a lid and cook over a gentle heat, shaking the pan from time to time for 10–15 minutes (depending on the thickness of the chops).

Cut 2 rashers of bacon into four strips. Roll them up, secure them with a skewer and cook them under a hot grill. Keep them hot.

Heap up the risotto in a hot serving dish. Arrange the chops round the risotto. Pour the wine into the hot butter the chops were cooked in. Stir in the tomato purée. Bring it to the boil. Taste and adjust the seasoning. Pour the sauce over the chops. Garnish with tiny bacon rolls and wafer thin slices of lemon. Dust over with finely chopped parsley.

Serve with a dish of grated cheese.

CÔTES DE VEAU AUX RAISINS ** (for 6 persons)

Ingredients:
6 good sized veal chops
250 g. white grapes (½ lb.)
1 liqueur glass brandy
90 g. butter (3 oz.)

¼ l. dry white wine (1½ gills)
seasoning
For the Garnish:
120 g. noodles (4 oz.)
60 g. butter (2 oz.)

Method: Heat 90 g. (3 oz.) butter in a sauté pan. Season the chops, place them in the pan and cook them for 3–4 minutes on each side. When they are well browned, pour in the wine and season to taste. Cover with grease-proof paper and the lid and cook very gently for ½ hour. Skin and pip the grapes. Ten minutes before the end of the cooking time, add them to the pan. Just before serving, heat the brandy, pour it over the chops and 'flame' it.

Meanwhile, cook the noodles in plenty of boiling salted water for 12–15 minutes or until they are done. Drain and refresh them in hot water. Drain again. Make 60 g. (2 oz.) butter hot in the pan, which has been rinsed out, and toss the noodles in this until they are coated and hot.

Arrange the noodles at each end of a hot serving dish, place the cutlets and grapes in the centre. Pour over the liquor they were cooked in. Serve at once.

ESCALOPES DE VEAU À LA CRÈME ** (for 6 persons)

Ingredients:
6 veal escalopes
125 g. unsalted butter (4 oz.)
180 g. button mushrooms (6 oz.)
1½ dl. white port (1 gill)
¼ l. thick cream (1½ gills)

1 teaspoon oil
beurre manié, made with 30 g.
    (1 oz.) butter and 15 g. (½ oz.)
    plain flour (see page 16)
a little Cayenne pepper
seasoning

Method: Flatten the escalopes under the blade of a heavy knife. Season them. Heat the butter in a sauté pan with the oil. When it is frothing put in the escalopes and cook them gently allowing 2–3 minutes on each side. Remove them and keep them hot in a hot serving dish. Put the mushrooms which have been wiped with a clean cloth, into the butter and cook them for 3–4 minutes. Lift them with a draining spoon and arrange them on the top of the veal. Pour the port into the pan, raise the heat and reduce the liquor by half. Add the cream, seasoning and a pinch of Cayenne pepper.

Bring to simmering point, whisk in the beurre manié and cook for a minute or two longer to allow it to thicken. Pour the sauce over the veal and mushrooms and serve at once.

ESCALOPES DE VEAU 'CHEZ SOI' *   (for 4 persons)

Ingredients:
4 veal escalopes
4 slices ham
60–90 g. unsalted butter (2–3 oz.)

60–90 g. Gruyère cheese (2–3 oz.)
seasoned flour
seasoning

Method: Flatten the escalopes under the blade of a heavy knife. Dip them in seasoned flour.

Heat the butter in a sauté pan, fry the escalopes in this for one minute on each side. Remove and drain them. Place each escalope on a slice of ham, fold over and arrange them in a hot buttered fireproof dish.

Slice the Gruyère cheese into wafer thin slices, lay them all over the top of the veal and ham. Place under a very hot grill or in the top of a very hot oven, gas mark 8 or 450° F. (230° C.) to 'gratiner' the top.

ESCALOPES DE VEAU ST. AFFRIQUE **   (for 4 persons)

Ingredients:
4 veal escalopes
60 g. unsalted butter (2 oz.)
1 teaspoon oil
1 dl. dry white wine (¾ gill)
2 tablespoons thick cream
1 teaspoon paprika
juice of 1 lemon

seasoned flour
seasoning
To finish:
120–170 g. noodles (4–6 oz.)
30 g. butter (1 oz.)
Sauce Tomate (Method I) (see page 38)
thin slices lemon

Method: Make the sauce tomate. Flatten the escalopes well under the blade of a heavy knife and dip each one into the juice of the lemon. Lay them in a dish. Cover and put them aside for ½ hour. At the end of this time, remove them and dip them into seasoned flour. Heat the butter and oil together in a pan. Lay the escalopes in this and brown them on each side. Pour in the wine and season well. Cover with greaseproof paper and the lid. Cook over a gentle heat for 15 minutes. Remove the escalopes. Sprinkle in the paprika and stir round well. Raise the heat and reduce the liquor slightly. Stir in the cream. Replace the escalopes and then heat them through. Rectify the seasoning and keep hot.

Meanwhile cook the noodles in plenty of boiling salted water. Drain them and refresh them in hot water. Drain again, return them to the pan, which has been rinsed out, and stir in the butter, using a fork. Then stir in the hot sauce tomate. Make a border with the noodles in a hot dish.

Arrange the escalopes and their sauce in the centre. Decorate the escalopes with thin slices of lemon.

FRICANDEAU AUX ENDIVES ** (for 4–6 persons)

Ingredients:

1 kg. cushion of veal (2 lb.)
larding bacon
60 g. butter (2 oz.)
2 carrots
1 onion

1½ dl. dry white wine (1 gill)
½ kg. chicory (1 lb.)
6–8 rashers lean bacon
1½ dl. Madeira (1 gill)
30 g. butter for the chicory (1 oz.)
seasoning

Method: Cut the larding bacon into strips and lard the meat (see page 13 for notes on larding). Heat the butter in a braising pan, put in the veal and brown it well on all sides, then add the carrots and onion cut into slices. Season and pour in the wine. Cover with greaseproof paper and the lid and cook in a moderate oven, gas mark 5 or 375° F. (190° C.) for 1 hour.

Meanwhile, wash the chicory and remove any bruised leaves. Wrap a rasher of bacon round each head and tie securely. Heat the butter in a shallow saucepan or sauté pan over a moderate heat. Put in the chicory and turn until the bacon is beginning to crisp. Season. Cover with grease-proof paper and the lid and cook in the oven beside the veal for 45 minutes. At the end of this time drain the chicory well and place it round the sides of the veal. Baste it in the juice from the meat and allow it 5 minutes further cooking.

To Serve: Re-dish the veal on a hot serving dish. Remove the string and arrange the chicory on each side. Pour off the excess fat from the braising pan. Pour in the Madeira and stir round well. Reheat and adjust the seasoning. Pour the sauce over the meat and chicory. Serve at once.

FRICANDEAU BOURGEOISE *** (for 4–6 persons)

Ingredients:

1 kg. centre cut of cushion of veal
  (2 lb.)
larding bacon
For the Braising Mirepoix:
1 medium sized onion
1 shallot
1 carrot
1 stick celery
1 tablespoon concentrated tomato
  purée
2 rashers streaky bacon

30 g. beef dripping (1 oz.)
bouquet garni
seasoning
veal stock
For the Garnish:
½ kg. carrots (1 lb.)
250 g. small onions (½ lb.)
125 g. streaky bacon (4 oz.)
45 g. butter (1½ oz.)
½ l. stock (1 pint)
seasoning

Method: Flatten the piece of veal, using a wet cutlet bat or the blade of a large kitchen knife. Cut lardons from the larding bacon, making them rather thinner than usual and lard the veal.

Prepare the mirepoix, cutting the vegetables and the bacon into 1 cm. ($\frac{1}{2}$ inch) squares. Make the dripping hot in a braising pan, toss the vegetables in this to cook them slightly. Add the tomato purée. Lay the veal on top, season well, add the bouquet garni and sufficient stock to cover the veal. Tuck a piece of greaseproof paper over the top and cover with the lid. Cook in a moderate oven, gas mark 4 or 350° F. (175° C.) for 1–1$\frac{1}{2}$ hours.

Peel the carrots and turn them to the size of large olives. Put them into a saucepan with half of the stock and 15 g. ($\frac{1}{2}$ oz.) butter. Season. Bring quickly to the boil and cook with the pan uncovered until all the stock has evaporated, and the carrots are tender and covered in a light glaze. Keep them hot.

Peel the onions and cook them in a similar way to the carrots, using the rest of the stock and 15 g. ($\frac{1}{2}$ oz.) butter. Keep them hot also.

Remove the rind. Cut the bacon across into lardons. Fry these gently in the rest of the butter until they are just tender. Keep them hot.

When the veal is tender, remove it from the braising pan, taking care not to pierce the meat. Place it on a hot serving dish. Arrange small clusters of carrots, onions and bacon alternately around the veal. Keep hot.

Remove the grease. Strain the braising liquor, and adjust the seasoning. Pour a little over the veal. Allow it to glaze in a hot oven, gas mark 8 or 450° F. (230° C.) for 5 minutes. Serve at once.

Comment: A fricandeau is a piece cut from the length of a cushion of veal (i.e. with the grain). It should not be more than 3 or 4 cm. (1$\frac{1}{2}$ inch) thick. A fricandeau should be larded, otherwise it is called a 'cushion' or 'noix de veau'.

It should be cooked carefully, but thoroughly, and served with two spoons, not cut with a knife, which connoisseurs believe spoils the flavour.

LONGE DE VEAU AUX NOIX **   (for 6 persons)

Ingredients:

1$\frac{1}{2}$ kg. loin of veal (3 lb.)	45 g. butter (1$\frac{1}{2}$ oz.)
90 g. shelled walnuts (3 oz.)	3 dl. thick cream ($\frac{1}{2}$ pint)
2 carrots, finely chopped	$\frac{1}{4}$ l. dry white wine (1$\frac{1}{2}$ gills)
2 onions, finely chopped	Cayenne pepper
	seasoning

Method: Have the veal boned and rolled. Make the butter hot in a fairly deep pan, put in the meat, brown it well on all sides. Take it out of the pan and put in the carrots and onions and allow them to brown quickly. Return the meat, pour in the white wine, season, adding a pinch of

Cayenne. Cover with a lid, lower the heat and allow the contents of the pan to simmer very gently for an hour and a half, turning the meat from time to time. When the veal is cooked, allow it to cool slightly in the liquor. Then remove it from the pan and carve it into slices ½ cm. (¼ inch) thick.

Meanwhile pass the nuts through a nut mill, add 2 or 3 tablespoons of cream to make a stiff purée. Season. Put one quarter of the nut mixture on one side. Using the remainder, spread each slice of veal and arrange them overlapping on a serving dish. Pass the sauce the meat has been cooked in through a strainer, pressing the vegetables down well so as to extract the full flavour and to thicken the sauce slightly. Add to it the remaining nut mixture, together with the rest of the cream, pour this over the meat. Reheat the dish in a fairly hot oven, gas mark 5–6 or 375–400° F. (190–200° C.).

Comment: If desired, this dish can be served with plain boiled Patna rice which has been dried and warmed through in a little butter.

NOIX DE VEAU AU PAPRIKA ** (for 6 persons)

Ingredients:

1 kg. cushion of veal (2 lb.)
piece of bacon fat
piece of pork fat
3–4 tablespoons oil
2 onions
1 carrot
1 clove garlic
3 shallots
3 dl. dry white wine (½ pint)

3 dl. veal stock (½ pint)
2 teaspoons paprika
bouquet garni
1 teaspoon fécule de pommes de
  terre or potato flour
5 large tomatoes
seasoning
To finish:
finely chopped parsley

Method: Season the veal with salt, pepper and paprika. Lard it with the larding bacon and bard it with the pork fat (see pages 11 and 13). Make the oil hot in a thick sauté pan and brown the meat on all sides in this. Remove the meat from the pan. Chop the onions and carrot coarsely and brown them quickly in the hot oil. Then add the garlic crushed with a little salt and the finely chopped shallots. Pour in the wine and stock. Add the bouquet garni, the remaining paprika and season well. Replace the meat and bring to simmering point. Cover with greaseproof paper and the lid and cook in a moderate oven, gas mark 4 or 350° F. (175° C.) for 1 hour approximately or until the meat is tender.

Meanwhile skin and pip the tomatoes and cut them into quarters.

When the meat is cooked, remove it from the pan and cut off the string. Carve the meat into fairly thick slices. Arrange them overlapping on a hot serving dish and keep them hot. Degrease the sauce and strain it into a clean pan. Mix the fécule de pommes de terre to a smooth paste with a little cold water, stir it into the sauce. Bring it to the boil, stirring all the time, and cook for a few minutes. Adjust the seasoning. Heat the tomatoes in the sauce. Remove them carefully and arrange them around the veal. Coat the meat with the sauce. Dust the tomatoes with a little finely chopped parsley. Serve hot.

PAUPIETTES DE VEAU À LA GRECQUE **

(for 6 persons)

Ingredients:
6 escalopes of veal
1 large onion, finely chopped
120 g. butter (4 oz.)
3 green olives, finely chopped
6 thin slices ham
1 carrot, sliced
6 tiny onions
¼ l. dry white wine (1½ gills)
seasoning
For the Garnish:
2 cups Patna rice

120 g. butter (4 oz.)
1 tablespoon finely chopped onion
240 g. sausage meat (½ lb.)
the hearts of 2–3 lettuces
3 green peppers – diced and
  blanched in boiling water
120 g. fresh peas, cooked in butter
  (4 oz.)
seasoned flour
To finish:
¼ l. dry white wine (1½ gills)
60 g. butter (2 oz.)

Method: Flatten the escalopes under the blade of a knife. Heat about an ounce of butter in a small saucepan and soften the finely chopped onion in this without colouring. Divide the onion into six and spread each escalope with it. Cover with a slice of ham and roll the excalopes up and tie with thin kitchen string.

Heat the rest of the butter in a sauté pan. Add the carrot and the onions and the escalopes and brown them well on all sides, turning them with a wooden spoon or spatula. Then pour in the wine and season. Cover with greaseproof paper and the lid and cook over a gentle heat for 25–30 minutes.

Whilst this is taking place, prepare the garnish. Heat 60 g. (2 oz.) butter in a large pan, add the onion and stir for a moment, then add the rice and continue to stir until it is well coated in the butter. Then pour in four cups of hot water. Cover and cook 20–25 minutes. Divide the sausage meat into pieces about the size of a walnut, roll them in seasoned flour and then in the rest of the butter, melted. Mix them gently in to the rice with a fork. Add also the peppers, peas and lettuce hearts. Pile this mixture in a mound in the centre of a hot dish. Untie the string and arrange the escalopes round the edge. Keep hot and meanwhile pour the wine into the pan the escalopes were cooked in and swill round well. Taste and adjust the seasoning. Remove from the heat and whisk in the butter, bit by bit. Pour over the escalopes and serve at once.

PAUPIETTES DE VEAU À LA MÉNAGÈRE **

(for 4 persons)

Ingredients:
4 veal escalopes
90 g. butter (3 oz.)
1 large tomato, skinned and
  pipped
½ large onion
3 cloves garlic
60 g. mushrooms (2 oz.)
9–12 stoned olives
3 dl. stock (½ pint)
1 tablespoon concentrated tomato
  purée
bouquet garni
seasoning

For the Farce:
180 g. minced pork or pork
  sausage meat (6 oz.)
1 shallot
1 clove garlic
a little dry white wine
1 tablespoon finely chopped
  parsley
seasoning
To finish:
finely chopped parsley

Method: Make the farce as follows – chop the shallot very finely and mix it with the pork or sausage meat, add the clove of garlic crushed with a little salt, together with the parsley and enough white wine to moisten. Season well.

Place the escalopes on a board and flatten them with a wet cutlet bat or with the blade of a heavy knife until they are thin enough to roll easily. Spread a quarter of the farce on each escalope, then roll them up and tie them with string.

Melt 60 g. (2 oz.) of butter in a sauté pan. When it is hot, put in the paupiettes and turn them quickly until they are brown on all sides. Remove them and add to the pan the finely chopped onion. Allow this to brown lightly in the hot butter, then stir in the 3 cloves of garlic crushed with a little salt, the stock, tomato purée, bouquet garni and seasoning. Bring to simmering point, then return the paupiettes, cover with the lid and cook gently over a low heat for 50–60 minutes.

Twenty minutes before the paupiettes are ready slice the mushrooms. Heat the remaining ounce of butter in a pan and cook them quickly without browning. When they are done, lift them with a draining spoon. Add the mushrooms, together with the roughly chopped tomato to the paupiettes. Just before serving, add the olives.

To Serve: Remove the string from the paupiettes and arrange them on a hot serving dish. Keep them hot. Reheat the sauce and adjust the seasoning. Remove the bouquet garni. Pour the sauce over the paupiettes, sprinkle with the finely chopped parsley and serve very hot.

PAUPIETTES DE VEAU À LA RICHELIEU **

(for 6 persons)

Ingredients:
6 veal escalopes
90 g. butter (3 oz.)
seasoned flour
1½ dl. dry white wine (1 gill)
3 dl. stock (½ pint)
90 g. mushrooms (3 oz.)
2 medium onions, coarsely
  chopped
2 cloves garlic, crushed with a
  little salt
2 shallots, finely chopped
1 teaspoon concentrated tomato
  purée
bouquet garni
seasoning

For the Farce:
180 g. minced pork (6 oz.)
2–3 finely chopped shallots
2 cloves garlic, crushed with a
  little salt
1 tablespoon finely chopped
  parsley
1 egg
pinch of mixed spice
seasoning
To finish:
3 large tomatoes
30–60 g. butter (1–2 oz.)
Pommes de Terre Château (see
  page 223)

Method: Put the minced pork together with the shallots, garlic, parsley, seasoning and spices into a bowl. Moisten with the beaten egg. Mix well.

Lay the escalopes on a board and flatten them well. Season. Divide the farce into 6 portions and place a portion on each escalope, smoothing it out well to the outside edges. Roll them up and tie with string, then roll them in seasoned flour.

Put about 60 g. (2 oz.) butter into a sauté pan, make it very hot and add the paupiettes. Cook, turning them occasionally for about 5 minutes. Remove them, reduce the heat and add the rest of the butter to the pan. Put in the onions and soften gently without browning. When they are practically cooked, add the shallots, together with the wine and the stock. Stir well and add the bouquet garni, tomato purée and the garlic. Mix well together. Season. Return the paupiettes to the pan. Cover with greaseproof paper and the lid and cook in a moderate oven, gas mark 5 or 375° F. (190° C.) for 20–30 minutes.

Slice the mushrooms into 1 cm. (½ inch) slices. When the veal has been cooking for ¼ hour, add the mushrooms. Stir round well and continue to cook for a further 20 minutes or until they are ready.

Cut the tomatoes in half and fry them carefully in the hot butter. Season them well. Keep them hot.

Remove the paupiettes from the pan and cut off the string. Arrange the tomatoes around a hot serving dish and place a paupiette neatly on each with the mushrooms in between. Strain the sauce into a clean saucepan. Make it hot, adjust the seasoning, and pour it carefully over the paupiettes. Garnish the centre of the dish with Pommes de Terre Château.

(*See Plate 6.*)

PAUPIETTES DE VEAU MELUNAISE ** (for 4 persons)

Ingredients:

4 veal escalopes
½ onion, finely chopped
1 shallot, finely chopped
60 g. minced pork (2 oz.)
60 g. minced veal (2 oz.)
a little thyme, finely chopped
seasoning
60 g. button mushrooms (2 oz.)
1 teaspoon lemon juice

1½ dl. veal stock (1 gill)
For the sauce:
60 g. butter (2 oz.)
30 g. plain flour (1 oz.)
60 g. grated Gruyère cheese (2 oz.)
1½ dl. thick cream (1 gill)
180 g. mushrooms or mushroom
stalks (6 oz.)
To finish:
a little grated Gruyère cheese

Method: Flatten the escalopes under the blade of a heavy knife. Prepare the farce with the minced meats, chopped onion, chopped shallot, thyme and seasoning. Spread a quarter of it on each escalope. Roll them up and tie them with fine kitchen string. Place in a buttered fireproof dish. Cover them with buttered greaseproof paper and cook in a moderate oven, gas mark 5 or 375° F. (190° C.) for ½ hour.

Heat the lemon juice, stock and seasoning in a pan. Put in the button mushrooms, cover with greaseproof paper and the lid and simmer gently for 5 minutes. Remove, drain and reserve the liquor.

Chop the 180 g. (6 oz.) mushrooms very finely. Place in a dry cloth and squeeze tightly to expel all the moisture. Heat 30 g. (1 oz.) butter in a pan and stir in the mushrooms, seasoning them well.

After the paupiettes have been cooking for ¼ hour, add the liquor from the button mushrooms. Turn the paupiettes over, replace the paper and return them to the oven. Make 30 g. (1 oz.) butter hot in a pan, draw aside from the heat, stir in the flour and return to the heat. Cook the roux gently for 2–3 minutes. Strain on the cooking liquor from the paupiettes. Keep the paupiettes hot. Cook the sauce over a good heat for 5 minutes, stirring all the time. Remove it from the heat and stir in the cream and the grated Gruyère cheese. Lastly stir in the chopped mushrooms. Taste and season as required.

Pour half of this sauce in the bottom of a fireproof dish. Untie the paupiettes and lay them on top and coat them with the rest of the sauce. Sprinkle with a little grated Gruyère cheese and brown quickly under a hot grill or in the top of a hot oven, gas mark 7 or 425° F. (220° C.). Serve at once.

SAUTÉ DE VEAU À L'AIXOISE ** (for 3–4 persons)

Ingredients:

¾–1 kg. stewing veal (1½–2 lb.)
90 g. butter (3 oz.)
120 g. lean bacon cut into strips (4 oz.)
½ l. white stock (¾ pint)

1 small head celery
12 small carrots
4–5 small turnips
4 small onions
seasoning

Method: Heat the butter in a thick stewpan. Put in the bacon and fry it quickly. Cut the veal into 3–5 cm. (1½–2 inch) cubes. Add it to the pan and turn it in the hot butter until it is brown on all sides. Pour on the stock and season very well. Cover with greaseproof paper and the lid. Simmer gently for ¾ hour. Put in the celery cut into 2½ cm. (1 inch) lengths, the onions cut into quarters and the carrots and turnips 'turned'. Cover again with greaseproof paper and the lid and simmer for a further ¾ hour.

To Serve: Pile the meat in the centre of a hot dish and surround it with the vegetable garnish. Keep it hot. Strain the liquor into a clean saucepan over a good heat and reduce it quickly by one-third. Adjust the seasoning. Pour over the meat and serve at once.

SAUTÉ DE VEAU CHASSEUR ** (for 3–4 persons)

Ingredients:

½–¾ kg. stewing veal (1–1½ lb.)
1 small onion
1 teaspoon plain flour
1 teaspoon concentrated tomato
  purée
3 dl. white stock (½ pint)
1½ dl. dry white wine (1 gill)
120 g. button mushrooms (4 oz.)

45–60 g. butter (1½–2 oz.)
1 tablespoon oil
1 clove garlic
bouquet garni
seasoned flour
seasoning
To finish:
fried croûtons
chopped parsley

Method: Cut the veal into convenient sized pieces, discarding the fat and gristle. Dip each piece into seasoned flour. Put 45 g. (1½ oz.) butter and the oil into a thick sauté pan. When it is hot add the veal and turn it quickly until it is brown on all sides. Remove the veal from the pan, add a little more butter if needed and brown the finely chopped onion. Stir in the flour and the tomato purée and cook for 2–3 minutes, keeping it well stirred. Stir in the wine and stock together with the bouquet garni, seasoning and the garlic crushed with a little salt. Bring it to simmering point. Return the veal to the pan, cover with greaseproof paper and the lid and cook over a very low heat or in a moderate oven, gas mark 5 or 375° F. (190° C.) for approximately 1 hour. At the end of this time adjust the seasoning, add the mushrooms and cook for a further 10 minutes.

    Remove the bouquet garni. Pile the veal in the centre of a hot serving dish. Pour the sauce over the meat and garnish with the mushrooms. Sprinkle lightly with finely chopped parsley and arrange the fried croûtons around the sides of the dish. Serve hot.

BOUDIN À LA FLAMANDE * (for 4 persons)

Ingredients:

1 black pudding, approx. ½ kg.
  (1 lb.)
150 g. butter (5 oz.)
2 small onions
¾ kg. apples (1½ lb.)

2 cups Patna rice
3½ cups stock or water
120 g. sultanas (4 oz.)
bouquet garni
seasoning

Method: Put the sultanas to soak in boiling stock or water. Chop the onions finely. Heat approximately 60 g. (2 oz.) of the butter in a fairly large pan, put in the onions and move them in the hot butter until they begin to soften, then stir in the rice until it is thoroughly coated in the butter. Pour on the hot stock or water. Add the bouquet garni and season well. Bring to simmering point on top of the stove, stirring occasionally to prevent the rice sticking. Cover with greaseproof paper and the lid then place it in a moderate oven, gas mark 5 or 375° F. (190° C.) for 25–30 minutes.

Peel the apples, cut them into quarters and remove the cores. Heat the remaining butter in a pan and sauter the apples in this until they are soft. Remove them carefully with a draining spoon and keep them hot.

Slice the black pudding in half and cut each slice in half again. Heat it through in the butter the apples were cooked in.

To Serve: Remove the bouquet garni and arrange the rice on a hot serving dish. Drain the sultanas and sprinkle them over the top. Group the apple quarters at each end of the dish. Lay the pieces of black pudding on the top of the rice and serve very hot.

CERVELLES DE VEAU EN MATELOTE **

(for 3–4 persons)

Ingredients:

½ kg. calves brains (1 lb.)
3 dl. red wine (½ pint) ⎱ for the
1 onion stuck with 2 cloves ⎰ Court
1 carrot sliced ⎱ Bouil-
bouquet garni ⎰ lon
60 g. butter (2 oz.)

15–20 tiny onions
250 g. button mushrooms (½ lb.)
beurre manié (see page 16)
seasoning
To finish:
triangular croûtons of bread fried
  in a little butter

Method: Soak the brains in cold salt water for 3–4 hours, changing the water frequently. Pull off the membrane and return to fresh cold water. Remove any trace of blood.

Meanwhile mix the wine and 3 dl. (½ pint) water together in a pan. Add the carrot, onion, bouquet garni and seasoning. Bring to simmering point and simmer gently for $\frac{1}{2}$ hour, keeping the pan covered. Add the brains to this court bouillon and poach over a very gentle heat for 20 minutes. At the end of this time, remove them, drain and cut them into escalopes. Strain the court bouillon and reduce it by half. Whisk in sufficient beurre manié to make a coating sauce and adjust the seasoning.

Heat the butter in a sauté pan, add the tiny onions, which have been peeled and left whole. Cook them gently without colouration until they are soft and then add the mushrooms and soften them also. Stir in the sauce.

Lay the brains carefully in the sauce and allow them to heat through.

To Serve: Place the brains in a hot shallow dish. Pour over the sauce with the onions and mushrooms. Arrange the croûtons round the side of the dish and serve hot.

FRITOT DE CERVELLES DE VEAU ** (for 4 persons)

Ingredients:
$\frac{1}{2}$ kg calves' brains (1 lb.)
1 teaspoon wine vinegar
1 bayleaf
seasoned flour
Fritter Batter (see page 20)

deep fat for frying
To finish:
chopped parsley
Sauce Tomate (Method I)
(see page 38)

Method: Soak the brains in cold salted water for 3–4 hours, changing it frequently. Remove as much as possible of the membrane covering them. Place the brains in a saucepan with the vinegar, bayleaf and sufficient cold water to cover. Bring slowly to the boil and poach gently for ten minutes. Drain well. Allow them to cool and then cut them into equal sized pieces. Cover them carefully with seasoned flour.

Make the Sauce Tomate.

Meanwhile prepare the fritter batter. Coat the pieces of brain with the batter and fry them in deep fat until golden. Drain them on kitchen paper.
To Serve: Pile the brains in a hot serving dish on a napkin or dish paper and sprinkle them with chopped parsley. Serve hot with the sauce tomate separately.

FOIE DE PORC À LA MOUTARDE * (for 2–4 persons)

Ingredients:
4 slices of pig's liver
60 g. butter (2 oz.)
2 tablespoons Dijon mustard
$1\frac{1}{2}$ dl. thick cream (1 gill)
pinch of nutmeg

seasoning
To finish:
wedges of lemon
tiny croûtons of bread fried in
butter

Method: Heat the butter in a sauté pan. Turn the slices of liver in this to seal all sides. Season with salt and pepper. Lower the heat and cook gently for 3–4 minutes. Remove the liver to a hot serving dish and keep it hot.

Pour off any excess butter from the pan. Add the mustard, nutmeg and cream, stir well and adjust the seasoning. Pour the sauce over the liver. Arrange the croûtons and wedges of lemon round the dish. Serve very hot.

FOIE DE VEAU À LA BONNE FEMME *

(for 3–4 persons)

Ingredients:

½ kg. slices calves' liver (1 lb.)
60 g. butter (2 oz.)
125 g. mushrooms (4 oz.)
12 small onions
12 small new potatoes
125 g. lean bacon or ham (4 oz.)

1 dessertspoon plain flour
3 dl. veal stock (½ pint)
1 dl. red wine (½ gill)
bouquet garni
1½ dl. thin cream (1 gill)
seasoning

Method: Heat the butter in a thick stewpan and sauter the liver quickly on all sides for 2–3 minutes over a good heat. Remove and keep on one side. Wipe the mushrooms and cut off the stalks. Add the stalks, together with the bacon cut into lardons, the potatoes and the onions to the fat in the pan. Sauter them together until they begin to turn a pale golden colour. Scatter in the flour and brown this carefully, stirring all the time. Stir in the stock and wine, bring to the boil, lower the heat and return the liver to the pan with the bouquet garni and seasoning. Cover with a closely fitting lid. Simmer over a low gas or cook in a moderate oven, gas mark 5 or 375° F. (190° C.) for 10 minutes. Then add the mushrooms, cut into slices, and cook for a further 10 minutes. Just before serving, remove the bouquet garni, stir in the cream and adjust the seasoning.

To Serve: Arrange the liver in the centre of an entrée dish and pour over the sauce and the garnish.

FOIE DE VEAU À LA PROVENÇALE *

(for 4 persons)

Ingredients:

½ kg. calves' liver cut into thin
   slices (1 lb.)
2 tablespoons oil
3 medium onions
½ kg. firm ripe tomatoes (1 lb.)

1–2 tablespoons wine vinegar
a little French mustard
30–45 g. butter (1–1½ oz.)
thyme, bayleaf
seasoning

Method: Heat the oil in a sauté pan. Put in the liver and seal it quickly on both sides. Chop the onions very finely and slice the tomatoes. Butter a fireproof dish, place half the liver in the bottom, cover with half the onions, then half the tomatoes. Season well. Repeat again with the other half of the ingredients. Season again. Sprinkle over the vinegar, spread a little French mustard on the top and dot with small pieces of butter. Lay a sprig of thyme and a bayleaf on the top. Cook in a moderate oven, gas mark 5 or 375° F. (190° C.) for 30–35 minutes. Remove the bayleaf and the thyme before serving.

GRATIN DE RIS DE VEAU SULLYLOISE **

(for 4–5 persons)

Ingredients:
¾ kg. veal sweetbreads (1½ lb.)
125 g. cooked lean ham (4 oz.)
125 g. button mushrooms (4 oz.)
1½ dl. thick cream (1 gill)
60–75 g. butter (2–2½ oz.)

lemon juice
2–3 tablespoons brandy
seasoning
To finish:
60 g. grated Gruyère cheese.
(2 oz.)

Method: Soak the sweetbreads in cold water for 1–2 hours, changing the water frequently. Place them in a pan of cold water, bring them to the boil and boil them for 1–2 minutes. Remove and plunge them into cold water. Trim the sweetbreads and remove the membranes. Put the sweetbreads between two plates, place a heavy weight on the top and leave them until they are quite cold.

Wipe the mushrooms with a clean cloth and cut them into quarters. Put them in a pan with about 30 g. (1 oz.) butter, a few drops of lemon juice and seasoning. Cover with greaseproof paper and the lid. Cook them over a very gentle heat for 5 minutes. Remove and keep them hot.

Cut the ham into ½ cm. (¼ inch) dice.

Slice the sweetbreads into thick escalopes. Heat the butter in a sauté pan. When it is hot put in the sweetbreads and cook them gently, allowing 2–3 minutes on each side. Remove them and keep them hot. Heat the brandy, pour it into the pan the sweetbreads were cooked in and 'flame' it. Stir in the cream together with the ham and the mushrooms and their liquor. Stir them gently whilst heating them through. Taste and adjust the seasoning.

Arrange the sweetbreads overlapping in the centre of a hot fireproof serving dish. Pour the sauce and garnish over them. Sprinkle with grated cheese. Brown under a hot grill or in the top of a hot oven, gas mark 7 or 425° F. (220° C.). Serve at once.

RIS DE VEAU PRINCESSE *** (for 4 persons)

Ingredients:

¾ kg. calves' sweetbreads (1½ lb.)
1 large onion
1 large carrot
1 large tomato
1 bundle asparagus
60 g. butter (2 oz.)

½ l. approx. white stock (½–1 pint)
1 tablespoon brandy
truffles
bouquet garni consisting of
    bayleaf and parsley
seasoning

Method: Soak the sweetbreads for 2–3 hours in cold water, changing it frequently. Place them in a pan of cold water, bring it to the boil and cook for 2–3 minutes. Drain, refresh them in cold water and remove the skin and any sinews. Press them under a weighted plate until cold.

Heat the butter in a strong sauté pan. Slice the carrot and onion thinly and cook them gently in the butter without browning for 5–10 minutes. Add the tomato, roughly chopped. Place the sweetbreads on top of the vegetables and add sufficient stock to cover. Season and add the bouquet garni. Cover with a buttered paper and the lid and simmer very gently for 20–30 minutes.

Meanwhile, wash and scrape the asparagus. Tie in a bundle and cut off the stalks to leave the top 8 cms. (3 inches). Cook in boiling salted water until tender, or for about 10 minutes. Drain and keep it hot.

When the sweetbreads are cooked, remove from the pan and keep warm. Strain the liquor and reduce over a good heat to the consistency of thin cream. Add the brandy and adjust the seasoning.

To Serve: Cut the sweetbreads into thick escalopes. Arrange them in the centre of a hot dish with bouquets of asparagus round the sides. Spoon the sauce over the sweetbreads. Place a slice of truffle on each slice of sweetbread. If liked, Pommes de Terre Noisette (see page 228) may be served as an extra garnish.

RIS DE VEAU ÎLE DE FRANCE ** (for 4–6 persons)

Ingredients:

¾ kg. veal sweetbreads (1½ lb.)
90–100 g. butter (3–3½ oz.)
2–3 tablespoons Calvados
1½ dl. thick cream (1 gill)
seasoned flour

seasoning
For the Garnish:
1 small bunch of asparagus
30 g. butter (1 oz.)
fried croûtons

Method: Soak the sweetbreads in cold water for 2–3 hours, changing it frequently. Place them in a pan of cold water, bring to the boil and boil them for 2–3 minutes. Remove them and plunge them into cold water.

Trim them and remove the membranes. Press the sweetbreads between two plates under a weight, until cold.

Scrape the asparagus and cut off the hard stalks, tie in a bundle and cook gently in boiling salted water until it is just tender. Keep hot.

Slice the sweetbreads carefully. Season them. Dip them in seasoned flour. Heat the butter in a sauté pan. Cook them in this for 5–7 minutes, until they are pale gold on both sides. Remove them and keep them hot.

Pour the Calvados into the pan the sweetbreads were cooked in, bring up to simmering point then add the cream. Season. Raise the heat and allow it to thicken slightly. Return the sweetbreads to the pan, heat them through gently.

Toss the asparagus in a little hot butter.

To Serve: Dish the sweetbreads in the centre of a hot serving dish. Arrange the asparagus at each side and the croûtons at each end. Serve at once.

ROGNONS DE MOUTON À LA PARISIENNE **

(for 3 persons)

Ingredients:
6 sheep's kidneys
250 g. button mushrooms (½ lb.)
a few drops of lemon juice
180 g. butter (6 oz.)

1 glass Madeira
seasoning
To finish:
finely chopped parsley

Method: Wipe the mushrooms. Heat half the butter in a medium sized saucepan. Add the mushrooms with the lemon juice and seasoning. Cover with buttered paper and the lid and cook over a gentle heat, shaking the pan from time to time for 5–7 minutes.

Cut the kidneys in halves. Remove the cores and skin. Heat the rest of the butter in a sauté pan and sauter the kidneys quickly in this until they are just cooked. Season. Remove the kidneys. Pour off any excess fat from the pan, then pour in the Madeira and the mushroom liquor and reduce it quickly over a good heat. Adjust the seasoning. Arrange the kidneys in the centre of a hot dish. Surround with a border of mushrooms. Pour over the juice from the sauté pan. Dust the kidneys with finely chopped parsley and serve very hot.

ROGNONS DE MOUTON AU FOUR **

(for 4 persons)

Ingredients:
6 sheeps' kidneys
250 g. pork sausage meat (½ lb.)
1 dessertspoon brandy
1 medium sized onion
1 egg

1 teaspoon finely chopped parsley
90 g. butter (3 oz.)
juice of ½ lemon
125 g. button mushrooms (¼ lb.)
¾ dl. dry white wine (½ gill)
seasoning

Method: Chop the onion very finely. Mix with the sausage meat, beaten egg, brandy, wine and plenty of seasoning. Butter a fireproof dish well and arrange the farce down the centre.

Slice the mushrooms and cook them in about 30 g. (1 oz.) of butter, seasoning them well. Arrange them in a border round the farce. Pour over the top the butter they were cooked in. Cover the whole with a piece of buttered greaseproof paper and cook in a moderate oven, gas mark 5 or 375° F. (190° C.) for 25–30 minutes.

Meanwhile, skin and halve the kidneys, removing the cores. Fry them in the remainder of the butter. When done arrange them on the top of the farce. Sprinkle with lemon juice and finely chopped parsley.

SALADE DE LANGUE ** (for 4 persons)

Ingredients:

120–150 g. cooked ox tongue (4–5 oz.)
1 head of celery
1 lettuce
5–6 gherkins

2 hardboiled eggs
250 g. tomatoes (8 oz.)
2 old potatoes or 4–5 new ones
Sauce Mayonnaise (see page 36)
seasoning

Method: Scrub the potatoes and cook them until they are just done, but still firm. Plunge them into cold water and remove their skins. Cut them into slices and cool them completely.

Cut the tongue into dice. Dip the tomatoes into boiling water for a few seconds, remove their skins and pips and cut the flesh into small dice.

Slice the hardboiled eggs. Chop the gherkins. Slice the celery.

Remove the outside leaves of the lettuce. Wash the remaining leaves well and put them on a clean cloth to drain thoroughly. Then arrange them in a salad bowl.

Using two forks, mix all the other ingredients, including the sauce mayonnaise, together. Season to taste. Pile up in the centre of the lettuce leaves. Serve very cold.

SAUCISSES À LA PARMENTIÈRE * (for 3–4 persons)

Ingredients:

½ kg. pork sausages (1 lb.)
2 shallots
3–4 large potatoes
60–90 g. butter (2–3 oz.)

1½ dl. dry white wine (1 gill)
a little lemon juice
1 tablespoon finely chopped fresh herbs
seasoning

Method: Heat about half the butter in a frying pan. Put in the sausages and cook them over a very gentle heat. This will take from 20–30 minutes. In this way the sausages will not burst.

Whilst they are cooking chop the shallots very finely, peel the potatoes and slice them into rounds ½ cm. (¼ inch) thick. Heat the remaining butter in a thick sauté pan, put in the potatoes and the shallots and cook them gently without letting them brown, for 2–3 minutes. Pour in just enough water to cover the potatoes, season and sprinkle in the herbs. Cover with a piece of greaseproof paper and the lid of the pan. Cook for about 15 minutes over a medium heat until the potatoes are soft but not mushy.

Meanwhile pour off the fat from the sausages, pour in the wine and cook for a further 5 minutes. Arrange the potatoes piled up in the centre of a hot dish. Place the sausages all round. Add a squeeze of lemon juice to the sausage gravy, season, swill round and pour over the top. Serve very hot.

SAUCISSES EN RIZOT ** (for 3–4 persons)

Ingredients:
½ kg. pork sausages (1 lb.)
60 g. butter (2 oz.)
Sauce Demi-Glace (see page 34)
Rice Pilaf made with:
1 cup Patna rice
1 medium onion, finely chopped

1 dl. dry white wine (½ gill)
2 cups stock
1 dl. oil (½ gill)
seasoning
To finish:
finely chopped parsley

Method: Make the sauce demi-glace in the usual way.

Make the pilaf – heat the oil in a thick pan, add the onion and stir over a gentle heat to soften it without colouration. Stir in the rice and season well. Pour in the hot stock and the wine. Bring slowly up to simmering point. Cover with greaseproof paper and the lid. Cook in a moderate oven, gas mark 5 or 375° F. (190° C.) for 25–30 minutes. Do not disturb whilst it is cooking.

Heat the butter in a frying pan. Put in the sausages and cook very slowly over a gentle heat. (If the sausages are allowed to cook for about the same time as the rice instead of being fried quickly, they are less likely to split open.)

When the rice is cooked, form it into a ring in a hot serving dish. Pile the sausages in the middle and coat with the sauce demi-glace. Serve very hot sprinkled with finely chopped parsley.

Poultry and Game

Poultry prices have dropped – and are now less than the cheapest cuts of carcase meat. Fresh killed chickens are available from at least two notable supermarkets, which enables the housewife in town to buy cheap fresh meat. The majority of these and frozen birds are battery produced. Free range fowl are still only available from specialist retailers or from the farm.

Turkeys are now obtainable at all seasons and provide an even more economical source of animal protein.

Game on the other hand becomes more and more expensive and difficult to obtain.

All poultry is susceptible to infection from salmonella virus and for this reason it is essential to make sure that all frozen birds are completely thawed out before cooking, and that they are thoroughly cooked through.

PURCHASING POULTRY

Before giving the recipes, it is important to know some of the points to be observed in purchasing the birds. Most chickens should have been hung for twenty-four hours or longer. Turkeys are hung for longer – upwards of five days. The birds are not drawn before they are hung, but they are generally plucked directly after they have been killed. Birds should be singed by holding over a gas flame or spirit stove after plucking.

Poultry should always be perfectly fresh. There should be no unpleasant smell. Young poultry has white skin free from wrinkles and the breast should be plump and white and the breast bone pliable. The quills should come out easily when lightly pulled. Young birds have small combs and wattles. When a chicken has been recently killed, its eyes are clear and they should on no account be sunken. The feathers should be soft and abundant and there should be plenty of down. The scales on the leg should be small and only just overlapping. The feet should be pliable.

TO DRAW A BIRD

1. Cut off the head, leaving about four inches of the neck.
2. Lay the bird on its back on a board.

3. With a sharp pointed knife, slit the skin down the neck for three or four inches. Free the skin from the muscle and bone.
4. Cut off the neck as close to the body as possible, leaving the flap of skin, and remove the crop and wind pipe.
5. Turn the bird over with the neck facing you. Insert one finger and loosen the inside. Do not draw it from this end.
6. Turn the bird again, make a slit between the vent and tail. Cut away the vent.
7. Insert two fingers, being careful not to stretch the opening. Turn them round, grip the gizzard firmly by bending the fingers and draw it out with the rest of the intestines, as well as the heart, liver and gall bladder. Remove any soft fat. Take out the spongy lumps which are embedded in the bony case.
8. Wipe the bird out with a damp cloth.
9. Remove the gall bladder from the liver. Care should be taken to remove it whole. The heart, neck, gizzard and liver must be rinsed in cold water. Before the gizzard can be used, it should be cut open. The stony bag and contents are discarded, leaving the muscular wall. These are known as the giblets.

TO JOINT A CHICKEN

1. Lay the bird on its back with the neck end to the left.
2. Take a sharp cook's knife and cut the skin of the groin, bend the thigh towards you so as to dislocate the hip joint. It is then quite easy to cut the flesh close to the body and detach the whole leg, cutting through the tendons between the ball and socket joint.

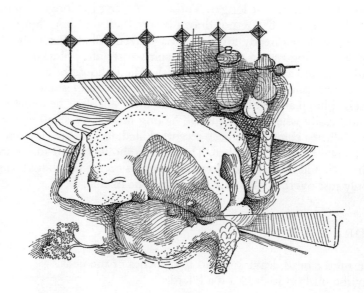

3. Turn the bird round and remove the left leg in the same manner.
4. With the neck facing you, remove the left wing, cutting a good fillet of the breast and continuing to cut down through the tendons of the shoulder joint.

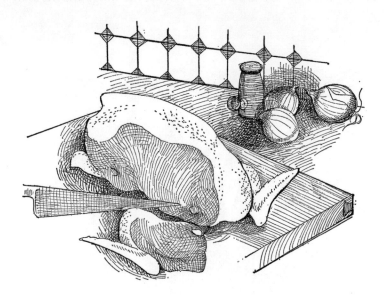

5. Remove the right wing in the same manner.
6. With a pair of scissors separate the breast from the keel by cutting through the ribs from the vent to the shoulder joint on each side.

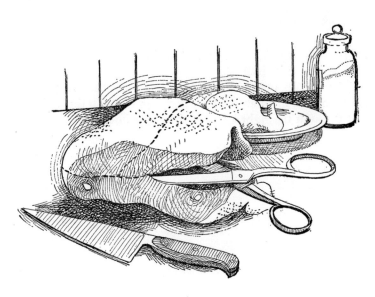

7. Use the sharp knife to divide the breast in half with a diagonal cut. Divide the keel into three, cutting at right angles to the backbone.
8. Lay the legs flat on the board and separate the thighs from the drumsticks by cutting through the knee joints.
9. Finally cut off and discard the top joints of the wings and the scaly legs.

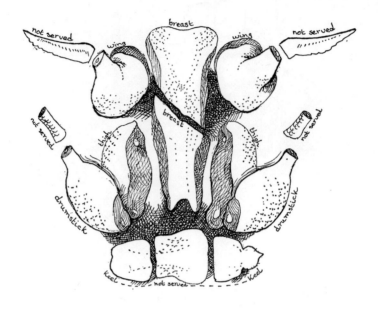

TO TRUSS A BIRD

Using a trussing needle threaded with string:
1. Lay the bird on its back.
2. Hold the two legs up with one hand and press back and down.
3. Pass the needle through the left knee then through the body and bring it out through the right knee on the opposite side.

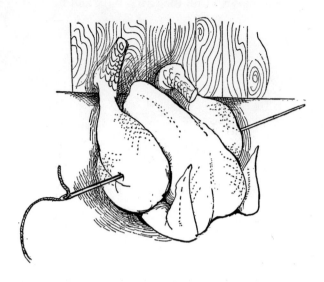

4. Turn the bird over on its breast. Draw the loose skin from the neck over the back to close the opening. Bend the wings so that the neck skin is held in place by the wing tips.

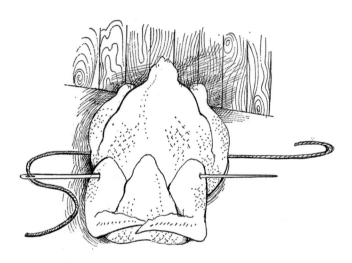

5. Turn the bird on its back. Take the needle and continue with the same piece of string through the right 'elbow', back through the body and through the left 'elbow'. Pull the string tight and tie it off in a bow.

6. With the bird still on its back, turn it with the tail towards you. Take another piece of string and hold it between your two hands. Stretch it under the legs and loop it round the 'parsons nose'. Bring each end of the string around each leg and tie firmly with a bow.

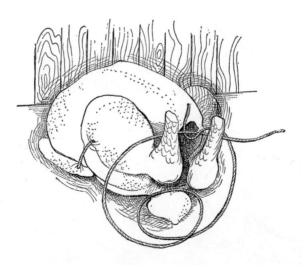

Comment: In France, the wishbone is removed before trussing. This is for easier carving. To remove this bone, use a sharp pointed knife, insert the point under the flap of skin at the neck end and gently free the skin from above the bone and the flesh from below the bone. Care must be taken not to pierce the skin. The bone will easily be freed by severing the ligaments at each end. The skin will fall back naturally into place.

CHICKEN STOCK

To make a well flavoured stock in which to cook a chicken, put the chicken into a large pan, cover with cold water and add two carrots cut into four, an onion stuck with a clove, a bouquet garni, four or five peppercorns, a little coarse salt and if liked a strip of lemon peel. If available a leek cut up and a stick of celery can be included.

This stock can then be used as a basis of a sauce, as in Poulet à la Vigneronne.

POULTRY AND GAME

CANARD AU CHOCOLAT **   (for 4–5 persons)

Ingredients:

1 duck, approx. 2 kg. (4 lb.)
12 chipolata sausages
3 dl. dry white wine (½ pint)
1½ dl. white stock (¼ pint)
1 tablespoon wine vinegar
60 g. butter (2 oz.)
1 dessertspoon oil
2–3 carrots

juice of 1 lemon
60 g. sweetened chocolate powder
  (2 oz.)
bouquet garni
seasoning
To finish:
1 dl. rum (½ gill)
120 g. Patna rice (4 oz.)

Method: Have the duck drawn and trussed. Peel the carrots and slice them evenly. Prick the sausages. Make the butter and oil hot in a deep sauté pan. Put in the duck and brown it well on all sides. This should take about 15–20 minutes. At the end of this time, add the carrots and the sausages. Pour in the wine, stock, vinegar and lemon juice. Add the bouquet garni and the chocolate, which has been mixed to a paste with a little cold water. Season, cover with greaseproof paper and the lid and cook it in a moderately cool oven, gas mark 3–4 or 325–350° F. (160–180° C.) for 1 hour.

    Meanwhile cook the rice in plenty of boiling salted water for 12–16 minutes. When it is cooked drain it and refresh it with cold running water, drain it again and put it to dry in a lightly buttered dish in a cool oven covered with buttered greaseproof paper.

Form a ring with the rice on a hot serving dish and put the duck in the centre. Pile the carrots and chipolatas at each end of the dish. Remove most of the fat from the liquor the duck was cooked in and stir in the rum. Rectify the seasoning. Strain some sauce over the duck and serve the rest separately.

CANARD AUX FRUITS **   (for 4–5 persons)

Ingredients:

1 young duck, drawn and trussed
165 g. butter (5½ oz.)
2 tablespoons oil
5 small oranges
1 cucumber
2 grapefruit

240 g. cooked black cherries (½ lb.)
120 g. Patna rice (4 oz.)
1 tablespoon port, optional
2 tablespoons brandy
paprika
seasoning

Method: Make 60 g. (2 oz.) butter and the oil hot in a sauté pan. Put in the duck and turn it until it is brown on all sides. Cover it with a piece of buttered greaseproof paper, tucking it down well all round and with a lid. Cook it on a low heat for 35–40 minutes. Shake the pan from time to time to prevent it from sticking.

Squeeze the juice from one orange and one grapefruit. Mix it well. Divide three oranges into sections and the other grapefruit. Cut the remaining orange into thin slices.

Cook the Patna rice in plenty of boiling salted water for 12–16 minutes. When it is done, remove, rinse and drain it on a clean cloth. Place it in a hot bowl and stir in 30 g. (1 oz.) butter using a fork, then stir in the orange and grapefruit sections. Keep hot.

Peel the cucumber and cut it into 3 cm. (1 inch) dice. Season and sauter them in 60 g. (2 oz.) butter until they are just tender. Remove and drain them. Keep them hot.

To Serve: Place the duck on a hot serving dish. Arrange the rice in a border all round.

Remove the excess grease from the pan the duck has been cooked in. Pour in the brandy and port. Add the orange and grapefruit juice. Stir well over a good heat, taste and season. Remove from the heat and beat in 15 g. (½ oz.) butter. Pour this over the duck.

Arrange the cherries in a ring in between the rice and the duck. Pile up the slices of orange and the cucumber at each end. Dust them lightly with paprika. Serve at once. (*See Plate 8.*)

CANETON AUX PÊCHES *** (for 4–5 persons)

Ingredients:

1 duckling
60 g. butter (2 oz.)
6 even sized peaches
syrup for poaching made with 1 l.
  (1¾ pint) water (see page 24)
For the Sauce:
stomach, neck, liver, heart of
  duckling
1 onion
1 clove garlic
30 g. (1 oz.) butter

½ l. white stock (¾ pint)
1 tablespoon plain flour
60 g. sugar (2 oz.)
1 shallot
4 tablespoons brandy
1 tablespoon concentrated tomato
  purée
bouquet garni
2 tablespoons wine vinegar
1 tablespoon Madeira
seasoning

Method: Remove the wishbone from the duckling. Truss it firmly. Lay the duckling on its side in a roasting tin, season well and spread with the butter. Roast it in a hot oven, gas mark 7 or 425° F. (220° C.) for 20 minutes, then turn the duckling over on to the other side, reduce the heat to gas mark 6 or 400° F. (200° C.) and continue to cook for a further hour. When it is almost cooked, lay the bird on its back so that the breast browns lightly.

Make the sauce, chop roughly the stomach, neck, heart, wing tips, liver, onion and shallot. Melt the butter in a thick pan and sauter them all together until they are lightly browned. Then add the clove of garlic crushed with salt and the flour. Stir well, pour in 3 tablespoons of brandy and flame it. Stir in the stock and the tomato purée and add the bouquet garni. Bring the sauce to the boil, stirring continuously, season well. Reduce the heat and allow it to cook slowly for about ½–¾ hour.

Make the syrup. Skin the peaches by plunging them into boiling water for a few seconds. Remove them and gently peel off the skins. Cut them in half and remove their stones. Poach the peaches in the syrup until they are just tender, then leave them to cool slightly in the syrup.

When the duckling is cooked, remove it from the roasting tin and keep it hot. Take off all the grease from the tin and add the remaining liquid to the sauce. Strain and reheat it. In another pan dissolve the sugar in a little water and boil it to a light caramel. Add the vinegar with care so that the caramel dissolves. Use a little of this to give piquancy and a rich colour to the sauce. Stir in the Madeira and the rest of the brandy. Correct the seasoning.

Remove the trussing strings from the duckling and serve it on a hot dish. Drain the peaches and arrange them round the duckling. Pour a little sauce over the duckling and serve the remainder in a sauceboat.

FAISAN À LA MONÉGLAS **   (for 3–4 persons)

Ingredients:
1 pheasant, drawn and trussed
1 sliced carrot
1 sliced onion
60 g. butter (2 oz.)
bacon for barding
Farce made with:
the pheasant's liver
60 g. white breadcrumbs (2 oz.)
1 egg
1 dessertspoon chopped parsley
60 g. mushrooms (2 oz.)
2 rashers streaky bacon

seasoning
For the Sauce:
120 g. chicken livers (4 oz.)
2 oranges
1 tablespoon finely chopped
   parsley
Sauce Demi-glace (see page 34)
3 dl. well flavoured chicken stock
   ($\frac{1}{2}$ pint)
seasoning
To finish:
2 oranges

Method: First make the sauce demi-glace.

Make the farce – chop the pheasant liver, bacon, mushrooms and parsley finely and mix with the breadcrumbs and sufficient egg to bind it. Season well and stuff the breast of the pheasant with this, then fasten with a skewer.

Place the pheasant in a roasting tin with the butter, the carrot, and onion. Season and cover with rashers of bacon. Roast in a moderate oven, gas mark 5 or 375° F. (190° C.) for 45 minutes. A quarter of an hour before the end of the cooking time remove the bacon to allow the breast to brown.

Meanwhile, take a pan with the stock and seasoning. Put in the chicken livers, bring to simmering point and cook until tender. Drain the livers and put them through a fine sieve. Using a sharp vegetable knife, pare the zest from one orange and cut it into fine julienne strips. Put these in a pan of cold water, bring them to the boil and drain well. Squeeze the juice from both oranges. Mix it with the sauce demi-glace, add the sieved livers, the chopped parsley and the strips of blanched orange peel. Taste and season.

When the pheasant is cooked, remove the trussing strings. Serve on a hot dish and keep it hot.

To Finish: Cut off all the skin and pith from the oranges. Divide them into sections by cutting between the skin and the pulp. Coat the pheasant with the sauce allowing it to run over the bottom of the dish. Arrange the orange segments on each side of the bird. Serve hot.

FAISAN AUX CANNEBERGES **   (for 3–4 persons)

Ingredients:

1 young pheasant, drawn and trussed
120 g. lean bacon (4 oz.)
1 tablespoon finely chopped fresh herbs
2 chicken livers
½ beaten egg
3 rashers streaky bacon for barding
60 g. white breadcrumbs (2 oz.)
45 g. butter (1½ oz.)

2 tablespoons brandy
seasoning
To finish:
2 tablespoons brandy
For the Garnish:
Compôte de Canneberges made with:
    240 g. cranberries (½ lb.)
    a good pinch of cinnamon
    120 g. castor sugar (4 oz.)
Pommes de Terre Chips (see page 223)

Method: Chop the chicken livers finely together with the 120 g. (4 oz.) bacon. Put them into a bowl with the herbs and breadcrumbs. Mix in the brandy and sufficient beaten egg to make a moist stuffing. Season well. Stuff the body of the pheasant with this mixture. Lay the rashers of streaky bacon over the breast of the bird. Tie down with string.

Heat the butter in a deep sauté pan and when it is hot put in the pheasant and turn it carefully until it is brown on all sides. Then butter a piece of greaseproof paper and tuck it well down over the bird. Roast it in a moderate oven, gas mark 5 or 375° F. (190° C.) for 40 minutes.

Whilst it is cooking make the pommes de terre chips and keep them hot.

Now prepare the compôte de canneberges. Place the cranberries in a thick pan with a little water and sugar and the cinnamon and stew them gently over a low heat until they are tender, but not broken. Drain them carefully if necessary and keep hot.

To Serve: When the pheasant is cooked, remove it from the pan, untie the string and take off the bacon. Place it on a hot serving dish. Pour the remaining two tablespoons of brandy into the pan, heat through and 'flame' it and adjust the seasoning. Pour this over the pheasant. Arrange the pommes de terre chips at each end of the dish and the compôte de canneberges at each side. Serve very hot. (*See Plate* 11.)

LAPIN À LA FORESTIÈRE **   (for 4–5 persons)

Ingredients:

1 rabbit, approximately 1½ kg. (3 lb.)
6 small onions
60 g. streaky bacon (2 oz.)
1½ dl. dry white wine (1 gill)
700 g. tiny new potatoes (1½ lb.)

240 g. button mushrooms (½ lb.)
5 rashers back bacon
240 g. butter (½ lb.)
stock
bayleaf
a pinch of powdered thyme
seasoning

Method: Have the rabbit cut into joints. Cut the streaky bacon into lardons. Put about 3 tablespoons of butter into a deep thick stewpan. Make hot and put in the rabbit with the bacon and the onions and brown well. Season well and add the thyme and the bayleaf. When the rabbit is well browned on all sides, pour in the white wine. Tuck a piece of buttered paper over the top. Cover with the lid. Place in a moderate oven, gas mark 5 or 375° F. (190° C.) for 50 minutes.

Whilst it is cooking, plunge the well washed potatoes into boiling water. Boil rapidly for 7–8 minutes, then remove their skins. Heat 60 g. (2 oz.) butter in a saucepan and brown the potatoes gently over a moderate heat. Season well. Melt the rest of the butter in another pan and add the mushrooms and season. Cook over a very gentle heat for 3–4 minutes. Lightly fry the rashers of back bacon. Keep all hot.

When the rabbit is cooked, arrange the joints in a deep serving dish. Garnish with the browned potatoes and the mushrooms. Cut the back rashers in half and place them round the sides of the dish. Strain the liquor from the rabbit and mix it with the butter the mushrooms were cooked in and a little stock. Make it hot, season well and pour it over the rabbit. Serve very hot.

LAPIN À LA PAYSANNE *   (for 6 persons)

Ingredients:

1 rabbit, approximately 1½ kg. (3 lb.)
60 g. butter or dripping (2 oz.)
120 g. lean back bacon rashers (4 oz.)
450 g. carrots (1 lb.)
1 l. white stock (1¾ pints)
1 large onion, unpeeled and stuck
  with 2 cloves

24 small onions
2 tablespoons oil
1 teaspoon arrowroot
1 bouquet garni
pinch of sugar
seasoning
To finish:
finely chopped parsley

Method: Have the rabbit jointed, and the carrots diced. Heat the butter in a thick pan. Put the joints in this and turn them quickly in the hot fat until they are well browned. Lift them from the pan and put in the bacon, cut into lardons. Brown these quickly, lift them out also, and put in the carrots. Turn them in the hot fat. As soon as they begin to brown, pour in the stock and bring it to the boil. Replace the rabbit and bacon. Season and add the bouquet garni and the onion with the cloves. Cover with a lid and cook gently over a low heat for 45–50 minutes, or until the rabbit is tender.

Whilst this is taking place, peel the little onions and brown them in a thick pan with the sugar and the oil, stirring from time to time so that they do not burn. When they are partially cooked, add about 1 dl. (¾ gill) of water and a pinch of salt. Cover the pan and finish cooking them over a low heat. When they are tender, lift them out of the pan and pour the cooking liquor into the pan with the rabbit.

When the rabbit is cooked, remove the onion and the bouquet garni. Arrange the rabbit joints on a hot serving dish with the little onions round them. Keep them hot. Slake the arrowroot with a little cold water and add to the rabbit liquor. Continue to cook until it thickens. Taste, season if necessary. Pour the sauce over the rabbit. Sprinkle with finely chopped parsley and serve hot.

OIE À LA MECKLEMBOURGEOISE ** (for 8 persons)

Ingredients:

1 medium sized goose
1–1½ kg. dessert apples (2–3 lb.)
2 shallots, finely chopped
450 g. chestnuts (1 lb.)
1 red cabbage

90 g. sultanas or seedless raisins (3 oz.)
180–240 g. butter, approximately (6–8 oz.)
seasoning

Method: Peel the apples and cut them into quarters. Melt about 90 g. (3 oz.) butter in a sauté pan and put in the apples. Cook them very gently over a low heat until they are just transparent and not in any way cooked to a pulp. It is advisable not to stir them, but to shake the pan to prevent them from sticking.

Whilst this is taking place heat a little butter in a small pan and cook the shallots until they are soft, but not brown. When the apples are ready put one-third of them on one side. Mix the remaining two-thirds with the sultanas or raisins and shallots. Season well. Stuff the breast of the goose with this mixture.

Rub the goose over with butter and wrap it with aluminium foil. Stand the goose on its side on a rack in a deep roasting tin. Put it in a fairly hot oven, gas mark 6 or 400° F. (200° C.). Allow it to cook for half an hour on one side, then turn it over and cook it the other side for a further half hour, then reduce the heat to gas mark 3 or 325° F. (160° C.) and finish cooking it, with the breast up and the foil removed. Baste it frequently.

Shred the cabbage finely, removing the hard stalks. Cook it in a pan of boiling salted water for 3–5 minutes. Drain off the water and dry the cabbage well on a clean cloth. Melt about 60–90 g. (2–3 oz.) of butter in the pan, return the cabbage and season well. Cover it with greaseproof paper and the lid and allow it to cook either in a fairly cool oven, gas mark 3 or 325° F. (160° C.), or over a low heat for about an hour. Shake the pan from time to time. Peel the chestnuts and cook them in boiling salted water until they are just tender. Just before the cabbage is ready, add the chestnuts and allow them to heat through with the cabbage. Add more butter if needed. Heat the remaining apples.

To Serve: Drain the goose well and place it on a hot serving dish. Arrange the apples on one side of the dish and the red cabbage on the other. Serve very hot.

OIE AUX CERISES ** (for 6–8 persons)

Ingredients:

1 goose, about 3½–4 kg. (6–8 lb.)
60–90 g. butter (2–3 oz.)
1 kg. red cherries (2 lbs.)
60 g. sugar (2 oz.)
3 dl. red wine (½ pint)

12 even sized dessert apples
12 lumps sugar
seasoning
To finish:
finely chopped parsley

Method: Rub the goose all over with about a third of the butter. Season it well. Wrap it with aluminium foil. Place a rack in a deep roasting tin. Lay the goose on its side on this. Put it in a fairly hot oven, gas mark 6 or 400° F. (200° C.). Cook it at this temperature for the first 45 minutes, turning it half the way through the cooking time to allow it to cook evenly. Now reduce the oven heat to gas mark 3 or 325° F. (160° C.). Remove the foil and with its breast uppermost, baste the bird well and finish cooking for a further hour.

Peel the apples and remove their cores without damaging the apples. Put them in another roasting tin and brush them over with a little melted butter. Place a knob of butter and a lump of sugar in each apple. Stand the roasting tin in the oven below the goose and bake until the apples are tender.

Stalk and stone the cherries, put them into a pan with the red wine and sugar. Bring them to the boil and then simmer gently until they are tender. Keep them hot.

When the goose is cooked, take it from the oven. Hold it up and allow the fat to drain off. Pour off the excess fat from the roasting tin. Strain in the red wine in which the cherries were cooked, déglace the pan with this. Taste and adjust the seasoning.

Dish the goose on a large hot serving dish. Arrange the apples all round. Place the cherries in between them and put one or two cherries on the top of each apple. Dust the goose with finely chopped parsley. Hand the gravy separately.

OIE ROTIE AUX PRUNEAUX ** (for 6–8 persons)

Ingredients:

1 medium sized goose
100 g. butter (3½ oz.)
2 onions
1 orange
3 large cooking apples
12–15 prunes, soaked
30 g. castor sugar (1 oz.)
1 teaspoon finely chopped thyme

½ teaspoon quatre épices or mixed spice
2 tablespoons Madeira
2 tablespoons brandy
170 g. white breadcrumbs (6 oz.)
3–4 tablespoons milk
3 dl. stock made from the giblets, a slice of onion and carrot and bouquet garni (½ pint)
seasoning

Method: Chop the onions finely. Melt 90 g. (3 oz.) butter in a large pan, cook the onions slowly in this without allowing them to brown. Remove the peel and pips from the orange, chop it roughly and cook it with the onions for 2–3 minutes without raising the heat. Peel and core the apples, stone the soaked prunes and chop both of these finely. Remove the pan from the heat and stir in the apples, prunes, sugar, quatre épices and thyme. Chop the goose liver finely and soak the breadcrumbs in the milk, the brandy and the Madeira. Mix these all together in the pan and season to taste.

Stuff the goose with this mixture. Rub it all over with the rest of the butter. Season it well. Wrap the goose with aluminium foil. Stand the goose on its side on a rack in a deep roasting tin. Put it in a fairly hot oven, gas mark 6 or 400° F. (200° C.) and allow it to cook for half an hour on one side, then turn it over and cook the other side for a further half hour. Then reduce the heat to gas mark 3 or 325° F. (160° C.), remove the foil and finish cooking it for a further hour with the breast uppermost. Baste it frequently.

Whilst it is cooking make a stock with the giblets, the sliced vegetables, bouquet garni and seasoning. Cook for half an hour, strain it off and reduce it in a clean pan to about ½ l. (1 pint).

When the goose is cooked, remove it from the oven, hold it up and allow the fat to drain from it. Serve it on a hot dish.

Pour off most of the fat from the roasting tin and pour in the stock. Stir it well. Taste and season. Heat quickly and serve separately in a sauceboat.

Comment: Serve accompanied by pommes de terre frites or pommes de terre chips, followed by a green 'salade de saison'.

PERDREAUX À LA TITANIA ** (for 4 persons)

Ingredients:

a brace of partridges	1 dl. chicken or game stock (½ gill)
30 g. butter (1 oz.)	240 g. white grapes (8 oz.)
2 slices larding bacon	1 tablespoon brandy
4 oranges	2 tablespoons redcurrant jelly
	seasoning

Method: Tie a slice of larding bacon over the breast of each bird with string. Melt the butter in a casserole and when it is hot, turn the partridges in this. When they are brown on all sides remove them. Add the brandy, the stock and the juice of one orange to the pan. Heat them to boiling point. Season well. Return the partridges to the pan, together with the grapes, which have been skinned and pipped. Peel the rest of the oranges and divide them into sections. Add these to the pan also. Cover the partridges with greaseproof paper and the lid and cook in a fairly hot oven, gas mark 6 or 400° F. (200° C.) for 20 minutes. At the end of this time, strain the liquid from the partridges into a pan. Reduce this slightly over a good heat.

Meanwhile, remove the larding fat and string from the partridges and place them on a hot dish surrounded by the grapes and orange segments.

Whisk the redcurrant jelly into the sauce. Adjust the seasoning and pour it over the partridges. Serve at once.

Comment: If the age of the birds is doubtful, cook them at gas mark 4 or 350° F. (180° C.) for 40–45 minutes to make them more tender.

PIGEONS AU VERMOUTH *   (for 4 persons)

Ingredients:
2 pigeons
60 g. butter (2 oz.)
120 g. lean bacon, cut into strips (4 oz.)
1 dozen small onions
1 dl. white stock (½ gill)

6 black olives
4 green olives
1 wine glass dry vermouth
seasoning
To finish:
finely chopped parsley

Method: Have the pigeons cleaned and singed. Make the butter hot in a sauté pan and put in the bacon and onions. Turn them all together quickly until they are well browned. Cut the pigeons in half and add them to the pan. Season. Reduce the heat slightly and brown them well on all sides, taking about 20 minutes to do so. At the end of this time the pigeons should be cooked. Remove them from the pan and keep them hot on a serving dish.

Stone the olives and chop the black ones, leaving the green ones whole. Put them in the pan with the vermouth and stock. Stir round over a low heat for 1–2 minutes. Taste and season. Pour all over the pigeons. Sprinkle with finely chopped parsley and serve hot.

POULE À LA LOUISIANE ***   (for 6 persons)

Ingredients:
1 boiling fowl, drawn and trussed
460 g. sweetcorn (canned or deep frozen) (1 lb.)
2 tablespoons thick cream
1 green or red pepper
120 g. butter (4 oz.)

90 g. Patna rice (3 oz.)
3 dl. chicken stock (½ pint)
2 tablespoons Madeira
4 medium sized bananas
seasoning
8 tartlet cases made from Pâte Brisée Method I (see page 338)

Method: If the sweet corn is uncooked, cook it and drain and refresh it under running cold water. Drain again. Mix the cream with the corn.

Cut the pepper in half and remove the pith and seeds. Chop the flesh into dice. Put it into a pan of cold salted water. Bring it to the boil and cook until it is just tender, probably 2–3 minutes. Drain and refresh it, drain again. Mix it with three-quarters of the sweet corn and cream. Season well, stuff the body of the bird with this.

Heat 60 g. (2 oz.) of the butter in a braising pan or large saucepan. Put in the fowl and brown it lightly. Pour in the hot stock and the Madeira. Season well. Cover with greaseproof paper and the lid and cook in a moderate oven, gas mark 5 or 375° F. (190° C.) for 2–2½ hours, or until the fowl is tender.

Meanwhile cook the rice in plenty of boiling salted water. Drain and refresh it under cold running water. Drain again. Put it to dry, covered with buttered greaseproof paper, in a lightly buttered dish in a cool oven.

Make the tartlet cases and a quarter of an hour before serving time, fill them with the remainder of the sweetcorn. Put them in the oven to heat thoroughly.

Peel the bananas and cut them in half lengthwise. Heat the rest of the butter in a frying pan, and fry the bananas in this.

Press the hot rice into timbale moulds. Leave them in a warm place.

When the fowl is cooked, remove the trussing strings and dish it on a large hot serving dish. Unmould the rice timbales and arrange them round the edge. Place the tartlets at each end.

Remove the fat from the liquor the fowl was cooked in. Reduce the liquor over a good heat, taste and adjust the seasoning. Serve this separately. (*See Plate 12.*)

POULE AUX POIRES FLAMBÉES AU WISKY ***

(for 4–8 persons)

Ingredients:

1 boiling fowl
120 g. butter, approx. (4 oz.)
½ l. thick cream (¾ pint)
3 yolks of egg
120 g. button mushrooms (4 oz.)
4 ripe pears

syrup for poaching made with
  120 g. (4 oz.) sugar, 3 dl. (½ pint)
  water (see page 24)
¼ l. dry white wine (1½ gills)
1 dl. whisky (½ gill)
seasoning
castor sugar

Method: Have the chicken jointed. Place about 90 g. (3 oz.) butter in a deep pan. Heat gently. When it is hot put in the chicken joints and move them in the hot butter until they are just beginning to turn a pale gold. They must not burn. Season well, pour in the wine. Seal the pan with a 'repère' paste (see page 23). Place it in a moderate oven, gas mark 5 or 375° F. (190° C.) and cook it very gently for 1–1½ hours.

Meanwhile peel the pears, cut them in half and remove the cores. Poach them very gently in a syrup until they are cooked but still firm. Remove them carefully and place them on a cloth to drain. Sprinkle them with a little castor sugar.

Wipe the mushrooms with a clean cloth. Put them in a small saucepan with about 1 dl. (¾ gill) water. Season them. Cover with greaseproof paper and the lid. Cook very gently for 5 minutes, shaking the pan from time to time. Strain off the liquor and reserve it.

When the chicken is cooked, take it out of the pan, and put it aside to keep hot. Pour the cream together with the mushroom liquor into the pan. Heat it through. Whisk the yolks in a bowl, pour on a little of the hot cream. Whisk well and return to the pan. Stir over a very gentle heat until it thickens. Do not allow it to boil. As soon as it has thickened return the joints of chicken to the pan, off the heat, but keep the pan covered.

Well butter a chafing dish and place it over the heat, put the pears in this and heat them through, allowing the sugar to brown a little, then pour in the whisky and 'flame' the pears.

Dish the chicken on a hot serving dish. Strain over the cream sauce. Arrange the pears down the side of the dish. Serve at once.

GELINE DE TOURAINE EN FRICASSÉE VOUVRIONNE **

(for 4–6 persons)

Ingredients:

1 roasting chicken, 1½–2 kg. jointed (2–3½ lb.)
60–90 g. butter (2–3 oz.)
12–15 small onions
2 tablespoons plain flour
1½ dl. dry Vouvray (1 gill)
bouquet garni, containing at least 3 sprigs tarragon

1 small clove garlic
4–6 button mushrooms
seasoning

For the Liaison:

3 yolks of egg
1–2 tablespoons brandy
3 tablespoons thick cream

Method: Heat the butter in a large thick pan. Put in the chicken joints and move them in the hot butter until they are a pale gold. (It is not correct to brown them.) Lift them out with a draining spoon and add the small onions to the butter. Cover with greaseproof paper and the lid of the pan and shake them over a gentle heat until they are tender. (The length of time required for this process will depend on the size of the onions – probably about 8–10 minutes.) Remove the greaseproof paper and sprinkle in the flour. Stir whilst allowing it to colour slightly. Pour in the Vouvray and 3 dl. (½ pint) water. Season, add the garlic, crushed with a little salt and the bouquet garni. Bring it up to simmering point, replace the chicken joints and add the mushrooms, which have been wiped with a clean cloth and cut into quarters. Cover again with greaseproof paper and the lid, cook gently over a low heat, or in the oven, gas mark 5 or 375° F. (190° C.) for ¾–1 hour. At the end of this time, remove the chicken and pile it up in a hot serving dish. Keep hot.

Make the liaison. Whisk the yolks of egg with the cream and the brandy. Pour a little of the hot liquor the chicken was cooked in on to them. Stir round well, and pour back again into the chicken pan, keeping well stirred. Thicken over a low heat, stirring all the while. It must not boil. Taste and adjust the seasoning.

Lift the onions and mushrooms with a draining spoon. Arrange them at each end of the dish. Pour the sauce over the chicken. Serve at once.

Comment: Geline is Old French for chicken. Dry Vouvray should be used, but other dry white wine would do as a substitute.

POULET À LA CATALANE ** (for 5–6 persons)

Ingredients:

1 roasting chicken, 1½–2 kg. approx. (3–3½ lbs.)
¼ l. olive oil (1½ gills)
2 onions
30–60 g. butter (1–2 oz.)
1 clove of garlic
¼ l. vin blanc sec du Roussillon or dry white wine (1½ gills)
3 aubergines
2 green peppers
12 button mushrooms
6 tomatoes, skinned and pipped
bouquet garni, composed of thyme, bayleaf, tarragon and celery
120 g. green olives (4 oz.)
seasoning
To finish:
fried croûtons
finely chopped parsley

Method: Have the chicken jointed. Heat the butter and half the oil in a sauté pan. Season the joints and turn them quickly in the hot fat until they are browned on all sides. Then add the onions finely chopped and the garlic crushed with a little salt. Continue the cooking for a further 5–7 minutes. Pour in the wine. Season. Cover the chicken with greaseproof paper and the lid and place in a moderate oven, gas mark 5 or 375° F. (190° C.) for approximately 45 minutes.

Meanwhile, peel the aubergines and cut them into fairly large cubes. Cut the peppers in half, remove the pith and the seeds. Blanch them in boiling salted water for 2–3 minutes. Cut them into similar sized pieces. Cut the tomatoes into strips. Halve the mushrooms.

Put these vegetables into a sauté pan with the rest of the oil and the bouquet garni. Season well. Simmer gently until they are soft. Stone the olives. Blanch them in simmering water for 1–2 minutes. Drain the vegetables and add them to the pan with the chicken, together with the olives. Stir round well and remove any surplus grease with kitchen paper. Season to taste. Cook together for 3–4 minutes.

Dish the chicken and vegetables in a large hot dish. Arrange the fried croûtons round the edge. Sprinkle with finely chopped parsley.

Comment: This recipe is a speciality of M. Michel Bonneil of The Grand Hôtel Thermal, Molitg-les-Bains.

POULET À LA HONGROISE **   (for 4–6 persons)

Ingredients:
1 roasting fowl, 1½–2 kg. (3–
   3½ lbs.)
240 g. Patna rice (½ lb.)
240 g. tomatoes (½ lb.)
1 medium sized onion
1 tablespoon concentrated tomato
   purée

1 l. chicken stock (1½ pints)
1 tablespoon paprika
90 g. butter (3 oz.)
1 clove garlic
bouquet garni
seasoning
To finish:
finely chopped parsley

Method: Have the chicken jointed. Melt 60 g. (2 oz.) of the butter in a large sauté pan. When it is hot, fry the chicken joints in it until they are lightly brown on all sides. Remove them from the pan and add the other 30 g. (1 oz.) of butter and allow it to heat, then add the onion which has been thinly sliced. Cook it gently, stirring frequently until it is tender. It must not brown. Put the rice into the pan and stir this also until it is well coated in the butter. Remove the pan from the heat and pour in the stock. Skin and pip the tomatoes and cut them into quarters. Crush the garlic with a little salt. Mix in the paprika, garlic, tomato purée and the tomatoes with the rice. Add the bouquet garni, season well. Stirring all the time, bring the mixture to the boil.

Place the joints of chicken on top of the rice mixture, cover with grease-proof paper and the lid. Put it to cook in a moderate oven, gas mark 5 or 375° F. (190° C.) for 30 minutes. By this time the chicken should be tender and the rice will have absorbed the liquid and be dry and fluffy.

To Serve: Remove the chicken joints and keep them hot. Remove the bouquet garni. Stir the rice mixture with a fork, adjust the seasoning. Pile this in the centre of a hot serving dish. Arrange the chicken joints around the rice. Dust with finely chopped parsley. Serve hot.

POULET À LA NOIX DE COCO **   (for 4–6 persons)

Ingredients:
1 roasting fowl, 1½–2 kg. approx.
   (3–3½ lb.)
1 small red pepper
1 large onion
1 small coconut
pinch or sugar

¼ l. white stock (1½ gills)
2 teaspoons curry powder
pinch of saffron
90 g. butter (3 oz.)
seasoning
To finish:
finely chopped parsley

Method: Have the chicken jointed. Remove the pips and pith from the pepper and chop it finely. Blanch it for 2–3 minutes in boiling salted water. Remove and drain it. Slice the onion very finely.

Heat the butter in a fairly large pan, add the onion and soften it gently over a low heat until it is transparent looking, but not browned. Remove and put it to one side. Add the chicken to the pan together with the seasoning, curry powder, sugar and saffron. Raise the heat and move the chicken quickly in the hot fat. When it is brown on all sides, remove it carefully, pour in the stock and add the onion and pepper. Cover the pan and allow the contents to simmer gently for 15 minutes. Return the pieces of chicken. Cover with greaseproof paper and the lid. Cook for a further 25 minutes over a low heat.

Whilst the chicken is cooking, split open the coconut. Reserve the milk and add to it approximately 1½ dl. (1 gill) of warm water. Grate the coconut meat with a cheese grater, or chop it finely, and mix it well with the milk and water. Just before serving pour it into the pan with the chicken. Heat through thoroughly and adjust the seasoning.

To Serve: Pile the joints of chicken in a hot dish. Pour over the coconut mixture. Dust with the parsley. Serve very hot.

POULET À LA VIGNERONNE ***   (for 4–6 persons)

Ingredients:

1 roasting fowl, 1½–2 kg. approx. (3–3½ lb.)
60 g. white breadcrumbs (2 oz.)
a little milk
1 tablespoon finely chopped tarragon
1 clove garlic
2 onions
60 g. plain flour (2 oz.)
60 g. butter (2 oz.)
3 yolks of egg

1½ dl. thin cream (1 gill)
seasoning
For the Garnish:
6 or 8 tartlet cases made from Pâte Brisée (Method I) (see page 338) or Flaky Pastry (see page 335)
240 g. black grapes (½ lb.)
salade de pommes de terre made with 1 kg. (2 lbs.) new potatoes, etc. (see page 236)

Method: Soak the breadcrumbs in the milk, then press them between the hands to expel the excess moisture. Chop the chicken liver and mix it with the breadcrumbs in a bowl together with the tarragon and the garlic, which has been crushed with a little salt. Season well. Truss the chicken, stuffing the breast with this mixture.

Peel and slice the onions thinly. Place them in the bottom of a deep casserole. Put the bird on top and season it well. Pour in enough boiling water to come ½–¾ of the way up the sides of the chicken. Cover with buttered greaseproof paper and the lid. Cook in a moderate oven, gas mark 5–6 or 375–400° F. (190–200° C.) for 1–1¼ hours, until the chicken is tender.

Whilst it is cooking make the tartlet cases and the salade de pommes de terre, which should be served with the chicken whilst it is still warm.

When the chicken is cooked, remove it from the oven and strain off the liquor it has been cooked in. If necessary, make it up to 6 dl. (1 pint) with more chicken stock or water. Keep the chicken hot on a serving dish.

Melt the butter in a small saucepan. Remove it from the heat and stir in the flour. Return it to the heat and cook gently for 1–2 minutes, stirring continuously with a wooden spoon or spatula. Remove from the heat and pour in the chicken liquor gradually, stirring all the time. Bring it to the boil and simmer for 5 minutes, still stirring.

Beat the yolks with the cream and pour on a little of the sauce and beat all together. Return the egg mixture to the sauce and thicken it very gently over a low heat. It must not boil.

Skin and pip the grapes and fill the tartlet cases with them.

Coat the chicken lightly with some of the sauce. Pour the rest into a sauce boat and serve separately. Arrange the tartlets round the sides of the dish. Serve hot with the warm salade de pommes de terre.

Comment: A boiling fowl may be used for this dish, in which case it should be cooked considerably longer, according to the age and size of the bird.

POULET ARCHIDUC **   (for 4–6 persons)

Ingredients:

1 roasting fowl, 1½–2 kg. approx. (3–3½ lb.)
60 g. butter (2 oz.)
3 tablespoons white port
2 tablespoons brandy

1½ dl. Sauce Béchamel (see page 34) (1 gill)
1½ dl. thick cream (1 gill)
seasoning

To finish:

30 g. butter (1 oz.)
small bundles of asparagus

Method: Have the chicken jointed. Heat 60 g. (2 oz.) of butter in a sauté pan. Turn the joints of chicken quickly in the butter to brown them lightly on all sides. Season well. Cover the chicken with greaseproof paper and the lid. Reduce the heat and cook slowly for 35 minutes, shaking the pan from time to time to prevent the chicken from sticking.

Meanwhile make the sauce Béchamel and cook the asparagus (see page 194).

Remove the joints to a serving dish and keep them hot. Pour the port and brandy into the sauté pan, stir well and then add the sauce Béchamel and the cream. Mix well together and allow the sauce to simmer over a good heat for 3–4 minutes, stirring occasionally. Remove from the heat, adjust the seasoning, and whisk in 30 g. (1 oz.) of butter.

Pour the sauce over the chicken. Arrange the bundles of asparagus round the dish. Serve hot. (*See Plate 10.*)

POULET 'BONNE VIEILLE' *** (for 4–5 persons)

Ingredients:

1 roasting fowl, approx. 1½ kg. (3 lb.) drawn and trussed
120 g. small onions (4 oz.)
360 g. button mushrooms (¾ lb.)
a little lemon juice
8 tartlet cases, made with Flaky Pastry (see page 335) or Pâte Brisée (Method I) (see page 338)

8 small tomatoes
1½ dl. Sauce Tomate (Method II) (see page 39)
8 black olives
120 g. butter (4 oz.)
1½ dl. dry white wine (1 gill)
seasoning

Method: Rub the breast of the chicken with 60 g. (2 oz.) butter. Season well. Put it in a roasting pan and cook it in a fairly hot oven, gas mark 6 or 400° F. (200° C.) for 1 hour or until the chicken is tender.

Make the tartlet cases, and the sauce tomate. Melt 60 g. (2 oz.) of butter in a pan, skin the tomatoes and toss them carefully in the hot butter, then pour in the sauce tomate and keep hot.

When the chicken is cooked, keep it hot. Drain off the fat from the roasting tin into a saucepan. Cook the mushrooms in this, with a few drops of lemon juice and salt and pepper. When they are tender, remove and drain them and keep hot. Sauter the onions in the remaining fat.

Cut the chicken into neat joints and arrange these with the mushrooms and onions in a hot serving dish. Keep them hot.

Place a tomato in each tartlet case, pour a little sauce over and decorate with a black olive on the top of each. Arrange the tartlets around the dish. Keep hot.

Pour the wine into the pan in which the mushrooms and onions were cooked. Heat it through and remove the excess grease. Stir round well. Taste and season. Pour it over the chicken. Serve very hot.

(See Plate 9.)

POULET D'ARTAGNAN ** (for 4–6 persons)

Ingredients:

1 roasting fowl, 1½–2 kg. approx. (3–3½ lb.)
60 g. ham (2 oz.)
90 g. butter (3 oz.)
bouquet garni
2 yolks of egg
1 teaspoon arrowroot

10 tiny onions
10 button mushrooms
1 dl. dry white wine (½ gill)
1½ dl. thick cream (1 gill)
2 teaspoons lemon juice
2 teaspoons pâté de foie
10 tiny fried croûtons
seasoning

Method: Have the chicken jointed. Season the joints well. Make the butter hot in a deep sauté pan. Put in the chicken and the ham cut into dice. Turn the joints quickly until they are browned on all sides. Add the mushrooms and the tiny onions. Cover the pan with greaseproof paper and the lid and place over a gentle heat for 10–15 minutes, shaking the pan from time to time. Pour in the wine and add the bouquet garni. Season well. Continue cooking for a further 25 minutes or until the bird is tender.

Remove the joints and keep them hot on a serving dish. Lift out the garnish carefully and keep it hot as well. Remove the bouquet garni. Slake the arrowroot with a little water. Sieve the pâté de foie and mix it well with the cream, lemon juice and egg yolks. Raise the heat under the pan, scrape the bottom well, stir in the arrowroot and allow to cook for 2–3 minutes. Stir in the cream mixture. Allow the sauce to thicken gently, without boiling and stirring all the time. Rectify the seasoning. Pour the sauce over the chicken and surround it with the onions, mushrooms and croûtons arranged alternately.

POULET DRAP D'OR ** (for 6–8 persons)

Ingredients:

1 roasting fowl, 1½–2 kg. approx. (3–3½ lb.)
60 g. butter (2 oz.)
1 tablespoon oil
2 sticks celery
250 g. tomatoes (½ lb.)
120 g. mushrooms (4 oz.)
2 oranges
3 black olives
3 green olives
½ clove garlic

2 red peppers
2 green peppers
1½ dl. brandy (1 gill)
1½ dl. dry white wine (1 gill)
1½ dl. chicken stock (1 gill)
2 tablespoons thick cream
2 teaspoons paprika
3 sprigs thyme
1 sprig rosemary
½ bayleaf
seasoning

Method: Joint the chicken. Make the butter and oil hot in a deep sauté pan. Put in the chicken and turn it in the hot fat until it is a rich brown. This will take some minutes. Whilst this is happening, skin and pip the tomatoes and chop them roughly. Cut the peppers into strips. Remove the pith and seeds. Blanch them for 2–3 minutes in boiling water. Drain them well. Grate the rind of one orange. Blanch this also and drain. Reserve the juice from this orange and cut the other in thin slices. Put it aside. Stone the olives. Cut the mushrooms into halves or leave whole if they are very small. Chop the celery roughly. Crush the garlic with a little salt.

When satisfied that the chicken is sufficiently brown, pour in the brandy and 'flame' it. Stir well. Now add the celery, the peppers and pour on the wine and stock. Add the garlic and the herbs tied together with a piece of string. Put the tomatoes on top of the chicken. Season. Cover with greaseproof paper and the lid and cook slowly for half an hour. At the end of this time, add the blanched orange rind and 2 tablespoons of orange juice, together with the mushrooms and the paprika. Continue to cook for a further 10 minutes.

To Serve: Dish the chicken joints on a large hot serving dish. Remove the herbs from the pan. Stir well and add the cream. Rectify the seasoning. Pour the sauce over the chicken. Place slices of orange round the sides of the dish and put an alternate black and green olive on each slice.

POULET FARCI AUX OLIVES **   (for 4–6 persons)

Ingredients:

1 roasting fowl, drawn and trussed
  1½–2 kg. approx. (3–3½ lb.)
75 g. butter (2½ oz.)
juice of ½ orange
seasoning

For the Farce:

60 g. black olives (2 oz.)
1 egg
1 hardboiled egg
150 g. pâté de foie (5 oz.)
½ teaspoon powdered aniseed
  (optional)

1 tablespoon grated orange rind
2 tablespoons white breadcrumbs
seasoning

For the Garnish:

3 small oranges
6 stoned black olives
Sauce Vinaigrette (see page 40)
sieved yolk of 1 hardboiled egg
1 tablespoon chopped chervil
½ cucumber
a pinch of sugar
seasoning

Method: Make the farce – sieve the hardboiled egg, stone the olives and pass them through a vegetable mill. Mix them together in a bowl. Add the pâté de foie, aniseed, grated orange rind, breadcrumbs and seasoning. Stir in the beaten egg. Stuff the chicken with this mixture. Spread the butter all over the breast. Season well. Place the chicken in a roasting tin, cover it with greaseproof paper and roast it in a hot oven, gas mark 7 or 425° F. (220° C.) allowing 20 minutes to the pound. After 10 minutes of cooking, add the juice of half an orange to the pan (not more) and baste the chicken frequently with this. Fifteen minutes before the chicken is cooked, remove the buttered paper and allow the breast to become golden.

Make up the sauce vinaigrette, using 3 parts oil to 1 part wine or tarragon vinegar. Whisk in the sieved yolk of egg and the chopped chervil. See that it is well seasoned with salt, black pepper and a pinch of sugar.

Cut the oranges for the garnish in half and remove the peel without damaging it. Take the flesh from the inner skin and chop it roughly. Cut the cucumber into 1 cm. (½ inch) dice and mix it lightly with the orange sections and the vinaigrette. Put this salad back into the peel. Top each with a stoned black olive.

When the chicken is cooked, remove the trussing strings and serve it on a hot dish. Arrange the garnish round the sides of the dish. Serve at once.

POULET SAUTÉ AU GRATIN ** (for 4–6 persons)

Ingredients:

1 roasting fowl, 1½–2 kg. (3–3½ lb.)
120 g. butter (4 oz.)
180 g. button mushrooms (6 oz.)
3 medium sized onions
2 tablespoons plain flour
3 dl. chicken stock (½ pint)

juice ½ lemon
1½ dl. thick cream (1 gill)
90 g. grated Gruyère cheese
  (3 oz.)
1 wine glass dry white wine
seasoning

Method: Wipe the mushrooms on a clean cloth. If they are small button mushrooms leave them whole, otherwise cut them in half.

Melt 30 g. (1 oz.) butter in a small pan, add the mushrooms. Season. Cover with greaseproof paper and the lid and toss them for 2–3 minutes over a gentle heat. Remove from the stove and place them on one side.

Peel and slice the onions very thinly. Have the fowl ready jointed. Heat the remaining butter in a fairly deep strong pan. Put in the onions and the chicken joints. Move them in the hot butter, using a wooden spoon, until they are just beginning to turn a pale gold. It is important not to let the onions brown. Sprinkle in the flour and stir round well. Then add the stock and bring up to simmering point. Pour in the wine together with the cream which has been mixed with the lemon juice, the mushrooms and their liquor. Return to simmering point. Taste and adjust the seasoning. Put all together in a deep fireproof dish, arranging the chicken joints neatly. Sprinkle over the grated cheese. Wipe round the sides of the dish to prevent unsightly browning. Cover with the lid or with aluminium foil. Put into a moderate oven, gas mark 5 or 375° F. (190° C.) for 45–50 minutes. Ten minutes before serving, remove the lid, or the foil, to allow the cheese to become crisp and brown. Serve hot in the dish in which it has been cooked.

POULET PICASSO ** (for 4–6 persons)

Ingredients:

1 roasting fowl, 1½–2 kg. approx.
  (3–3½ lb.)
2 tablespoons oil
90 g. butter (3 oz.)
12 green olives
12 black olives
4 tomatoes, peeled, pipped and
  quartered

1 teaspoon concentrated tomato
  purée
1½ dl. dry white wine (1 gill)
1 dl. stock (½ gill)
seasoning
To finish:
Pommes de Terre Dauphine (see
  page 225)
1 green pepper

Method: Joint the chicken. Make the oil and 30 g. (1 oz.) butter hot in a sauté pan. Season the chicken joints and turn them quickly in the hot fat to brown them on all sides. Cover with a piece of greaseproof paper, well tucked down over the chicken, and the lid. Place on a low heat. Cook for 35 minutes, shaking the pan from time to time to prevent the chicken from sticking.

Whilst it is cooking remove the pips and pith from the pepper, cut it into strips and blanch for 2–3 minutes in boiling salted water. Drain. Prepare the pommes de terre Dauphine and keep hot.

When the chicken is cooked, arrange the joints on a hot serving dish and keep them hot. Add the remaining butter to the pan and heat the olives and pepper in this. Remove them and toss the tomatoes in the same pan. Season well. Keep all hot.

Pour the wine and stock into the pan, raise the heat and add the tomato purée. Stir round well, adjust the seasoning and pour over the chicken. Arrange the peppers and olives down each side of the dish, pile the tomatoes and potatoes at each end.

Comment: This dish is a speciality of Chez Camille Renault in Puteaux and is served with a garnish of chicken shaped croûtons of pâte feuilletée with a tiny sausage in the middle of each.

POULET SAUTÉ BAGATELLE *** (for 4–6 persons)

Ingredients:
1 roasting fowl, 1½–2 kg. approx. (3–3½ lb.)
60 g. butter (2 oz.)
1 tablespoon oil
1 small onion, finely chopped
1 dl. dry white wine (½ gill)
1½ dl. Madeira (1 gill)
2 yolks of egg

3 dl. thick cream (½ pint)
seasoning
For the Garnish:
fried croûtons
small bunch asparagus
460 g. young carrots (1 lb.)
60 g. butter (2 oz.)
pinch of sugar

Method: Have the chicken jointed and season it well. Heat the butter and oil in a deep sauté pan. Put in the chicken and sauter it on all sides without allowing it to brown. Remove the joints. Cook the onion in the pan over a low heat and soften it gently without allowing it to brown.

Return the chicken to the pan with the wine and seasoning. Cover with greaseproof paper and the lid, or if liked, seal the pan with a 'repère' paste (see page 23). Place it in a moderate oven, gas mark 5 or 375° F. (190° C.). Cook for a further 45–50 minutes.

Whilst it is cooking, wash and scrape the carrots and cut them into even sizes. Place them in a saucepan and just cover them with boiling salted water. Add 30 g. (1 oz.) butter and a pinch of sugar. Cook them as for Carottes Vichy.

Scrape the asparagus. Cut it to lengths about 7–10 cm. (3–4 inches). Tie in a bundle and cook for 15–20 minutes in fast boiling salted water. Drain, untie, and toss it in melted butter.

Fry the croûtons and drain them on kitchen paper. Keep them hot.

To Finish: Remove the chicken from the pan and keep it hot on a serving dish. Whisk up the yolks with the Madeira and cream, pour into the pan the chicken was cooked in. Stir round well while thickening the sauce over a low heat. Do not boil on any account. Taste and adjust the seasoning. Pour the sauce over the chicken. Arrange the carrots and asparagus tips alternately round the edges of the dish. Serve hot.

POULET SAUTÉ BONNE FEMME ** (for 5–6 persons)

Ingredients:
1 roasting fowl, 1½–2 kg. approx. (3–3½ lb.)
¼ l. dry white wine (1½ gills)
1 heaped teaspoon plain flour
1 chopped shallot
60 g. butter (2 oz.)
bouquet garni
seasoning

For the Garnish:
Pommes de Terre Cocotte made with 700 g. (1½ lb.) potatoes (see page 224)
30 tiny onions
120 g. back bacon rashers cut into squares (4 oz.)
90 g. butter (3 oz.)
finely chopped parsley

Method: Have the chicken jointed. Make the butter hot in a sauté pan. Put in the chicken, together with the shallot. Cook over a moderate heat, turning them occasionally until the chicken is well browned on all sides. Sprinkle the flour into the pan and stir well. Pour in the wine, add the seasoning and the bouquet garni. Bring to simmering point stirring all the time. Cover with greaseproof paper and the lid and cook gently for 30–35 minutes.

Whilst it is cooking, prepare the garnish. Melt 60 g. (2 oz.) of the butter in a pan, put in the peeled onions. Season and cover with greaseproof paper and the lid. Sweat them over a gentle heat until they are tender. Keep them hot.

Make the pommes de terre cocotte. Keep these hot also.

Heat the remaining 30 g. (1 oz.) of butter and gently fry the bacon in this.

When the chicken is cooked, arrange it on a large hot dish. Adjust the seasoning and strain over the gravy. Place the pommes de terre cocotte at each end of the dish and the onions and bacon at each side. Sprinkle lightly with the parsley. Serve hot.

POULET SAUTÉ CRÉCY ** (for 4–6 persons)

Ingredients:
1 medium sized roasting fowl, 1½–2 kg. approx. (3–3½ lb.)
90 g. butter (3 oz.)
3 dl. (½ pint) Sauce Veloutée made with chicken stock (see page 39)
700 g. carrots (1½ lb.)
3 dl. thin cream (½ pint)
40–60 g. butter (2–3 oz.)
seasoning

Method: Joint the chicken. Melt the butter in a deep sauté pan. Put in the chicken joints and sauter them gently without letting them colour. Keep them well turned to prevent them from browning. Pour off the excess butter and add 3–4 tablespoons of water. Season. Cover with greaseproof paper and the lid, or if liked, seal with a repère or flour and water paste (see page 23). Place in a moderate oven, gas mark 5 or 375° F. (190° C.) and cook gently for 45 minutes–1 hour, until the chicken is tender.

Meanwhile peel the carrots and cut them into paysanne strips. Melt the butter in a thick pan, add the carrots. Season. Cover them with grease-proof paper and the lid and sweat them over a gentle heat until tender. Shake the pan from time to time to prevent them from sticking. Make the sauce Veloutée. When the carrots are cooked, stir in the cream, heat through and then stir in the sauce Veloutée. Keep it hot.

When the chicken is cooked, lift the joints on to a hot dish. Pour over the sauce and carrots. Serve at once.

POULET SAUTÉ GRAND MONARQUE **

(for 5–6 persons)

Ingredients:

1 roasting fowl, 1½–2 kg. approx. (3–3½ lb.)
60 g. butter (2 oz.)
1 tablespoon oil
2 tablespoons brandy
2 medium carrots, diced
1 onion, finely chopped
a little chicken stock
3 dl. dry white wine (½ pint)
2 shallots, finely chopped
1 ripe tomato, skinned and pipped
2 tablespoons thick cream
120 g. mushrooms (4 oz.)

bouquet garni
seasoning
For the rice pilaf:
1 teacupful Patna rice
3–4 chicken livers (as available)
2½ cups chicken or veal stock
60 g. chopped ham (2 oz.)
1 small onion
2 tomatoes, skinned and pipped
2 tablespoons sultanas
60 g. butter (2 oz.)
pinch of saffron
seasoning

Method: Joint the chicken and make the butter and oil hot in a deep sauté pan. Put in the chicken joints and brown them quickly on all sides over a good heat. Remove them and put aside, then brown the shallots, carrots and onion in the same pan over a lower heat. When they are brown, return the chicken joints to the pan. Heat through. Pour in the brandy and 'flame' it. Then pour in the white wine and add just sufficient stock to cover the chicken. Place the bouquet garni down the side and add the tomato. Season well. Cover with greaseproof paper and the lid. Cook gently in a moderate oven, gas mark 5 or 375° F. (190° C.) for 30–35 minutes.

Whilst it is cooking, make the pilaf – melt the butter in a thick pan. Add the onion finely sliced. Soften over a low heat without allowing it to colour. Then add the chicken livers lightly chopped and turn them in the hot fat for one minute. Add the rice and stir this also over a low heat. Now add the diced ham, the roughly chopped tomato, sultanas and the hot stock, to which has been added the saffron. Season. Cover with greaseproof paper and the lid and put into a moderate oven, gas mark 5 or 375° F. (190° C.) for 25–30 minutes. When the rice is cooked, remove it from the oven and form it into a border on a hot serving dish, leaving enough room for the chicken to be placed in the centre. Keep hot. Take out the chicken joints and place them in the centre of the rice. Strain the liquor in which the chicken was cooked into a clean pan, and reduce it quickly over a good heat. Stir in the cream and rectify the seasoning. Add the mushrooms to the sauce and pour it over the chicken. Serve at once.

POULET ST. MACLOU ** (for 4–6 persons)

Ingredients:

1 roasting chicken drawn and trussed, 1½–2 kg. approx. (3–3½ lb.)	1½ dl. white stock (1 gill)
	1 dl. brandy (½ gill)
	6 mushroom caps
a few sprigs of tarragon	120 g. chicken livers (4 oz.)
1 carrot	a little lemon juice
1 onion	seasoning
120 g. butter (4 oz.)	**To finish:**
4 rashers bacon	1 tablespoon brandy
	watercress

Method: Place the tarragon inside the body of the chicken. Put it in a roasting tin together with the carrot sliced, the onion and the stock. Season well and dot with 60 g. (2 oz.) of the butter. Cover the breast with the rashers of bacon. Roast in a moderate oven, gas mark 6 or 400° F. (200° C.) for one hour, basting from time to time. Twenty minutes before the end of the cooking time remove the bacon to allow the breast to brown.

Meanwhile prepare the garnish. Melt 30 g. (1 oz.) of butter in a small pan and add a few drops of lemon juice and 2 tablespoons of water and seasoning. Add the mushroom caps and cover with greaseproof paper and the lid. Cook gently for 4–5 minutes. Chop the chicken livers finely. Melt the rest of the butter in a small pan and sauter the livers gently until they have changed colour. Pour in the 1 dl. (½ gill) brandy and simmer for 5 minutes. Season well.

To Serve: Lift the chicken on to a hot serving dish. Fill the mushrooms with the chicken livers and arrange them around the dish. Pour the brandy into the roasting tin and 'flame' it. Taste and season and strain over the chicken. Arrange a bunch of watercress at either end of the dish.

SALADE DE POULET ** (for 4 persons)

Ingredients:

1 small cold roast chicken
60 g. browned almonds (2 oz.)
60 g. currants or sultanas (2 oz.)
1 root celeriac

1 bunch watercress
Sauce Mayonnaise (see page 36)
1 orange
seasoning

Method: Put the currants or sultanas to soak in warm water several hours in advance.

Make the sauce mayonnaise and stir in finally the juice of the orange.

Wash the watercress well and divide it into small sprigs. Wash and peel the celeriac, and cut it into fine julienne strips.

Remove the skin from the chicken, carve off the meat carefully and cut it into even sized strips.

Place the chicken, celeriac, watercress, drained currants or sultanas, almonds and the sauce mayonnaise in a bowl. Using two forks, carefully mix all together. Taste and season as desired. Serve very cold piled up in a salad dish.

Vegetables

If the influx of immigrants from warmer climates has brought us no other benefits, it has at least increased the demand for an even greater variety of vegetables to be available in our greengrocers: even quite remote or rural places are now able to supply such previously exotic things as green peppers, aubergines, fresh chillies, fennel, yams, fresh ginger and courgettes.

The best vegetables are those which are grown in one's own garden, freshly picked and cooked. Quick freezing has made many vegetables available at all times of the year, and not much inferior to the garden produce.

VEGETABLES

VEGETABLES

ARTICHAUTS À LA GRECQUE *   (for 4 persons)

Ingredients:

4 globe artichokes, young and
   tender
1½ dl. olive oil (1 gill)
3 dessertspoons coriander seed
1 teaspoon black peppercorns,
   crushed

bouquet garni containing 3–4
   sprigs thyme, 3–4 sprigs fennel,
   a stick of celery, 1 bayleaf
juice of 3 lemons
4 cloves garlic (optional)
a little salt

Method: Wash the artichokes well. Pull off the outside leaves and cut off the top – if the stalks are tender leave them on.

Put 1 l. (2 pints) of water, the oil, herbs, pepper, coriander, salt and lemon juice in a large deep pan. Bring them quickly to the boil and boil them for 10 minutes before adding the artichokes and the cloves of garlic. Simmer for 40–45 minutes, keeping the pan covered. At the end of this time remove the artichokes and place them on a clean dry cloth to drain.

Raise the heat under the pan and reduce the liquid quickly until about ¼ l. (½ pint) or a little less remains.

Dish the artichokes upside down on a large serving dish with the cloves of garlic. Strain over the liquid. Serve very cold as an hors d'œuvres.

ARTICHAUTS À LA MARAÎCHÈRE *   (for 3–4 persons)

Ingredients:

2 globe artichokes
2 tomatoes
8–9 small new potatoes
a handful sorrel
a handful spinach

4 new carrots
6 spring onions
4 young turnips
¼ l. dry white wine (1½ gills)
30 g. butter (1 oz.)
seasoning

Method: Pull off the outside leaves. Cut the artichokes into four and take out the choke from each quarter. Trim the centre leaves to 3 cm. (1 inch) length. Blanch the artichokes in boiling salted water for 5 minutes.

Meanwhile peel the other vegetables and 'turn' the carrots and turnips to the same size as the potatoes and onions. Wash the spinach and sorrel in several waters and chop them finely. Cut the tomatoes into four.

When the artichokes are blanched, drain them well and put them in a clean pan with all the other vegetables, together with the white wine, butter and seasoning. Cover with greaseproof paper and the lid and cook in a moderate oven, gas mark 5 or 375° F. (190° C.) for 30–35 minutes. At the end of this time, adjust the seasoning and serve in a hot dish.

POINTES D'ASPERGES À LA CRÈME **   (for 4–5 persons)

Ingredients:

½ kg. approx. asparagus (1–1½ lb.)
½ l. thin cream (1 pint)
75 g. butter (2½ oz.)
30 g. plain flour (1 oz.)

3 yolks of egg
seasoning
To finish:
fleurons of Pâte Feuilletée (see
    page 337)

Method: Wash and scrape the asparagus and trim it into equal lengths. Tie it in small bundles and cook it gently in plenty of boiling salted water until tender.

Meanwhile heat 45 g. (1½ oz.) butter in a saucepan, draw it from the heat and stir in the flour, then carefully add all but one decilitre (½ gill) of the cream. Return it to the heat and bring it slowly to simmering point, stirring all the time. Beat the yolks of egg, mix them with the rest of the cream and stir them into the sauce. Allow it to thicken over a low heat, without boiling, for 2–3 minutes, keeping it well stirred. Season.

When the asparagus is cooked, lift it carefully from the pan and allow it to drain. Remove the strings. Lay the asparagus in a hot dish, coat it with the rest of the butter, melted, and pour over the sauce. Garnish with puff pastry fleurons and serve at once.

AUBERGINES À LA MEUNIÈRE *   (for 2–3 persons)

Ingredients:
3 aubergines
salt
seasoned flour

90–120 g. butter (3–4 oz.)
finely chopped parsley
1 tablespoon lemon juice
seasoning

Method: Peel the aubergines and cut them into slices about 1 cm. (¼ inch) thick. Sprinkle them with salt and place them on a wire rack to drain. At the end of 15 minutes turn them over and dust the other side equally with salt. Allow them to drain again for a further 15 minutes. Remove and dry them thoroughly on a clean cloth and coat them in seasoned flour.

Make the butter very hot indeed in a large sauté pan. Lay the aubergine slices side by side. Cook them for 4–5 minutes before turning to cook the other side. When they are cooked pile them up in a hot dish and keep them hot. Add the finely chopped parsley and lemon juice to the pan. Season, stir round over the heat and then pour it over the aubergines. Serve at once.

Comment: Exactly the same method can be used for cooking cucumbers.

AUBERGINES AU GRATIN *   (for 3–4 persons)

Ingredients:
4 aubergines
1 l. Sauce Béchamel (see page 34)
    (1½ pints)
120 g. grated Gruyère cheese (4 oz.)

browned breadcrumbs
oil for frying
seasoned flour
seasoning

Method: Peel the aubergines. Cut them into even slices about 1 cm. (¼ inch) thick. Dust them with salt and put them on a wire rack to drain, turning them from time to time. Make about 1 dl. (¾ gill) of oil very hot, dry the aubergines on a clean dry cloth, dip them into seasoned flour and fry quickly in the hot oil. Do not fry more aubergines at a time than will conveniently cover the bottom of the pan. As the oil is used add more to the pan if needed.

Make up the sauce Béchamel as usual. Remove it from the heat as soon as it is cooked and whisk in three-quarters of the grated Gruyère cheese. Taste and season well.

Butter a shallow fireproof dish. Pour in a layer of the sauce, cover with a layer of the fried aubergines, continue in this way with alternate layers until the dish is full, finishing with a layer of the sauce. Sprinkle over the top with the rest of the cheese, mixed with the browned crumbs. Brown in the top of a fairly hot oven, gas mark 6 or 400° F. (200° C.) for 5–10 minutes. Serve very hot.

AUBERGINES FARCIES À LA BOSTON *   (for 3–6 persons)

Ingredients:

3 aubergines
1 egg
olive oil for frying
seasoned flour
3 dl. Sauce Béchamel (see page 34) (½ pint)

60 g. grated cheese (2 oz.)
1 dl. thick cream (½ gill)
1 tablespoon finely chopped parsley
seasoning

Method: Cut the aubergines in half lengthwise. Run a knife all round between the skin and the flesh. Make several cuts across the flesh, dust them with salt and turn upside down on a wire rack to drain for 30 minutes.

Make the sauce Béchamel in the usual way. Remove from the heat and stir in the beaten egg, together with half the cheese. Season.

Dry the aubergines with a clean cloth. Dip them into the seasoned flour. Heat the oil in a frying pan and fry the aubergines, cut side down, in the hot oil. (They will take about 10 minutes.) When they are cooked, remove them from the pan and scoop out the flesh carefully without damaging the skins. Chop the flesh coarsely. Mix it with the sauce and add the finely chopped parsley. Adjust the seasoning. Put the mixture back into the skins. Sprinkle over the remainder of the cheese and brown quickly under a hot grill. Dish the aubergines in a hot dish and at the moment of serving put a spoonful of cream on the top of each.

Comment: Sometimes the sauce Béchamel is made with half milk and half thin cream. When this is the case, it is as well to use Gruyère for the cheese. The result is superb.

BETTERAVES À L'AUVERGNATE *   (for 4 persons)

Ingredients:

500 g. cooked beetroots (1 lb.)
1 small onion, finely chopped
60 g. lean bacon (2 oz.)
15 g. plain flour (½ oz.)

15 g. butter (½ oz.)
3 dl. white stock, approx. (½ pint)
pinch of mixed spice (quatre épices)
2 teaspoons wine vinegar
seasoning

Method: Remove the rind and cut the bacon into lardons. Heat the butter in a pan, put in the bacon and the onion and cook over a low heat until the onion is completely soft, but not brown. Draw the pan aside from the heat and stir in the flour. Return the pan to the heat and continue to cook, stirring all the time until the flour takes on a blond colour. Then pour in the stock, bring it to the boil, season well and simmer in an uncovered pan for 15 minutes.

Meanwhile skin the beetroots and cut them into slices or into 1 cm. (½ inch) dice. Add them to the sauce with the vinegar and simmer for a further 5–10 minutes. Stir in the mixed spices. Taste and adjust the seasoning. Serve hot in a vegetable dish.

BETTERAVES AU VIN * (for 4 persons)

Ingredients:
½–1 kg. cooked beetroots (1–1½ lb.)
120 g. lean bacon (4 oz.)
30 g. butter (1 oz.)
1 level tablespoon plain flour
12 small onions

¼ l. red wine (1½ gills)
1 large sprig of thyme
seasoning
To finish:
2 tablespoons finely chopped fresh
   herbs

Method: Peel the beetroots and cut them into 1 cm. (½ inch) cubes. Melt the butter in a saucepan, add the bacon, cut into lardons, and the onions. Season. Cover with greaseproof paper and the lid. Cook them over a gentle heat until the onions are tender and very lightly brown. Draw aside from the heat and sprinkle in the flour. Stir well. Return the pan to the heat and stirring all the time allow the flour to colour slightly. Pour in the wine, add the thyme. Bring up to simmering point, put in the beetroot cubes. Simmer all together for 10 minutes. At the end of this time remove the thyme. Adjust the seasoning.

Dish in a hot serving dish with the sauce. Lastly sprinkle over the finely chopped herbs.

BROCOLIS À LA PAYSANNE ** (for 4–5 persons)

Ingredients:
1 kg. sprouting broccoli (2 lb.)
120 g. streaky bacon rashers (4 oz.)
120 g. butter (4 oz.)
240 g. carrots (½ lb.)

180 g. mushrooms (6 oz.)
3 dl. white stock (½ pint)
seasoning
To finish:
finely chopped parsley

Method: Wash the broccoli in several waters and remove the hard stalks. Put it into a pan of boiling salted water and cook for 5–6 minutes. Drain it and refresh it in cold water. Drain again and press out as much water as possible with the hands.

Lay the bacon on the bottom of a casserole, cover it with half the broccoli and dot with half the butter in small knobs. Peel the carrots and cut them into very fine slices. Melt the rest of the butter in a pan, toss the carrots in this until they are well coated. Remove the carrots carefully and lay them on top of the broccoli. Chop the mushrooms very finely, toss these also in the butter the carrots were tossed in, stir them to make sure that they are well coated. Put them in a layer on top of the carrots, season all very well. Cover with the rest of the broccoli. Pour in the well flavoured stock. Cover with buttered greaseproof paper and the lid and cook in a moderate oven, gas mark 5 or 375° F. (190° C.) for 40–45 minutes. Serve hot, well sprinkled with finely chopped parsley.

Comment: When broccoli is out of season, frozen broccoli can be used.

CAROTTES À LA POULETTE ** (for 4 persons)

Ingredients:

½ kg. carrots (1 lb.)
60 g. butter (2 oz.)
20 g. plain flour (¾ oz.)
3 dl. water (½ pint)
1 onion
bouquet garni

½ teaspoon sugar
little grated nutmeg
seasoning
To finish:
2 yolks of egg
30 g. butter (1 oz.)

Method: Wash and peel or scrape the carrots and slice them thinly. Cook them in a pan of boiling salted water for 10 minutes. Remove and drain them. Peel the onion.

Heat 60 g. (2 oz.) butter in a pan and cook the carrots in this for a few minutes over a low heat without colouration, stirring occasionally. Add the flour and stir well and then add the water and mix thoroughly. Put in the whole onion, the bouquet garni and the sugar. Season well. Continue to cook the carrots gently over a low heat until they are tender. Now remove the bouquet garni and the onion. Mix a little of the liquor with the beaten egg yolks and pour it over the carrots. Return the pan to a low heat and stir gently, without boiling, until the sauce thickens slightly. Remove from the heat. Adjust the seasoning, adding a pinch of nutmeg. Stir in the rest of the butter and serve very hot.

CAROTTES À LA PROVENÇALE * (for 6 persons)

Ingredients:

½ kg. carrots (1 lb.)
240 g. small onions (½ lb.)
60 g. butter (2 oz.)
12–16 green olives

Persillade made with 30 g. (1 oz.)
white breadcrumbs, 1 clove
garlic, 2 tablespoons finely
chopped parsley, seasoning

Method: Wash and peel the carrots and cut them into very fine slices. Peel the onions and leave them whole. Heat the butter in a saucepan and stir the carrots and the onions to coat them with butter. Season. Cover them with a piece of buttered greaseproof paper and the lid and cook for 1 hour over a very gentle heat. Shake the pan from time to time to prevent their sticking.

Mix the breadcrumbs with the parsley and the garlic crushed with salt. Season well. When the carrots and onions are soft, stir in the stoned olives. Pile up the vegetables in a hot dish. Sprinkle the persillade over the top and serve at once.

CAROTTES ANDALOUSE ** (for 2–3 persons)

Ingredients:
240 g. carrots (½ lb.)
30 g. butter (1 oz.)
1 whole egg
1 teaspoon plain flour

1 teaspoon brandy
pinch of nutmeg
butter for frying
seasoning

Method: Wash and peel the carrots and cut them to even sized pieces. Cook them in boiling salted water for 30 minutes or until they are tender. Drain them and pass them quickly through a sieve or vegetable mill. Mix them with the yolk, flour, butter, nutmeg and brandy. Season and if liked add a pinch of sugar. Whisk the egg white stiffly and fold it lightly in to the carrot purée. Heat a nut of butter in a frying pan. Pour in the carrot mixture. Allow it to brown on the bottom and heat through. Turn onto a hot serving dish. Serve at once.

CAROTTES NOUVELLES AU RIZ * (for 4–5 persons)

Ingredients:
½ kg. new carrots (1½ lb.)
4 dessertspoons olive oil or 45 g. butter (1½ oz.)
4 small onions
1 teacup Patna rice

2½ teacups boiling stock or water
bouquet garni
seasoning
To finish:
1 oz. butter

Method: Peel and slice the onions. Wash and peel or scrape the carrots and slice them lengthwise to make rather thick matchlike strips. Heat the butter or oil in a thick pan. Add the onions and carrots and turn them in the butter for several moments. When they are just beginning to colour, add the rice, the stock and the bouquet garni. Season well. Bring up to simmering point on the top of the stove. Cover with greaseproof paper and the lid. Then place the pan in a moderate oven, gas mark 5 or 375° F. (190° C.) for 25–30 minutes or until the rice and vegetables are cooked.

Remove the pan from the oven. Take out the bouquet garni. Taste and season the mixture. Then, using a fork, mix in the remaining ounce of butter bit by bit. Serve at once.

CAROTTES PAUL-BAYLE ** (for 5–6 persons)

Ingredients:

¾–1 kg. carrots (1½–2 lb.)
1 large onion
2 yolks of egg
2 lumps sugar
1 dl. olive oil (½ gill)

1 tablespoon plain flour
2–3 tablespoons finely chopped
   parsley
1 tablespoon wine vinegar
seasoning

Method: Wash and peel or scrape the carrots and slice them thinly. Peel the onion and chop it finely. Make the oil hot in a pan, add the carrots and cook them gently over a very low heat. Keep them well stirred. When they are three parts cooked, make a small well in the centre and place the chopped onion in this. Leave a moment or two and when the onion begins to turn gold, mix it all well together with a wooden spoon. Stir in the flour carefully, then add ½ l. (¾ pint) hot water. Season well, add the sugar and parsley. Cover the mixture with greaseproof paper and the lid and simmer over a gentle heat until the onion and carrots are quite tender. Just before serving, beat the yolks with the vinegar. Pour in a little of the vegetable liquor, stir well and return to the pan. Heat gently without boiling, stirring the mixture carefully. Adjust the seasoning. Serve at once.

CAROTTES VALENTIGNEY * (for 6 persons)

Ingredients:

¾–1 kg. new carrots (1½ lb.)
90 g. butter (3 oz.)
30 g. castor sugar (1 oz.)
200 g. Patna rice (7 oz.)

60 g. grated Gruyère cheese (2 oz.)
1–2 tablespoons browned breadcrumbs
seasoning

Method: Wash and scrape the carrots. Slice them thinly. Heat 60 g. (2 oz.) of the butter in a saucepan, add the carrots, stir them over a low heat until they are well coated in the butter. Pour on sufficient boiling water to cover them, season well and add the sugar. Cook them gently in an un-covered pan until all the water has evaporated and the carrots are soft.

Meanwhile cook the rice in boiling salted water for approximately 15 minutes. When it is ready, drain it, refresh it in hot water, drain it again and keep it hot. When the carrots are tender mix them with the rice and half the grated cheese. Use a fork to ensure that the rice stays fluffy. Taste and season. Put this mixture into a greased fireproof dish. Cover the surface with a mixture of the remaining cheese and the browned crumbs.

Melt the rest of the butter and sprinkle it over the top. Put the dish in the top of a hot oven, gas mark 8 or 450° F. (230° C.) or under a hot grill to brown the top. Serve very hot.

CÉLERIS À LA GRECQUE * (for 5-6 persons)

Ingredients:

3-4 heads of celery
20 tiny onions
1 large tomato
¼ l. white wine (1½ gills)
bouquet garni
juice of ½ lemon

3 tablespoons oil
1½ dl. stock (1 gill)
seasoning
To finish:
½ lemon cut into thin slices
finely chopped parsley

Method: Remove the discoloured outside sticks of the celery. Scrape the remainder, wash it well and cut it into lengths of about 3 inches. Peel the onions. Blanch the celery for 5-6 minutes in boiling salted water, then refresh it in cold water and drain well. Place it in the bottom of a thick pan with the onions, the roughly chopped tomato and the bouquet garni. Pour in all the other ingredients. Season well, using a good proportion of pepper. Boil rapidly until the vegetables are tender. Remove the bouquet garni.

Arrange the celery down the length of a long dish with the onions round the sides. Pour the liquor over the top. Cut the remaining half lemon into thin slices and arrange it on top of the celery. Sprinkle with chopped parsley and serve very cold indeed.

Comment: This is served as a cold hors d'œuvres and is preferred by some, as it has less oil than Champignons à la Grecque.

CÉLERIS-RAVES EN PURÉE * (for 4 persons)

Ingredients:

2 medium sized roots of celeriac
3-4 medium sized potatoes
½ l. approx. well flavoured stock
  (½-¾ pint)

75 g. butter (2½ oz.)
1½ dl. milk (1 gill)
seasoning

Method: Scrub the potatoes, prick them well with a fork. Bake them in a moderate oven, gas mark 4-5 or 350-375° F. (175-190° C.) until they are tender.

Whilst they are cooking, wash and peel the celeriac. Cut them into even sized pieces and cook them in the stock. Drain them and pass through a sieve or vegetable mill. Skin the potatoes and sieve them also. Place both mixtures in a pan. Add half the butter, stirring well. Add sufficient hot milk to make a creamy purée. Beat well over a gentle heat. Season, and lastly beat in the remainder of the butter. Pile up in a hot dish. Serve at once.

CHAMPIGNONS À LA BELLE GIRONDINE **

(for 4–5 persons)

Ingredients:
½ kg. mushrooms (1 lb.)
5 tablespoons oil
45 g. butter (1½ oz.)
2 cloves garlic
2 or 3 large sprigs of parsley

4–5 tablespoons chopped chives
seasoning
To finish:
fleurons of Pâte Feuilletée (see
   page 337)

Method: Cut the mushrooms into slices, put them into a bowl and pour over 4 tablespoons of the oil. Season well. Allow them to macerate for approximately 2 hours. At the end of this time, put the mushrooms and the oil, together with the butter, into a saucepan. Cover with greaseproof paper and the lid and cook over a gentle heat for 15 minutes.

Crush the garlic with a little salt. Chop the parsley and the chives finely. Pour the remaining spoonful of oil into a pan and heat it gently, stir in the chives and parsley and warm them through for 2–3 minutes.

Lift the mushrooms on to a hot serving dish and keep them hot, whilst reducing their cooking liquor by half. Then add the herbs to the reduced liquor, taste and season. Pour it over the mushrooms and arrange the fleurons around the edge of the dish. Serve hot.

FEUILLETÉES AUX CHAMPIGNONS **

(for 2–3 persons)

Ingredients:
Flaky Pastry (see page 335)
For the Filling:
90 g. mushrooms (3 oz.)
90 g. bacon (3 oz.)
30 g. butter (1 oz.)
1 tablespoon chopped parsley
1 tablespoon chopped onion
seasoning

For the Sauce:
15 g. butter (½ oz.)
15 g. plain flour (½ oz.)
1 small egg
1½ dl. milk (1 gill)
seasoning

Method: Make up the flaky pastry in the usual way and put it aside to relax.

Wipe the mushrooms, chop them fairly finely and cut the bacon into dice. Heat the butter in a small pan. Put in the bacon and the finely chopped onion. Cook over a gentle heat for 5 minutes, stirring all the time. Now stir in the mushrooms. Season and cover with a piece of greaseproof paper and the lid. Cook gently for a further 5 minutes, shaking the pan from time to time.

Prepare the sauce – melt the butter in a pan, draw from the heat and add the flour. Return the pan to the heat and stir well for 2–3 minutes. Stir in the milk gradually, bring it slowly to the boil, keeping it well stirred, then simmer for 5 minutes. Season well. Remove the pan from the heat. Beat the egg, reserving a little of it to brush over. Stir the rest with the mushroom mixture into the sauce. Taste and adjust the seasoning. Allow it to get quite cold.

Roll out the pastry ½ cm. (¼ inch) thick. Cut it into squares of approximately 12 cm. (5 inches). Divide the filling into as many equal portions as there are pieces of pastry. Place a portion in the centre of each piece. Moisten all the edges and fold up the four corners to meet in the centre, pinching the edges well to make them stand up and adhere. Mix the remainder of the egg with a teaspoon of water and brush it over the pastries. Cook in a hot oven, gas mark 7 or 425° F. (220° C.) for 15–20 minutes. Serve hot or cold.

Comment: These make useful snacks for picnics. This quantity makes 5–6.

CHOUFLEUR À LA MIRABEAU ** (for 3–4 persons)

Ingredients:

1 firm white cauliflower
240 g. French beans (½ lb.)
120 g. tin tunny fish (4 oz.)
100 g. unsalted butter (3½ oz.)
2 tablespoons thick Sauce Mayonnaise (see page 36)

12 green olives
2 tablespoons olive oil
juice of a lemon
2–3 tablespoons finely chopped chervil
seasoning

Method: Wash the cauliflower well in salted water and divide it into flowerets. Cook them gently in boiling salted water until they are just tender but still firm. Prepare the French beans, cut them into lozenge shapes and cook them also in boiling salted water. When they are cooked, drain both vegetables and dry them on a clean cloth.

Sieve the tunny fish with the butter. Beat well with a wooden spatula, then stir in the well seasoned sauce Mayonnaise. Pile the mixture up in the centre of a large round dish and decorate with olives, previously stoned. Round this mixture arrange the French beans, sprinkling them with a little oil to give them a glossy appearance. Mix the remaining oil with the lemon juice.

Now arrange the flowerets of cauliflower round the edge of the dish. Sprinkle them with the lemon juice and oil and dust them with the finely chopped chervil. Serve very cold. (*See Plate 15.*)

CHOUFLEUR À LA PONT DE CÉAISE * (for 3–4 persons)

Ingredients:
1 good sized cauliflower
120 g. grated Gruyère cheese
  (4 oz.)
120 g. chopped ham (4 oz.)

double quantity Sauce Tomate,
  Method I (see page 38)
30–60 g. butter (1–2 oz.)
white breadcrumbs
seasoning

Method: Wash the cauliflower well and divide it into flowerets. Cook these in boiling salted water until they are firm, but not in any way broken. Drain them on a clean dry cloth and season them well.

Butter a fireproof dish and sprinkle the bottom with grated Gruyère cheese. Cover with half the cauliflower then half the ham, then a layer of sauce tomate and a good sprinkling of grated cheese. Now repeat the process using the rest of the cauliflower, ham, grated cheese and finishing with a thick covering of sauce tomate. Cover with white breadcrumbs and place knobs of butter on the top. Put in the top of a fairly hot oven, gas mark 6 or 400° F. (200° C.) for ¼ hour to brown the top.

CHOUFLEUR MONTOIS ** (for 4–6 persons)

Ingredients:
1 good sized cauliflower
½ kg. potatoes made into Pommes
  de Terre Mousseline (see page
  228) (1 lb.)

60 g. butter (2 oz.)
4 eggs
seasoning
To serve:
Sauce Hollandaise (see page 35)

Method: Wash the cauliflower well and remove the outside leaves. Cook it in boiling salted water for 15–20 minutes. When it is just tender, drain it well and pass it through a sieve or vegetable mill. Return it to a clean pan and stir in the butter over a good heat. Make the Pommes de Terre Mousseline as usual and mix it with the cauliflower purée. Season well. Remove it from the heat. Whisk the eggs and beat them into the purée.

Pour the mixture into a buttered 15 cm. (6 inch) charlotte mould or cake tin. Stand it in a bain-marie or roasting tin containing boiling water and bake it for 1 hour in a moderate oven, gas mark 5 or 375° F. (190° C.). When it is cooked unmould it carefully in a hot dish and serve at once with a sauceboat of sauce Hollandaise.

CHOUFLEUR NORMANDE ** (for 2–3 persons)

Ingredients:
1 small cauliflower
240 g. cooking apples (½ lb.)

120 g. butter (4 oz.)
lemon juice
seasoning

Method: Wash the cauliflower and divide it into flowerets, discarding the stalk. Cook them carefully in boiling salted water for 10 minutes. Drain them well. Meanwhile peel the apples and cut them into slices about ½ cm. (¼ inch) thick. Heat half the butter in a pan and sauter the apple slices in this, allowing them to cook slowly for about 20 minutes. Heat the rest of the butter in a second pan, and rissoler the flowerets carefully in this without breaking them. Season well.

Mix the flowerets and apple slices carefully together. Sprinkle with lemon juice, rectify the seasoning and serve at once.

Comment: This recipe is especially good served with pork or veal.

CROÛTES À LA DUBARRY * (for 3 or 6 persons)

Ingredients:
1 medium sized cauliflower
Sauce Béchamel, made with 45 g.
 (1½ oz.) flour, 45 g. (1½ oz.)
 butter, 3 dl. (½ pint) milk (see
 page 34 for method)

6 slices of toasted bread
30–60 g. grated Gruyère cheese
 (1–2 oz.)
pinch of nutmeg
seasoning

Method: Wash the cauliflower and divide it into flowerets. Cook it in boiling salted water for 15 minutes. Make the sauce Béchamel. When the cauliflower is cooked, drain it well and pass it through a sieve or vegetable mill. Mix it with the sauce Béchamel. Season very well, adding a pinch of nutmeg.

Cut the slices of toast into 10 cm. (4 inch) circles and spread the mixture on these. Cover with a thick layer of grated cheese. Arrange the croûtes in a well buttered fireproof dish. Place it in the top of a hot oven, gas mark 7 or 425° F. (220° C.) or under the grill until the tops are well browned. Serve very hot.

PAIN DE CHOUFLEUR ** (for 4–5 persons)

Ingredients:
1 cauliflower
2 eggs
1 yolk of egg
thick Sauce Béchamel (see page
 34) made with 45 g. (1½ oz.)

flour, 45 g. (1½ oz.) butter,
3 dl. (½ pint) milk, seasoning
and pinch of nutmeg
To finish:
Sauce Tomate (Method I) (see
 page 38)

Method: Wash the cauliflower and remove the hard stalk and outside leaves. Cook it in a pan of boiling salted water for 20–25 minutes. Drain it very well and pass it through a sieve or vegetable mill.

Make the sauce Béchamel in the usual way. Beat in the eggs and yolk and season it very well, adding a pinch of nutmeg. Mix it with the cauliflower purée and pour it into a well buttered charlotte mould or 15 cm. (6 inch) cake tin.

Stand it in a bain-marie or in a roasting tin containing boiling water and bake it in a moderate oven, gas mark 5 or 375° F. (190° C.) for 40 minutes. When it is cooked unmould it in a hot serving dish and pour over a well flavoured sauce tomate.

COURGETTES À LA LYONNAISE * (for 5–6 persons)

Ingredients:
2 large courgettes or 1 medium
   sized marrow
120 g. grated cheese (4 oz.)

240 g. onions (½ lb.)
60 g. butter (2 oz.)
seasoning

Method: Peel the courgettes or marrow and cut into slices about one centimetre (½ inch) thick. Remove the centre pith and seeds very carefully. Cook in boiling salted water for 12–15 minutes or until they are just done, lift carefully and drain on a clean cloth. Slice the onions very thinly. Heat the butter in a pan. Cook the onions in this over a low heat until they are soft and transparent looking. Do not let them brown. Well butter a fireproof dish. Cover with a layer of the cooked courgettes, sprinkle with grated cheese, season well. Place a layer of onions on the top. Repeat in this way until the dish is full. Finish with a layer of grated cheese. Put it in the top of a fairly hot oven, gas mark 8 or 450° F. (230° C.) for about 10 minutes or until the top is browned. Serve hot.

Comment: If it is possible to use Gruyère cheese for this dish the flavour will be much improved.

COURGETTES À L'ITALIENNE * (for 4–6 persons)

Ingredients:
4 courgettes of equal size
1½ dl. olive oil (1 gill)
2 large onions
1 clove garlic
460 g. ripe tomatoes (1 lb.)

bouquet garni containing thyme,
   bayleaf, and a sprig of basil
90 g. grated Gruyère cheese (3 oz.)
seasoned flour
seasoning

Method: Wash and dry the courgettes and cut them in half lengthwise. Dip them in seasoned flour.

Make half the oil hot in a sauté pan. Gently fry both sides of the courgettes in this. Drain them and keep them hot in a hot fireproof dish.

Add the remaining oil to the pan and thoroughly soften the onions, which have been sliced into thin rings. Remove eight of the best rings and put them aside for the garnish. Add to the pan the tomatoes, skinned and pipped, the garlic crushed with salt and the bouquet garni. Allow the mixture to simmer until the tomatoes are quite soft. Taste and season well. Remove the bouquet garni. Pour this mixture over the courgettes and sprinkle the top evenly with the grated Gruyère cheese. Place the dish in the top of a hot oven, gas mark 6–7 or 400–425° F. (200–220° C.) for 10–15 minutes or until the top is browned. Just before serving, arrange two onion rings on the top of each courgette.

COURGETTES AU LARD *   (for 4–5 persons)

Ingredients:
1 kg. courgettes (2 lb.)
¼ l. olive oil (1½ gills)
30 g. butter (1 oz.)
8 slices streaky bacon
1 onion

1 bayleaf
1 sprig thyme
seasoning
To finish:
finely chopped parsley

Method: Wash the courgettes. Cut them into fairly thick slices. Drain them, and dry them thoroughly. Chop the onion very finely. Heat the oil in a sauté pan, add the bayleaf, thyme and the courgettes. Stir them carefully to coat them in the oil. Lower the heat and continue to cook, stirring from time to time, for 10 minutes. Now add the onion, season and cook for a further 10 minutes, or until the vegetables are soft. Remove the bayleaf and thyme.

Cut the rind off the bacon. Fry the rashers in the butter until they are crisp.

To Serve: Arrange the courgettes and onion in a hot vegetable dish. Lay the rashers of bacon on the top. Sprinkle over with the parsley and serve at once.

COURGETTES AUX POIS ET AU LARD *   (for 4–6 persons)

Ingredients:
3 good sized courgettes
170 g. lean bacon (6 oz.)
2 small onions
1½ kg. peas (3 lb.)

60 g. butter (2 oz.)
1½ dl. white stock (1 gill)
bouquet garni
a little oil
seasoning

Method: Peel the courgettes and cook them in boiling salted water for 15 minutes according to their size. Drain them well. Make the oil hot in a pan, 'rissoler' them in the oil. Keep them hot.

Whilst this is taking place, cut the bacon into lardons and chop the onions finely. Heat the butter in a pan and put in the bacon and the onions and cook them gently until the onions are soft but not coloured, then add the peas and the stock, together with the bouquet garni. Cover with thickly buttered greaseproof paper and the lid and cook over a low heat for 15 minutes, shaking the pan from time to time. (If the peas are old, a little longer will be needed for cooking as well as a little more stock.) Put the courgettes into the pan with the peas, etc. Taste and adjust the seasoning. Remove the bouquet garni. When the courgettes have heated through serve at once in a hot dish.

COURGETTES FARCIS AUX CHAMPIGNONS *

(for 4 persons)

Ingredients:
2 courgettes or 1 medium sized thick marrow
thick Sauce Béchamel made with 45 g. (1½ oz.) flour and 45 g. (1½ oz.) butter to 3 dl. (½ pint) milk (see page 34 for method)

120–180 g. mushrooms (4–6 oz.)
a little lemon juice
60 g. butter (2 oz.)
seasoning
To finish: a little grated cheese

Method: Peel the courgettes or marrow, cut them in half lengthwise and remove the pips and the pith. Cook the courgettes in boiling salted water and boil them until they are just done, but still firm. Lift them carefully on to a clean cloth to drain.

Meanwhile, cut the mushrooms into ½ cm. (¼ inch) slices. Melt the butter in a pan. Add the mushrooms, seasoning and lemon juice. Cover with greaseproof paper and the lid to cook over a gentle heat for 5–7 minutes, shaking the pan from time to time.

Make up the sauce Béchamel in the usual way – it must be of a thick consistency and well seasoned.

Mix two-thirds of the sauce Béchamel with the mushrooms and the liquor they were cooked in. Fill this mixture into one half of each courgette and cover with the other half. Arrange them in a well buttered dish. Pour the rest of the sauce over the top and sprinkle with the finely grated cheese. Put in the top of a hot oven, gas mark 7–8 or 425–450° F. (220–230° C.), or under a hot grill to brown the top slightly. Serve hot either as a vegetable dish or as an entrée.

COURGETTES VENITIENNE *

(for 4–6 persons)

Ingredients:
1 kg. courgettes (2 lb.)
1 small tin tunny fish
120 g. cottage cheese (¼ lb.)
120 g. fresh white breadcrumbs (4 oz.)

3 tablespoons dry white wine
oil
chopped parsley
seasoning

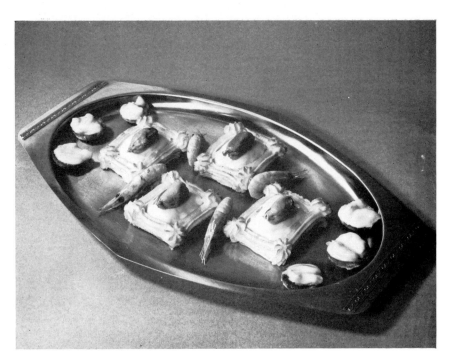

1. Filets de Sole à la Duchesse
(see page 95)

2. Casserolettes de Filets de Sole
(see page 93)

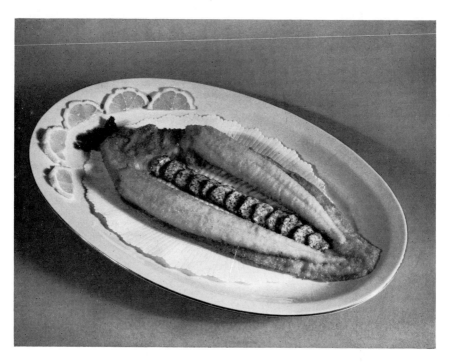

3. Sole Colbert
(see page 102)

4. Sole Braisée Champenois
(see page 103)

5. Filets de Sole Carmelite
(see page 97)

6. Paupiettes de Veau à la Richelieu
(see page 147)

7. Entrecôte à la Mirabeau
(see page 121)

8. Canard aux Fruits
(see page 167)

9. Poulet Archiduc
(see page 181)

10. Poulet 'Bonne Vieille'
(see page 182)

11. Faisan aux Canneberges
(see page 170)

12. Poule à la Louisiane
(see page 175)

13. *Pommes de Terre*

Château   Cocotte

Pont Neuf   Noisette   Paille

Allumettes

14. *Pommes de Terre*

Brioche   Duchesse

Dauphine   Lorette

15. Choufleur à la Mirabeau
(see page 203)

16. Condé de Tomates
(see page 238)

17. Vacherin: Method
(see pages 277*f*)

18. Vacherin à l'Ananas
(see page 277)

19. Charlotte aux Fraises
(see page 287)

20. Gâteau Bissextile
(see page 297)

21. Poires Brillat Savarin
(see page 302)

22. Mousse au Citron et au Caramel
(see page 288)

23. Fromage de Brie
(see page 364)

24. Gâteau Fragaria
(see page 371)

25. Gâteau Nougatine
(see page 378)

26. Gâteau à l'Ananas Tourangelle
(see page 366)

27. Gâteau Thérésa
(see page 381)

28. Petites Religieuses
(see page 360)

29. Gâteau Grand Armée
(see page 373)

30. Gâteau au Chocolat Saint Philippe du Roule
(see page 367)

31. Gâteau Faidherbe
(see page 370)

32. Gâteau d'Automne de Sarlat
(see page 366)

Method: Cut the courgettes in half lengthwise and remove the seeds. Soak the breadcrumbs in the white wine and mix them with the tunny fish, the cheese, parsley and seasoning. Fill the halved courgettes with this stuffing and re-form them. Lay them in a fireproof dish, brush them with oil and bake them in a moderate oven, gas mark 4 or 350° F. (175° C.) for half an hour. Serve hot.

CONCOMBRES FARCIES *   (for 2–3 persons)

Ingredients:
1 large cucumber
45 g. butter (1½ oz.)
1 small clove garlic
2 tablespoons finely chopped
   onion
1 tablespoon finely chopped ham
1 tablespoon finely chopped
   tongue
120 g. finely chopped mushrooms
   (4 oz.)

1 dessertspoon white breadcrumbs
1 tablespoon finely chopped fresh
   herbs
1 teaspoon plain flour
a little grated cheese
seasoning
To finish:
Sauce Tomate (Method II) (see
   page 39)

Method: Cut the cucumber in half and then cut it again lengthwise. Scoop out the pith and seeds and place the four pieces in a well buttered roasting tin.

Heat the butter in a pan, add the onion and cook it gently until it is soft and transparent looking. Now add the garlic, crushed with a little salt, together with the ham, tongue, mushrooms, flour, breadcrumbs and herbs. Continue cooking for a few minutes over a low heat, allowing just enough time for the mushrooms to soften. Season.

Pile the farce on top of each piece of cucumber. Sprinkle with grated cheese. Cook in the top of a fairly hot oven, gas mark 6 or 400° F. (200° C.) for 15–20 minutes, or until well browned. Serve hot in a hot dish with a well seasoned sauce tomate poured round.

ENDIVES À LA MEUNIÈRE *   (for 2–3 persons)

Ingredients:
2–3 heads chicory
60 g. butter (2 oz.)
juice of ½ lemon
seasoning

To finish:
beurre noisette made with 45–
   60 g. (1½–2 oz.) butter (see page
   33)

Method: Wash the chicory in several waters removing any damaged leaves. Place the chicory in a saucepan of cold salted water, bring it to the boil and boil it for 5 minutes. Remove and drain it well. Lay it in the bottom of a hot fireproof dish. Melt the butter and pour it over the chicory. Strain the lemon juice and sprinkle it over the top. Season well. Cover with buttered greaseproof paper and cook in a moderate oven, gas mark 5 or 375° F. (190° C.) for about 20–25 minutes. At the end of this time the chicory should be fairly dry and beginning to brown slightly. Arrange the chicory on a clean hot dish. Pour the beurre noisette over the top and serve at once.

SOUFFLÉ D'ENDIVES À LA POMPADOUR ***

(for 4 persons)

Ingredients:

6 heads chicory

For the Soufflé:

100 g. butter (3½ oz.)

1½ dl. milk (1 gill)

1 tablespoon thick cream

Sauce Béchamel made with 1½ dl. (1 gill) milk, 20 g. (¾ oz.) plain flour, 20 g. (¾ oz.) butter (see page 34)

2 teaspoons concentrated tomato purée

6 eggs

seasoning and a pinch of sugar

For the Sauce Pompadour:

2 tablespoons Sauce Béchamel (see page 34)

1 tablespoon concentrated tomato purée

4 yolks of egg

60 g. butter (2 oz.)

3 tablespoons thick cream

60 g. chopped truffle (optional) (2 oz.)

Method: Take the chicory, separate the leaves and wash them well. Do not soak them in the water as this develops a bitter flavour.

Place in a saucepan, the butter, hot milk, chicory and thick cream. Season well adding a pinch of sugar. Simmer gently, keeping stirred, until the chicory is tender. Add the thick sauce Béchamel mixed with the tomato purée. Stir well and allow to reduce over a moderate heat until the mixture is thick. Sieve the mixture through a nylon or hair sieve. (It is not advisable to use a metal one as it will cause discolouration.)

Separate the eggs, add the yolks, one at a time, to the purée and mix well. Season. Whisk the egg whites very stiffly and fold them lightly into the purée. Pour the mixture into a buttered 18 cm. (7 inch) soufflé dish. Wipe round the edges carefully to prevent unsightly browning. Cook in a moderate oven, gas mark 5 or 375° F. (190° C.) for 20–25 minutes.

Meanwhile prepare the sauce. Put into a saucepan the 2 tablespoons sauce Béchamel, tomato purée and egg yolks. Whisk well and then stir over a low heat to thicken the mixture, without allowing it to come to boiling point (great care is required here).

Remove the mixture from the heat and whisk in the butter a little at a time. Add the cream and the chopped truffle. Whisk all well together to obtain a foaming sauce. Colour with a drop of carmine if necessary.

When the soufflé is cooked remove from the oven and coat the top with a little of the sauce. Hand the remainder of the sauce separately. Serve at once.

Comment: For economy, the truffle may be replaced by chopped cooked mushroom, but the flavour will be in no way comparable.

ÉPINARDS À LA VIEILLE MODE *   (for 3–4 persons)

Ingredients:
250 g. spinach (½ lb.)
250 g. chicory (½ lb.)
250 g. dandelion leaves (½ lb.)
250 g. watercress (½ lb.)
½ l. Sauce Béchamel (see page 34) (¾ pint)
seasoning

Method: Remove the hard stalks from the spinach and wash all the vegetables well in several waters. Cook them in a large pan of boiling salted water for 5–7 minutes. Remove and refresh them in cold water. Squeeze to remove excess moisture. Put them in a dish which has been well greased with butter and pour over the well seasoned sauce Béchamel. Put in a moderate oven, gas mark 5 or 375° F. (190° C.) for 10 minutes. Serve hot.

Comment: This recipe is an excellent way of cooking spinach. The dandelion leaves and the chicory impart a very piquant flavour.

ÉPINARDS AU GRATIN *   (for 3–4 persons)

Ingredients:
1 kg. spinach (2 lb.)
thick Sauce Béchamel made with 60 g. (2 oz.) flour, 60 g. (2 oz.) butter and ½ l. (¾ pint) milk (see page 34)
30 g. butter (1 oz.)
2 eggs
120 g. grated Gruyère cheese (4 oz.)
seasoning
To finish:
browned crumbs

Method: Wash the spinach in several waters, removing the hard stalks and cook it in boiling salted water until tender – this will be about 7–10 minutes. When it is cooked refresh it in cold water and squeeze it to remove all excess moisture. Chop it roughly.

Make a very well seasoned sauce Béchamel. Pour this sauce into the bottom of a hot fireproof dish. Keep it hot. Melt the butter in a pan, add the spinach and toss it gently in this until it is well coated, then draw it aside from the heat. Beat the eggs with three-quarters of the cheese, season and add them to the spinach little by little, stirring all the time. Taste again, season well. Spread the spinach on the top of the sauce. Cover with browned crumbs and the rest of the cheese. Cook in the top of a hot oven, gas mark 7 or 425° F. (220° C.) for 5–10 minutes to heat through and brown the top. Serve very hot.

HARICOTS VERTS À LA LYONNAISE * (for 2–3 persons)

Ingredients:
500 g. French beans (1 lb.)
2 large onions
3–4 tablespoons olive oil
1 tablespoon finely chopped chives

1 tablespoon finely chopped
  parsley
1–2 tablespoons vinegar
seasoning

Method: Top and tail the beans and cut them into 'lozenges'. Cook them in boiling salted water for 10 minutes. Drain well.

Peel the onions and cut them into very thin slices. Heat the oil in a sauté pan. Add the onions and soften them over a low heat. Stir frequently. When they are soft and transparent, add the beans and continue to cook in the oil for a further 5 minutes, shaking the pan from time to time. Add the chives, parsley and seasoning. Lift the beans and onions from the pan with a draining spoon and pile them up in a hot serving dish. Pour the vinegar into the pan. Swill it round, taste and season if necessary, then pour it over the beans and serve at once.

HARICOTS VERTS À LA TOURANGELLE *

(for 6–8 persons)

Ingredients:
1 kg. French beans (2 lb.)
Sauce Béchamel – thin consistency,
  made with 30 g. (1 oz.) flour,
  30 g. (1 oz.) butter and ½ l. (¾ pint)
  milk (see page 34 for method)

1 clove garlic
seasoning
To finish:
finely chopped parsley

Method: Make up the sauce Béchamel in the usual way. Season well. Top and tail the beans and if they are young cook them whole in boiling salted water. If, however, they are past their best, cut them into two or three pieces. At the end of 7–8 minutes, drain off the water and mix the beans with the sauce Béchamel, adding the clove of garlic crushed with a little salt. Return to the saucepan, cover with greaseproof paper and the lid and continue cooking for a further 15–20 minutes, or until the beans are tender.

Serve in the sauce in a hot vegetable dish, sprinkled with finely chopped parsley.

HARICOTS VERTS EN COCOTTE * (for 4–5 persons)

Ingredients:
750 g. French beans (1½ lb.)
120–150 g. streaky bacon (4–5 oz.)
2–3 large tomatoes

2–3 tablespoons finely chopped
  parsley
3 dl. white stock, approx. (½ pint)
seasoning

Method: Top and tail the beans and if they are large cut them in two. Cut the bacon into lardons. Skin and pip the tomatoes and cut them into dice.

Well butter a fireproof dish. Put in the bacon and the beans, together with the tomatoes. Season them well and sprinkle with the finely chopped parsley. Fill the dish three-quarters full with white stock. Cover with greaseproof paper and cook in a moderate oven, gas mark 5 or 375° F. (190° C.) for 1–1½ hours. Remove the greaseproof paper and serve hot.

HARICOTS VERTS LIÉS ** (for 3–4 persons)

Ingredients:
½ kg. French beans (1 lb.) 1 tablespoon finely chopped parsley
60 g. butter (2 oz.) 2 yolks of egg
30 g. plain flour (1 oz.) 2 tablespoons thick cream
3 dl. white stock, approx. (½ pint) pinch of nutmeg
 seasoning

Method: Top and tail the beans and if they are rather large, cut them in half. Put them to cook in boiling salted water. When they are just cooked, drain them and refresh them in cold water. Drain again.

While the beans are cooking, melt the butter in a fairly large pan, remove it from the heat and stir in the flour. Return it to the stove and cook the roux for 2–3 minutes. Stir in the stock and parsley and cook for 5 minutes, stirring all the time, then add the beans and mix them in carefully. Season, adding a pinch of nutmeg.

Whisk the yolks with the cream and mix in a little of the sauce, then stir them in to the beans in the pan. Heat gently without allowing the sauce to boil, stirring all the time until it thickens slightly. Serve at once in a hot vegetable dish.

LAITUES BRAISÉES ** (for 2–3 persons)

Ingredients:
1 or 2 large cos lettuce 1 carrot
90 g. cooked meat, veal, beef or 30 g. butter (1 oz.)
  pork (3 oz.) 3 dl. stock (½ pint)
3–4 slices fat bacon bouquet garni
1 shallot seasoning
1 egg **To finish:**
1 small onion finely chopped parsley

Method: Remove the outer green leaves. Wash the lettuces in water to which a little vinegar has been added and then cook them in boiling salted water for 5 minutes. At the end of this time, remove them from the pan and refresh them in a bowl of cold water, then press them lightly with the hands to remove excess moisture.

Mince the meat and the shallot. Mix and season very well and bind with a little beaten egg.

Make an incision in the lettuces and fill them with the farce. Press the leaves together again and tie the slices of bacon round them with string. Heat the butter in a sauté pan, put in the lettuces with the sliced onion and carrot. Cook over a low heat to rissoler the lettuces slightly. Pour in the stock, add the bouquet garni and cover with greaseproof paper and the lid. Cook in a fairly hot oven, gas mark 6 or 400° F. (200° C.) for 10–15 minutes. When the lettuces are cooked, remove them from the pan to a hot serving dish. Remove the strings, and keep them hot. Strain the liquor into a clean pan and reduce it over a good heat to about half its volume. Pour it over the lettuces and sprinkle with finely chopped parsley. Serve at once.

LAITUES MIMOSA *   (for 2–3 persons)

Ingredients:
1 cos lettuce
2 hard boiled eggs

1½ dl. Sauce Vinaigrette (see page 40) (1 gill)
seasoning

Method: Wash the lettuce, separate the leaves and tear the larger ones into two or three pieces. Dry well. Make the sauce vinaigrette. Shell the eggs and separate the whites from the yolks. Chop the white finely and sieve the yolks. Pour the sauce vinaigrette into a salad bowl, stir in the chopped white of egg and allow it to macerate for a full 10 minutes. Then put in the lettuce and turn it carefully, using two forks, until it is well coated in the dressing. Sprinkle the sieved yolks of egg on the top, mix gently and serve at once.

POIREAUX À LA GRECQUE *   (for 4 persons)

Ingredients:
8–10 very young leeks
juice of 1 lemon
3 dl. white stock (½ pint)
1½ dl. dry white wine (1 gill)
1 tomato

1 bayleaf
12 small onions
1½ dl. olive oil (1 gill)
seasoning
To finish:
finely chopped parsley

Method: Remove the outer green leaves from the leeks and discard them. Wash the leeks well. Peel the onions. Cut the tomato into quarters. Put the leeks, onions and all the other ingredients into a saucepan. Season well. Cover the pan with a lid, bring to the boil and cook quickly over a good heat for approximately 8 minutes, or until the leeks and onions are tender. Remove from the heat and allow it to become quite cold. Remove the bayleaf. Adjust the seasoning. Arrange the leeks and onions in a shallow serving dish. Pour over the liquor. Sprinkle with the parsley. Serve very cold.

Comment: This makes an excellent hors d'œuvre. More tomato can be added if liked. It is important to use really young leeks. If large ones are used, it is better to cut them into slices.

POIREAUX BÉRENGÈRE *   (for 4 persons)

Ingredients: (½ pint) milk, 30 g. (1 oz.) butter
8 leeks   30 g. (1 oz.) flour (see page 34)
3 hardboiled eggs, sliced   seasoning
1 tablespoon chopped parsley   **To finish:**
Sauce Béchamel made with 3 dl.   sprigs of parsley

Method: Clean and trim the leeks, washing them well in running water. Tie them in two bundles and cook them in a pan of boiling salted water until tender. While the leeks are cooking, make the sauce Béchamel in the usual way and keep it hot.

When the leeks are cooked, drain, remove the string and refresh them quickly in cold water. Drain again thoroughly and squeeze them lightly to remove excess moisture. Arrange them in a buttered fireproof dish, cover them with the sliced hardboiled eggs. Season. Sprinkle with the chopped parsley and then coat all over with the hot sauce Béchamel. Serve hot, garnished with sprigs of parsley at each end of the dish.

POIREAUX BRAISÉS AU GRAS *   (for 6 persons)

Ingredients: well seasoned stock
18 small leeks   seasoning
90 g. butter (3 oz.)   **To finish:**
150 g. lean bacon (5 oz.)   60 g. butter (2 oz.)

Method: Clean and trim the leeks into even lengths. Wash and dry them well. Melt the butter in a fairly large pan. Put in the leeks and allow them to soften in the butter without colouration, turning them carefully. When they are ready, pour over sufficient stock to cover them. Cut the bacon into lardons and add it to the leeks. Cover the pan with a lid, bring to the boil, and simmer for 30–40 minutes. At the end of this time lift the leeks carefully with a draining spoon and arrange them neatly in a hot serving dish. Keep them hot. Reduce the liquor by three-quarters over a good heat. Adjust the seasoning. Pour it over the leeks.

To Finish: Melt the butter and pour it over the leeks also. Serve very hot.

POIREAUX OLIVETTE *   (for 4 persons)

Ingredients:

1 kg. leeks (2 lb.)
3–4 anchovy fillets
1 tablespoon finely chopped thyme
3 tablespoons brandy

240 g. black olives (½ lb.)
1 large teaspoon French mustard
3 tablespoons olive oil
seasoning

Method: Wash and prepare the leeks as usual. Tie them in two bundles and place them in a pan of boiling salted water. Cook them for 15–20 minutes. Remove and refresh them in cold water. Press gently with the hands to dispel the excess moisture. Lay them on a clean cloth to drain. Allow them to get perfectly cold.

Stone the olives. Crush the anchovy fillets with a pestle and mortar, add the olives, the mustard and the thyme. Mix well. Rub this through a fairly coarse sieve, or put it through a vegetable mill. Stir into the purée thus obtained the olive oil and the brandy. Season with a little pepper.

Arrange the leeks in a long serving dish. Spoon the mixture on top. Serve very cold.

OIGNONS FARCIS **   (for 4–6 persons)

Ingredients:

4–6 medium sized onions
½ l. white stock, approx. (1 pint)
60–90 g. butter (2–3 oz.)
white breadcrumbs
seasoning
For the Duxelle:
60 g. butter (2 oz.)
1 dessertspoon oil

1 shallot
¼ small onion
60 g. mushrooms (2 oz.)
pinch nutmeg
seasoning
To finish:
Sauce Demi-glace (see page 34)
finely chopped parsley

Method: Cut off the top quarter and skin the onions. Place them in a pan of cold salted water, bring them slowly to the boil and boil them gently for ¾–1 hour, according to the size of the onions.

Meanwhile make the duxelle – chop the mushrooms finely and squeeze them in a cloth to remove the moisture. Heat the butter and oil in a pan. Finely chop the remaining onion and soften it in the hot fat, browning it lightly. Add the mushrooms and shallot, finely chopped, together with a pinch of nutmeg and seasoning. Continue stirring over a good heat until all the moisture has evaporated.

When the onions are cooked, remove them from the pan and drain them well. With a vegetable ball cutter or teaspoon remove the centres from the onions, leaving about ½ cm. (¼ inch) all round the sides and the bottom. Chop the centres finely. Melt about half the butter in a pan, add the chopped

216

onion and soften it over a low heat. Stir in the duxelle mixture, season well and mix thoroughly. Fill this back into the onion shells. Place them in a well buttered fireproof dish. Pour round enough stock to come half way up the sides of the onions. Cover them with a piece of well buttered greaseproof paper and cook them in a moderate oven, gas mark 5 or 375° F. (190° C.) for a further ½ hour. At the end of this time remove the paper and drain off the stock. Cover the farce with breadcrumbs. Melt the remaining butter and pour it over the top. Return the onions to a hot oven, gas mark 6–7 or 400–425° F. (200–220° C.), until golden brown.

Dish the onions in a hot serving dish. Pour round a well flavoured sauce demi-glace and dust the onions with finely chopped parsley. Serve very hot.

PETITS POIS À L'ESPAGNOLE *   (for 4 persons)

Ingredients:

1 kg. peas (2 lb.)	1 tablespoon oil
2 onions	1 bayleaf
3 tomatoes	seasoning
60 g. butter (2 oz.)	**To finish:**
	finely chopped basil or parsley

Method: Shell the peas. Peel the onions and slice them finely. Skin and pip the tomatoes and cut them into shreds. Heat the butter and oil in a fairly large pan, add the tomatoes, onions and bayleaf. Season. Allow to cook gently over a low heat, without in any way browning. Stir frequently. At the end of about 15 minutes add the peas and mix well. Cover with greaseproof paper and the lid and simmer very gently for 25 minutes or until the vegetables are just ready. Stir them from time to time.

Remove the bayleaf and serve the vegetables in a hot dish, dusted with the basil or parsley.

PETITS POIS AU MADÈRE *   (for 4–6 persons)

Ingredients:

1½ kg. fresh peas (3 lb.)	4 rashers bacon
60 g. butter (2 oz.)	1 teaspoon plain flour
1 onion	1½ dl. Madeira (1 gill)
bouquet garni	seasoning

Method: Heat the butter in a fairly large pan, add the shelled peas together with an onion cut into quarters and the bouquet garni. Cover the whole with a piece of thickly buttered greaseproof paper and the lid. Cook over a very low heat for 15 minutes, shaking the pan from time to time.

Chop the bacon roughly and fry it in a pan until it is crisp. Stir in the flour until it is well mixed with the bacon fat. Pour in the Madeira and bring it to the boil, stirring all the time. Season. Simmer for 1 minute.

When the peas are cooked serve them in a hot dish and remove the onion and the bouquet garni. Pour over the bacon and Madeira sauce. Serve at once.

POIVRONS VERTS FARCIS AU FROMAGE *

(for 6 persons)

Ingredients:
6 green peppers
For the Filling:
240 g. cheese (8 oz.)
2 eggs
60 g. plain flour (2 oz.)

salt
black pepper
pinch of Cayenne
a little milk
a little butter

Method: Wash the peppers, which should be of a good shape and free from blemish or holes. Cut them in halves lengthwise and scoop out the pips and pith. Put them into a pan of cold salted water, bring them to the boil and boil them for 2–3 minutes. Remove and drain them on a dry cloth.

Beat the eggs in a bowl. Grate the cheese and stir two-thirds of it in to the beaten eggs, then add the flour, stirring it in well, and season to taste. Beat with a wooden spoon or spatula adding a little milk if needed (it should be the consistency of thick cream). Arrange the halved peppers, cut side uppermost, in a shallow, buttered fireproof dish. Fill them with the cheese mixture. Sprinkle over the remaining grated cheese and dot with knobs of butter. Cook them in a fairly hot oven, gas mark 6 or 400° F. (200° C.) for ½ hour, by which time the filling will have risen and become crisp and brown on top. Serve at once.

Comment: Serve, if liked, with a well flavoured fresh sauce tomate.

GRATIN DAUPHINOIS **

(for 5–6 persons)

Ingredients:
½ kg. firm potatoes (1 lb.)
30 g. Gruyère cheese (1 oz.)
1–2 eggs

3 dl. milk (½ pint)
good pinch nutmeg
seasoning

Method: Cut the cheese into wafer thin slices. Peel the potatoes and using a very sharp knife, slice them as finely as possible. It is important that the slices should be of uniform thickness, otherwise the potatoes will cook unevenly and the result will be disappointing.

Butter a fireproof dish and lay the rounds of potato very neatly in this, packing them down well. Season well, adding the pinch of nutmeg. Whisk the eggs lightly and pour the milk on to them. Making a small place at the side of the potatoes, strain the egg and milk into the dish. It is advisable not to pour the milk all over the potatoes. Lay the slices of Gruyère cheese over the top. Put the dish in a hot oven, gas mark 6–7 or 400–425° F. (200–220° C.) for approximately 40 minutes. Serve in the dish.

Comment: This is a very well known French method of cooking potatoes. If they are cut correctly it is delicious, but if they are carelessly sliced, the result is most unappetizing.

POMMES DE TERRE ADRIENNE * (for 4 persons)

Ingredients:
3 dozen small new potatoes
1 dozen spring onions
3 rashers streaky bacon

½ l. chicken or veal stock, approx.
(½–¾ pint)
100 g. butter (3½ oz.)
bouquet garni
seasoning

Method: Scrape, or rub the skins off the potatoes. Wash the onions. Cut the bacon into lardons. Place the bacon lardons in a frying pan over a good heat and rissoler them, adding a little butter if needed. Put the bacon, onions and potatoes into a thick pan. Just cover with the stock. Add the bouquet garni, butter and seasoning. Cook over a good heat until nearly all the liquid has evaporated and the vegetables are covered with a light glaze. Remove the bouquet garni and serve at once.

POMMES DE TERRE ALLUMETTES **

The same as for Pommes de Terre Paille (see page 230) except that the potatoes are cut the size of matchsticks. They are used as a garnish. (*See Plate 13.*)

POMMES DE TERRE ANGLAISE or (for 3–4 persons)
POMMES DE TERRE VAPEUR *

Ingredients: salt
700 g. potatoes (1½ lb.)

Method: Wash and peel the potatoes and cut them into even sized olive shapes. Place them in a steamer over boiling water. Sprinkle over with a little salt. Cover with a lid and steam them until tender. They will take half as long again to cook as boiled potatoes, approximately 30–35 minutes. When they are done, remove the steamer, place a dry folded cloth over the potatoes and cover partially with the lid. Leave in a warm place for a few moments before serving.

Comment: New potatoes can be used for this recipe equally well.

POMMES DE TERRE À LA DIJONNAISE *

(for 4 persons)

Ingredients:

1 kg. potatoes (2 lb.)
90 g. butter (3 oz.)
1–2 tablespoons finely chopped
    fresh herbs

30–60 g. unsalted butter (1–2 oz.)
½ dl. thick cream (½ gill)
1 tablespoon Dijon mustard
seasoning

Method: Wash and peel the potatoes and cut them into very thin slices. Make the 90 g. (3 oz.) butter hot in a thick shallow pan. Add the potatoes and sauter them over a good heat, turning them carefully from time to time with a metal spatula or fish slice. When they are lightly brown pour into the pan approximately ¼ l. (1½ gills) of hot water. Season well. Lay a piece of greaseproof paper on the top, cover with the lid and cook the potatoes over a low heat for a further 20 minutes. Meanwhile, beat together the herbs, unsalted butter, cream and mustard in a bowl. Pile the potatoes up in a hot dish. Top with the herb, cream and mustard mixture. Serve at once.

POMMES DE TERRE À LA HORTY *

(for 4–5 persons)

Ingredients:

1 kg. old potatoes (2 lb.)
60 g. butter (2 oz.)
2 tablespoons finely chopped
    parsley
1 large onion

2–3 tablespoons thin cream
3 hardboiled eggs
seasoning
To finish:
a little finely chopped parsley

Method: Peel the potatoes and cut them into even sized pieces. Put them in a pan of cold salted water, bring them to the boil and cook until they are done. Whilst they are cooking, peel and chop the onion finely. Melt the butter in a saucepan. Stir the onion in this over a gentle heat until it is perfectly soft. Do not let it brown in any way. Strain the potatoes, add the onion and pass all together through a vegetable mill or sieve into a hot bowl. Beat in the cream, then the finely chopped parsley. Season well. See that the mixture is creamy and light. Chop the hardboiled eggs finely. Reserving a little chopped egg for decoration, stir them into the potato mixture. Pile it on a serving dish. Sprinkle with chopped parsley and hardboiled egg and serve hot.

POMMES DE TERRE À LA NORMANDE *

(for 4 persons)

Ingredients:

1 kg. potatoes (2 lb.)
120 g. streaky bacon (4 oz.)
3 dl. water or white stock (½ pint)
1 onion

1 leek
3 dl. milk (½ pint)
30 g. butter (1 oz.)
seasoning

Method: Peel the onion and cut it into fine dice. Wash the leek thoroughly and slice the white part finely. Wash and peel the potatoes. Melt the butter in a pan, add the onion and leek and the bacon cut into lardons. Cover with greaseproof paper and the lid and cook slowly without colouration. When the onion is soft, add the potatoes cut into thin slices, the stock or water and the milk. Season well and cook for 30–40 minutes, simmering gently. When the potatoes are done, remove from the heat, taste and season, and place them in a hot serving dish.

POMMES DE TERRE À LA PARISIENNE **

(for 3–4 persons)

Ingredients:

700 g. potatoes (1½ lb.)
60–90 g. butter (2–3 oz.)
glace de viande (see page 21)

seasoning
To finish:
finely chopped parsley

Method: Select large potatoes if possible. Wash and peel them and, using a small vegetable ball cutter, scoop out small balls. Place them in a sauce-pan containing cold salted water. Bring them to the boil and boil for 2–3 minutes. Drain well and dry them on a clean dry cloth.

Heat the butter in a shallow pan and when it begins to turn a nutty colour, add the potatoes and seasoning. Place the lid on the pan and cook the potatoes, shaking the pan to prevent them from sticking: this will probably take about 5 minutes. Pour off any excess butter from the pan. Add 1–2 tablespoons of glace de viande and coat the potatoes in this. Season. Dust with finely chopped parsley and serve at once.

Comment: These potatoes are usually used as a garnish for suitable meat or fish dishes.

POMMES DE TERRE À LA TRIPE *

(for 4 persons)

Ingredients:

1 kg. potatoes (2 lb.)
½ kg. onions (1 lb.)
Sauce Béchamel (see page 34)

1½ dl. thick cream (1 gill)
60 g. butter (2 oz.)
seasoning

Method: Choose potatoes of the same size. Peel them and boil them in the usual way.

Whilst they are cooking, peel the onions and cut them into rings. Melt the butter in a pan, add the onions, season well and soften them over a low heat, without allowing them to brown. Make the sauce Béchamel.

When the potatoes are just cooked, remove them and drain them well. Cut them into thin slices and, using a fork, stir them gently into the sauce Béchamel, which must be hot. Taste and season. Add the onions and the butter to the potatoes and lastly stir in the cream. Heat gently and pour into a hot serving dish. Serve hot.

POMMES DE TERRE AU PAPRIKA * (for 4–6 persons)

Ingredients:
1 kg. potatoes (2 lb.)
2 medium sized tomatoes
3 medium onions

2 teaspoons paprika
3 tablespoons oil
stock
seasoning

Method: Peel the onions and chop them finely. Heat the oil in a large pan, add the onions and soften them over a low heat without allowing them to brown. Skin and pip the tomatoes and cut them into shreds. Add them, with the paprika, to the onions.

Peel the potatoes, slice them thinly and add them to the onion and tomato mixture. Pour over sufficient hot stock to cover. Season well. Cover with greaseproof paper and the lid of the pan and cook in a moderate oven, gas mark 5 or 375° F. (190° C.) for 40–45 minutes or until the potatoes are tender when tested with the point of a sharp knife. Remove the dish from the oven, carefully pile the mixture in a hot dish and serve at once.

POMMES DE TERRE BADOISE ** (for 4–5 persons)

Ingredients:
1 kg. potatoes (2 lb.)
2 eggs

60–90 g. cheese (2–3 oz.)
seasoning

Method: Wash and peel the potatoes. Place them in a pan of cold salted water, bring to the boil and boil them until tender. Drain them well and pass through a sieve or vegetable mill into a hot bowl. Separate the eggs. Beat the yolks, grated cheese and seasoning into the potato.

Whisk the egg whites until very stiff and fold them into the potato mixture. Spread three-quarters of the mixture in a buttered fireproof dish. Fill the remainder into a forcing bag with a rosette tube and pipe a design on the top. Place it in a moderate oven, gas mark 5–6 or 375–400° F. (190–200° C.) for 20 minutes until it is risen and golden brown. Serve at once.

POMMES DE TERRE BRIOCHE * (for 4–5 persons)

Ingredients:
Pommes de Terre Duchesse,
  Method I, made with 1 kg.

(2 lb.) potatoes, etc. (see page 226)
beaten egg

Method: Make the pommes de terre duchesse in the usual way. Season it well. Turn out on a floured board and allow it to cool. When it is cool enough to handle, divide it into pieces the size of an egg, and an equal number of pieces the size of a hazel nut. Roll each piece into a ball shape, place a small ball on the top of each large one to resemble a brioche. Press lightly on the top. Brush over with beaten egg. Put them on a baking sheet and bake them in a fairly hot oven, gas mark 6 or 400° F. (200° C.) to heat them through and brown them. (*See Plate 14.*)

POMMES DE TERRE CHÂTEAU * (for 2–3 persons)

Ingredients:
500 g. old potatoes (1 lb.)
salt

60 g. good dripping or melted butter (2 oz.)

Method: Wash and peel the potatoes, cut them to even sized pieces and turn them to barrel shapes, approximately 5 cm. (2 inches) long by 3 cm. (1¼ inches) as greatest width. Place them in a pan of cold salted water, bring them to the boil and boil for 2–3 minutes. Remove and drain and dry them on a clean cloth.

Heat the dripping in a roasting tin, turn the potato shapes in this and cook in a moderate oven, gas mark 6 or 400° F. (200° C.) turning them from time to time until they are evenly brown, approximately 40–45 minutes. Drain the potatoes free of the dripping, sprinkle them with salt and serve immediately. (*See Plate 13.*)

POMMES DE TERRE CHIPS **

Ingredients:
potatoes as required

deep fat
salt

Method: Peel the potatoes and cut them into cylindrical shapes. The diameter of each potato should be approximately the same. Slice them very thinly, using a very sharp knife and keeping each slice the same thickness. Place in a bowl of cold water. Remove, drain and dry them thoroughly on a clean, dry cloth.

Heat the fat until it is barely smoking. Place the potatoes in a drying basket and lower them into the fat. Cook for approximately 3 minutes. Remove. Raise the heat under the pan until the fat has a faint blue haze, or test with a piece of bread as for Pommes de Terre Pont-Neuf (see page 231). Replace the basket and fry the potatoes quickly until gold. Drain on white kitchen or tissue paper. Sprinkle with salt. Serve at once.

POMMES DE TERRE CLEO * (for 4–6 persons)

Ingredients:
6 large potatoes
90 g. butter (3 oz.)
1½ dl. dry white wine (1 gill)

1 small onion
2 tablespoons finely chopped
    parsley
seasoning

Method: Peel the potatoes and cut them into quarters. Peel the onion and cut it into small dice.

Heat the butter in a sauté pan, add the wine together with the onion and the seasoning. Place the potatoes on top. Cover firmly with greaseproof paper and the lid. Cook in a moderate oven, gas mark 5 or 375° F. (190° C.) for approximately one hour. At the end of this time, remove the pan from the oven and take off the lid and remove the paper. Allow the cooking liquor to evaporate over a good heat. (Prevent the potatoes from sticking to the bottom of the pan by shaking it vigorously.) As soon as the potatoes are a golden brown, dish them up in a hot dish and sprinkle them thickly with the chopped parsley.

POMMES DE TERRE COCOTTE * (for 3–4 persons)

Ingredients:
750 g. potatoes (1½ lb.)

60–90 g. butter (2–3 oz.)
seasoning

Method: Peel the potatoes, cut them into even sized pieces and 'turn' them to the size of large olives. Place them in a pan of cold salted water, bring them to the boil and then drain them well. Heat the butter in a roasting tin, put in the potatoes and turn them until they are well coated in butter. Cook in a moderate oven, gas mark 5 or 375° F. (190° C.) for about half an hour or until they are golden brown. Drain, sprinkle with salt and use as required. (*See Plate 13.*)

Comment: These potatoes are usually used as a garnish for suitable meat or fish dishes, but can be served as a vegetable.

POMMES DE TERRE COLOMBINE * (for 2–3 persons)

Ingredients:
½ kg. new potatoes (1 lb.)
1–2 green peppers

60 g. butter (2 oz.)
seasoning

Method: Scrape the potatoes in the usual way. Cut the peppers in half, remove the pith and seeds and blanch them for 5 minutes in boiling salted water. Remove and drain them and cut into julienne strips. Slice the potatoes into wafer thin slices. Melt the butter in a thick pan. Add the potatoes and peppers. Season. Cover with buttered greaseproof paper and a lid and cook over a gentle heat, shaking the pan from time to time. Do not allow them to burn. Pile them up in a hot dish and serve at once.

POMMES DE TERRE DANOISE **   (for 4–5 persons)

Ingredients:

¾–1 kg. new potatoes (1½–2 lb.)   90 g. sugar (3 oz.)
60 g. butter (2 oz.)   a little salt

Method: Wash the potatoes well and put them into a pan of fast boiling salted water. Boil them until they are just done but still quite firm. Drain them and then peel off the skins. Cut them into slices about 1 cm. (½ inch) thick.

Put the sugar into a strong pan with a little water and cook it over a good heat until it turns to a caramel. Add the butter to the caramel and as soon as it has melted, put in the potato slices and turn them quickly until they are well coated. It is important not to allow them to break up. Serve at once.

POMMES DE TERRE DAUPHINE **

Ingredients:

Pâte à Choux (see page 336)
750 g. potatoes (1½ lb.)
2 yolks of egg
pinch of nutmeg   for Pommes de Terre Duchesse
seasoning   Method I (see page 226)
deep fat for frying

Method: Make the pâte à choux in the usual way. Prepare the pommes de terre duchesse. Mix the pâte à choux and the pommes de terre duchesse together. Beat them thoroughly and season very well.

Place the mixture in a forcing bag with a 1 cm (½ inch) plain pipe and pipe out, cutting it into 2 cm. (¾ inch) lengths, and allowing them to fall gently into a pan of hot fat. Fry until they are golden brown. Drain well on white kitchen or tissue paper and serve at once. (*See Plate 14.*)

Comment: These potatoes are used as a garnish to a dish.

POMMES DE TERRE DUCHESSE * (Method I)

(for 2–3 persons)

Ingredients:
½ kg. old potatoes (1 lb.)
2 yolks of egg
30 g. butter (1 oz.)

seasoning
a pinch of nutmeg
beaten egg to brush over

Method: Peel the potatoes, cut them into even sized pieces and place them in a pan of cold salted water. Bring them to the boil and boil until tender. Pass them quickly through a sieve or vegetable mill into a *hot* basin. Beat in the butter, yolks and seasoning. Beat the mixture very well.

Put the mixture into a forcing bag with a large rosette pipe. Pipe out into cone shapes on a lightly greased baking tin. Place them in the top of a hot oven, gas mark 6–7 or 400–425° F. (200–220° C.) for 10 minutes. Remove, brush them over lightly with beaten egg. Return them to the oven to brown. (*See Plate 14.*)

Comment: These potatoes can be sprinkled with finely chopped parsley or paprika before serving.

POMMES DE TERRE DUCHESSE * (Method II)

Ingredients:
½ kg. potatoes (1 lb.)
1 egg
30 g. butter (1 oz.)

a little hot milk
seasoning
a pinch of nutmeg
beaten egg to brush over

Method: Follow directions given for Method I (see above) but use a whole egg in place of the yolks and a little hot milk. This method is more suitable when using pommes de terre duchesse as a piped border for a dish. (*See Plate 14.*)

POMMES DE TERRE FARCIES À LA VIENNOISE *

(For 6 persons)

Ingredients:
6 large even sized potatoes
60 g. butter (2 oz.)
1 dl. thick cream (½ gill)
1 egg
45 g. Gruyère cheese (1½ oz.)

1 teaspoon chopped fresh herbs
seasoning
To finish:
white breadcrumbs
30 g. butter (1 oz.)

Method: Wash and scrub the potatoes thoroughly. Prick the skins with a fork and rub them with butter. Sprinkle with salt. Place them on a baking tin and cook in a hot oven, gas mark 7 or 425° F. (220° C.) for approximately one hour, or until just cooked. Cut them in half and remove the flesh with a spoon, being careful not to pierce the skins. Pass the potato pulp through a sieve or vegetable mill into a hot bowl.

Add the beaten egg, grated cheese and the cream to the potato and season it well. Beat it until light and creamy. Stir in the finely chopped herbs. The mixture should be soft without being liquid. Season to taste. Replace it in the potato skins, coat the top with breadcrumbs, and dot with knobs of butter. Brown under the grill or in the top of a hot oven, gas mark 7 or 425° F. (220° C.). Serve hot.

POMMES DE TERRE LORETTE **   (for 4–6 persons)

Ingredients:
Pâte à Choux, (see page 336)
Pommes de Terre Duchesse,
   Method I, made with 750 g.

(1½ lbs.) potatoes, 2 yolks of
   egg, etc. (see page 226)
deep fat for frying

Method: Make up the pâte à choux. Make the pommes de terre duchesse. Mix the two together, beat very well. Season and allow the mixture to cool.

Fill it into a forcing bag with 2 cm. (¾ inch) pipe.

Heat the deep fat. Pipe little finger lengths into the fat. Fry them until they are golden brown. Lift them out carefully with a draining spoon, drain them well on white kitchen or tissue paper. Serve very hot. (*See Plate 14.*)

Comment: Escoffier says that they should be formed into crescent shapes by rolling them on a floured board with the hands before frying.

POMMES DE TERRE MONT D'OR *   (for 4–5 persons)

Ingredients:
1 kg. potatoes (2 lb.)
90 g. butter (3 oz.)

3 yolks of egg
60 g. grated cheese
seasoning

Method: Peel the potatoes and cut them into even sized pieces. Place them in a pan of cold salted water and bring them to the boil. Boil until just cooked. When they are cooked, drain well and pass them through a sieve or vegetable mill into a hot bowl. Beat them well and add the egg yolks, butter and grated cheese. Beat again. Season to taste.

Pile the potatoes in a pyramid or mountain in a fireproof dish and brown under a hot grill or in the top of a hot oven, gas mark 7 or 425° F. (220° C.). Serve at once.

POMMES DE TERRE MOUSSELINE *   (for 2–3 persons)

Ingredients:
750 g. potatoes (1½ lb.)
30 g. butter (1 oz.)

boiling milk as required
seasoning

Method: Wash and peel the potatoes. Cut them into even sized pieces. Cover with cold water and add a good teaspoon of salt. Bring to the boil and boil them until tender. Drain at once. Put a folded dry cloth under the lid of the pan, which should not be completely on, and stand it over a very low heat. Put the milk on to heat. When the potatoes are quite dry, pass them quickly through a sieve or vegetable mill into a hot bowl. Make a well in the centre, put in the butter, then beat in the boiling milk a little at a time. The exact quantity will depend on the type of potatoes used. Beat *very well indeed* with a wooden spoon or spatula. The more vigorous the beating the lighter and fluffier the result will be. Season to taste. Pile them up in a hot serving dish.

Comment: A tiny pinch of grated nutmeg can be added with the seasoning if desired.

POMMES DE TERRE NINON *   (for 4–5 persons)

Ingredients:
1 kg. old potatoes (2 lb.)
30 g. butter (1 oz.)
60 g. finely chopped cooked ham
   (2 oz.)

2 yolks of egg
1 dessertspoon concentrated
   tomato purée
a little beaten egg
seasoning

Method: Peel the potatoes and cut them into even sized pieces. Place them in a pan of cold salted water. Bring them to the boil and cook until they are just done but still fairly firm. Remove and drain them thoroughly. Pass them through a sieve or vegetable mill into a hot bowl. Beat in the butter, egg yolks, tomato purée and chopped ham. Season well. Beat very well until all are perfectly mixed.

Turn the mixture out on to a floured board. Form it into small croquettes two inches long. Place them on a lightly greased baking sheet and bake them in the top of a hot oven, gas mark 7 or 425° F. (220° C.) for 10 minutes. Brush them with beaten egg and return them to the oven until they are golden brown. Serve hot.

POMMES DE TERRE NOISETTE * (for 3–4 persons)

Ingredients:
750 g. potatoes (1½ lb.)

60–90 g. butter (2–3 oz.)
seasoning

Method: Select large potatoes if possible. Wash and peel them and then using a vegetable ball cutter, scoop out small balls. Place them in a pan of cold salted water, bring them to the boil and boil them for 2–3 minutes. Remove, and drain and dry them on a clean dry cloth. Heat the butter in a sauté or shallow pan and when it begins to turn a golden brown, add the potatoes and seasoning. Place the lid on the pan and cook the potatoes, shaking the pan from time to time. They will probably take from 5–7 minutes to finish cooking. Drain them on plain kitchen or tissue paper. Serve at once. (*See Plate 13.*)

POMMES DE TERRE NOUVELLES ALBARÈNE *
(for 3–4 persons)

Ingredients:
12 medium sized new potatoes
6 very small onions
135 g. lean bacon (4½ oz.)
60 g. butter (2 oz.)

¼ l. dry white wine (1½ gills)
seasoning
To finish:
60 g. butter (2 oz.)

Method: Wash and scrape the potatoes. Peel the onions. Cut the bacon into lardons. Heat the butter in a fairly large pan, add the onions and the bacon, and stir over a gentle heat until the onions are beginning to turn gold. Add the potatoes, whole, and allow them to turn a golden colour, keeping them stirred from time to time. Season and pour in the wine. Cover with greaseproof paper and the lid. Simmer very gently for 25–30 minutes, or until the potatoes are cooked.

Lift the potatoes, etc., with a draining spoon. Pile them up in a hot dish and keep them hot.

Return the pan to a good heat and reduce the liquor by half. Remove from the heat and whisk in the remaining butter bit by bit. Taste and adjust the seasoning. Pour over the vegetables and serve very hot.

POMMES DE TERRE O'BRIEN ** (for 4–5 persons)

Ingredients:
1–1½ kg. new potatoes (2–3 lb.)
90 g. butter (3 oz.)

1 red and 1 green pepper
seasoning

Method: Wash the potatoes well and place them in a pan of boiling salted water. Cook them rapidly until they are done, but still firm. Remove and drain them and peel off the skins. Chop the potatoes into coarse dice.

Cut the peppers in half and remove the pith and seeds. Discard these and chop the peppers fairly finely. Place them in a pan of boiling salted water and blanch them for 5 minutes. Remove them and refresh them in cold water. Dry them thoroughly on a clean dry cloth.

Heat the butter in a large thick pan. Add the potatoes and allow them to brown gently without breaking up. Just before serving, stir the peppers gently with the potatoes. Season well. When they are coated in the butter, remove them and pile them up in a hot serving dish. Serve at once.

POMMES DE TERRE PAILLE **

These potatoes are used as a garnish. They should be firm and waxy. Peel them and cut them into very fine julienne strips, the thickness of straw. Dry them thoroughly on a clean cloth and fry them in the same way as for Pommes de Terre Pont-Neuf (see page 231), except that the first frying is omitted and the cooking time will be shorter. Drain them on kitchen or tissue paper. Dust them with salt before using them. (*See Plate 13.*)

POMMES DE TERRE PAVESANE *   (for 4–6 persons)

Ingredients:
1 kg. potatoes (2 lb.)
120 g. Parmesan or Gruyère
   cheese (4 oz.)

60 g. plain flour (2 oz.)
90–120 g. butter (3–4 oz.)
a little white stock
seasoning

Method: Peel the potatoes and cut them into wafer thin slices.

Grate the cheese and mix it with the flour and seasoning. Heat about half the butter in a frying pan. Dip the potato slices into the mixture of flour and cheese. Sauter them in the hot butter.

Butter a fireproof dish. Make a layer of potatoes in the bottom and cover with a good sprinkling of the flour and cheese mixture. Dot small knobs of butter on top. Repeat this process until the dish is full, finishing with the flour and cheese mixture.

Using a funnel, pour in sufficient stock to three-quarters fill the dish. Cook in a moderate oven, gas mark 5 or 375° F. (190° C.) for one and a half hours. Serve very hot.

POMMES DE TERRE PONT-NEUF ** (for 3–4 persons)

Ingredients:
750 g. potatoes (1½ lb.)

salt
deep fat

Method: Select large, waxy potatoes. Peel them and cut them into even sizes, the thickness and length of the little finger. They should *all* be exactly the same length and thickness. Dry them thoroughly on a clean dry cloth.

Heat the fat until it is barely smoking (test with a cube of bread which will bubble gently but not agitatedly.) Place the potatoes in the frying basket, being careful not to put too many in at once. Lower gently into the fat. Cook for 7–8 minutes, or until the potatoes are soft when tested. They should not colour. Remove the frying basket, raise the heat under the pan until it is smoking, test again with a piece of bread and if it bubbles quickly, return the potatoes and fry them for a further 2–3 minutes until they are a light gold. Remember that they will continue to brown for a moment or two after they have been taken out of the pan. Drain them on a piece of plain kitchen or tissue paper. Dust them with salt before serving. (*See Plate 13.*)

POMMES DE TERRE SAUTÉES À LA LYONNAISE *
(for 4–5 persons)

Ingredients:
¾–1 kg. potatoes (1½–2 lb.)
1 large onion
60–90 g. butter (2–3 oz.)
1 tablespoon oil

pinch nutmeg
seasoning
To finish:
finely chopped parsley

Method: Wash the potatoes well and cook them in boiling salted water. When they are just cooked, drain and peel them. Cut the potatoes into slices about ½ cm. (¼ inch) thick. Melt half the butter in a sauté pan, add the oil and make it very hot. Add the potatoes and brown them, turning them occasionally. Chop the onion finely. Melt the remainder of the butter in another pan, add the onion and soften it gently. When the onion is a pale yellow colour and quite tender, combine it with the potatoes. Season, adding a pinch of nutmeg. Cook all together for a further 5 minutes, shaking the pan from time to time. Heap up in a hot vegetable dish. Sprinkle with very finely chopped parsley and serve hot.

POMMES DE TERRE VIEILLE MODE * (for 4 persons)

Ingredients:
1 kg. potatoes (2 lb.)
1 kg. ripe tomatoes (2 lb.)
1 clove garlic
bouquet garni

60 g. butter (2 oz.)
seasoning
To finish:
Finely chopped parsley

Method: Peel the potatoes and cut them into wafer thin slices. Leave them in cold water.

Skin and pip the tomatoes, and divide them into quarters. Place them in a pan with seasoning, the bouquet garni, and the garlic roughly chopped. Put them over a moderate heat and simmer, stirring frequently, for 20 minutes. Pass them through a sieve or vegetable mill. Drain and dry the potatoes and pack them tightly in a well buttered fireproof dish. Pour the sauce over. Place the butter in knobs over the top and put in a moderate oven, gas mark 5 or 375° F. (190° C.) for 1–1¼ hours, or until the potatoes are done.

PFLUTTERS (CUISINE ALSACIENNE) **

(for 5–6 persons)

Ingredients:

1 kg. potatoes (2 lb.)
2 tablespoons plain flour
2 eggs
1 clove garlic

1 tablespoon finely chopped parsley
a little grated nutmeg
seasoning
To finish:
60 g. butter (2 oz.)

Method: Peel the potatoes. Cut them into even sized pieces and cook them in boiling salted water for 20 minutes or until they are done. Drain and pass them through a sieve or vegetable mill into a hot bowl. Whilst they are still hot beat in the flour, eggs, parsley and garlic crushed with a little salt. See that the mixture is well seasoned, adding a little grated nutmeg. Using two dessertspoons, form it into oval shapes. Arrange them in a buttered fireproof dish, seeing that there is a good space in between each. Put them in a fairly hot oven, gas mark 5–6 or 375–400° F. (190–200° C.) for 10–15 minutes.

Melt the butter, pour it over the top and serve at once.

RATATOUILLE DE POMMES DE TERRE **

(for 4–6 persons)

Ingredients:

750 g. new potatoes (1½ lb.)
500 g. tomatoes (1 lb.)
180 g. lean bacon, in one piece
    (6 oz.)
2 large onions

60 g. butter (2 oz.)
1 tablespoon oil
2 cloves garlic
bouquet garni, to include, thyme,
    bayleaf and sage seasoning

Method: Scrape the potatoes. Peel the onions and cut them into fine rings. Cut the bacon into 1 cm. (½ inch) dice.

Heat the butter and oil in a deep, strong pan. Put in the bacon and cook it gently for 5 minutes. At the end of this time lift it out with a draining spoon. Put it aside and keep hot. Place the onions in the pan and stir them continuously over a low heat until they are soft. (This process cannot be hurried or the onions will become scorched and brown.)

Return the bacon to the pan together with the potatoes and tomatoes, which have been cut into quarters, and the garlic crushed with a little salt. Lay the bouquet garni on top. Season well adding plenty of black pepper. Pour in sufficient water, just to cover the potatoes. Cover with grease-proof paper and the lid and simmer gently for $\frac{3}{4}$ hour. Remove the bouquet garni and arrange the vegetables neatly in a hot dish. Serve very hot.

CRUDITÉS NATURISTE *   (for 4 persons)

Ingredients:

4 large firm tomatoes
9–12 white button mushrooms
1 small cooked beetroot
1 head celery
1 lemon
6–8 radishes
½ cucumber

3–4 young carrots
1 large lettuce
Sauce Vinaigrette made with:
    8 tablespoons oil, 3 tablespoons
    tarragon vinegar, to which has
    been added 1 tablespoon finely
    chopped fresh herbs (see page 40)
seasoning

Method: Wash and dry the lettuce well and arrange the outside leaves on a large flat platter.

Make up the sauce vinaigrette in the usual way, seasoning it well. Place it in a small pot in the centre of the dish.

Slice the tomatoes thinly. Rub the lemon over the mushrooms and slice them thinly also.

From one side of the dish, radiating towards the centre, arrange the slices of tomato, placing a slice of mushroom between each.

Slice the carrots thinly and cut the celery into small slices. Arrange these slices of carrot and celery alternately on the opposite side, also radiating towards the centre.

Using a lemon zester, peel the radishes and cucumber to give a decorative effect. Arrange them together in a similar way at right angles to the tomatoes etc.

Lastly, opposite the radishes and cucumber, arrange the beetroot cut into thin slices and in between each slice place a little of the heart of the lettuce.

This is a particularly pretty salad if it is cut neatly and arranged with care. All the vegetables, with the exception of the beetroot, are served raw.

SALADE AUX ANCHOIS ET ŒUFS *　　　　(for 4 persons)

Ingredients:
350 g. new potatoes (¾ lb.)
6 hardboiled eggs
1½ dl. (¼ pint) approx. Sauce
　Vinaigrette (see page 40) to
　which has been added a good

teaspoon Dijon mustard and
a good pinch of chopped
tarragon seasoning
To finish:
1 small tin anchovy fillets

Method: Wash the potatoes well and put them to cook in boiling salted water. As soon as they are cooked and whilst they are still firm, place them in a bowl of cold water and remove their skins. Cut them into slices. Whilst they are still warm, put them into a bowl and pour over the sauce vinaigrette. Chop two of the hardboiled eggs. Mix them carefully with the potatoes, using two forks, and season.

To Serve: Pile up the potato salad in a salad bowl. Cut the remaining four eggs into slices and decorate round the edge of the salad with these. Using the anchovy fillets make a lattice design all over the top. Serve very cold.

SALADE AUX NOIX *　　　　　　　　(for 4–6 persons)

Ingredients:
1–2 large lettuces
2 green peppers
1 handful chopped walnuts

Sauce Vinaigrette, to which has
　been added 2 tablespoons
　chopped fresh herbs (see page
　40)

Method: Cut the peppers into halves and remove the pith and seeds. Cut the peppers into fine shreds and cover them with cold water in a small pan. Bring them to the boil and cook for a minute or two. Drain them well and refresh them in cold water. Drain again.
　　Wash the lettuces well, having removed the coarse outside leaves. Drain the lettuces well.
　　Mix the lettuce with the peppers and the walnuts. Add the well seasoned sauce vinaigrette. Toss the salad in this and serve very cold.

SALADE BEAUCAIRE **　　　　　　(for 4–5 persons)

Ingredients:
1 small root celeriac
1 large head of celery
2 cooked potatoes
2 cooked beetroots
2 slices cooked ham
12 hazelnuts

Sauce Mayonnaise (see page 36)
seasoning
To finish:
rounds of cooked beetroot
2 tomatoes
heart of celery
1 truffle, or slices of black olive

234

Method: Cut the celeriac into thin slices. Add to it the thinly sliced celery, using equal proportions as far as possible. Cut the ham into small squares, dice the potatoes and beetroot. Mix all together in a bowl with the hazelnuts. Season well.

Make the sauce Mayonnaise and fold it in so as to coat the salad evenly. Turn the mixture carefully into a serving bowl.

To Finish: Decorate the salad with rounds of beetroot, slices of tomato and the sliced truffle or black olive. In the centre place the celery heart.

SALADE CÉSAR ** (for 4 persons)

Ingredients:
3 artichoke hearts
3–4 large sprigs of cooked cauli-
    flower
1 green or red pepper
1 dessert apple

90 g. sultanas (3 oz.)
60 g. chopped hazel nuts (2 oz.)
1 lemon
6 tablespoons olive oil
seasoning

Method: If using fresh artichokes, prepare and cook them in the usual way (see page 238, Salade Orloff).

Cut the pepper in half, remove the seeds and pith. Slice it into fine julienne strips. Place these in a pan of cold salted water, bring it to the boil and boil for 2–3 minutes. Drain and refresh the strips under cold running water. Drain them again.

Slice the artichoke hearts and the cauliflower thinly. Dice the apple, leaving the peel on. Mix these with the sultanas, nuts and pepper. Place the mixture in a salad bowl.

Whisk the lemon juice and oil together. Season well. Pour the dressing over the salad. Toss lightly and serve immediately.

SALADE DE CHOUFLEUR * (for 4–5 persons)

Ingredients:
1 large cauliflower
1½ dl. Sauce Vinaigrette (see page
    40) (1 gill)

4–5 gherkins
1 tablespoon capers

Method: Wash the cauliflower well in salted water. Divide it into flower-ets and cook them in boiling salted water until just tender. Refresh them in cold water and dry on a clean cloth. Whilst they are still hot arrange them in a salad bowl and pour over the sauce vinaigrette, then allow them to become quite cold. Finally decorate with finely sliced gherkins and sprinkle with chopped capers. Serve very cold.

SALADE DE MAIS ** (for 4 persons)

Ingredients:

60 g. poached smoked haddock
(2 oz.)
250 g. cold roast veal or pork
($\frac{1}{2}$ lb.)
1 kg. shelled peas (2 lb.)
2 red peppers

1 cucumber
juice of 1 lemon
1 large packet frozen sweetcorn
Sauce Mayonnaise (see page 36)
paprika
seasoning

Method: Cook the peas in boiling salted water, to which has been added a pinch of sugar. Drain them well when done and put them aside to get quite cold.

Cut the peppers in half, remove the pith and seeds and plunge them into boiling water and cook them for 2–3 minutes. Remove them, drain and refresh with cold water. Drain again. Cut them into dice.

Peel the cucumber and cut this into dice also.

Cut the meat into thin strips. Flake the haddock. Cook the sweetcorn as usual, drain and refresh with cold water. Drain again and cool thoroughly.

Make the sauce Mayonnaise, adding the juice of a lemon.

Using two forks, mix all the ingredients thoroughly in a bowl. Season to taste. Pile up the salad in a bowl. Sprinkle generously with paprika. Serve very cold.

SALADE DE POMMES DE TERRE * (for 4 persons)

Ingredients:

1 kg. new potatoes (2 lb.)
3 dl. Sauce Vinaigrette (see page
40)

3–4 tablespoons finely chopped
fresh herbs
salt

Method: Select potatoes of relatively the same size. Wash them well and place them in a pan of boiling, salted water. Cook them until just done, but still firm. Rub off their skins and cut them into neat dice. Mix with the sauce vinaigrette whilst they are still hot. Sprinkle with chopped herbs, or the herbs may be mixed in with the sauce vinaigrette. Serve cold.

Comment: Another way to make a Salade de Pommes de Terre is to cook them in exactly the same way. Peel and dice them. Then when they are quite cold, incorporate them into a well seasoned sauce Mayonnaise (see page 36).

SALADE ÉGYPTIENNE * (for 5–6 persons)

Ingredients:
1 teacup Patna rice
120–170 g. chicken livers (4–6 oz.)
60 g. cooked ham (2 oz.)
3 cooked artichoke hearts
60 g. mushrooms (2 oz.)
2 red peppers
60 g. butter (2 oz.)

a little lemon juice
1½ dl. Sauce Vinaigrette (see
   page 40) (1 gill)
seasoning
To finish:
250 g. cooked peas (½ lb.)
3–4 tomatoes

Method: Cook the rice in plenty of boiling salted water for 12–16 minutes. When it is cooked drain and refresh it in cold water. Drain well. Melt the butter and sauter the chicken livers in this. Remove them and chop them roughly.

Cut the peppers into strips, removing all the pith and pips, place them in cold salted water, bring to the boil and boil them for 2–3 minutes. Drain, refresh in cold water. Drain well. Cut the mushrooms into quarters. Cook them lightly in the butter the livers were cooked in, adding seasoning and a few drops of lemon juice. Remove and drain them. Dice the ham and artichoke hearts. Mix them into the rice with the livers, mushrooms and peppers. Stir in the vinaigrette dressing lightly with a fork. Taste and adjust the seasoning. Pile up in a dome in a serving dish and decorate with the cooked peas and sliced tomatoes. Serve cold.

Comment: If fresh artichokes are not available, tinned ones can be used instead.

SALADE IMPÉRATRICE * (for 4 persons)

Ingredients:
2 grapefruit
lettuce
2 red peppers
2 slices of pineapple NO
60–90 g. cooked white fish
   (turbot, hake or halibut) (2–3 oz.)

90–120 g. grapes (3–4 oz.)
Sauce Vinaigrette (see page 40)
2 tablespoons whisky
To finish:
finely chopped fresh herbs

Method: Cut the grapefruit in half and remove the flesh, keeping the peel whole. Separate the grapefruit flesh from the inner skin. Skin and pip the grapes. Cut the peppers into dice, having removed all pith and pips. Blanch them in boiling water for 2–3 minutes. Drain and refresh them in cold water. Drain again and dry on a clean cloth. Dice the pineapple. Flake the fish, being careful to remove all bones. Mix all these together with the sauce vinaigrette.

Roll the lettuce leaves like a cigar and cut crosswise to make long fine julienne strips. Arrange a little shredded lettuce in each grapefruit case and pile up the mixture on top. Pour over the whisky and dust with finely chopped fresh herbs. Serve very cold.

Comment: This salad should be eaten within 2 hours of making, as the lettuce tends to become 'sad' quickly.

SALADE ORLOFF ** (for 2–3 persons)

Ingredients:

2–3 large globe artichokes
120 g. cooked macaroni (4 oz.)
240 g. mushrooms (8 oz.)
Sauce Mayonnaise (see page 36)

1 head celery
170 g. cooked cold chicken (6 oz.)
6 large tomatoes
2 tablespoons tarragon vinegar

Method: Wash the celery. Blanch the tomatoes and skin, pip and cut them into shreds. Remove the leaves from the artichokes. Take out the choke carefully, thus exposing the 'fonds'. Put these to cook in cold water containing salt and a few drops of vinegar. This should take about 20 minutes.

When the artichoke fonds are cooked, drain them and chop them roughly. Cut the chicken meat into shreds, add the uncooked mushrooms cut into thin strips, together with the celery cut similarly. Mix all together with the macaroni. Sprinkle with vinegar and allow to become quite cold. Just before serving fold in the sauce Mayonnaise.

CONDÉ DE TOMATES * (for 3–4 persons)

Ingredients:

460 g. tomatoes (1 lb.)
125 g. Patna rice (4½ oz.)
6 new carrots
30–45 g. butter (1–1½ oz.)
sprig of thyme, parsley and rosemary
1 finely chopped clove garlic
1 tablespoon finely chopped parsley

pinch of sugar
1 dl. oil (½ gill)
Sauce Tomate (Method II) (see page 39)
seasoning
To finish:
finely chopped parsley
1 finely chopped clove garlic

Method: Heat the oil in a pan. Cut the tomatoes into two and turn them quickly in the oil, then add the finely chopped garlic, the parsley, pinch of sugar and the herbs. Lower the heat and cook gently for 4–5 minutes. Stir occasionally.

Cook the rice in fast boiling salted water, drain and refresh it in hot water and drain again. Return it to the pan. Fold a clean cloth and place it over the pan with the lid on top and allow the rice to rest for a few minutes, keeping it hot.

Cook the carrots also in boiling salted water, then cut them into slices when they are done. Toss them in hot butter, using about half the quantity. Add them to the rice, stirring in the rest of the butter at the same time. Season. Press the rice mixture into a greased ring mould and unmould it on to a hot dish. Place the tomatoes in the centre, sprinkle with the chopped garlic and parsley. Serve the sauce tomate separately. (*See Plate 16.*)

TOMATES À LA MOSCOVITE *   (for 6 persons)

Ingredients:
12 small tomatoes
2 medium onions
2 tablespoons oil
3 hardboiled eggs
1 tablespoon chopped parsley

1 tablespoon chopped chives
1 tablespoon chopped capers
paprika
seasoning
To finish:
lettuce leaves

Method: Cut a lid off the top of the tomatoes, remove the pulp carefully with a teaspoon or vegetable ball cutter. Dust out with salt. Turn upside down to drain for 15–20 minutes.

Peel the onions and chop them finely.

Heat the oil in a pan, soften the onions in this without colouration. Meanwhile chop the eggs. Add them to the onions, together with the parsley, chives and capers. Season well, adding a good pinch of paprika. Fill the mixture into the tomatoes. Leave to become quite cold. Serve cold on a bed of lettuce leaves.

TOMATES AUX OLIVES *   (for 4–8 persons)

Ingredients:
4 good sized tomatoes
120 g. black olives (4 oz.)
90–120 g. butter (3–4 oz.)
3 shallots

seasoning
To finish:
lettuce leaves
anchovy fillets

Method: Cut the tomatoes in half and scoop out the pulp carefully. Dust them out with salt and turn them upside down on a wire rack to drain for 15–20 minutes.

Beat the butter until it is soft. Chop the shallots very finely indeed and add them to the butter. Add the stoned olives, which have been chopped finely. Season well. Fill into the tomato shells. Decorate with crossed strips of anchovy fillet. Serve them very cold on a bed of lettuce leaves.

TOMATES FARCIES À LA LANGUEDOCIENNE *

(for 6 persons)

Ingredients:
6 large firm tomatoes
1 tablespoon white breadcrumbs
Farce made with:
240 g. pork sausage meat (8 oz.)
1 chopped hardboiled egg yolk

1 finely chopped onion
1 tablespoon oil
1 clove garlic
1 tablespoon finely chopped
  parsley
seasoning

Method: Cut the tomatoes in half and scoop out the pulp carefully. Sprinkle them inside with salt and turn them upside down on a wire rack to drain for 15–20 minutes.

Meanwhile heat the oil in a pan, add the onion and cook gently without browning until soft. Mix it together with the sausage meat, chopped hardboiled egg yolk, parsley, and the clove of garlic crushed with a little salt. Taste and season. Fill this mixture into the tomato cases and place them in a buttered fireproof dish. Sprinkle them with breadcrumbs and a little oil. Cook in a moderate oven, gas mark 5–6 or 375–400° F. (190–200° C.) for 30 minutes. Serve hot.

TOMATES FARCIES PEREZ *

(for 4 persons)

Ingredients:
8 large tomatoes
2 hardboiled eggs
120 g. mushrooms (4 oz.)
45 g. butter (1½ oz.)
2 tablespoons fresh or tinned crab
  meat

1 tablespoon finely chopped fresh
  herbs
4–5 tablespoons Sauce Béchamel
  (see page 34)
a few drops of anchovy essence
30 g. grated cheese (1 oz.)
seasoning

Method: Cut a thin slice off the top of each tomato. Scoop out the pulp. Season them well inside and turn them upside down on a wire rack to drain for 15–20 minutes.

Prepare the filling. Chop the mushrooms finely. Heat the butter in a pan and cook the mushrooms in this until they are soft. Season with black pepper. Add the chopped hardboiled eggs. Stir well, then add the crab meat and the herbs. Stir in half of the sauce Béchamel and the anchovy essence. Taste and adjust the seasoning. Fill the tomatoes with this mixture. Place them in a lightly buttered fireproof dish. Put a little sauce Béchamel on the top of each tomato and sprinkle with the grated cheese. Cook them in a moderate oven, gas mark 5 or 375° F. (190° C.) for 20–25 minutes. Serve hot.

Comment: *Really* large tomatoes must be used for this recipe.

RATATOUILLE À LA NIÇOISE *   (for 4 persons)

Ingredients:

2 large aubergines
1 small marrow or 2 courgettes
1 large green pepper
3 cloves garlic or more if preferred
2 large onions

3 large tomatoes
4 tablespoons olive oil
1 large bouquet garni
seasoning
To finish:
finely chopped parsley

Method: Peel the marrow or courgettes. Cut it into quarters lengthwise and then into 2–3 cm. (1 inch) cubes. Peel the aubergines and cut them in the same fashion, dust them with salt, leave to stand for 20 minutes. Drain the aubergines and dry on a cloth.

Skin the tomatoes and cut them into as large dice as possible. (The marrow, aubergines and tomatoes should be in fairly equal proportions.)

Cut the pepper into quarters, remove all seeds and pith. Then cut across into thin julienne strips. Peel the onions and slice them very thinly.

Heat the oil in a sauté pan. Add the onions and the pepper, cover with the lid and cook slowly, without allowing them to brown. When they are almost cooked, add the marrow or courgettes, the aubergines and the bouquet garni, together with the cloves of garlic crushed with a little salt. Season well. Replace the lid and cook for a further ½ hour over a low heat, shaking the pan from time to time. Remove the bouquet garni. Adjust the seasoning.

To Serve: Pour the ratatouille into a hot serving dish, dust with finely chopped parsley and serve at once.

REGAL D'ANNA *   (for 5 persons)

Ingredients:

1 kg. ripe tomatoes (2 lb.)
1 kg. aubergines (2 lb.)
180 g. lean bacon – in one piece
  (6 oz.)
1 medium sized onion

6 shallots
2 cloves garlic
3 tablespoons oil
bouquet garni
seasoning

Method: Cut the bacon into fairly large dice. Peel the onion and shallots and chop them finely. Cut the tomatoes and aubergines into slices without peeling them. Heat the oil in a sauté pan and fry the bacon quickly in this. Then add the onion, shallots and the garlic crushed with a little salt. Turn them in the oil without allowing them to colour. Add the tomatoes and aubergines. Season, bearing in mind that the bacon will be salt. Add the bouquet garni. Cover with greaseproof paper and a tightly fitting lid and cook in a moderate oven, gas mark 5 or 375° F. (190° C.) for 1½ hours. Remove the bouquet garni and serve hot in a shallow dish.

Eggs

The egg is the original pre-packed food, and is still relatively cheap in price as well as being essential in practically every branch of cookery.

Many domestic refrigerators have egg storage space in the door. If eggs are refrigerated, they should be removed some hours before use so that they acquire the same temperature as the other ingredients with which they are to be used. There are obvious exceptions to this, of course, i.e. scrambled eggs, meringues.

EGG DISHES

POACHING EGGS

Poaching eggs needs care and practice. Egg poachers sold in shops containing little individual cups set in a tray which rest in a pan of boiling water, do not produce an 'Œuf Poché'. They steam the eggs and a quite different consistency is obtained. I have seen these poachers greeted with enthusiasm in France, but I still disapprove, knowing full well that this neat little egg, with its solid white and semi-solid yolk, is far removed from that mysterious object, a correctly poached egg, enclosed in a veil of white, the yolk being soft and runny. There is a fascination in making a whirlpool in the pan, dropping the egg in and seeing how, with stirring, the white encloses the yolk entirely (see page 26).

ŒUFS MOLLETS

When cooking a dish of Œufs Mollets, care must be taken not to over-boil the eggs. They should boil only for 5–6 minutes. The white should always be firm and solid, the yolk barely set. As soon as the eggs have been boiled for the required time, remove them at once from the pan and place them in cold water to arrest further cooking. Shell them carefully. If the rest of the dish is not ready, keep the eggs hot after shelling by letting them stand in a bowl of hot water until they are required.

ŒUFS EN COCOTTE

Eggs to be cooked in small individual ramekin dishes should never be broken into a cold dish. Place the dish in the oven first of all to heat it through. If the egg is to rest on a purée of some sort, let this be hot when the egg is placed on the top. Again only cook until the egg is just set. It should be remembered that the egg will continue to cook after it has been removed from the oven.

OMELETTES

Making an omelette is at once the easiest and the most tricky process. I have eaten delicious omelettes. I have also eaten thick, solid, tough blankets. Certain points should be observed in omelette making.

    1. *The choice of a Pan.* A French iron pan is the best. Cast aluminium is very good.

    When a new pan is bought it should be thoroughly washed, heated with a spoonful or so of oil, removed from the stove and allowed to stand with the oil in it for twenty-four hours. This is then poured off. After use the pan should only be wiped with tissue paper or a damp cloth. If it has become very dirty, coarse salt can be used to clean it.

The pan should be thick and have a level base, otherwise the omelettes will cook unevenly and burn.

2. *The Eggs*. These should be only lightly beaten, so as to break up the yolks and whites, adding a tablespoon of cold water to each three eggs.

Omelettes are usually made with 2–6 eggs. More than 6 eggs are unwieldy and do not cook evenly. The eggs should be lightly beaten with the water and seasoned.

3. *The Fat*. Butter is the BEST fat to use for cooking omelettes.

The pan should be put over a good heat. When it is very hot, drop a nut of butter into it. Allow it to froth and tip the pan so that the butter runs all over the surface.

Pour in the eggs. Tilt the pan so they run smoothly over the surface. With a fork, stroke the mixture from the sides towards the centre, like the spokes of a wheel, at the same time giving the pan an occasional bang, to settle the eggs. Lift the edges of the omelette with a thin bladed knife and allow the liquid egg to run underneath. As soon as the underside is a light golden brown colour and the surface of the omelette is moist and resembles scrambled eggs – the whole process of cooking should take from 35–45 SECONDS – fold over and place a nut of butter in the pan. Lift the omelette slightly, so as to allow the butter to run underneath, thereby giving a crisp brown surface. Then holding a hot dish or plate in the left hand and the pan in the right hand, turn the omelette with a quick flick of the wrist onto the hot dish.

Any fillings to be added to the omelette should be made and kept hot and spread on the surface just before it is folded over. In some cases the flavouring, or an additional ingredient, is added to the actual egg mixture before it is cooked, for example Omelette Jardinière.

ŒUFS BROUILLÉS – SCRAMBLED EGGS (Method I) *

To 2 eggs allow 30 g. butter (1 oz.) and seasoning

Method: Divide the butter in half and spread one half round the sides and base of the pan. Beat the eggs lightly with a fork. Season well and strain into the pan. Add the rest of the butter cut into small pieces and stir with a wooden spoon over a very gentle heat, scraping the bottom of the pan with the spoon. When the eggs resemble a thick mass, remove the pan from the heat and continue to stir for a moment or two longer. Use at once.

ŒUFS BROUILLÉS – SCRAMBLED EGGS (Method II) *

For 3 eggs allow 45 g. butter (1½ oz.), 1 tablespoon of thick cream and
seasoning

Method: Spread the butter round the sides and base of the pan. Break
the eggs into the pan without whisking them. Add the seasoning and cream
and cook, stirring with a wooden spoon, over a very low heat, or over a
pan of boiling water. Remove from the heat whilst it is still creamy. Stir
a little longer and use at once.

Comment: This is the classical French method for Œufs Brouillés.

ŒUFS ARGENTEUIL **   (for 6 persons)

Ingredients:
6 eggs
Flaky pastry (see page 335)
1 bundle green asparagus or 1
   large packet frozen green
   asparagus

30 g. butter (1 oz.)
Sauce Béchamel made with 3 dl.
   (½ pint) milk, etc. (see page 34)
1½ dl. thick cream (¼ pint)
seasoning

Method: Make the flaky pastry in the usual way and put it aside to relax
in a cool place. Make the sauce Béchamel.

Roll out the pastry and line it into six 9 cm. (3½ inch) tartlet cases. Prick
them very well and bake them blind in a hot oven, gas mark 7 or 425° F.
(220° C.) for 15 minutes. Remove the beans and keep the tartlets hot in a
cooler oven.

Meanwhile, prepare the asparagus and cook it in plenty of boiling salted
water for 10 minutes or until just tender. Take care not to over cook it.
Drain and refresh with cold water, drain again. Take half the asparagus
and keep it hot in the melted butter. Pass the tips of the remaining asparagus through a sieve or vegetable mill and stir the purée into the sauce
Béchamel, together with the cream. Taste and adjust the seasoning. Keep
hot.

Cook the eggs as for Œufs Mollets (see page 244). Meanwhile cut off the
tips of the remaining asparagus and arrange them like the spokes of a
wheel in the tartlet cases. Keep hot. Shell the eggs when they are cooked
and place one carefully in each tartlet case. Cover the eggs with the sauce.
Serve at once.

Comment: If frozen asparagus is used, cook in accordance with directions on the packet. This is not a complicated recipe but it is essential that
the eggs should not be cooked until just before serving.

ŒUFS EN CÔTELETTES ** (for 2–3 persons)

Ingredients:

4 hardboiled eggs
Sauce Béchamel made with 3 dl.
  (½ pint) milk, 45 g. (1½ oz.)
  butter, 45 g. (1½ oz.) plain flour,
  seasoning (see page 34)
3 slices ham, chopped
2 yolks of egg

1 beaten egg
1 tablespoon oil
white breadcrumbs
seasoned flour
deep fat for frying
To Garnish:
fried parsley
halved grilled tomatoes

Method: Make the sauce Béchamel, stir in the two yolks and allow to thicken slightly over a gentle heat. Chop the hardboiled eggs finely and add them, with the chopped ham, to the sauce Béchamel. Season well. Spread the mixture on a plate and allow it to get quite cold. Divide it into even sized portions, roll them in seasoned flour and make them into cutlet shapes. Then dip them in the egg which has been beaten with the oil and coat them with breadcrumbs. Fry them in hot deep fat until they are pale gold. Serve on a hot dish garnished with halved tomatoes and fried parsley (see page 20).

ŒUFS À LA TRIPE * (for 4 persons)

Ingredients:

6 hardboiled eggs
3 medium onions
½ l. milk (¾ pint)
60 g. flour (2 oz.)

75 g. butter (2½ oz.)
60 g. grated cheese (2 oz.)
finely chopped parsley
seasoning

Method: Peel and slice the onions thinly. Heat the butter in a pan and cook the onions in this over a low heat, stirring them from time to time, until they are soft but uncoloured. Stir in the flour, gradually add the milk, stirring all the time and boil for 2–3 minutes. Season. Whisk in the cheese.

Separate the whites from the eggs and cut them into slices. Keep the yolks on one side.

Put the white in a shallow serving dish, pour over the hot sauce. Sieve the hardboiled yolks all over and sprinkle with some chopped parsley.

ŒUFS FARCIS CHIMAY ** (for 2–4 persons)

Ingredients:

4 hardboiled eggs
Duxelles: 1 onion
  120 g. mushrooms (4 oz.)
  1 tablespoon finely chopped
    parsley
  30 g. butter (1 oz.)

2 tablespoons thick cream
seasoning
Sauce Mornay (see page 36)
To finish:
60 g. Gruyère cheese (2 oz.)
a little melted butter

247

Method: Make the duxelles by chopping the onion finely and frying it gently in the butter. Chop the mushrooms finely and squeeze them in a cloth to remove the excess moisture. Add them to the onion and cook gently until the mixture is dry, stirring from time to time. Cut the cold hardboiled eggs in half lengthwise. Remove the yolks, sieve them and mix them well with the duxelles. Moisten with the cream, add the parsley and season. Fill the whites with this mixture.

Make the sauce Mornay in the usual way. Arrange the eggs in a buttered fireproof dish. Coat them with the sauce. Sprinkle with the grated Gruyère cheese and melted butter and brown under a grill or in the top of a hot oven. Serve at once.

ŒUFS À LA LANDAISE * (for 4 persons)

Ingredients:

4 eggs
2 tablespoons oil
120 g. sausage meat (4 oz.)
4 tomatoes

1 onion, finely chopped
2 tablespoons chopped parsley
30–60 g. grated Gruyère cheese
(1–2 oz.)
seasoning

Method: Make the oil hot in a saucepan. Add the onion and cook without colouration until quite soft. Add the sausage meat, the tomatoes, skinned and cut into slices and the parsley. Season well. Mix and heat through thoroughly. Spread this farce at once into a hot shallow fireproof dish. Make four indentures in the mixture. Cook in the top of a hot oven, gas mark 7 or 425° F. (220° C.) for 15 minutes. After this time remove the dish from the oven and break an egg into each indenture. Sprinkle over with the grated Gruyère cheese. Return the dish to the oven for a further 10 minutes or until the eggs are just set. Serve at once.

ŒUFS MÊLÉS ** (for 6 persons)

Ingredients:

6 eggs
60 g. button mushrooms (2 oz.)
180 g. diced carrots (6 oz.)
180 g. chopped onions (6 oz.)
180 g. diced celeriac (6 oz.)
120 g. chopped ham (4 oz.)

3 tablespoons Madeira
120 g. butter, approx. (4 oz.)
3 tablespoons thick cream
a squeeze of lemon juice
seasoning
To finish:
finely chopped parsley

Method: Prepare the onions, carrots and celeriac and cut them into 1 cm. ($\frac{1}{2}$ inch) dice. Heat about two-thirds of the butter in a thick pan, add the vegetables and seasoning. Cover with greaseproof paper and the lid and 'sweat' them over a gentle heat until tender. Now add the ham cut into dice, together with the Madeira. Mix well, keep hot.

Wipe the mushrooms with a cloth and put them in a pan in which the rest of the butter has been melted, and add the lemon juice and seasoning. Cover with greaseproof paper and the lid and sweat these also over a gentle heat for 5–7 minutes. Butter a large hot fireproof dish, then pour in the vegetables and ham, etc. to cover the base. Make six indentures in the vegetables. Crack each egg into a cup and carefully slide them into the indentures. Put in the top of a hot oven, gas mark 6 or 400° F. (200° C.) until the eggs are just set. Remove from the oven, spoon a little cream over each egg. Make a border of the mushrooms round the sides of the dish. Sprinkle with a little finely chopped parsley. Serve at once.

Comment: Peas, French beans, small broad beans and tiny new potatoes can all be used in this dish when they are in season. The green vegetables should, of course, be cooked in boiling salted water.

ŒUFS MOLLETS À LA LYONNAISE *   (for 2–6 persons)

Ingredients:
4–6 eggs
60 g. butter (2 oz.)
45 g. flour (1½ oz.)
2–3 medium sized onions
¼ l. white stock (1½ gills)

¼ l. milk (1½ gills)
seasoning
To finish:
30 g. grated Gruyère cheese (1 oz.)
30 g. fresh butter (1 oz.)

Method: Chop the onions finely and put them to blanch in boiling salted water for 5 minutes. Remove and drain them. Heat the butter in a thick stewpan. Add the onions and cook them gently without allowing them to colour. When they are completely soft, stir in the flour to make a 'roux'. Cook for 2–3 minutes, stirring all the time. Pour in the hot stock and milk. Bring to the boil, keeping it well stirred. Season the sauce and allow it to simmer for 5 minutes.

Meanwhile, cook the eggs in boiling water for 5–6 minutes. Plunge them into tepid water to arrest the cooking. Shell them.

Spread half the onion sauce in the bottom of a buttered fireproof dish. Place the eggs on this and cover with the rest of the sauce. Sprinkle over with the grated Gruyère cheese and put small knobs of butter on the top. Brown quickly in the top of a hot oven, gas mark 7 or 425° F. (220° C.) or under a hot grill. Serve at once.

ŒUFS POCHÉS À LA NIÇOISE **   (for 4 persons)

Ingredients:
4 eggs
¼ l. Sauce Mayonnaise (see page 36) (1½ gills)
concentrated tomato purée
For the Salade Niçoise:
180 g. French beans (6 oz.)

120 g. tomatoes (4 oz.)
120 g. cooked potatoes (4 oz.)
Sauce Vinaigrette (see page 40)
green stuffed olives
anchovy fillets
1 lettuce

Method: Lightly poach the eggs (see page 26). Trim them neatly. Dry on a clean cloth.

Make the Salade Niçoise. Cook the beans in the usual way. Drain and refresh them in cold water. Cut them into lozenge shapes. Drain and dry them on a clean cloth. Skin and pip the tomatoes and cut them into shreds. Cut the potatoes into small dice. Make up the sauce vinaigrette, seasoning well, adding, if liked, some chopped chervil and tarragon. Combine the dressing with the vegetables.

Make the sauce Mayonnaise and colour it with tomato purée so that it is a good pink.

Lay some lettuce leaves in the centre of a serving dish, pile the Salade Niçoise on these. Arrange the eggs all round the salad and coat them with a spoonful of the pink sauce Mayonnaise. Decorate the eggs with anchovy fillets and olives. Serve cold.

ŒUFS À LA PORTUGAISE *   (for 4 persons)

Ingredients:
4 eggs
350 g. tomatoes (¾ lb.)
1 clove garlic
60 g. butter (2 oz.)

seasoning
To Serve:
Sauce Tomate (Method I) (see
    page 38)

Method: Skin the tomatoes and cut them into thin slices. Melt the butter in a pan, add the tomatoes. Season well. Cook until just soft, and then stir in the clove of garlic which has been crushed with a little salt. Pour at once into the bottom of a hot 15 cm. (6 inch) fireproof dish. Make four indentures in the tomato mixture. Break the eggs and drop one in each indenture. Cook in the top of a hot oven, gas mark 7 or 425° F. (220° C.) until the eggs are just set. Serve at once with a 'cordon' of sauce tomate round each egg.

ŒUFS POCHÉS À LA SUZETTE **   (for 4 persons)

Ingredients:
4 eggs
4 large potatoes
½ quantity Sauce Mornay (see
    page 36)

2–3 tablespoons thick cream
30 g. butter (1 oz).
seasoning

Method: Scrub the potatoes well and bake them in their skins in a moderate oven, gas mark 5 or 375° F. (190° C.) for approximately 1 hour or until cooked. Remove them from the oven and cut a slice off the top of each. With a teaspoon scoop out most of the pulp. Pass the potato pulp through a sieve or vegetable mill. Beat in the cream and seasoning. Put a layer of this mixture back in the shells. Keep them hot.

Lightly poach the eggs (see page 26). Drain and trim them. Pour a layer of sauce Mornay in each potato case. Place an egg on the top and coat the eggs with the rest of the sauce Mornay. Sprinkle with melted butter. Brown quickly for a few minutes under a hot grill or in the top of a hot oven, gas mark 7 or 425° F. (220° C.). Serve at once.

ŒUFS À LA RUSSE ***   (for 8 persons)

Ingredients:
8 eggs
1 tablespoon vinegar
For the Salade Russe:
3 small carrots
2 small turnips
60 g. French beans (2 oz.)

60 g. peas (2 oz.)
seasoning
Sauce Mayonnaise (see page 36)
1 l. Aspic Jelly (see page 17)
   (2 pints)
1 truffle

Method: Make the aspic jelly and the sauce Mayonnaise.

Poach the eggs in simmering salted water to which has been added the vinegar, for about 3 minutes. Lift them carefully with a draining spoon on to a clean dry cloth. Allow them to become quite cold.

Cut the carrots and turnips into ½ cm. (¼ inch) dice and slice the beans into similar sized pieces. Cook all the vegetables in separate pans in boiling salted water. Drain and refresh them. Drain again and dry on a clean cloth. Allow them to become quite cold.

Have eight cocotte moulds iced, then coat all over the insides with aspic jelly, which should be on the point of setting. Decorate the base of each with a neat slice of truffle. Trim the eggs and place one in each cocotte and fill with aspic jelly. Put in a cold place to set.

Mix the vegetables with sufficient sauce Mayonnaise to coat and make a mound with the salade in the centre of a serving dish. Unmould the eggs and arrange them all around the salade russe. Chop the rest of the aspic jelly and decorate between the eggs with this. Serve ice cold.

OMELETTE À LA FERMIÈRE *   (for 1–2 persons)

Ingredients:
to a 3–4 egg mixture add:
60 g. diced ham (2 oz.)

2 tablespoons finely chopped fresh
  herbs
seasoning

Method: Add the ingredients to the eggs. Cook as usual, but leave the omelette flat. Do not fold over. Dish on a hot dish and serve at once.

OMELETTE JARDINIÈRE *   (for 1–2 persons)

Ingredients:

4 eggs
1 tablespoon cooked peas
1 tablespoon cooked diced French
  beans
1 tablespoon cooked diced carrots
1 large onion

2 tablespoons oil
a little butter
seasoning
To finish:
2 or 3 firm tomatoes
parsley

Method: Peel and chop the onion *very* finely. Heat the oil in an omelette pan. Add the onion and soften it over a low heat, without allowing it to colour. Beat the eggs lightly with a fork. Add all the cooked vegetables. Season. As soon as the onion is tender, raise the heat and pour in the egg mixture. Stir the omelette in the usual way, but as soon as it is cooked, slide it onto a hot dish, keeping it flat. Dot the surface with knobs of butter and decorate with thin slices of tomato and small bunches of parsley. Serve at once.

OMELETTE AU LARD *   (for 1 person)

Ingredients:
For a 3 egg mixture:
3 slices of lean bacon, cut into lardons

a good slice of gammon
seasoning

Method: Fry the bacon quickly and when crisp add to the eggs, season and cook in the usual way. Meanwhile grill the gammon and serve it on a hot dish with the omelette on top.

OMELETTE À L'OSEILLE *   (for 1–2 persons)

Ingredients:
For 3–4 egg mixture:

1 handful shredded sorrel leaves
  tossed in 30 g. butter (1 oz.)
seasoning

Method: Wash the sorrel. Chop it finely. Toss it in the hot butter for 2–3 minutes. Add to the seasoned egg mixture. Cook as before.

OMELETTE PARMENTIER *   (for 1–2 persons)

Ingredients:
To a 3–4 egg mixture add:

3 tablespoons diced potatoes
  'sweated' in 30 g. butter (1 oz.)
seasoning

Method: Cook the potatoes in boiling salted water for 5 minutes. Drain them and cut them into 1 cm. (½ inch) dice. Make the butter hot in a pan and sauter the potatoes in this. Make the omelette in the usual way with the potatoes added to the beaten eggs before cooking.

OMELETTE AUX POINTES D'ASPERGES *

(for 1–2 persons)

Ingredients:
For a 3–4 egg mixture:
15 small heads of asparagus in
  1 cm. lengths (½ inch)

45 g. butter (1½ oz.)
seasoning
To finish:
a tiny bunch of asparagus heads

Method: Cook the asparagus in boiling salted water until it is tender. Drain and refresh it in cold water. Drain again and toss it in the melted butter. Add the asparagus to the eggs. Season. Cook in the usual way. Decorate the top of the omelette with a small bunch of cooked asparagus. Serve at once.

PIPERADE BASQUAISE *

(for 2–3 persons)

Ingredients:
700 g. ripe tomatoes (1½ lb.)
2 red peppers
2 green peppers
6 eggs
1 clove garlic

pinch of sugar
oil for frying
seasoning
To finish:
triangular or heart shaped
  croûtons of fried bread

Methods: Cut the peppers in half and remove the seeds and pith. Chop fairly finely and plunge them into a pan of boiling salted water, allowing them to simmer for 5–7 minutes. Drain them and dry them on a clean cloth. Reserve three even sized tomatoes. Skin, pip and quarter the others. Crush the garlic with a little salt. Put about 4 tablespoons of oil in the bottom of a sauté pan. (The exact amount of oil will depend on the size of the pan used.) Make it hot, put in the peppers and cook them slowly for 3–4 minutes. Then add the quartered tomatoes, garlic, seasoning and sugar. Cover the pan and cook for a further 10–15 minutes. Slice the three tomatoes, heat a little oil in a separate pan, and fry them carefully in this. Fry the croûtons in oil. Keep both hot. When the tomatoes and peppers are soft and mushy, pour off any excess liquid. Beat the eggs very lightly with a fork, add them to the tomatoes and peppers, return the pan to a low heat and stir with a wooden spoon until the eggs are just beginning to set. Serve in a hot dish with the slices of tomato at each end and the croûtons at each side.

Light Luncheon and Supper Dishes

LIGHT LUNCHEON AND SUPPER DISHES

PÂTE À CRÊPES **

Ingredients:
150 g. plain flour (5 oz.)
3 dl. milk (½ pint)
1 tablespoon oil or melted butter

1 whole egg and 1 yolk
(salt and pepper if a savoury
   mixture is required)

Method: Sift the flour into a bowl, make a well in the centre, drop in the whole egg, the yolk and the oil. (If butter is added it must be liquid but not hot.) Beat in the milk by degrees, using either a wooden spatula or a small sauce whisk. Stir rather rapidly at first, then more slowly whilst mixing the flour from the sides of the bowl. The mixing of the liquid into the flour is of the utmost importance for at no time should the mixture in any way resemble a dough. A little more flour is incorporated all the time until a batter is obtained which should be the consistency of thin cream. If it is too thick, add a little more milk.

TO COOK CRÊPES

A strong iron pan is needed with a flat bottom. Heat the pan until it is very hot, pour in a little oil and tilt the pan so that the oil runs all over the surface of the pan. Pour off the superfluous oil, then using a small jug or measure, pour in just sufficient batter to run all over the surface, making a *very* thin coating. Replace over the heat. Cook until the upper surface looks dry. Loosen the edges with a thin bladed knife or palette knife, toss, or turn with the knife, and cook the other side. The side cooked first is always the right side of the crêpe. The idea of tossing the crêpes or pancakes is that they can be made rather thinner than if they were turned with a knife, but provided the knife is thin and flexible it can equally well be employed.

Probably the best way to keep crêpes hot after cooking is as follows: as they are fried, stand each one on a reversed saucer, which in turn is stood on a plate over a pan of hot water. As each crêpe is cooked, slip it on top of the previous one, thereby keeping them hot and a good shape. To re-heat place a pudding basin large enough to cover the saucer over them, and heat the water in the pan. In this way it will be found that the crêpes will heat through perfectly.

IMPORTANT

3 dl. (½ pint) of pâte à crêpes will make approximately 10–15 crêpes, according to the size of the pan used. Most of the recipes are intended for 3–4 persons.

CASSOULETTES SUZANNE *   (for 6 persons)

Ingredients:
500 g. spinach (1 lb.)
250 g. chopped cooked chicken
  or white meat (½ lb.)
125 g. mushrooms (¼ lb.)
Sauce Béchamel made with ½ l.
  (1 pint)

milk, etc. (see page 34)
90 g. butter (3 oz.)
seasoning
squeeze of lemon juice
To serve:
6 cooked mushroom caps

Method: Wash the spinach thoroughly and remove the tough stalks. Blanch it for 2–3 minutes in boiling salted water, drain it and refresh with cold water. Drain again and squeeze between the hands to expel as much water as possible. Make 60 g. (2 oz.) butter hot in a large pan, turn the spinach in this until it is tender.

Meanwhile, make the sauce Béchamel. Chop the mushrooms roughly, cook them slowly in the rest of the butter with a squeeze of lemon juice and seasoning.

Take six individual fireproof dishes and spread a layer of spinach in each. Keep hot. Mix the meat and the mushrooms with enough sauce Béchamel to bind. Make it hot. Adjust the seasoning. Divide the mixture equally between the six dishes. Coat each with hot sauce Béchamel and decorate with a cooked mushroom cap. Serve at once.

CROQUE MONSIEUR *   (for 2 persons)

Ingredients:

4 slices of bread
2 slices of ham

2 thin slices hard cheese (Gruyère for preference)
seasoning
150 g. butter, approx. (5 oz.)

Method: Spread the bread with butter and make a sandwich for each person with the ham and cheese. Season and press firmly together.

Make the rest of the butter hot in a frying pan and fry the sandwiches quickly on both sides, until crisp and golden brown. Serve at once.

Comment: This is a classic hot sandwich.

CROQUETTES DE FROMAGE **   (for 3–4 persons)

Ingredients:

Sauce Béchamel made with:
45 g. butter (1½ oz.)
45 g. plain flour (1½ oz.)
3 dl. milk (½ pint)
        (see page 34)
3 yolks of egg
60–90 g. grated cheese (2–3 oz.)

beaten egg to which has been added 1 tablespoon oil
seasoned flour
white breadcrumbs
deep fat for frying
seasoning
For the Garnish:
Fried parsley (see page 20)

Method: Make a thick sauce Béchamel in the usual way. When it is cooked, stir in the egg yolks and the cheese. Season well. Pour out on a buttered plate and allow it to become quite cold.

When it is firm, turn it on to a floured board and cut it into equal sized pieces about 5 cm. (2 inches) square. Coat them in seasoned flour, then dip into the beaten egg. Roll them in the breadcrumbs and fry quickly in hot deep fat. Drain on kitchen paper. Serve at once piled up in a dish on a dish paper. Garnish with sprigs of fried parsley.

FICELLE DE NORMANDIE **   (for 4–6 persons)

Ingredients:
Pâte à Crêpes (see page 255)
For the Filling:
6 large slices of ham
For the Sauce:
125 g. button mushrooms (4 oz.)

30 g. unsalted butter (1 oz.)
1 heaped teaspoon flour
1–2 tablespoons Calvados
1½ dl. thick cream (1 gill)
a little extra butter
seasoning

Method: Make up the pâte à crêpes in the usual way. Warm the slices of ham through by placing them between two plates and standing them over a pan of boiling water.

Make the sauce. Cut the mushrooms into fairly thick slices and cook them in the butter over a gentle heat for 3–4 minutes, stirring all the time. They do not want to be too well done. Scatter in the flour, stir round, then stir in the Calvados and the cream, bring to the boil and simmer for 2–3 minutes, stirring all the time. Taste and season. Keep hot.

Fry the crêpes, making 6 approximately the size of the slices of ham. Place a slice of ham on each crêpe. Roll them together like a cigar. Arrange them down the centre of a fireproof dish and pour over the sauce. Place knobs of butter on the top and glaze under a hot grill.

GÂTIS DE ST. AFFRIQUE **   (for 4 persons)

Ingredients:
Flaky Pastry made with 240 g.
  plain flour, etc. (see page 335)
  (8 oz.)

For the Filling:
120 g. Roquefort cheese (4 oz.)
120 g. Cantal cheese (4 oz.)
1–2 tablespoons single cream
1 beaten egg

Method: Make up the pastry in the usual way and put it aside to relax.

Grate the Cantal cheese and place it in a bowl with the Roquefort, which has been mashed with a fork. Mix the two cheeses together, adding a little cream.

Roll out the pastry on a floured board and divide it into two rectangles, approximately 25 × 15 cm. (10 × 6 inches). Place one rectangle on a baking sheet. Spread the cheese mixture on this, leaving a border of about 1 cm. (⅓ inch) all round. Brush this with beaten egg, lay the second half of pastry on the top, pressing the edges together to make them adhere. Lightly brush with beaten egg. Mark with the back of a knife into fingers. Put in a hot oven, gas mark 7 or 425° F. (220° C.) and bake for 12–15 minutes. Serve hot.

Comment: This is a speciality of the Hôtel Moderne in St. Affrique in the Roquefort country where it appears on the menu on Wednesdays and Fridays only.

Roquefort cheese is very expensive in England and Cantal is hard to obtain as well. Any blue veined and hard cheese can be used, but of course the result will never be quite the same.

GNOCCHIS À LA FLORENTINE ** (for 4–5 persons)

Ingredients:

Pâte à Choux made with 60 g. (2 oz.) plain flour, etc. (see page 336)
Pommes de Terre Duchesse made with 500 g. (1 lb.) potatoes, etc. (see page 226)
90 g. grated Parmesan cheese (3 oz.)

60 g. chopped ham (2 oz.)
2 tablespoons chopped herbs
seasoning
To finish:
grated cheese
60 g. melted butter (2 oz.)

Method: Make the pâte à choux in the usual way and the pommes de terre duchesse. Mix them together very smoothly, then stir in the herbs, grated cheese and finely chopped ham. Season well.

Using a forcing bag and a 1 cm. (⅜ inch) tube, pipe this mixture in short lengths about 2 cm. (¾ inch) long into simmering salted water, cutting the mixture off with a sharp knife dipped in water. Allow the gnocchis to poach gently for 10 minutes. At the end of this time remove them with a draining spoon and put them into a bowl of cold water to stop their cooking.

When all the mixture has been cooked, drain the gnocchis well. Put them in a well buttered fireproof dish with grated cheese between each layer. Sprinkle the top with melted butter. Reheat them in the top of a hot oven. Serve at once.

Alternatively, the gnocchis may be folded into a well seasoned sauce Mornay, put in a fireproof dish, sprinkled with cheese and browned in the top of the oven as above.

KAROLYS AUX CREVETTES ** (for 3–4 persons)

Ingredients:

Pâte à Choux made with 60 g. (2 oz.) plain flour etc. (see page 336)
Sauce Béchamel made with 3 dl. (1 gill) thin cream and seasoning etc. (see page 34 for method)

a little beaten egg
180 g. unshelled prawns (6 oz.)
To finish:
paprika or prawn heads

Method: Make up the pâte à choux in the usual way. Using a forcing bag and a 1 cm. (⅜ inch) plain pipe, pipe the mixture out into fingers about 7 cm. (3 inches) long on a greased baking sheet. Brush them over with a little beaten egg and bake them in a hot oven, gas mark 7–8 or 425–450° F. (220–230° C.) for 10 minutes. After this time reduce the heat to gas mark 5 or 375° F. (190° C.) for a further 20 minutes.

While the karolys are cooking shell the prawns. Make up the sauce Béchamel, seasoning it well. Add the prawns to the sauce and keep hot.

When the karolys are well risen and crisp and have been cooked for the required time, remove them from the oven. At once take a sharp knife and cut lengthwise down one side near the top, thus leaving a good depth for the filling. Using a teaspoon fill them with the prawn sauce. If available use 3–4 prawn heads to decorate each opening, otherwise a touch of paprika may be used. Serve at once while they are still very hot.

LES MARQUISES DE SEVIGNÉ ** (for 3–4 persons)

Ingredients:

Flaky Pastry made with 120 g. (4 oz.) plain flour, etc. (see page 335)

For the filling:
1 small onion finely chopped
30 g. butter (1 oz.)
1½ dl. thin cream (1 gill)

2 eggs
1 level teaspoon curry powder
a little dripping for frying
1½ dl. milk (1 gill)
15 g. flour (½ oz.)
4–6 chipolata sausages
seasoning

Method: Make up the pastry in the usual way. Line carefully into a flan ring 18 cm. (7 inches) in diameter. Heat the butter in a pan, add the onion and soften it over a low heat without allowing it to colour. Stir in the flour and curry powder. Cook for 2–3 minutes, stirring all the time. Add the milk and cook for a further 5 minutes, stirring continuously. Remove from the heat. Beat the eggs with the cream and strain them into the mixture. Season. Meanwhile fry the chipolatas in the dripping until they are just brown. Lay them in the pastry case. Pour over the egg mixture and bake in a hot oven, gas mark 7 or 425° F. (220° C.) for 10 minutes. Reduce the heat slightly and continue cooking for a further 20 minutes. Serve hot.

QUICHE BOURGUIGNONNE ** (for 4–5 persons)

Ingredients:

Flaky pastry made with 120 g. (4 oz.) plain flour, etc. (see page 335)

For the Filling:
¼ l. thin cream (1½ gills)
2–3 eggs

120 g. prawns (4 oz.)
15 g. grated cheese (½ oz.)
a tiny pinch of nutmeg
seasoning

To finish:
a little chopped parsley

Method: Make up the pastry in the usual way. Put it aside to relax. Prepare the filling – shell all the prawns with the exception of 6–8, which are to be used for the decoration. Whisk the eggs. Stir in the cream and add the nutmeg. Season well, bearing in mind that the prawns will be salt.

Roll out the pastry and line into an 18 cm. (7 inch) flan ring. Cover the bottom with the shelled prawns. Strain on the egg and cream mixture. Scatter the grated cheese on top. Put to bake in a hot oven, gas mark 7 or 425° F. (220° C.) for 10 minutes, reduce the heat to gas mark 5 or 375° F. (190° C.) and cook for a further 20 minutes. Just before serving, decorate with the whole prawns and a little finely chopped parsley. Serve warm or cold.

TARTE PANACHÉE **   (for 5–6 persons)

Ingredients:

Flaky pastry made with 180 g. (6 oz.) plain flour, etc. (see page 335)
For the Filling:
$\frac{1}{4}$ l. Sauce Mornay (see page 36) ($\frac{1}{2}$ pint)
60 g. shelled prawns (2 oz.)
1 dl. thick cream ($\frac{1}{2}$ gill)
pinch of nutmeg
seasoning
4 hardboiled eggs
4–5 medium sized tomatoes
30 g. butter (1 oz.)
45 g. Gruyère cheese (1$\frac{1}{2}$ oz.)
Dijon mustard
For the Garnish:
15–20 cooked whole prawns

Method: Make the flaky pastry in the usual way. Line it into a 27 cm. (9 inch) flan ring. Prick the base very well. Bake blind in a hot oven, gas mark 7 or 425° F. (220° C.). Remove on to a wire rack to cool.

Whilst it is cooking, make the sauce Mornay. Remove from the heat and stir in the shelled prawns and the cream. Taste and adjust the seasoning, adding a pinch of nutmeg.

Skin the tomatoes, cut them into fairly thick slices and toss them in about 30 g. (1 oz.) melted butter. Season. Slice the hardboiled eggs.

Spread the base of the flan with a thick covering of Dijon mustard. Cover with a layer of eggs, then with the tomatoes. Pour over the sauce Mornay to cover the filling completely. Sprinkle over the grated cheese. Put it in the top of a fairly hot oven, gas mark 6 or 400° F. (200° C.) for about 15 minutes to heat through and lightly brown the top. Just before serving arrange a ring of whole prawns all round the edge. Serve hot.

TARTLETTES DE CREVETTES AU FROMAGE **
(for 4–6 persons)

Ingredients:

12 Flaky pastry tartlet cases
2 large or 4 small petit Suisse cheeses
100 g. Coulommiers cheese (3$\frac{1}{2}$ oz.)
240 g. shelled shrimps (8 oz.)
seasoning

Method: Using a fork, mash the petit Suisse with the Coulommiers cheese. Reserve 12 shrimps and very finely chop the remainder. Mix the chopped shrimps with the cheeses. Season. Pile the mixture up into domes in the tartlet cases. Lay a shrimp on the top of each. Serve cold.

Comment: Coulommiers cheese is a French whole milk round soft cheese, after the 'Façon Brie'. It is made in Seine-et-Marne, the Brie country. It is smaller than the average Brie, about 30 cm. (10 inches) or less in diameter. It is mostly made from October to May when Brie Gras is not made.

TIMBALE À LA ORLOFF *** (for 4–6 persons)

Ingredients:

¼ l. Pâte à Crêpes (see page 225) (½ pint)

100 g. semolina (3½ oz.)

½ l. chicken stock (¾ pint)

4 yolks of egg

120 g. mushrooms (4 oz.)

120 g. cooked ham (4 oz.)

180–240 g. cooked chicken (6–8 oz.)

3 dl. Sauce Veloutée (see page 39) (½ pint)

30 g. butter (1 oz.)

a little lemon juice

seasoning

To Serve:

Sauce Soubise (see page 38)

Method: Make 9 thin crêpes. Cut 6 of them in half and arrange them over the base and sides of a 21 cm. (8 inch) moule à manqué or round cake tin, radiating from the centre and overlapping.

Boil the stock in a pan and shoot in the semolina while stirring vigorously. Bring back to the boil and, still stirring, continue to cook for 5 minutes to ensure the semolina is thoroughly cooked. Remove the mixture from the heat and beat in 2 yolks of egg.

Make up the sauce veloutée, remove from the heat and beat in the other 2 yolks of egg.

Wipe the mushrooms on a clean cloth, cut them into strips. Heat the butter in a small saucepan, add a squeeze of lemon juice, put the mushrooms in this, cover with greaseproof paper and the lid and cook them over a gentle heat for 2–3 minutes. Put them on one side. Cut the chicken and the ham into julienne strips. Mix them with the mushrooms and sufficient sauce veloutée to cohere. Taste and season.

Pour half the semolina mixture into the crêpe-lined tin. Smooth over. Cover with a crêpe and then pour in the chicken, ham and mushroom mixture. Cover with a second crêpe and complete the filling with the remaining semolina mixture. Cover with the remaining crêpe and turn the ends of the crêpes lining the sides of the tin over this.

Bake in a bain-marie or roasting tin containing boiling water, in a moderately hot oven, gas mark 6 or 400° F. (200° C.) for 25–30 minutes.

To Serve: Unmould on a hot serving dish and serve accompanied by sauce soubise.

Sweets

A subtle change has come over the taste of the British, in that sweets are less sweet than they used to be. This is possibly due to the craze for slimming. Nevertheless, less sugar is desired than has previously been the case. Bearing this in mind, the Crème Anglaise and some syrups have reduced quantities of sugar as compared with Book I.

It is not possible to take too much trouble over the presentation of an attractive sweet course, which often can be prepared in advance, and can well be the 'pièce de résistance' of a meal.

Another change which has occurred, is the enormously increased consumption of wine by the British. This could well lead to the French custom of taking the cheese course before the dessert; the cheese making an excellent partner for the wine which is left in the glass after the meat course.

SWEETS

GELATINE

Many cooks prefer the leaf or sheet gelatine, principally because it dissolves more easily and has no taste – the reason it is not used more generally may be due to the fact that some may not know how to adapt the weight – say of half an ounce into leaves or else find it difficult to obtain. Nowadays, when most of the leaf gelatine is of a standard thickness and we do not meet that very thick, almost yellow kind, I think it is fairly safe to use 5 sheets to set one pint of liquid in place of 15 g. ($\frac{1}{2}$ oz.) of granulated gelatine. It is recognized that half an ounce of most of the best known granulated gelatines will stiffen one pint of liquid. There are exceptions to this and it is important to read the directions on the outside of the packets of gelatine.

In all cases it is most important to soften the gelatine first in cold water and then dissolve it in hot liquid. When using leaf gelatine, place it in a bowl of cold water and soften first, gently squeeze with the hands to dispel the excess moisture and then stir into the hot liquid. With the granulated gelatine, after softening it in cold water, place it in a small basin over a pan of boiling water and stir until dissolved completely. To test if it is dissolved, stir with a clean metal spoon. Any undissolved granules will easily be detected on the back of the spoon. This is a more satisfactory way of dissolving it than heating it in a pan over a direct heat which may result in overheating or boiling the gelatine: this will make it sticky and stringy. The gelatine should be added lukewarm to the mixture to be set. Many sweets which contain gelatine have whipped cream or whisked egg whites added when the main mixture has begun to set. In this case pour the mixture with the added gelatine, into a large bowl and put in a cool place. From *time to time* stir the mixture, so that it thickens evenly. It will be found that it will begin to set round the edges of the bowl first. Do not attempt to add the cream or whisked egg whites to a mixture which has become too solid as it will not mix properly and be lumpy and unpleasant. Should the mixture become too thick, place the bowl for a few moments over a pan of hot, not boiling water. Stir until it is liquid again, pour into a clean bowl and then wait until it thickens a second time. This may seem a lot of bother, but it is the only way to get a satisfactory result.

DECORATING SWEETS

Even if the main part of the work is done well in advance, the decoration should be left as far as possible until the last moment. Decorations always look their best when fresh. Cream should be whisked gently, adding a spoonful of cold milk in hot weather to prevent it from becoming too stiff. When whisking cream for piping, watch it whilst whisking and visualise the type of texture required for piping. Once the cream has been over-whisked, it will not pipe satisfactorily. It should stand up in spikes from the end of the whisk. Cream for whipping bought from dairies is called 'double cream' – this means that it must have at least 48 per cent fat content. Flavouring, such as vanilla, should be added *after* the cream has been whipped.

CRÈME CHANTILLY

Crème Chantilly is whipped cream. Vanilla sugar and sugar are added after the whipping is completed.

GLACÉ CHERRIES AND ANGELICA

Glacé cherries are nearly always halved when used as a decoration. Angelica should be cut in bold diamonds, never tiny spikes. The sides should be about 1 cm. ($\frac{1}{2}$ in.). It is best to wash the angelica first to remove the sugary deposit on the outside, then dry carefully and cut as required.

PISTACHIO NUTS

Are expensive, but only small quantities are used. They should be blanched in boiling water first and the purple-brown skins removed. Afterwards dry and chop them finely or cut crosswise when they can be used three slices at a time to give a clover leaf effect.

CRYSTALLIZED VIOLETS, ROSES AND MIMOSA

These can all be used as decoration, in moderation. When they are put on to a moist surface the colour often runs and for that reason it is especially important only to decorate with them just before serving.

ABRICOTS À L'ANCIENNE ** (for 2–4 persons)

Ingredients:
4 tinned apricot halves
Pâte à Génoise Commune made
   with 2 eggs, etc. (see page 333)
   baked in a swiss roll tin.
1 tablespoon rum
For the apple purée:
250 g. apples ($\frac{1}{2}$ lb.)
1 dl. water ($\frac{1}{2}$ gill)

15 g. butter ($\frac{1}{2}$ oz.)
30 g. sugar (1 oz.)
To finish:
30 g. chopped blanched almonds
   (1 oz.)
1 tablespoon sieved icing sugar
30 g. melted butter (1 oz.)
3 tablespoons sieved apricot jam
1 tablespoon rum

Method: Cut the cake into rounds about 6–7 cm. (2$\frac{1}{2}$–3 in.) in diameter and arrange them in a large shallow fireproof serving dish. Sprinkle each round with rum.

Make the apple purée. Peel and core the apples and cut them into slices. Put them into a pan with the water and butter. Cook them until they are soft and mushy, stirring occasionally. Pass them through a sieve or vegetable mill. Beat in the sugar at once.

Put a quarter of the apple purée on each round of cake with a half apricot on top.

Scatter over the chopped almonds. Dust with sieved icing sugar and sprinkle a little melted butter over each.

Put the dish in the top of a hot oven, gas mark 7 or 425° F. (220° C.) for a few minutes to caramelise the sugar.

Meanwhile melt the apricot jam over a low heat. Remove it from the stove and stir in the tablespoon of rum.

Remove the dish from the oven. Carefully pour in the apricot sauce so as to surround the cake bases.

ABRICOTS À LA BANVILLE ** (for 6 persons)

Ingredients:
6 ripe, firm apricots
12 small Macarons (see page 356)
syrup for poaching made with
   3 dl. ($\frac{1}{2}$ pint) water, 120 g. (4 oz.)

sugar and 1 vanilla pod
   (see page 24)
To finish:
1$\frac{1}{2}$ dl. thick cream ($\frac{1}{4}$ pint)
glacé cherries
angelica

Method: Make the syrup. Cut the apricots in half. Remove the stones. Poach the apricots lightly in the syrup; do not let them boil or they will become broken and a bad shape. When they are cooked, lift them carefully out of the syrup, drain and allow to cool.

Make the macarons and arrange them in a ring in a serving dish. Reduce the syrup until it is fairly thick. Spoon a little over each macaron. Place a halved apricot in the centre of each, cut side downwards and brush over with the rest of the syrup. Decorate each apricot with a halved glacé cherry and leaves cut from angelica. Stiffly whip the cream and using a forcing bag with a rosette tube, pipe a design in the centre of the dish. Serve very cold.

ABRICOTS À LA MASCOTTE ** (makes 10–12 tartlets)

Ingredients:
Pâte Sucrée made with 75 g. plain
  flour (2½ oz.), etc. (see page 339)
450 g. fresh apricots (1 lb.),
syrup for poaching made with
  3 dl. water (½ pint), and 180 g.
  sugar (6 oz.) (see page 24)
  OR
1 tin halved apricots

Crème Pralinée made with:
1 yolk of egg
a good 15 g. crème de riz (½ oz.)
30 g. sugar (1 oz.)
1½ dl. milk (1 gill)
30 g. powdered praline (1 oz.)
  (see page 348)
30 g. butter (1 oz.)
To finish:
a few chopped browned almonds
1–2 tablespoons sieved apricot jam

Method: Make up the pâte sucrée in the usual way. Put it aside to relax. Roll it out and line it into tartlet tins. Prick the bases well. Bake the tartlets in a fairly hot oven, gas mark 6 or 400° F. (200° C.) for 15 minutes. When the pastry is golden brown, remove the tartlets from the tins and place them on a wire rack to cool.

Halve and stone the apricots and poach them very gently in the syrup until they are cooked. Lift them carefully and drain them on a wire rack or clean cloth. Make the crème pralinée – work the sugar, crème de riz and egg yolk in a bowl. Heat the milk and pour it over the mixture, stirring well. Return it to the pan and bring it to the boil, stirring all the time. Simmer until it thickens and the crème de riz is cooked. Remove it from the heat and whilst it is still hot, beat in the praline and the butter. Pour the crème on to a plate and allow it to cool.

Heat the jam and thin it with a little of the syrup the apricots were cooked in. Put a spoonful of the crème pralinée in each tartlet. Arrange a halved apricot on the top. Brush all over with the apricot jam. Scatter over a few chopped almonds.

ABRICOTS À LA PARISIENNE ** (for 6 persons)

Ingredients:

6 tinned apricot halves
2 whites of egg
75 g. castor sugar (2½ oz.)
60 g. plain flour (2 oz.)
60 g. butter (2 oz.)

60 g. chopped almonds (2 oz.)
1 teaspoon vanilla sugar
1 dessertspoon icing sugar
240 g. sieved raspberry jam (½ lb.)
4–5 tablespoons redcurrant jelly
1½ dl. thick cream (1 gill)

Method: Melt the butter until it runs, then put it aside to cool. Whisk the whites until frothy, but not stiff. Add the sugar and continue to whisk for 3–4 minutes. Fold in the flour, sifted with the vanilla sugar, together with the almonds coarsely chopped and the butter.

Using a teaspoon, place the mixture in heaps on a greased baking sheet. Spread out into rounds, about 5–7 cm. (2–3 inches) apart, making 18 in all. See that each round is of even size. Dust over with icing sugar and cook in a fairly hot oven, gas mark 6 or 400°F. (200° C.) for 4–5 minutes. When they are brown round the edges, remove them and place them on a wire rack to harden off.

Take the biscuits and spread them with a layer of raspberry jam, sandwiching 3 together. On the top of each place a halved apricot, cut side uppermost. Spoon over melted redcurrant jelly. Whisk the cream stiffly and, using a forcing bag with a rosette tube, pipe a star of cream in the centre of each. Serve cold.

ABRICOTS AU RIZ CRÉOLE ** (for 4–6 persons)

Ingredients:

135 g. Carolina rice (4½ oz.)
75 g. castor sugar (2½ oz.)
3 dl. milk (½ pint)
30 g. butter (1 oz.)
1 teaspoon vanilla sugar

1 tin apricot halves
1 egg
To finish:
glacé cherries
angelica
1 tablespoon sieved apricot jam

Method: Put the apricots on a wire rack to drain and reserve the syrup. Put the rice into a pan of boiling water and boil for 5 minutes. Drain it well. Heat the milk in a saucepan until it boils. Stir in the rice, the sugar, vanilla sugar and butter. Lay a piece of greaseproof paper on the top of the rice and cover with the lid. Put the pan in a moderate oven, gas mark 4–5 or 350–375° F. (180–190° C.) and cook for 25 minutes. During this time do not disturb the rice in any way or it will cook unevenly. When it is ready, remove it from the oven and whilst it is still hot stir in the beaten egg. Turn the rice on to a serving dish and with a palette knife, form it into a flat cake or galette shape. Arrange the halved apricots all over the top.

Boil the apricot syrup over a good heat until it is reduced by half. Stir in the apricot jam which must be mixed in whilst the syrup is still hot. Cool slightly. Arrange a decoration of halved glacé cherries and leaves cut from the angelica on the top of the apricots and coat with the syrup. Serve very cold.

MOUSSE À LA CONFITURE ** (for 4 persons)

Ingredients:
4 whites of egg
450 g. apricot jam (1 lb.)
caramel made with 120 g.

sugar, (4 oz.) 1 dl. water ($\frac{1}{2}$ gill)
(see page 16)
1 wine glass rum

Method: Make a caramel with the sugar and water. Line a 15 cm. (6 inch) charlotte mould with this, holding it in a cloth and turning to allow the caramel to coat the sides and the base.

Sieve the jam and reserve one tablespoon for finishing. Whisk the egg whites very stiffly, then fold in the sieved apricot jam.

Fill this mixture into the lined charlotte mould and stand it in a bain-marie or roasting tin containing boiling water. Cook in a moderate oven, gas mark 5 or 375° F. (190° C.) for $\frac{1}{2}$ hour.

When it is cooked allow it to get quite cold before unmoulding on a serving dish. Melt the tablespoon of jam in a small pan and stir in the rum. Allow it to cool and pour it over the mousse. Serve cold.

NAPPES AUX ABRICOTS ** (for 4 persons)

Ingredients:
Pâte Sucrée (see page 339)
450 g. tin apricots (1 lb.)

sieved apricot jam for glaze
a little white of egg

Method: Make up the pastry in the usual way and put it aside to relax.
Pour off their syrup and drain the apricots well on a clean cloth.

Roll the pastry fairly thinly and cut it into squares of approximately 6 cm. (2$\frac{1}{2}$ inches). Place a half apricot on opposite corners of each square, fold over the other two corners to overlap slightly and seal the join with a little white of egg.

Bake the 'nappes' in a fairly hot oven, gas mark 6 or 400° F. (200° C.) for 15–20 minutes or until the pastry is a pale golden colour. When they are cooked remove them from the oven and place them on a wire rack to cool. When they are quite cold brush them all over with hot apricot glaze.

TARTE AUX ABRICOTS ET AUX CERISES **

(for 4–5 persons)

Ingredients:
Flaky pastry made with 120 g. (4 oz.)
  plain flour, etc. (see page 335)
Crème Pâtissière (see page 344)
1 small tin apricot halves
1 small tin cherries

To finish:
sieved apricot jam and redcurrant
  jelly for glazing
glacé cherries
angelica

Method: Make up the pastry in the usual way. Put it aside to relax. Make up the crème pâtissière and allow it to cool.

Roll out the pastry and line it into an 18 cm. (7 inch) flan ring. Spread the crème pâtissière in an even layer in the bottom of the case. Bake it in a moderate oven, gas mark 6–7 or 400–425° F. (200–220° C.) for 30 minutes. When it is cooked remove it and place it on a wire rack to cool.

Drain the apricots and drain and stone the cherries. Arrange the apricots in a ring all round the edge of the flan. Then place a double or treble ring of cherries inside the ring of apricots. Place an apricot in the centre of the tart. Heat the apricot jam and redcurrant jelly separately. Brush the apricots with apricot glaze and the cherries with redcurrant glaze. Decorate between the apricots with the glacé cherries and leaves cut from angelica. Serve cold.

CRÈME PRISE AUX AMANDES **

(for 3–4 persons)

Ingredients:
½ l. milk (¾ pint)
2 eggs
2 yolks of egg
60 g. ground almonds (2 oz.)
60 g. castor sugar (2 oz.)

1 teaspoon vanilla sugar
1 dessertspoon kirsch
To finish:
1½ dl. thick cream (1 gill)
30 g. split or chopped almonds
  (1 oz.)

Method: Put the eggs, yolks, ground almonds and sugars into a bowl and work all well together until perfectly mixed. Heat the milk to simmering point. Pour it on to the eggs a little at a time, stirring continuously. Add the kirsch. Stir again and pour the mixture into individual buttered fireproof pots. Stand them in a bain-marie or roasting tin containing boiling water and cook in a moderate oven, gas mark 5 or 375° F. (190° C.) for about 25–30 minutes, or until set. Remove them and cool completely. When they are cold, decorate each pot with whipped cream and the almonds. Serve ice cold.

CHARLOTTE PRALINÉE **   (for 5–6 persons)

Ingredients:
3 eggs
1 tablespoon castor sugar
90 g. praline (3 oz.) (see page 348)
¼ l. thick cream (1½ gills)

15 g. gelatine (½ oz.)
Biscuits à la Cuillère (see page 331)
To finish:
1 dl. thick cream (½ gill)

Method: Place a round of buttered paper in the bottom of a 15 cm. (6 inch) charlotte mould or cake tin. Make the biscuits à la cuillère and line the sides of the mould with these. Put the gelatine to soften in cold water. Pound the praline in a mortar. Separate the eggs. Beat the yolks and sugar over a pan of hot water until thick and creamy. Remove and continue to beat until they are quite cold.

Dissolve the gelatine in 1 dl. (½ gill) of hot water. Cool slightly and then stir it into the yolk and sugar mixture. Mix thoroughly and put it aside in a cold place stirring from time to time. When it begins to set fold in the praline. Lightly whip the cream and fold this in also. Whisk the whites stiffly and fold these in lightly, but thoroughly. Pour this mixture into the prepared charlotte mould. Place in a refrigerator or cold place until set. When it is set, trim the biscuits to the level of the filling. Turn out the charlotte carefully on a serving dish. Using a forcing bag and rosette tube, decorate the top with the stars of whipped cream. Serve very cold.

FLAN FRANGIPANE **   (for 4–5 persons)

Ingredients:
Pâte Sucrée (see page 339)
For the Filling:
¼ l. milk (1½ gills)
60 g. castor sugar (2 oz.)
1 teaspoon plain flour
15 g. ground almonds (½ oz.)

1 egg
2 yolks of egg
1 tablespoon kirsch or Grand
   Marnier to flavour
To finish:
sieved apricot jam for glaze

Method: Make up the pâte sucrée in the usual way. Put it aside to relax.

Meanwhile make the crème Frangipane for the filling. Mix the sugar, the flour and the ground almonds together with the egg yolks in a bowl. Heat 1½ dl. (1 gill) of milk and pour it into the mixture. Stir well and return the mixture to the pan, which has been rinsed out. Cook over a gentle heat, keeping well stirred until it thickens. Remove from the heat. Beat the remaining egg with the rest of the milk and stir it in, together with the liqueur to flavour.

Bake the pastry blind in an 18 cm. (7 inch) flan ring (see page 326), in a fairly hot oven, gas mark 6 or 400° F. (200° C.) approximately 20–25 minutes or until pale gold. Then pour in the filling and replace in the oven, gas mark 4 or 350° F. (180° C.) for 10 minutes to set the crème. When ready, remove and cool slightly. Brush all over with warm apricot glaze. Serve warm or cold.

FROMAGE BLANC AUX NOISETTES *   (for 5–6 persons)

Ingredients:
450 g. cream cheese (1 lb.)
120 g. browned hazel nuts (4 oz.)

150 g. castor sugar (5 oz.)
1½ dl. thick cream (1 gill)
2 tablespoons Grand Marnier

Method: Chop the nuts finely. Sieve the cheese, mix it with the cream, sugar and the Grand Marnier. Beat well together. Fold in the nuts. Serve ice cold piled up in 'coupe' glasses.

PUDDING AUX AMANDES **   (for 4 persons)

Ingredients:
60 g. butter (2 oz.)
60 g. plain flour (2 oz.)
3 dl. milk (½ pint)
60 g. castor sugar (2 oz.)
2 eggs

60 g. ground almonds (2 oz.)
To finish:
3 dl. Crème Anglaise (½ pint)
flavoured with lemon (see
page 40)

Method: Melt the butter in a saucepan, draw it aside from the heat and then work in the flour. Add the milk gradually, stirring well to prevent it from forming lumps. Bring it to the boil, stirring continuously until it thickens. Remove it from the heat and pour it into a mixing bowl. Stir in the sugar and the yolks of the eggs. Mix well. Whisk the whites stiffly, then fold them in with the ground almonds.

Pour the mixture into a buttered and sugared 18 cm. (7 inch) moule à manqué or deep sandwich tin, stand it in a bain-marie or baking tin containing hot water. Cook it in a fairly hot oven, gas mark 6 or 400° F. (200° C.) for 30–35 minutes. Turn out the pudding on a warm serving dish and pour over the lemon flavoured crème Anglaise. Serve hot.

TARTE AUX AMANDES **   (for 4–5 persons)

Ingredients:
Pâte Brisée Method I (see page 338)
For the Filling:
3 eggs

100 g. castor sugar (3½ oz.)
90 g. ground almonds (3 oz.)
1 liqueur glass kirsch or rum

Method: Make up the pâte brisée in the usual way and put it aside to relax.

Prepare the filling – whisk the eggs until they are light and fluffy. Stir in the sugar, almonds and the liqueur. Roll out the pastry and line it into a well greased 18 cm. (7 inch) moule à manqué or deep sandwich tin. Pour in the filling. Roll out the trimmings from the pastry very thinly indeed and cut them into *very* narrow strips. Arrange these in a lattice work on the top of the filling. Bake in a hot oven, gas mark 7 or 425° F. (220° C.) for the first 7–10 minutes, then lower the heat to gas mark 5 or 375° F. (190° C.) and continue cooking for a further 15–20 minutes until the filling is set. Unmould carefully and serve hot or cold.

ANANAS 'ALI BAB' **   (for 5–6 persons)

Ingredients:

1 Savarin (see page 339)
3 dl. Crème Pâtissière (½ pint) (see
   page 344)

melted redcurrant jelly
1 tin pineapple slices, approx.
   450 g. tin (1 lb.)
3–4 crushed macaroons

Method: Cut the savarin into 1 cm. (¼ inch) slices, twice as many as there are pineapple slices. Arrange them overlapping in a ring in a round serving dish. Pour over the crème pâtissière. Put aside to get completely cold.

Drain the slices of pineapple on a clean cloth. Cut them in half and arrange one half on each slice of savarin. Spoon over the melted redcurrant jelly. Sprinkle all over with crushed macaroons and serve very cold.

Comment: Whereas tinned pineapple is economical and readily available, fresh pineapple should be used for a formal dinner.

ANANAS À LA VIRGINIE **   (for 4 persons)

Ingredients:

1 medium sized pineapple
2 yolks of egg
60 g. castor sugar (2 oz.)

15 g. gelatine (½ oz.)
1½ dl. milk (¼ pint)
1½ dl. thick cream (¼ pint)
250 g. strawberries (½ lb.)

Method: Soften the gelatine in 1 tablespoon water. Then dissolve it in 2 tablespoons of boiling water. Beat the yolks and sugar together with a wooden spatula. Heat the milk and pour it on to the yolks, etc. Stir it well. Return it to the saucepan, which has been rinsed out with cold water. (It is helpful to use a double boiler if available). Cook, stirring constantly until the mixture coats the back of a wooden spoon. It must on no account be allowed to boil. Strain the mixture on to the gelatine. Stir it very well. Stand it in a cold place or a refrigerator. Stir the mixture from time to time. When it is beginning to set, whisk the cream lightly. Sieve the strawberries and gently fold these into the custard mixture. Leave it until on the point of setting.

Meanwhile, slice off the top of the pineapple with the leaves, and put it aside. Scoop out the flesh from the pineapple using a vegetable ball cutter or tablespoon, discard the core. Leave 1 cm. (½ inch) of the outside and the base. Cut the flesh into even sized pieces, and stir them into the nearly set bavarois mixture. Pour the mixture into the pineapple, and replace the top slice. Leave to set in a cold place or refrigerator. Serve very cold on a folded napkin.

Comment: If a smaller or larger pineapple is used, more or less filling will be required.

ANANAS MAURICE * (for 4 persons)

Ingredients:

1 tin pineapple slices (approx. 450 g.) (1 lb.)
Crème Pâtissière made with 3 dl. (½ pint) milk and 45 g. (1½ oz.) plain flour (see page 344)

5–6 sponge finger biscuits
1 yolk of egg
30 g. grated chocolate (1 oz.)
3–4 tablespoons Grand Marnier
To finish:
a little extra Grand Marnier

Method: Make the crème pâtissière. Butter a heatproof serving dish and spread over the base 2–3 tablespoons of the crème pâtissière. Soak the sponge finger biscuits in the Grand Marnier and lay these on the top of the crème. Cut the drained pineapple slices into 2–3 pieces. Lay these neatly on the biscuits. Mix the egg yolk thoroughly with 2 tablespoons of pineapple juice, and the remaining crème pâtissière. Pour it over the pineapple and sprinkle with grated chocolate. Place the dish in a hot oven, gas mark 7 or 425° F. (220° C.) for 5–10 minutes to set the crème and melt the chocolate. Just before serving, heat a little Grand Marnier, pour it quickly over the surface and 'flame'. Serve at once.

CRÈME AUX ANANAS * (for 4 persons)

Ingredients:

1 tin pineapple rings (approx. 450 g.) (1 lb.)
1½ dl. sweet white wine (1 gill)
1 liqueur glass of kirsch or brandy
30 g. castor sugar (1 oz.)

30 g. plain flour (1 oz.)
3 yolks of egg
To finish:
glacé cherries
angelica

Method: Drain the pineapple and arrange the slices overlapping in a round serving dish.

Mix the yolks, sugar and flour together in a bowl. Heat the wine and the pineapple juice and pour it over the flour, yolks, etc., stirring all the time. Return it to the pan and cook over a moderate heat, continuing to stir, until the crème comes to the boil. Allow it to simmer for 2–3 minutes. Remove it from the heat and add the kirsch or the brandy.

Pour the crème over the pineapple slices. Leave to cool. Decorate lavishly with glacé cherries and angelica leaves. Serve ice cold.

SUPRÊME À L'ANANAS ** (for 4–6 persons)

Ingredients:

Pâte à Génoise Commune made
   with 3 eggs, etc. (see page 333)
1 small tin pineapple chunks
   (approx. 450 g.) (1 lb.)
apricot glaze made from sieved
   apricot jam

kirsch
a little sugar
To finish:
3 dl. thick cream (½ pint)
a little sugar
vanilla sugar
crystallised violets

Method: Make up the pâte à Génoise commune in the usual way. Pour it into a greased 18 cm. (7 inch) moule à manqué or deep sandwich tin and bake it in a moderate oven, gas mark 4–5 or 350–375° F. (180–190° C.) for about 30–35 minutes or until it is firm to touch and begins to shrink from the sides of the tin. Turn it out on a wire rack to cool.

Prepare the filling. Drain and chop the pineapple finely. Reserve the syrup. Mix the fruit with approximately two tablespoons apricot glaze and about the same amount of kirsch. Add a little sugar if necessary.

When the cake is cool, cut it into 3 layers. Macerate the base in the pineapple juice, then spread with half the fruit. Cover with the next layer of cake and then the remaining fruit and replace the top. Allow to stand for 2–3 hours.

Just before serving, whisk the cream stiffly. Sweeten it with a little sugar and vanilla sugar. Fill it into a forcing bag with a rosette tube and pipe stars of cream round the base of the cake and round the top. Pipe a rosette in the centre. Decorate the base and top with crystallised violets.

TARTE À L'ANANAS ** (for 4–8 persons)

Ingredients:

half quantity Pâte Brisée Method
   I (see page 338)
1 small tin pineapple rings
1 dl. thin cream (½ gill)

60 g. castor sugar (2 oz.)
2 eggs
sieved apricot jam
glacé cherries
angelica

Method: Make up the pastry. Line it into an 18 cm. (7 inch) flan ring. Prick the base. Drain the pineapple well, put aside two or three rings for decoration. Cut the rest into quarters, arrange them neatly on the bottom of the flan. Beat up the eggs with the cream and add the juice from the pineapple together with the sugar. Stir well and strain on to the fruit in the flan. Cook in a fairly hot oven, gas mark 6 or 400° F. (200° C.) for 30–35 minutes.

Whilst it is cooking melt two or three tablespoons of apricot jam with a little water. When the tart is cooked remove it to a wire rack and cool. Decorate with slices of pineapple, glacé cherries and leaves made from angelica. Brush all over with the apricot jam. Serve warm or cold.

TARTELETTES MERINGUÉES À L'ANANAS **

(for 4–6 persons)

Ingredients:
Pâte Sucrée (see page 339)
1 egg
1 yolk of egg
45 g. castor sugar (1½ oz.)
45 g. ground almonds (1½ oz.)
pineapple jam

To finish:
1 white of egg
1 dessertspoon castor sugar
sieved pineapple jam for glaze
angelica
a little icing sugar

Method: Make up the pâte sucrée in the usual way. Put it aside to relax and then roll out ½ cm. (¼ inch) thick on a lightly floured board and line into greased tartlet tins. Put a thin layer of pineapple jam in the bottom of the pastry cases. Beat together the egg, yolk, castor sugar and ground almonds and fill this mixture into the tartlet cases. Place a small teaspoon of jam in the centre of each and bake in a fairly hot oven, gas mark 6 or 400° F. (200° C.) for approximately 15 minutes, or until the pastry is a pale gold. Remove from the tins.

Whisk the white very stiffly, fold in the sugar. Place this meringue into a forcing bag with a small plain pipe and pipe six pear shaped points on the top of each tartlet. Dust with icing sugar. Place them on a baking sheet and put it in the top of a hot oven, gas mark 7 or 425° F. (220° C.) for a few minutes to brown the peaks. When they are cooked brush over thickly with pineapple glaze and arrange stalks of angelica to resemble pineapple leaves.

VACHERIN À L'ANANAS ***

(for 6 persons)

Ingredients:
9 whites of egg
580 g. castor sugar (1 lb. 4 oz.)
icing sugar
1 small fresh pineapple or 1 tin

pineapple (about 450 g. size)
(1 lb.)
3 dl. thick cream (½ pint)
1–2 tablespoons kirsch
1 teaspoon vanilla sugar

Method: Although the making of a vacherin case is a lengthy process, it need not be made at the one time. The cooking is divided into three distinct parts and, as will be seen from the following method, each part can be undertaken when time and ingredients permit.

The completed vacherin case or its component parts will keep well in an airtight container until required.

Brush 3 baking trays with melted lard and lightly dust them with flour. Turn them upside down and tap to remove excess flour. Mark two 15 cm. (6 inch) circles on each tray with a saucepan lid. Using three whites of egg and a third of the castor sugar proceed as follows:

Part I Whisk the egg whites until they stand in stiff peaks. Add 1 tablespoon of sugar and continue to whisk for 3–4 minutes until the mixture becomes stiff again. Fold in the rest of the sieved castor sugar in two lots. Place the meringue in a forcing bag with 1 cm. (⅜ inch) plain tube. Pipe a ring of mixture on all six circles, filling in one circle to make the base. Dust with icing sugar and tap to remove the excess sugar. Place them in a cool oven, gas mark ¼ or 200° F. (90° C.) for at least 2 hours until the meringue is dry and crisp. When cooked remove carefully from the baking sheets and cool on a wire rack.

Part II Make some more meringue using the same quantities and method as before. Replace the base of the vacherin on a greased and floured baking tray. Using the same sized tube, pipe a 6 inch circle of meringue on the base. Stick one of the cooked rings on top of this. Then pipe another circle on top of the ring. Build up in this way until all the rings have been used. Spread a smooth layer of meringue over the outside of the vacherin case. Dust with icing sugar and bake and cool as before.

Part III Make more meringue using the same quantity and method. With a large rosette pipe in a forcing bag, decorate the outside and top of the vacherin case. Dust with icing sugar and bake as before. When it is cooked, remove from the baking sheet and cool on a wire rack.

To serve: Cut the pineapple into dice, or drain the tinned pineapple, and macerate in kirsch. Whisk the cream moderately thick. Fold in the vanilla sugar, then the pineapple and kirsch and fill into the centre of the vacherin just before serving. (*See Plates 17 and 18.*)

Comment: Other fillings such as crème chantilly with strawberries or other fruits or marrons glacées may be used.

BANANES À LA CHANTILLY *　　　　　　　　(for 4–5 persons)

Ingredients:

4–5 bananas

1 liqueur glass kirsch or rum

1½ dl. thick cream (1 gill)

Method: Remove a strip of peel about 2½ cm. (1 inch) wide along one side of each banana. Remove the flesh, cut it into 1 cm. (½ inch) slices and macerate them in kirsch or rum for about an hour.

Refill the skins with the fruit together with any of the liqueur.

Whisk the cream lightly and using a forcing bag with a rosette tube, pipe a thick line of cream along the fruit in each banana. Serve very cold.

BANANES À LA MERINGUE *   (for 3 or 6 persons)

Ingredients:
6 bananas
4 whites of egg
240 g. castor sugar (8 oz.)
1 teaspoon vanilla sugar

1–2 tablespoons kirsch or rum
a little icing sugar
To finish:
glacé cherries
angelica

Method: Choose firm bananas. Peel and cut them in half lengthwise. Arrange them in a fireproof dish cut side down. Sprinkle them with vanilla sugar and the kirsch or rum and leave them for one hour to macerate in the liqueur.

Whisk the whites very stiffly and fold in the sugar carefully. Using a forcing bag with a rosette tube, pipe a line of meringue on each halved banana. Sift over a little icing sugar. Bake in a cool oven, gas mark 2 or 300° F. (150° C.) to set the meringue. Serve very cold, decorated with halved glacé cherries and leaves cut from angelica.

COUPES DE BANANES CAROLINE **   (for 4 persons)

Ingredients:
6 bananas
1 tablespoon Grand Marnier
For the Crème:
3 yolks of egg

60 g. castor sugar (2 oz.)
½ liqueur glass Grand Marnier
To finish:
chopped browned almonds

Method: Peel the bananas. Cut them into fairly thin slices and sprinkle them with the tablespoon of Grand Marnier. Leave them in a cool place to macerate for one hour. After this time, place them with the liqueur in four coupe glasses.

Meanwhile put the egg yolks, the sugar, half a glass of Grand Marnier together with five tablespoons of water in a bowl over a pan of boiling water. Whisk well and continue until the mixture thickens and becomes light and fluffy, and will hold the impression of the whisk when lightly pressed on the surface.

Pour the egg mixture over the bananas. Sprinkle with chopped browned almonds. Serve very cold.

DÉLICE AUX BANANES **   (for 6 persons)

Ingredients:
Pâte Sucrée (see page 339)
For the Filling:
6–8 bananas
90 g. icing sugar (approx.) (3 oz.)

¼ l. thick cream (1½ gills)
To finish:
1 banana
glacé cherries

Method: Make the pâte sucrée in the usual way and put it aside to relax. Roll it out thinly, cut it into rounds with a fluted cutter and line them into individual tartlet moulds. Prick them well and bake in a moderate oven, gas mark 4 or 350° F. (180° C.) for 10–15 minutes or until firm and golden brown.

Skin the bananas and pass them through a fine nylon sieve. For each banana add one tablespoon of icing sugar and mix to a smooth paste.

Whisk the cream fairly stiffly and fold in the banana mixture lightly. With a large rosette tube and forcing bag pipe the mixture into the tartlets in a dome shape. Decorate each tartlet with a slice of banana and half a glacé cherry. Serve cold.

PUDDING GLACÉ À LA FARNESE ***   (for 5–6 persons)

Ingredients:
Crème Praliné made with:
3 egg yolks
¼ l. milk (1½ gills)
100 g. castor sugar (3½ oz.)
2 leaves gelatine (approx. 7 g.)
  (¼ oz.)
100 g. praline, pounded finely
  (see page 348) (3½ oz.)
1½ dl. thick cream (1 gill)
Crème de Bananes made with:
6 large bananas

100 g. icing sugar (3½ oz.)
juice of ½ lemon
2 leaves gelatine (approx. 7 g.)
  (¼ oz.)
1 dl. thick cream (½ gill)
3–4 sponge finger biscuits
2 tablespoons rum
To finish:
2 bananas
1 dl. Crème Chantilly (½ gill)
  (see page 266)
approx. 12 glacé cherries

Method: Prepare the crème praliné. Put all the gelatine to soften in a bowl of cold water. Using a wooden spoon or spatula, cream the egg yolks and the sugar. Add the hot milk and stir well. Put the mixture into a clean pan and stirring continuously over a low heat allow it to thicken, but not boil. Squeeze half the gelatine with the hands to expel all the excess moisture, add this to the hot custard mixture and stir until it is dissolved. Strain into a clean bowl, and leave in a cool place, stirring it occasionally until it begins to set round the edges. When it is almost set fold in the pounded praline and the lightly whipped cream.

Now make the crème de bananes. Pass the 6 bananas through a nylon or hair sieve. Mix this purée with the icing sugar and lemon juice. Dissolve the remaining gelatine, which has been previously squeezed out, in 2 tablespoons of very hot water and add it to the purée. Stir well and put aside to cool. When it is on the point of setting, fold in the lightly whipped 1 dl. (½ gill) of cream together with the sponge finger biscuits, which have been broken into 3 or 4 pieces and soaked in the rum.

Take a domed ½ l. (1 pint) mould, cut the bananas into very thin slices and arrange them overlapping over the base of the mould. Stand the mould in a bowl of salted ice. Carefully spoon a layer of crème praliné, which is just on the point of setting to coat the banana slices. Leave to set. Gradually tilting the mould in the ice, coat the whole of the base and sides with the crème praliné, to form a good 1 cm. (½ inch) layer.

Fill the centre with the crème de bananes, using it as it reaches setting point. Leave in a cold place until it is quite firm.

To Serve: Unmould by dipping the mould into very hot water for 2–3 seconds and turn carefully on to a serving dish. Using a forcing bag and rosette pipe, pipe a decorative border of crème chantilly round the base of the pudding. Place a slice of glacé cherry on each banana slice showing on the top. Serve very cold.

BAVAROIS À LA DIPLOMATE AUX FRUITS **

(for 3–4 persons)

Ingredients:
3 dl. milk (½ pint)
135 g. castor sugar (4½ oz.)
4 yolks of egg
8 g. leaf gelatine (¼ oz.)
1½ dl. thick cream (1 gill)
90–120 g. finely chopped crystallised fruits (3–4 oz.)

5–6 sponge finger biscuits
1 vanilla pod
2–3 tablespoons kirsch
To finish:
a few extra crystallised fruits
a little whipped cream

Method: Put the gelatine to soften in a bowl of cold water. Make the bavarois. Cream the egg yolks and the sugar together, using a wooden spoon or wooden spatula. Heat the milk with the vanilla pod until it reaches simmering point. Remove the vanilla pod and pour the milk on to the egg mixture. Stir well and return it to the pan which has been rinsed out. Stirring all the time allow the custard to thicken over a low heat until it coats the back of a wooden spoon. Do not allow it to reach boiling point. Remove it from the heat.

Squeeze the gelatine with the hands to expel the excess moisture. Stir it in to the custard mixture until it is completely dissolved, then strain it into a clean bowl and leave it in a cold place, stirring it from time to time.

Macerate the crystallised fruits in about half the kirsch. Break up the biscuits into small pieces and soak them in the remainder of the kirsch.

When the custard is on the point of setting, whisk the cream lightly so that it is of the same consistency as the custard. Fold it in quickly and lightly. Put a layer of this mixture in the bottom of a glass serving dish. Stand the dish in crushed ice to set, or put it aside again in a very cold place. When it has set sprinkle over the crystallised fruits, with the kirsch in which they have been macerating, then make a layer on the top with the biscuits and the kirsch they have been soaking in. Pour over the rest of the bavarois mixture and put it aside to set completely.

To Finish: Whisk the cream for decorating rather more stiffly. Using a star pipe, decorate as desired. Arrange a few pieces of crystallised fruit on the top of each star. Serve very cold, but if liked with a hot apricot sauce, flavoured with kirsch.

Comment: This sweet can be made in a 15 cm. (6 inch) charlotte mould or cake tin and, when it is set, unmoulded on a serving dish. The sauce should be poured round just before serving.

SURPRISE AU CAFÉ ** (for 4–5 persons)

Ingredients:
3 yolks of egg
4 whites of egg
3 dl. thick cream ($\frac{1}{2}$ pint)
4 tablespoons strong coffee
1 tablespoon Tia Maria
8 g. leaf gelatine ($\frac{1}{4}$ oz.)

135 g. castor sugar ($4\frac{1}{2}$ oz.)
To finish:
2–3 crushed meringue shells
1–2 tablespoons Tia Maria
a little extra whipped cream
crystallised violets

Method: Put the gelatine to soak in a basin of cold water. When it is soft drain it well and then dissolve it in 2 tablespoons of hot coffee.

Separate the eggs and place the yolks and sugar in a bowl together with the rest of the coffee. Stand the bowl over a saucepan of boiling water and whisk energetically. When the mixture is thick and fluffy, remove the bowl from the pan of water, add the gelatine and coffee mixture and continue to whisk until it is quite cool. Stir in the tablespoon of Tia Maria. Put the mixture in a cold place, stirring from time to time to prevent it from setting unevenly. When it is on the point of setting, fold in the cream, lightly whisked, together with the stiffly beaten egg whites.

Pour into a soufflé or fairly deep dish and carefully stand an oiled 450 g. (1 lb.) size jam jar in the centre. Put the dish into a refrigerator or very cold place to set completely.

To Finish: Soak the crushed meringue shells in the Tia Maria. When the mixture is firmly set and ready to serve, loosen the jam jar in the centre and giving it a sharp twist, remove it gently and firmly. Fill the space thus left with the soaked meringue shells together with any Tia Maria remaining.

Pipe stars of whipped cream in a ring on top, and *just before* serving decorate with crystallised violets. (It is important *not* to put the violets on too far in advance, or to leave them in a damp place, as the colour tends to run.) Serve ice cold.

MOKATINE À LA CHANTILLY ** (for 5–6 persons)

Ingredients:
½ l. thick cream (¾ pint)
1½ dl. milk (1 gill)
120 g. castor sugar (4 oz.)

6 whites of egg
1 tablespoon instant coffee
dissolved in 2 tablespoons boiling
water

Method: Stand a large bowl in crushed ice. Pour in the cream, milk and coffee and whisk until it is thick. Whisk the whites stiffly and fold them into the cream, adding the sugar at the same time.

Pour the mixture into small serving bowls or coupes which have been chilled. Serve very cold.

Comment: This sweet should be served with tuiles, wafers or similar biscuits.

BOULES DE NEIGE AU CHOCOLAT *** (for 4 persons)

Ingredients:
4 whites of egg
135 g. castor sugar (4½ oz.)
1 teaspoon vanilla sugar
Crème Anglaise au Chocolat:
6 dl. milk (1 pint)

135 g. plain chocolate (4½ oz.)
4 yolks of egg
170 g. castor sugar (6 oz.)
To finish:
chopped browned nuts

Method: Heat the pint of milk to simmering point in a shallow pan. Meanwhile whisk the whites stiffly and fold in the sifted sugars very well. Make sure that the mixture is quite smooth. Form the egg mixture into balls with the aid of two dessertspoons and poach them in the hot milk turning them very carefully. Remove and drain them on a clean cloth.

Make up the crème Anglaise au chocolat – melt the chocolate in a basin over a pan of hot water. Work the yolks and the sugar together with a wooden spatula, and then add the melted chocolate. Pour in the milk the balls were poached in a little at a time and mix together very thoroughly. Return the crème to a clean pan. Cook, stirring continuously, until it thickens without allowing it to boil, then strain it into a clean bowl. Put it aside to get quite cold.

To Serve: Pour a little of the crème Anglaise au chocolat in the bottom of a shallow serving dish. Arrange the balls on top, spoon over the rest of the crème anglaise au chocolat. Scatter a few browned nuts over the whole. Serve cold.

CRÈME NÈGRE-BLANC * (for 3 persons)

Ingredients:

3 dl. milk (½ pint)
30 g. flour (1 oz.)
2 yolks of egg

30 g. castor sugar (1 oz.)
1 teaspoon vanilla sugar
120 g. plain chocolate (4 oz.)
1½ dl. thick cream (1 gill)

Method: Using a wooden spoon or spatula work the yolks and sugars together in a bowl. Then stir in the flour.

Break up the chocolate and melt it in a bowl over hot water. When it is quite melted, stir it into the egg mixture. Heat the milk and pour it also over the egg mixture, stirring well.

Rinse the pan and return the crème to it. Bring it to the boil, stirring well, then reduce the heat and allow it to simmer for 2–3 minutes so as to ensure that the flour is cooked.

Remove from the heat, cool the crème slightly and pour it into a shallow dish. Allow it to get quite cold.

Whip the cream fairly stiffly and, using a forcing bag with a rosette tube, pipe a design over the top. Serve very cold.

MARQUISE AU CHOCOLAT * (for 4–5 persons)

Ingredients:

150 g. plain chocolate (5 oz.)
60 g. castor sugar (2 oz.)
90 g. unsalted butter (3 oz.)
2 eggs
1 teaspoon vanilla sugar

1 packet, approx. 14 sponge finger
 biscuits
1½ dl. (1 gill) strong coffee,
 sweetened with 60 g. (2 oz.) sugar
To finish:
a little icing sugar

Method: Break the chocolate into small pieces and place them in a basin with the butter over a pan of hot water. When they are melted, remove the bowl from the pan and stir in the sugar and the vanilla sugar. Separate the eggs. Add the yolks to the chocolate and stir well. Whisk the whites until they are very stiff and fold them into the mixture very lightly.

Dip the biscuits, one at a time, into the coffee. Arrange half of them side by side in a row down the centre of an oval or oblong dish and spread them with half the chocolate mixture. Place the rest of the biscuits on top. Spread the remainder of the chocolate mixture so that it covers the top and sides evenly. Lastly dust with a little sieved icing sugar and serve very cold.

MOUSSE AU CHOCOLAT ** (for 4 persons)

Ingredients:

120 g. plain chocolate (4 oz.)
75 g. icing sugar (2½ oz.)

4 eggs
60 g. butter (2 oz.)
¼ l. thick cream (1½ gills)

Method: Break the chocolate into small pieces and place them in a bowl with the icing sugar and the butter over a pan of hot water. Stir well until they are melted. Remove from the heat.

Separate the eggs. Stir the yolks into the chocolate mixture thoroughly. Whisk the cream lightly and the whites stiffly. When the chocolate mixture is completely cool, fold in the cream and stiffly beaten whites. Pour into individual dishes or if preferred a glass bowl and serve very cold.

PETIT NÈGRE **   (for 4 persons)

Ingredients:
135 g. unsalted butter (4½ oz.)
135 g. grated plain chocolate
   (4½ oz.)
60 g. castor sugar (2 oz.)
1 packet of sponge finger biscuits

4 tablespoons sugar dissolved in
   ¼ l. (1½ gills) water to which has
   been added 1 tablespoon kirsch
To finish:
chocolate fondant icing (see page
   346)

Method: Butter a 15 cm. (6 inch) charlotte mould or cake tin.

Cream the butter and sugar together until they are light and creamy, then add the grated chocolate and cream again for a minute or two.

Take the sponge finger biscuits one at a time, dip them quickly into the kirsch flavoured syrup and line the inside of the mould with them. This must be done quickly otherwise the biscuits will become sodden and will break up.

Fill the chocolate mixture into the centre, tapping the mould gently on the table to allow the mixture to settle evenly. Put it aside in a cold place for 1½–2 hours to allow it to harden. At the end of this time, unmould it carefully. Pour the chocolate fondant icing all over it. Lift at once on to a serving dish.

CROÛTES MÉDICIS **   (for 6 persons)

Ingredients:
Pâte à Génoise Commune made
   with 3 eggs, etc. (see page 333)
   OR
Pain de Gênes (see page 334)
2 tablespoons sweetened chestnut
   purée

redcurrant jelly
6 marrons glacés (or 6 cooked
   whole chestnuts) soaked in
   kirsch
glacé cherries soaked in kirsch
castor sugar

Method: Line a swiss roll tin 23 × 30 cm. (9 × 12 inches), with greaseproof paper. Make the pâte à génoise or pain de gênes in the usual way. Spread it evenly in the prepared tin and cook it in a moderate oven, gas mark 5 or 375° F. (190° C.) for 15–20 minutes. Remove it from the oven and place it on a wire rack. When it is cool, cut it into rounds 6–7 cm. (2½–3 inches) in diameter.

Sprinkle each round with castor sugar. Place them on a baking sheet in a very moderate oven, gas mark 4 or 350° F. (180° C.) for ¼ hour. Remove them and allow to cool. Spread them thickly with the chestnut purée and coat all over with a little melted redcurrant jelly. Place a marron glacé or a cooked chestnut in the middle of each and arrange a glacé cherry, equally macerated, at each side. Serve warm with a jug of hot melted redcurrant jelly, to which has been added the kirsch left over from the marrons and cherries.

CROQUETTES DE RIZ FRUCTIDOR **

(for 4–5 persons approx.)

Ingredients:
120 g. Carolina rice (4 oz.)
3 yolks of egg
90 g. castor sugar (3 oz.)
½ l. milk (¾ pint)
vanilla pod
120 g. (4 oz.) chopped crystallised
1 fruits macerated in 4 tablespoons
   rum or kirsch

beaten egg
Sauce Abricot (see page 41)
   OR
Crème Anglaise (see page 40)
very finely chopped browned
   almonds
a little angelica

Method: Blanch the rice for 5 minutes in a pan of boiling water. Drain and rinse it in cold water. Cook the rice gently in the milk with the vanilla pod. Beat the yolks with sugar. When the rice is cooked remove the vanilla pod, draw it aside and using a fork stir in the yolks. Continue to stir over a *very* gentle heat until the rice leaves the side of the pan. Stir in the chopped fruits together with the rum or kirsch and pour it on to a marble slab or large plate. Allow it to become absolutely cold.

With lightly floured hands, form the rice into the shape of large pears. Brush them over with a little beaten egg and roll them in the chopped almonds. Arrange them on a paper doyley. Insert a small piece of angelica in the top of each to represent the stalk. Serve with a rum or kirsch flavoured sauce abricot or if preferred with a well flavoured Crème Anglaise.

FLAN AU LAIT À L'ANDALOUSE **   (for 4–5 persons)

Ingredients:
Pâte Sucrée (see page 339)
For the Filling:
90 g. sultanas (3 oz.)

150 g. castor sugar (5 oz.)
3 eggs
grated rind of 1 orange
1½ dl. milk (1 gill)

Method: Make up the pâte sucrée in the usual way and put it aside to relax for about ½ hour. Roll it out on a lightly floured board and line it into a 18 cm. (7 inch) flan ring. Prick the base well with a fork. Sprinkle over the sultanas.

Put the eggs and sugar into a bowl and work them well with a wooden spoon or spatula. When they are light and creamy looking, add the grated orange rind and the milk gradually. Mix all together thoroughly. Pour this mixture into the prepared flan case. Bake in a hot oven, gas mark 7 or 425° F. (220° C.) for 10 minutes, then lower the heat to gas mark 5 or 375° F. (190° C.) for a further 20 minutes. Serve warm or cold.

CHARLOTTE AUX FRAISES ** (for 4–5 persons)

Ingredients:
Pâte à Biscuits à la Cuillère (see page 331)
For the Filling:
350 g. strawberries (¾ lb.)
2 tablespoons thick cream
¼ l. water (½ pint)

18 g. leaf gelatine (½ oz.)
240 g. castor sugar (8 oz.)
2 whites of egg
carmine colouring
To Decorate:
6–8 whole strawberries
1 dl. thick cream (½ gill)

Method: Make up the pâte à biscuits à la cuillère in the usual way.

Put a round of buttered greaseproof paper in the bottom of a 15 cm. (6 inch) charlotte mould and line the sides with the sponge finger biscuits.

Rub the strawberries through a vegetable mill or nylon sieve. Make a syrup with the sugar and water. Bring to the boil and add the gelatine, which has been soaked in cold water. Stir until dissolved. Allow to cool, then stir into the strawberry purée and colour, if needed, with a little carmine colouring. Put in a cool place. When it begins to set, fold in the stiffly beaten whites and the cream. Pour into the lined mould. Put aside in a refrigerator or cold place to set.

Trim the biscuits to the level of the filling. Turn out the charlotte on a serving dish, and remove the greaseproof paper. Decorate the top with whole strawberries. Whip the cream lightly and using a forcing bag and a rosette tube, pipe stars of whipped cream in a decorative design. Serve very cold. (*See Plate 19.*)

CHOUX AUX FRAISES ** (for 4 persons)

Ingredients:
Pâte à Choux (see page 336)
Crème Chantilly (see page 266)
beaten egg

250 g. small firm strawberries (½ lb.)
To finish:
icing sugar

Method: Make up the pâte à choux in the usual way. Using a forcing bag and plain 1½ cm. (⅝ inch) tube, pipe the paste into ovals 2½ × 5 cm. (1 × 2 inches) on a greased baking sheet. Brush them over with beaten egg and bake them in a hot oven, gas mark 7 or 425° F. (220° C.) for

10 minutes. Then lower the heat to gas mark 5 or 375° F. (190° C.) for a further 20–25 minutes until they are crisp and golden brown.

Remove them from the oven, split them open down one side and allow them to get cold.

Meanwhile hull the strawberries and wash them if necessary. Let them drain well.

Prepare the crème Chantilly.

Put a layer of strawberries in each choux. (If the fruit is on the large side, cut the strawberries in half.) Cover with a thin layer of cream, then a second layer of strawberries, finally with a little more cream.

Dust the choux with icing sugar and serve immediately.

MELON EN SURPRISE *   (for 6–8 persons)

Ingredients:
1 large cantaloup melon
approx. ½ kg. (1 lb.) mixed fresh
   fruits, i.e. cherries, grapes, red
   and white currants, loganberries

4 tablespoons Grand Marnier
½ kg. ripe strawberries (1 lb.)
250 g. approx. castor sugar (½ lb.)
crushed ice

Method: Cut the top off the melon to form a lid and remove the seeds. Carefully scoop out the flesh and cut it into 1 cm. (½ inch) dice. Put it with the rest of the mixed fruits, add sugar to taste. Pour over the Grand Marnier and stir very gently from time to time.

Hull the strawberries and pass them through a nylon sieve. Mix them with sugar to taste.

Fill the melon with the macerated fruits and stand it in a bowl of crushed ice. Just before serving pour over the strawberry purée and replace the lid. Serve very cold.

MOUSSE AU CITRON ET AU CARAMEL ***
(for 4–6 persons)

Ingredients:
240 g. castor sugar (8 oz.)
2 lemons
8 g. leaf gelatine (¼ oz.)
3 eggs

2 yolks of egg
1½ dl. thick cream (1 gill)
To finish:
120 g. castor sugar (4 oz.)
1 dl. water (½ gill)
1 dl. thick cream (½ gill)

Method: Put the gelatine to soften in a bowl of cold water. Place 180 g. (6 oz.) sugar in a pan with 1 dl. (½ gill) of water and boil it to a caramel. Cool immediately by placing the pan in a bowl of cold water. Pour in 1 dl. (½ gill) hot water which will soften the caramel. Return the pan to the heat and stir until the caramel is all dissolved. Put it aside to get cold.

Whisk the eggs and yolks with 60 g. (2 oz.) sugar in a bowl over a pan of hot water until thick and fluffy. Remove from the heat and whisk until the mixture is cool.

Strain the juice from the lemons into a small pan and heat gently. Dissolve the softened gelatine in the warm lemon juice and stir it into the egg mixture.

Whip the cream lightly and fold it into the mixture together with the liquid caramel. Pour it into the serving dish and leave it in a cold place or refrigerator to set.

To Finish: Boil the water and sugar to a caramel and pour it on to an oiled tin. Allow it to become cold and crush finely.

Whisk the cream fairly stiffly. Using a forcing bag and rosette tube, pipe straight lines of stars across the top of the mousse, sprinkle lines of the crushed caramel between them and serve very cold. (*See Plate 22.*)

ŒUFS À LA NEIGE ** (for 2–3 persons)

Ingredients:

3 whites of egg
120 g. castor sugar (4 oz.)
1 teaspoon vanilla sugar
1 vanilla pod

½ l. milk (1 pint)
Crème Anglaise made with
  3 yolks of egg, etc.
  (see page 40)

Method: Bring the milk to simmering point with the vanilla pod over a low heat.

Whisk the egg whites stiffly, fold in the sugar and vanilla sugar. Using two tablespoons form the beaten whites into egg shapes, and drop them one by one into the simmering milk. Poach them for about 8–10 minutes. Remove and drain them on a clean cloth.

Make a Crème Anglaise using 3 dl. (½ pint) of the milk in which the 'eggs' have been simmered. Pour it into a shallow dish and float the 'eggs' on top. Serve very cold.

CRÈME CAPRICE ** (for 4 persons)

Ingredients:

3 oranges
120 g. castor sugar (4 oz.)
8 g. leaf gelatine (¼ oz.)
3 eggs

60–90 g. finely chopped crystallised orange peel (2–3 oz.)
1–2 tablespoons rum
To finish:
chocolate medallions made with
  60 g. plain chocolate (2 oz.)

Method: Put the gelatine to soak in cold water. Place the crystallised orange peel in a small bowl with the rum and leave it to macerate. When the gelatine is soft, lift it from the bowl and squeeze it out gently with the

289

hands to expel all the excess moisture. Stir it in two tablespoons of boiling water until it is quite dissolved. Put it aside to cool.

Separate the eggs. Work the yolks and the sugar together in a bowl until light and fluffy. Then add the grated rind of two oranges and the juice of all three. Stir in the gelatine and put it aside in a cold place, stirring it from time to time. When it begins to set whisk the whites stiffly and fold them in lightly, together with the rum in which the peel has been macerating.

Pour half of the mixture in a deep serving dish, put a layer of the peel on top, cover with the rest of the mixture and leave it in a cold place to set completely.

Whilst it is setting, make the chocolate medallions. Break the chocolate into small pieces and place it on a plate standing over a pan of boiling water. Allow it to melt completely. Take a piece of greaseproof paper, and using a 10p piece as a guide, trace 12–15 circles. Using a flexible knife spread the chocolate smoothly and evenly in the circles. Put aside in a cold place to harden for about half an hour.

To Finish: When the mixture is firmly set, peel the paper from the medallions, arrange them on the top and serve very cold.

CRÈME D'OR * (for 3–4 persons)

Ingredients:
240 g. cream cheese (½ lb.)
4 tablespoons castor sugar
juice of 3 blood oranges

1–2 tablespoons kirsch or coin-
    treau
To finish:
glacé cherries

Method: Sieve the cheese into a bowl, add the castor sugar and beat vigorously with a wooden spoon or spatula. When the mixture is smooth, add the strained orange juice, a little at a time, beating it in with a fork to make a lighter texture. When perfectly mixed, beat in the liqueur. Pour the mixture into little pots and stand them in a very cold place for 1 hour. Place half a glacé cherry on the top of each. Serve ice cold.

CRÈME MARGUERITE ** (for 4–6 persons)

Ingredients:
Crème Renversée au Caramel
    made with:
    ½ l. milk (¾ pint)
    90 g. castor sugar (3 oz.)
    4 yolks of egg
    2 eggs
    1 vanilla pod

Caramel made with:
    120 g. castor sugar (4 oz.)
    1½ dl. water (1 gill)
    (see page 16)
To finish:
3 large oranges
1½ dl. thick cream (1 gill)
3–4 meringue shells

Method: Make the caramel as usual. Wrap a thick cloth round a ring mould. Pour the caramel into the mould and turn it to allow the caramel to coat the sides.

Make the crème. Cream the eggs, yolks and sugar together in a bowl, using a wooden spoon. Bring the milk to the boil with the vanilla pod to flavour and then strain it on to the egg mixture. Stir well. Remove the froth which rises to the surface and pour the custard into the caramelized mould. Stand the mould in a bain-marie or roasting tin containing boiling water and cook in a very moderate oven, gas mark 4 or 350° F. (180° C.) for 40–45 minutes. At the end of this time insert a knife and if it comes out clean, the custard is cooked. Allow it to cool before unmoulding on a serving dish.

Peel the oranges and remove the segments, cutting in between each section. Whisk the cream until stiff and fold the broken-up meringue shells into half of it. Pile this mixture into the centre of the mould. Place the rest of the cream in a forcing bag with a rosette tube, and pipe stars over the mixture in the centre. Arrange orange slices around the cream and around the edge of the mould. Serve very cold.

RIZ À L'ORANGE * (for 3–4 persons)

Ingredients:

1 small teacup Carolina rice
3½ teacups (same size) creamy milk
45–60 g. sugar (1½–2 oz.)
2 oranges

3 tablespoons orange jelly marmalade
syrup made with 3 dl. (½ pint) water, 120 g. (4 oz.) sugar (see page 24)

Method: Put the rice into a pan with enough cold water to cover it well. Bring it to the boil and boil for 2–3 minutes. Strain the rice and rinse it in cold water. Heat the milk and add the grated rind of the oranges and sugar, then stir in the blanched rice. Cover with greaseproof paper and the lid and cook in a moderate oven gas mark 5 or 375° F. (190° C.) for 20–25 minutes. Do not disturb during cooking. At the end of this time the rice should be creamy and cooked but not too solid.

Whilst the rice is cooking, peel the oranges. Remove all pith and divide the fruit into sections. Poach them in the syrup over a low heat for about 10 minutes.

Form the rice into a flat cake shape on a serving dish. Decorate the top with the orange sections. Add the orange jelly to the syrup and stir until it is dissolved. Raise the heat and boil until it is of a thick syrupy consistency. Spoon over the orange sections. Serve cold.

TARTE À LA CRÈME AUX ORANGES ** (for 4–5 persons)

Ingredients:
Flaky pastry made with 120 g.
  plain flour (4 oz.), etc.
  (see page 335)
3 yolks of egg
120 g. castor sugar (4 oz.)

3 dl. milk (½ pint)
30 g. plain flour (1 oz.)
3–4 small oranges
To finish:
orange jelly marmalade

Method: Make up the pastry in the usual way. Put it aside to relax. Bake it blind (see page 326) in an 18 cm. (7 inch) flan ring, in a fairly hot oven, gas mark 7 or 425° F. (220° C.) for 20–25 minutes. Then place it on a wire rack to cool.

Make the cream as follows – cream the yolks, sugar and flour together with a wooden spatula. Heat the milk with the grated rind of one orange. When it is boiling pour it slowly on to the yolks, etc., stirring all the time. Return the mixture to the pan, which has been rinsed out, and simmer for 2–3 minutes over a low heat, stirring well. Allow it to cool slightly before pouring it into the pastry case. Peel the oranges and cut them into segments, cutting in between each section. Arrange them overlapping all over the top of the 'tarte'. Melt 2 or 3 tablespoons of the jelly marmalade over a gentle heat and spoon it over the oranges. Serve warm or cold.

Comment: To make a more exotic sweet add 2 tablespoons of Grand Marnier to the jelly before pouring it over the orange sections.

PÊCHES À L'AURORE ** (for 6 persons)

Ingredients:
3 ripe peaches
syrup for poaching, made with
  3 dl. (½ pint) water, 120 g. (4 oz.)
  sugar and 1 vanilla pod
Bavarois au Vanille made with:
½ l. milk (1 pint)
15 g. leaf gelatine (½ oz.)
2 teaspoons vanilla sugar

3 dl. thick cream (½ pint)
4 yolks of egg
1 teaspoon arrowroot
150 g. castor sugar (5 oz.)
Strawberry purée, made with:
250 g. strawberries (½ lb.)
75 g. icing sugar (2½ oz.)
To finish:
chopped browned nuts

Method: Prepare the bavarois. Put the gelatine to soften in a bowl of cold water. Using a wooden spoon or spatula, cream the egg yolks together with the sugar, vanilla sugar and the arrowroot. Pour in the hot milk and stir well. Put the mixture into a clean pan, cook, stirring all the time, over a low heat until it thickens without boiling. Squeeze the gelatine out with the hands to expel all the excess moisture, add this to the hot custard mixture, stir until it has dissolved. Strain into a clean bowl and leave in a cool place, stirring occasionally, until it is on the point of setting. Whisk the cream lightly and fold it into the custard. Take 6 coupe glasses and put an equal amount in each. Leave until set.

Meanwhile make the syrup for poaching the peaches. Dissolve the sugar in the water, add the vanilla pod, bring to the boil, then lower the heat to simmering point. Skin and halve the peaches, removing their stones. Poach them until they are just tender. Lift them carefully with a draining spoon and place them on a dry cloth.

Sieve the strawberries through a hair or nylon sieve. Mix with the icing sugar.

When the bavarois custard has set, place a half peach in each glass and coat with the strawberry purée. Sprinkle a few chopped, browned nuts on each and serve very cold.

PÊCHES À LA RÉJANE **   (for 9 persons)

Ingredients:
Pâte Frolle:
  135 g. plain flour (4½ oz.)
  75 g. ground almonds (2½ oz.)
  60 g. butter (2 oz.)
  75 g. castor sugar (2½ oz.)
  1 small egg
  grated rind of ½ lemon
  pinch of salt

For the filling and finish:
quince jelly
9 halved peaches
240 g. small strawberries or fraises
  des bois (½ lb.)
1½ dl. thick cream (¼ pint)
1 teaspoon vanilla sugar

Method: Make the pâte frolle – sift the flour on to a board, make a well in the centre and put in all the other ingredients. Work up with the tips of the fingers to make a smooth dough. Put the paste aside in a cool place or refrigerator for 1 hour to relax.

Butter and dust out with flour about 18 small tartlet tins. Roll out the paste thinly, stamp out with a suitably sized fluted cutter, line it into the tins. Prick very well. Bake them for about 15 minutes in a moderately hot oven, gas mark 6 or 400° F. (200° C.). When they are cooked, loosen them carefully with a thin bladed knife and unmould. Place on a wire rack to harden.

Place a teaspoonful of jelly in the bottom of each. Lay a halved peach on top, cut side uppermost. Arrange halved strawberries or whole fraises des bois round the edge. Whisk the cream with a little vanilla sugar. Fill it into a forcing bag with a large rosette tube. Pipe a star of cream in the centre of each peach. Serve very cold.

PÊCHES À LA SAVOYARD **   (for 3–6 persons)

Ingredients:

3 ripe peaches
6 rounds of Pâte à Génoise Commune (see page 333)

180 g. cream cheese (6 oz.)
1½ dl. thick cream (1 gill)
75 g. castor sugar (2½ oz.)
75 g. crystallised fruits (2½ oz.)

Method: Make up the pâte à Génoise commune in the usual way. Line a greased swiss roll or similar 23×30 cm. (9×12 inch) tin with greaseproof paper. Bake the pâte à Génoise commune in this in a moderately hot oven, gas mark 5–6 or 375–400° F. (190–200° C.) for 10–15 minutes. Turn out on a wire rack to cool and carefully remove the greaseproof paper.

When the cake is cool, cut it into 6 rounds, approximately the same size as the peaches. Hollow them out so that the peaches will sit on top.

Peel the peaches and cut them in half with a silver or stainless knife. Remove the stones. Arrange the peaches, cut side uppermost, on the rounds of cake.

Chop the crystallised fruits finely. Beat the cream cheese with the cream and stir in the sugar and the fruits. Pile this mixture on the hollowed peaches. Serve very cold.

PÊCHES CAPRICE **   (for 5 persons)

Ingredients:

5 ripe peaches
Flamri base made with:
¼ l. milk (1½ gills)
60 g. semoule de blé or fine semolina (2 oz.)
120 g. castor sugar (4 oz.)
3 whites of egg
8 g. leaf gelatine (¼ oz.)

2 tablespoons kirsch
Syrup for poaching:
(see page 24)
To finish:
2–3 tablespoons redcurrant jelly
20 halved, blanched almonds
1 dl. thick cream (½ gill)

Method: Put the leaves of gelatine to soak in cold water. Put the milk for the flamri base into a pan and bring it to the boil. Then shoot in all the semolina, stirring briskly at the same time. Continuing to stir, boil for 2–3 minutes until the semolina is thoroughly cooked. Remove from the heat, stir in the sugar, the leaves of gelatine and the kirsch. Pour the mixture into a bowl and allow it to cool until it begins to thicken round the edges. Whisk the whites of egg stiffly and fold them lightly into the semolina mixture. Pour this into a dampened moule à manqué or deep sandwich tin and put it in a cool place or refrigerator to set.

Meanwhile, lower the peaches carefully into boiling water for a few seconds. Remove them and peel off the skins. Poach the peaches, whole, in the syrup. When they are cooked, drain them on a clean cloth and allow them to become quite cold.

When the flamri base is set, dip the mould into hot water for a few seconds. Remove, dry the base and turn the flamri carefully on to a serving dish.

Arrange the five peaches on the flamri base and top each with a little of the melted redcurrant jelly. Place 4 halved almonds in a decorative design on each peach. Whisk the cream lightly and using a forcing bag and rosette tube, pipe a pyramid of cream in the centre of the flamri and a rosette between each peach towards the edge. Serve cold.

PÊCHES MASQUÉES *   (for 4 persons)

Ingredients:

1 kg. ripe peaches (2 lb.)

3 eggs

$\frac{1}{4}$ l. milk (1$\frac{1}{2}$ gills)

90 g. castor sugar (3 oz.)

1 tablespoon chopped, browned hazel nuts

Method: Peel the peaches with a silver or stainless knife. Cut them in half and remove their stones. Lay them in a large, shallow fireproof dish which has been buttered and dusted out with sugar.

Whisk the eggs with the milk and sugar, strain into another bowl and add the chopped hazel nuts. Pour this mixture over the peaches. Put them in a moderate oven, gas mark 5 or 375° F. (190° C.) for 30–35 minutes. Serve hot.

Comment: A tablespoon of kirsch can be added to the milk if desired.

TARTELETTES AUX PÊCHES AU FROMAGE **

(makes 12 tartlets)

Ingredients:

Pâte Sucrée (see page 339)

For the Filling:

120 g. cream cheese (4 oz.)

30 g. unsalted butter (1 oz.)

1 tablespoon castor sugar

$\frac{1}{2}$–1 level teaspoon vanilla sugar

1 tablespoon thin cream or top of milk

Syrup for poaching:

3 dl. water ($\frac{1}{2}$ pint)

120 g. sugar (4 oz.)

1 vanilla pod

} (see page 24)

6 small peaches

carmine to colour

angelica

apricot glaze (see page 41)

Method: Make up the pastry in the usual way and put it aside in a cool place to relax.

Meanwhile lower the peaches carefully into boiling water for a few seconds. Peel off the skins, cut them in half and remove the stones.

Make the syrup. Place the peaches gently in the syrup and poach them until they are tender. Lift them out and drain them on a wire rack.

Roll out the pastry and line it into twelve round tartlet tins. Prick well and bake them in a moderately hot oven, gas mark 6 or 400° F. (200° C.) until a golden brown, approximately 15 minutes.

Make the filling – sieve the cheese, cream the butter and sugars and mix them all together with the cream.

When the tartlets are cold, fill them with the cheese mixture and place one halved peach on each, cut side down. 'Blush' each with a little carmine colouring and decorate with a few leaves of angelica. Brush over with melted apricot glaze, and serve cold.

TIMBALE DE PÊCHES D'AREMBER *** (for 4–6 persons)

Ingredients:
1 small tin of sliced peaches
Pâte à Génoise Commune made with 3 eggs, etc. (see page 333)
Crème Pâtissière (see page 344)

a liqueur glass Cointreau
4 whites of egg
240 g. castor sugar (8 oz.)
To finish:
30 g. browned almonds (1 oz.)

Method: Make up the pâte à Génoise commune, pour it into a buttered 15 cm. (6 inch) charlotte tin and cook it in a moderate oven, gas mark 5 or 375° F. (190° C.) for 25–30 minutes. When it is cooked, remove it from the tin and place it on a wire rack to cool.

Whilst it is cooking make the crème pâtissière adding the Cointreau at the end. When the Génoise is cooled, carefully hollow out the centre without damaging the exterior and fill the cavity with alternate layers of crème pâtissière and peaches.

Make up the meringue cuite. Whisk the egg whites and the sugar over a pan of hot water until very thick indeed. Cover the sweet entirely with the meringue and decorate the top with a design, using a forcing bag and a large star pipe. Scatter a few browned almonds on the top. Put it in a cool oven, gas mark 3–4 or 325–350° F. (160–180° C.) for a few minutes to set the meringue.

FLAN À L'ALSACIENNE ** (for 4–5 persons)

Ingredients:
Pâte Sucrée (see page 339) to which is added a good pinch of nutmeg and cinnamon and a little vanilla sugar.
Crème Pâtissière (see page 344)
2 large apples

60 g. butter (2 oz.)
30 g. castor sugar (1 oz.)
To finish:
sieved apricot jam for glaze (see page 41)
leaves cut from angelica
glacé cherries

Method: Make up the pâte sucrée as usual but adding to the flour the three flavours as indicated. Put it aside in a cool place to relax. Bake 'blind' (see page 326) in an 18 cm. (7 inch) flan ring in a fairly hot oven, gas mark 6 or 400° F. (200° C.) for 20–25 minutes.

Make up the crème pâtissière as usual. Peel the apples and cut them in fairly thick slices. Melt the butter in a shallow pan and cook the apple carefully in this. When cooked sprinkle with the sugar. Lay the apple slices on the bottom of the flan case. Pour over the crème pâtissière and allow it to cool slightly. Brush all over with apricot glaze. Make a bold design of leaves with the angelica in the centre. Place a cluster of glacé cherries in the middle. Glaze heavily again. Serve hot or cold.

GÂTEAU BISSEXTILE **   (for 4–5 persons)

Ingredients:

Pâte Sucrée made with 225 g.
  plain flour (7½ oz.), etc.
  (see page 339)
¾ kg. apples (1½ lb.)
90 g. sugar (3 oz.)

1 dl. thick cream (½ gill)
1 teaspoon vanilla sugar
redcurrant jelly
sieved apricot jam
blackberry jelly

Method: Make the pâte sucrée in the usual way and put it aside in a cool place to relax.

Peel and core the apples and cut them into slices. Cook them in a thick saucepan with a very little water, keeping them well stirred so that they do not stick to the bottom of the pan. When they are soft and pulpy stir in the sugar and vanilla sugar until they are dissolved. Remove from the heat and pass the apple mixture through a sieve or vegetable mill. Spread the purée on a plate to cool.

Roll out two thirds of the pastry and line it into an 18 cm. (7 inch) flan ring, cut the remainder into ½ cm. (¼ inch) strips. Fill the flan case with the apple purée, which must be quite cold, and smooth it over. Wet the edges of the pastry and lay the strips over to form a fine lattice. Cook in an oven, gas mark 6 or 400° F. (200° C.) for 25–30 minutes. Remove and allow to cool

Whisk the cream fairly stiffly. When the flan is cold fill the jam, jellies and cream carefully into the diamonds of the lattice to form a harlequin effect. Serve cold. (*See Plate 20.*)

PETITS POTS DE POMMES AU RHUM*   (for 3–4 persons)

Ingredients:

½ kg. apples (1 lb.)
15 g. butter (½ oz.)
90 g. seedless raisins (3 oz.)
1 tablespoon apricot jam

1 tablespoon rum
To finish:
redcurrant or blackcurrant jelly
chopped browned nuts
a little whipped cream

Method: Peel and core the apples and cut them into slices. Put them with the butter and very little water into a thick pan and cook until they are soft and pulpy, stirring them well to prevent their sticking to the bottom of the pan. When they are cooked, pass them through a sieve or vegetable mill. Chop the raisins roughly and mix them with the apple purée in a clean thick pan; add the apricot jam and stir over a good heat until the mixture is thick. Remove the pan from the heat and allow the mixture to become quite cold. Then stir in the rum.

Fill the mixture into small pots. Melt the jelly and cover the surface of each with this. Sprinkle with chopped nuts and decorate with whipped cream.

POMMES À LA BOURGEOISE * (for 4 persons)

Ingredients:
4 good sized cooking apples
Crème Pâtissière made with ½ l.
 (1 pint) milk, 120 g. (4 oz.) castor
 sugar, 35 g. (1½ oz.) plain flour,
 2 eggs, 2 yolks of egg, 1 vanilla
 pod (see page 344 for method)

240 g. crystallised fruits (8 oz.)
60 g. chopped almonds (2 oz.)
30 g. melted butter (1 oz.)
a little castor sugar
syrup to poach the apples (see
 page 24)

Method: Make the syrup. Bring the water to the boil with the sugar and the vanilla pod, stirring occasionally to dissolve the sugar. Reduce the heat.

Meanwhile wash and peel the apples. Cut them in half crosswise and remove the cores carefully. Poach the halves in the prepared syrup and simmer them gently until they are just tender. Lift the apples with a draining spoon and arrange them, cut side uppermost, in a fireproof serving dish. Fill the centre of each halved apple with the finely chopped crystallised fruits.

Make the crème pâtissière. It should be slightly thinner than usual. Coat each apple half with an even layer. Scatter the chopped almonds over the surface, dust lightly with castor sugar and sprinkle with the melted butter.

Put the dish in the top of a hot oven, gas mark 7–8 or 425–450° F. (220–230° C.) for 5 minutes to brown lightly. Serve hot.

POMMES À LA PORTUGAISE * (for 4–6 persons)

Ingredients:
6 apples
60 g. crystallised lemon peel in
 the piece (2 oz.)
2 tablespoons apricot jam

3–4 crisp macaroons (see page 356)
60 g. castor sugar (2 oz.)
30 g. butter (1 oz.)
Crème Pâtissière (see page 344)
1 dl. white port (½ gill)

Method: Make up the crème pâtissière in the usual way. Remove it from the heat and add the port, together with the crushed macaroons, and the apricot jam. Mix all well together. Spread all of this, except about 4 table-spoons, in the bottom of a buttered fireproof dish. Peel the apples care-fully and remove their cores. Cut the lemon peel into thin strips and using the point of a knife, make holes in the sides of the apples. Insert the lemon peel in these allowing it to project slightly. Place the apples in the dish on the crème pâtissière. Fill the centres of the apples with the rest of the crème. Dust them over with the castor sugar. Put a knob of butter on each apple. Wipe round the sides of the dish carefully. Place in a fairly hot oven, gas mark 6 or 400° F. (200° C.) for about 30 minutes until they are cooked. The length of time will depend on the type of apples used. Serve hot in the dish in which they have been cooked.

POMMES ROSA ** (for 4 persons)

Ingredients:
4 sweet dessert apples
syrup made with 180 g. (6 oz.),

castor sugar ½ l. (1 pint), water
1 vanilla pod (see page 24)
¼ l. red wine (1½ gills)

Method: Peel and core the apples and cut them in half crosswise. Put them into the syrup and poach them very gently until they are transparent looking. Lift them carefully with a draining spoon and arrange them in a serving dish.

Pour the wine into the syrup. Raise the heat and boil it rapidly until it is thick.

Remove the vanilla pod, coat the apples with the wine syrup. Serve very cold.

Comment: Care must be taken when boiling the syrup not to caramelise it.

POMMES PRALINÉES ** (for 4 persons)

Ingredients:
4 medium cooking apples
8 tablespoons thick apple purée –
  Marmelade de Pommes (see
  page 21)
1 white of egg

135 g. castor sugar (4½ oz.)
60 g. (light weight) finely chopped
  blanched almonds (2 oz.)
¼ teaspoon plain flour
a little icing sugar
syrup for poaching (see page 24)

Method: Peel the apples and remove their cores. Cut them in half and poach them carefully in the syrup until they are just tender. Remove them from the syrup and drain them on a wire rack.

Spread the apple marmalade in the bottom of a heatproof serving dish. Arrange the apple halves on this.

Sieve the sugar and flour and mix with the nuts and egg white to give a fairly smooth paste. Pour a spoonful over each half apple.

Dust lightly with icing sugar. Bake in the top of a hot oven, gas mark 7 or 425° F. (220° C.) for 5 minutes to brown the coating.

TARTE AUX POMMES MERINGUÉS *** (for 4–5 persons)

Ingredients:
Pâte Sucrée (see page 339)
350 g. Marmelade de Pommes, (¾ lb.) approx. (see page 21)
Pâte à Meringue Suisse made with 2 egg whites, 150 g. (5 oz.)

castor sugar, a little icing sugar (see page 334)
To finish:
redcurrant jelly
sieved apricot jam for glaze
a little royal icing (optional) (see page 345)

Method: Make up the pâte sucrée in the usual way and put it aside in a cool place to relax. Bake blind (see page 326) in an 18 cm. (7 inch) flan ring, in a fairly hot oven, gas mark 5 or 375° F. (190° C.) for 20–25 minutes or until pale gold. When it is ready, slide it on to a serving plate. Fill with marmelade de pommes.

Make the meringue suisse in the usual way. Spread half of this on the top of the apple, smoothing it out with a palette knife until it is quite even. Fill a forcing bag with the remaining meringue and with a plain ½ cm. (¼ inch) tube, pipe a lattice design on the top. Then pipe again on the top of the first piping to make a raised design. Dust thinly with icing sugar. Place in a cool oven, gas mark 2–3 or 300–325° F. (150–160° C.) for approximately 30 minutes or until the meringue is set firmly without browning.

Whilst it is setting, melt down a few spoonfuls of redcurrant jelly and of apricot glaze, intensifying the colours of each with a little vegetable colouring if necessary. Remove the 'tarte' from the oven and carefully fill the jelly and apricot glaze into the lattice work in a chequered design. Serve hot or cold.

Comment: To finish – if liked, a little royal icing may be piped on the lattice work to emphasise the pattern.

COMPÔTE DE POIRES SAINT-HONORÉ *

(for 4 or 8 persons)

Ingredients:
4 ripe pears
syrup for poaching (see page 24)
75 g. plain flour (2½ oz.)
120 g. castor sugar (4 oz.)

2 yolks of eggs
½ l. milk (1 pint)
1 teaspoon vanilla sugar
To finish:
crushed sugared almonds

Method: Peel the pears, cut them in half and remove the cores. Poach them in the syrup. Remove, drain well and arrange them in the bottom of a deep serving dish.

Meanwhile work the flour, sugar, vanilla sugar and the yolks well together with a wooden spatula. Heat the milk and when it is just on the point of boiling, stir it gradually on to the yolks, sugar, etc. Stir well, return it to a clean pan. Stirring all the time bring to the boil over a gentle heat and simmer for 2–3 minutes. Pour it over the pears and put them aside in a cool place. Finally sprinkle the crushed sugared almonds round the edge. Serve very cold.

POIRES À LA CARMELITE ** (for 4 persons)

Ingredients:

4 ripe pears
syrup for poaching (see page 24)
90 g. glacé cherries or crystal-
    lised fruits (3 oz.)
1 tablespoon sieved apricot jam

120 g. Carolina rice (4 oz.)
90 g. sugar (3 oz.)
3 dl. milk (½ pint)
2 tablespoons redcurrant jelly
½ lemon

Method: Peel the pears and leave them whole. Rub them with half a lemon and poach in the syrup until tender, taking care not to break them up. Remove them from the syrup and drain on a wire rack. Cut off the top of each pear and scoop out the centre. Fill with the finely chopped crystallised fruits or glacé cherries mixed with one tablespoon of sieved apricot jam.

Put the rice into a saucepan of cold water, bring to the boil and boil for 2–3 minutes. Drain well. Return to the pan, pour on the milk previously brought to the boil. Cover and cook very gently, stirring from time to time until all the milk is absorbed, approximately 20 minutes. Stir in the sugar. Place the rice in a serving dish and arrange the pears on top. Brush them with redcurrant jelly, which has been melted with a little water. Serve at once.

Comment: This recipe can be made with tinned pears which are arranged on the rice, cut side uppermost and filled with the crystallised fruits. The jelly is then brushed over afterwards.

POIRES À LA SICILIENNE ** (for 4 or 8 persons)

Ingredients:

4 ripe pears
syrup for poaching (see page 24)
    OR
1 tin pears
For the Filling:
3 dl. milk (½ pint)

60 g. castor sugar (2 oz.)
60 g. browned almonds (2 oz.)
60 g. fine semolina (2 oz.)
2 yolks of egg
8 small meringue shells
1½ dl. thick cream (1 gill)

Method: Make the syrup by boiling the water, sugar and vanilla pod together. Peel the pears with a stainless knife. Cut them in half lengthwise and remove the cores and pips. Poach them gently in the syrup until they are soft but not broken. Drain well and arrange them in a shallow serving dish.

Make the cream filling – bring the milk to the boil with the sugar. Scatter in the semolina and cook until it thickens, stirring briskly. This should take 2–3 minutes. Remove from the heat, cool slightly, then beat in the egg yolks. Return to a gentle heat and cook for a moment or two longer, continuing to stir all the time. Remove and stir in the nuts, which have been pounded to a powder or put through a nut mill. Fill the centre of each half pear with this mixture and leave to cool. Place a meringue shell on the top of each pear. Whisk the cream stiffly, place in a forcing bag with a small rosette tube and pipe a design to form a border round each meringue shell. Serve very cold.

POIRES BRILLAT SAVARIN **   (for 6 persons)

Ingredients:
1 tin pears or 3 good sized pears
syrup for poaching (see page 24)
360 g. Marmelade de Pommes
    (¾ lb.) (see page 21)
1 lemon
30 g. butter (1 oz.)
a little rum

Pâte à Génoise Commune made
    with 3 eggs (see page 333)
To finish:
chopped browned nuts
glacé cherries
angelica
a little rum
2 tablespoons sieved apricot jam

Method: Peel the pears with a stainless knife. Cut them in half and remove the cores. Rub them over with a cut lemon to prevent them from turning brown. Make a syrup and poach the pears in this. Remove them and put on a wire rack to drain.

Split the cake across. Place the marmelade de pommes in a small pan. Melt gently. Remove from the heat and beat in the butter bit by bit. Stir in 1–2 tablespoons of rum. Fill the cake with ⅔ of this. Melt the apricot jam with 1–2 tablespoons of the pear syrup. Brush the sides of the cake with this and coat with the nuts. Place the cake on the serving dish and arrange the pears on the top, narrow end pointing inwards. Heap the remainder of the marmelade de pommes in the centre. Use the glacé cherries and leaves cut from angelica macerated in a little rum, to decorate the pears and to cover the marmelade de pommes in the centre. Brush all over with apricot jam. Serve very cold. (*See Plate 21.*)

POIRES FLAMBÉES À L'ORANGE * (for 2 or 4 persons)

Ingredients:

2 ripe pears
½ lemon
juice of 1 or 2 oranges
grated rind of 1 orange

2 tablespoons Grand Marnier
120 g. sugar (4 oz.)
1 vanilla pod
¼ l. water (1½ gills)

Method: Make a syrup by heating the sugar, water, orange juice, grated orange rind and vanilla pod in a shallow pan. Bring to simmering point and stir until the sugar is dissolved. Peel the pears, cut them in half and remove the cores. Rub them over quickly with the ½ lemon to stop their discolouring.

Place the pears carefully in the syrup and poach them gently until they are just cooked. Lift the pears carefully without breaking them and arrange them on a hot serving dish. Strain over the syrup and keep hot.

To Serve: Heat a ladle or very large spoon, pour in the Grand Marnier and light it. Pour it over the hot pears and baste them quickly with the flaming liquid.

Comment: This recipe is suitable for making in a chafing dish at the table.

POIRES FOURRÉES SUD AFRIQUE ** (for 4 persons)

Ingredients:

2 whole pears
syrup for poaching (see page 24)
    OR
4 halved tinned pears
8 halved tinned guavas
1 tablespoon Grand Marnier
2 tablespoons redcurrant jelly

For the Cream:

3 dl. milk (½ pint)
2 yolks of egg
60 g. castor sugar (2 oz.)
1 heaped teaspoon arrowroot

To finish:

1 dl. thick cream (½ gill)

Method: If using fresh pears, peel them carefully with a stainless knife, cut them in half and remove the cores. Poach them in syrup made with sugar, water and vanilla pod. Drain the fresh or tinned pears and arrange them, cut side uppermost, in the bottom of the serving dish.

Cut the guavas into small dice and mix them with the Grand Marnier and redcurrant jelly. Pile this mixture in the centre of each halved pear.

Make the crème – work the sugar and arrowroot with the egg yolks until it is a light colour. Heat the milk to simmering point, pour it on to the egg yolks, etc., stir well and return to the pan, which has been rinsed out. It must not boil. Cook over a gentle heat until it thickens. Cool slightly, then pour this crème over the pears, etc. Put it aside to get completely cold.

Whip the cream lightly and using a rosette tube decorate the pears with stars of whipped cream. Serve very cold.

POIRES GRAND MOGUL **   (for 4–5 persons)

Ingredients:
3–4 pears, depending on size
Pâte Sucrée (see page 339)
Crème Pâtissière (see page 344)
240 g. pineapple conserve or
  finely chopped fresh pineapple
  ($\frac{1}{2}$ lb.)
$\frac{1}{2}$ lemon

syrup for poaching using $1\frac{1}{2}$ dl.
  ($\frac{1}{4}$ pint) white wine, $1\frac{1}{2}$ dl.
  ($\frac{1}{4}$ pint) water, 120 g. (4 oz.),
  sugar 1 vanilla pod (see page
  24)
apricot glaze (see page 41)
1 dl. kirsch ($\frac{1}{2}$ gill)

Method: Make up the pâte sucrée in the usual way and put it aside in a cool place to relax.

Dissolve the sugar in the water and the wine, add the vanilla pod. Meanwhile, peel the pears carefully and rub them with a cut lemon to keep them white. Cut the pears in half and remove the pips and cores. Poach the pears carefully in the simmering syrup. When cooked, remove them and drain on a clean cloth.

Roll out the pâte sucrée and line it into a 7 inch flan ring. Prick the base well. Cover with greaseproof paper and beans and bake 'blind' in a fairly hot oven, gas mark 6 or 400° F. (200° C.) for 20–25 minutes. Remove the paper and beans and return the case to the oven for about 5 minutes to dry.

Make the crème pâtissière and flavour with vanilla and half the kirsch. Pour it into the flan case and allow to get quite cold and set.

Mix the chopped pineapple or the pineapple conserve with the rest of the kirsch and spread it over the crème pâtissière. Arrange the pears on this. Spoon a little apricot glaze carefully over each pear. Serve cold.

POIRES MARIE-ANNE ***   (for 6–8 persons)

Ingredients:
Pâte à Génoise Commune made
  with 3 eggs etc. (see page 333)
Riz au Lait made with 90 g.
  (3 oz.) Carolina rice, 3 dl. ($\frac{1}{2}$ pint)
  milk, 1 vanilla pod, 180 g.
  (5 oz.) castor sugar, 2 yolks of
  egg, 75 g. ($2\frac{1}{2}$ oz.) butter
6 fresh pears
syrup for poaching (see page 24)
  OR
1 tin pears (480 g.) (16 oz.)

Pâte à Meringue made with 2
  whites of egg, 135 g. ($4\frac{1}{2}$ oz.)
  castor sugar, 1 teaspoon
  vanilla sugar (see page 334)
To finish:
glacé cherries
leaves cut from angelica
$1\frac{1}{2}$ dl. sieved apricot jam (1 gill) for
  glaze, to which has been added
  2 tablespoons Grand Marnier

Method: Make up the Pâte à Génoise Commune in the usual way. Pour into a greased moule à manqué or deep sandwich tin and bake in a moderately hot oven, gas mark 5–6 or 375–400° (190–200° C.) for 30–35 minutes. Remove and place on a wire rack to cool.

If using fresh pears, peel, core and halve them and poach them in the syrup. If using tinned pears, warm them in their syrup.

Make the Riz au Lait – pour the rice in a pan of cold water. Bring it to the boil and boil for 2–3 minutes. Remove and drain. Boil the milk in a clean pan with the vanilla pod, remove from the heat and stir in the rice. Cover with greaseproof paper and the lid and put it in a moderate oven, gas mark 5 or 375° F. (190° C.). When the rice is cooked, which should be at the end of 25 minutes or so, take it out of the oven, remove the vanilla pod and stir in the castor sugar together with the beaten yolks and the butter. Keep it hot.

Place the Génoise base on a plate. Pile the rice on top. Beat the whites stiffly and fold in the sieved sugar and the vanilla sugar. Spread half of this on top of the rice. Put the remainder into a forcing bag with a large rosette pipe and pipe a design all over the top of the meringue. Return the mixture to the top of a cool oven, gas mark 2–3 or 300–325° F. (150–160° C.) to set the meringue. (It should not brown). Warm the liqueur flavoured apricot glaze with 2–3 tablespoons of the pear syrup. When the meringue is set, arrange the pears round the sides of the Génoise. Decorate with glacé cherries and angelica leaves. Glaze the fruit with the apricot glaze and serve at once.

Comment: It is possible to serve this sweet cold if desired.

POIRES NELUSKO *   (for 4–8 persons)

Ingredients:

4 pears
syrup for poaching (see page 24)
8 macaroons, about 8 cm. (3 in.) in
  diameter (see page 356)

Sauce Chocolat (see page 41)
To finish:
finely chopped browned nuts

Method: Peel the pears, using a stainless knife. Cut them in half and remove the cores. Poach the pears in the vanilla flavoured syrup. Cook them gently until they are just tender. Lift the pears carefully and drain them on a clean cloth.

Meanwhile make the sauce chocolat in the usual way.

Arrange the macaroons on a serving dish and place a halved pear on the top of each, cut side downwards. Coat each pear evenly with the sauce chocolat and decorate the top with a few chopped browned nuts. Serve cold.

POIRES PRINCESSES **   (for 4–8 persons)

Ingredients:

5 ripe pears
syrup for poaching (see page 24)
Sauce Abricot, flavoured with
  kirsch (see page 41)
½ l. Crème Pâtissière (1 pint)
  (see page 344)

8 glacé cherries
angelica leaves
16 fleurons of puff or flaky pastry
  (see page 12)
1½ dl. thick cream (1 gill)
carmine to colour

Method: Peel four of the pears, cut them in half and take out the cores. Peel the fifth pear and using a vegetable ball cutter carefully remove the core through the base of the pear. Poach them all in the syrup. Remove them carefully when they are just tender and place them on a wire rack to drain. Reserve some of the syrup to make the sauce abricot.

Make the crème pâtissière and allow it to cool. Heap it in the centre of a large round dish with a good margin all the way round.

When the pears are quite cold and dry, 'blush' them lightly with carmine so as to give them a pink cheek. Place the whole pear in the centre of the crème pâtissière – arrange the cut pears, round end inwards, around the central pear. Lightly brush each pear with thin sauce abricot. At the top of each halved pear, put a fairly large leaf of angelica. Using a large rosette tube pipe a star of whipped cream in between each pear. On each star place a halved glacé cherry and two leaves of angelica. Arrange the fleurons all round the edge of the dish. Serve very cold.

RIZ À LA LORRAINE **   (for 4–6 persons)

Ingredients:

120 g. Carolina rice (4 oz.)
3 dl. milk (½ pint)
6 tablespoons castor sugar
2 tablespoons kirsch
2 eggs

150 g. crystallised fruits or
  drained, chopped tinned fruit
  (5 oz.)
½ teaspoon vanilla sugar
pinch of salt

Method: Put the fruit to macerate in the kirsch. Wash the rice well and blanch it in boiling water for 2–3 minutes. Drain well and place it in a saucepan with the boiling milk, to which has been added a pinch of salt and the vanilla sugar. Cover with buttered greaseproof paper and the lid of the pan and place it in a moderately hot oven, gas mark 4–5 or 350–375° F. (180–190° C.) until the rice is cooked, approximately 25–30 minutes. Do not stir whilst it is cooking.

Separate the eggs and beat the yolks lightly with a tablespoon of milk.

When the rice is cooked, remove it from the oven and using a fork, stir in 4 tablespoons of castor sugar together with the yolks. Fold in the chopped fruits and form the rice mixture into a galette shape on a round dish.

Whisk the whites stiffly and lightly fold in the rest of the sugar. Using a forcing bag with a rosette tube, pipe a design to cover the rice completely with meringue. Dust with a little castor sugar. Put to brown for half an hour in the top of a very moderate oven, gas mark 3 or 325° F. (165° C.) Serve warm.

TARTE À LA RUSSE **   (for 3–4 persons)

Ingredients: **For the Filling:**
For the Pastry: 120 g. cream cheese (4 oz.)
135 g. plain flour (4½ oz.)   75 g. castor sugar (2½ oz.)
105 g. butter (3½ oz.)   45 g. butter (1½ oz.)
pinch of salt   45 g. sultanas (1½ oz.)
cold water to mix   1 yolk of egg
                                    1 teaspoon vanilla sugar

Method: Sift the flour and salt into a bowl. Rub in the butter with the tips of the fingers until the mixture resembles fine breadcrumbs. Using a round bladed knife, add just sufficient water to make a firm dough. Put it in a refrigerator or cold place to relax for ½ hour.

Make the filling. Melt the butter and put it aside to cool. Sieve the cream cheese and mix it to a smooth paste with the liquid, but not hot, butter, the sugar and the vanilla sugar. Stir in the yolk of egg and finally the sultanas. Mix well.

Roll out the pastry on a lightly floured board. Line it carefully into an 18 cm. (7 inch) flan ring. Pour in the filling.

Cook it in a hot oven, gas mark 7 or 425° F. (220° C.) for 15–20 minutes, until the pastry is crisp and the filling is just set. Serve warm or cold.

TARTELETTES AUX RAISINS **   (Makes about 10–12 tartlets)

Ingredients: **For the Filling:**
Pâte Sucrée (half quantity) (see   about 350 g. sweet white grapes
  page 339)   (¾ lb.)
                                    227 g. redcurrant jelly (½ lb.)

Method: Make the pâte sucrée in the usual way. Leave it to relax in a cold place. Roll it out ½ cm. (¼ inch) thick on a lightly floured board and line it into boat shaped moulds. Prick very well. Bake them in a moderate oven, gas mark 5–6 or 375–400° F. (190°–200 C.) for 15 minutes, until a light golden brown. When they are cooked remove them from the tins carefully and place them on a wire rack to cool.

Blanch the grapes in boiling water for a few moments. Remove their skins and pips. Put 2 or 3 grapes in each boat. Heat the redcurrant jelly and spoon it over the top and around the grapes.

FLAMRI DE SEMOULE * (for 4–5 persons)

Ingredients:

3 dl. white wine (1 gill)
3 dl. water (1 gill)
75 g. semoule de blé or fine
    semolina (2½ oz.)

75 g. castor sugar (2½ oz.)
3 whites of egg
1 teaspoon vanilla sugar
redcurrant jelly
kirsch to flavour

Method: Put the wine and water into a pan. Bring them to the boil and then shoot in all the semolina at once. Stir very briskly. Add the sugar and vanilla sugar and cook for 2–3 minutes, stirring all the time. Remove the pan from the heat and beat in one white. Whisk the remaining whites until they are stiff, fold them into the semolina mixture lightly. Pour the mixture into a shallow mould or cake tin which has been well buttered and dusted out with castor sugar. Stand the mould in a bain marie or roasting tin containing boiling water and place it in a moderate oven, gas mark 5 or 375° F. (190° C.) for 30–35 minutes. Remove it and let it get cold. Unmould it on a serving dish and pour over a sauce made with melted redcurrant jelly flavoured with kirsch.

PUDDING DE SEMOULE AU CARAMEL ** (for 5–6 persons)

Ingredients:

60 g. semolina (2 oz.)
½ l. milk (1 pint)
vanilla pod
60 g. butter (2 oz.)
60 g. castor sugar (2 oz.)
2 whites of egg

3 eggs
For the Caramel:
240 g. sugar (8 oz.)
    (see page 16)
To finish:
3 dl. Crème Anglaise (½ pint)
    (see page 40)

Method: Heat the milk slowly with the vanilla pod. When it comes to the boil remove the vanilla pod and shoot in the semolina all at once. Cook for 2–3 minutes, stirring all the time, until it has thickened. Then beat in the sugar and butter bit by bit. Remove the pan from the heat and stir in the whole eggs, which have been lightly beaten. Whisk the whites stiffly and fold them lightly into the semolina mixture.

Make the caramel as usual and pour it into a charlotte mould or 15 cm. (6 inch) cake tin. Holding it in a cloth, turn the mould quickly to allow the caramel to run all round the sides and the bottom. Pour the semolina mixture into the mould and stand it in a bain-marie or baking tin containing boiling water. Cook it for 20–30 minutes in a fairly hot oven, gas mark 6 or 400° F. (200° C.). When it is cooked allow it to cool in the mould. Turn it out carefully on a serving dish. Serve if liked with a Crème Anglaise to which has been added a little caramel to flavour.

SOUFFLÉ AU KIRSCH **   (for 3–4 persons)

Ingredients:

¼ l. milk (1½ gills)	4 eggs
75 g. castor sugar (2½ oz.)	1 dl. kirsch (½ gill)
45 g. flour (1½ oz.)	icing sugar

Method: Separate the eggs. Work the yolks, sugar and flour together with a wooden spoon or spatula. Heat the milk and pour it on the yolks, etc., stirring well. Return to the pan, which has been rinsed out. Bring to the boil, stirring all the time, and still stirring, cook over a low heat for 2 minutes. Remove from the heat and stir in the kirsch.

Prepare an 18 cm. (7 inch) soufflé dish (see page 24).

Whisk the whites and fold them carefully in to the hot mixture. Pour this into the prepared soufflé dish and level off the top. Bake it in a moderate oven, gas mark 5 or 375° F. (190° C.) for 20–25 minutes. Serve at once. Just before serving sprinkle the top with icing sugar.

SOUFFLÉ CAMARGO **   (for 4 persons)

Ingredients:

3 yolks of egg	60 g. hazel nuts (2 oz.)
4 whites of egg	1–2 tablespoons Grand Marnier
45 g. plain flour (1½ oz.)	1 vanilla pod
135 g. castor sugar (4½ oz.)	2 tangerines
¼ l. milk (1½ gills)	4 sponge finger biscuits

Method: Place the hazel nuts on a baking sheet in the top of a fairly hot oven, gas mark 6 or 400° F. (200° C.). Brown for a few minutes. Remove from the oven and rub off their skins in a clean dry cloth. Pass them through a nut or cheese mill. Put them on one side.

Well butter an 18 cm. (7 inch) soufflé dish and dust it out with castor sugar.

Crumble the sponge finger biscuits roughly and put them to macerate in the Grand Marnier.

Peel the tangerines and cut in between the sections so as to give slices without skin. Remove the pips and put the slices on one side.

Cream the egg yolks, sugar and flour together, using a wooden spoon or spatula. Put the milk with the vanilla pod in a saucepan and heat it slowly. When it reaches simmering point remove it from the heat and pour it on to the yolks, sugar etc. Stir, and return it to the pan, which has been rinsed out. Cook it over a gentle heat, keeping it well stirred, until it thickens. Remove from the heat, take out the vanilla pod and stir in the hazel nuts.

Whisk the whites very stiffly and fold the custard mixture into them as lightly and quickly as possible. Put three quarters of the mixture into the prepared soufflé dish. Lay half of the tangerine slices on top, then the sponge finger biscuits, together with the liqueur they have soaked in, then the rest of the tangerines. Cover with the remainder of the soufflé mixture. Wipe round the edges of the dish to prevent unsightly browning. Put it into a moderately hot oven, gas mark 5–6 or 375–400° F. (190–200° C.) for 20–25 minutes. Serve at once.

SOUFFLÉ TRIOMPHE DU CHEF **   (for 4–5 persons)

Ingredients:

3 yolks of egg
4 whites of egg
60 g. unsalted butter (2 oz.)
60 g. plain flour (2 oz.)
3 dl. milk (½ pint)
90 g. castor sugar (3 oz.)

90–120 g. crystallised fruits (3–4 oz.)
1 vanilla pod
liqueurs as follows to make 3 dl. (1 gill) Kirsch, Grand Marnier, Benedictine, Chartreuse, Fine Champagne Cognac

Method: Chop the fruits roughly and put them to macerate in the mixed liqueurs.

Butter an 18 cm. (7 inch) soufflé dish and dust it out with a little castor sugar.

Melt the butter in a pan, draw it aside from the heat, stir in the flour. Mix well and return it to the heat to cook the roux for 2–3 minutes. Heat the milk with the vanilla pod, pour it on to the roux and stirring all the time, bring it to the boil.

Boil it for approximately 5 minutes, stirring continuously. Remove the pan from the heat, take out the vanilla pod. Stir in the sugar at once whilst it is still very hot. Add the whisked egg yolks. Mix them in thoroughly. Put the mixture on one side to cool slightly. Whisk the whites stiffly and fold them in lightly and quickly. Spread a thick layer of the soufflé mixture in the bottom of the prepared dish. Cover with the crystallised fruits, together with the liqueurs in which they have been macerating. Spread the rest of the mixture on the top. Smooth it over with a palette knife. Put the soufflé into a moderately hot oven, gas mark 5–6 or 375–400° F. (190–200° C.) for 25–30 minutes. Serve immediately.

Comment: This soufflé is a speciality of M. Cazalis of Chartres.

CRÊPES AU GINGEMBRE **   (for 4–5 persons)

Ingredients

Pâte à Crêpes (see page 255)
For the Filling:
100 g. preserved ginger (3½ oz.)
¼ l. thick cream (1 gill)

For the Sauce:
4 oranges
2 tablespoons castor sugar
1 dl. preserved ginger syrup (½ gill)
To finish:
2 tablespoons brandy

Method: Make the pâte à crêpes in the usual way.

Make the filling – drain the ginger and chop it finely. Whisk the cream lightly and fold in the ginger.

Make the sauce – squeeze the juice from the oranges. Put it in a saucepan with the sugar and ginger syrup. Stirring occasionally, bring the sauce to the boil, then continue to boil it until it thickens to the consistency of thin cream. Keep it hot.

Fry the crêpes as thinly as possible.

Spread a layer of filling on each crêpe. Roll up each like a cigar. Arrange them side by side in a hot fireproof dish. Pour over the hot sauce.

Just before serving heat the brandy, pour it quickly over the crêpes and 'flame' them.

OMELETTE SOUFFLÉE GRAND MARNIER **

(for 4 persons)

Ingredients:

180 g. castor sugar (6 oz.)
3 yolks of eggs
5 whites of eggs
1 orange

4–6 tablespoons Grand Marnier
1 brioche or 2 macaroons or
   4 ratafias
a little extra castor sugar

Method: Peel the orange very thinly, being careful not to remove any of the white pith with the zest. Sprinkle a little sugar on the zest and chop it very finely. Now cut all the pith from the orange, removing the skin. Cut in between the sections and remove the flesh without any skin. Put this to macerate in 2–3 tablespoons of Grand Marnier. Slice the brioche or break the macaroons into small pieces. Put half the sugar on to the brioche, together with the peel and the rest of the liqueur and mix them all together.

Put the yolks into a bowl and add the remaining sugar. Work them well with a wooden spoon or spatula until thick and creamy. Butter a fireproof serving dish. Dust it out well with castor sugar.

Beat the whites very stiffly indeed. Sprinkle in about one tablespoon of castor sugar and continue to beat for a further 5 minutes. Fold the whites into the yolks in three lots. Spread one third of this on the bottom of the prepared dish. Cover with half of the brioche and peel mixture, then with half of the orange slices. Spread another layer of omelette mixture on the top. Cover with the rest of the brioche, peel and orange slices. Lastly cover the whole surface with the rest of the omelette mixture. Smooth the surface and make a design on the top with a palette knife. Dust with castor sugar. Cook in a moderate oven, gas mark 5 or 375° F. (190° C.) for 15 minutes. Serve immediately.

Ices

For a year or so before the time of writing, there has been a dramatic increase in the popularity of home freezing. This has put the home production of delicious ices made from pure ingredients within the grasp of many more people. It is still an advantage to have an ice cream bucket and with a home freezer one is not dependent on the diminishing supply of ice from the fishmonger. As an alternative, there are on the market various electrical ice cream machines which are small enough to fit into the freezing compartment of a domestic refrigerator, but large enough to make a ½ litre (1 pint) of ice cream or more.

Ices fall into two main categories: cream ices and water ices or sorbets. Cream ices have a basis of egg custard (Crème Anglaise) to which cream and flavouring are added. Water ices are made from fruit juices or purée or wine with a sugar syrup – having a specific gravity of 18 degrees Beaumé. Sorbets are not as sweet as cream ices and should have a soft texture, which makes them easy to eat with a spoon. Originally sorbets were served between the entrée and roast at large banquets consisting of many courses. The idea was to refresh the palate. In present times when such elaborate meals are not usual, the sorbet can be a pleasant finale.

It has been known to serve a Sorbet au Vin Blanc as an appetiser at the beginning of a meal.

Parfait is a particular form of cream ice which does not require an ice bucket. It can be made easily in the domestic refrigerator or home freezer.

ICES

BOMBES

A bombe is a moulded case of ice cream entirely enveloping some exotic rich mixture such as glacé fruits macerated in liqueurs.

BOMBE À LA MARIE-THÉRÈSE ***   (for 4–6 persons)

Ingredients:
Glace au Chocolat (see page 316)
¼ l. Creme Chantilly (1½ gills)
(see page 344)

60 g. Biscuits à la Cuillère (2 oz.)
(see page 331)
1 dl. kirsch (½ gill)
To finish:
crystallised pineapple

Method: Whilst preparing the ice cream, place a square bombe mould in the refrigerator. At the same time, break the biscuits à la Cuillère into even sized lengths and soak them in the kirsch. Put them in the refrigerator also.

Line the bombe mould with an even layer of the chocolate ice cream. Whisk the cream fairly thickly, fold in the soaked biscuits. Fill the centre of the bombe with this mixture. Smooth off and cover with greaseproof paper and the lid. Seal with lard and bury in a mixture of ice and salt to mature for at least 2 hours. If possible the bombe can be set in a deep freezer, in which case it will not be necessary to seal the bombe with lard.

To Serve: Unmould on to a cold serving dish. Decorate with the pineapple pieces, using discretion.

GLACE AUX ABRICOTS ***   (for 4–6 persons)

Ingredients:
500 g. fresh apricots (1 lb.)
OR
250 g. soaked dried apricots (½ lb.)
stewed in 3 dl. (½ pint) water
and 120 g. sugar (4 oz.)

3 dl. milk (½ pint)
1½ dl. thin cream (¼ pint)
4 yolks of egg
90 g. castor sugar (3 oz.)
1 vanilla pod

Method: Cream the yolks and sugar until they are light and thick. Heat the milk with the vanilla pod and pour over the yolks etc., removing the vanilla pod first. Stir well and return to the pan which has been rinsed out. Cook slowly until the custard thickens enough to coat the back of a wooden spoon. Strain into a large bowl. Put it aside to cool. When completely cold, add the cream and the purée of sieved apricots and put the container in the prepared bucket and freeze.

When the ice cream has stiffened, remove the paddle; reseal the container and leave it covered with a thick layer of sacking until required.

Serve the glace in coupes accompanied by tuiles, gaufrettes, biscuits à la cuillère or other suitable crisp biscuits.

GLACE AU CASSIS *** (for 6–8 persons)

Ingredients:
½ l. milk (¾ pint)
4–5 yolks of egg
90 g. castor sugar (3 oz.)

500 g. blackcurrants (1 lb.)
   cooked in 180 g. sugar (6 oz.)
   and 1 dl. water (½ gill)
1 vanilla pod

Method: Cream the yolks and sugar until they are light and thick. Heat the milk with the vanilla pod and pour over the yolks, etc., first removing the vanilla pod. Stir well and return to the pan which has been rinsed out. Cook slowly until the custard thickens enough to coat the back of a wooden spoon. Strain into a large bowl and add the sieved blackcurrant purée. Put it aside to cool. When cold, place in the refrigerator. When completely cold, put into the container in the prepared ice bucket and freeze as already described.

GLACE AU PRALINE *** (for 4–6 persons)

Ingredients:
½ l. milk (¾ pint)
4–5 yolks of egg

90 g. castor sugar (3 oz.)
120 g. crushed praline (4 oz.)
(see page 348)
1 vanilla pod

Method: Cream the yolks and sugar together until they are light and thick. Heat the milk with a vanilla pod and pour it over the yolks, etc., first removing the vanilla pod. Stir well and return to the pan which has been rinsed out. Cook slowly until the custard thickens enough to coat the back of a wooden spoon. Strain it into a bowl and put it aside to cool. When it is cool, place it in a refrigerator. When completely cold, stir in the crushed praline and pour into the container in the prepared bucket and freeze as already described.

A richer ice cream may be made by using thin cream in place of milk.

GLACE À LA VANILLE ** (for 3–4 persons)

Ingredients:
½ l. milk (¾ pint)
4–5 egg yolks

90 g. castor sugar (3 oz.)
1 vanilla pod

Method: Cream the yolks and sugar until they are light and thick. Heat the milk with the vanilla pod and pour over the yolks, etc., first removing the vanilla pod. Stir well and return to the pan which has been rinsed out. Cook slowly until the custard thickens enough to coat the back of a wooden spoon. Strain into a large bowl. Put it aside to cool. When cold, place in the refrigerator. When completely cold, put into the container in the prepared bucket and freeze as already described.

A richer ice cream may be made by adding ½ l. (¾ pint) slightly whipped thick cream to the custard when it is cold, prior to freezing.

GLACE AU CHOCOLAT ** (for 3–4 persons)

As for Glace à la Vanille, but dissolve 180 g. (6 oz.) chocolate in the milk before making the custard.

PARFAIT AU CAFÉ *** (for 3–4 persons)

Ingredients:
120 g. castor sugar. (4 oz.)
strong coffee or instant coffee to
　taste
5 yolks of egg

3 dl. thick cream (½ pint)
To finish:
Crème Chantilly (see page 344)
sugar coffee beans

Method: Put the sugar in a pan with sufficient water to dissolve it. Stir it over a moderate heat until the sugar crystals have dissolved. Boil without stirring until it forms a thread (215–220° F. (103° C.)) when tested between the finger and thumb. Pour it in a steady stream on to the beaten yolks, whisking all the time. Continue whisking until the mixture is quite cold and thickens and is white and fluffy. Stir in the whipped cream and flavour with coffee to taste.

Pour the mixture into a parfait mould and close it firmly, sealing the lid with lard. Plunge the mould into a mixture of salt and ice and freeze for 2–3 hours, or place it in a home freezer for 2–3 hours or in the freezing compartment of a domestic refrigerator for 5 or 6 hours.

To Serve: Turn out and decorate with crème Chantilly, using a forcing bag and a small rose tube. Arrange the coffee beans around.

Comment: A parfait may be flavoured alternatively with chocolate using 150 g. (4–6 oz.) melted chocolate, or praline using 100–125 g. (3–4 oz.) powdered praline.

OMELETTE NORVÉGIENNE ***   (for 6–8 persons)

Ingredients:

Pâte à Génoise Commune made with 3 eggs, etc. (see page 333)
La Glace Amandine made with:
  120 g. ground almonds (4 oz.), 6 yolks of egg and 180 g. castor sugar (6 oz.), 60 g. chopped browned almonds (2 oz.), ½ l. milk (1 pint)

For the Meringue:

4 whites of egg
270 g. castor sugar (9 oz.)
a little icing sugar

Method: Make up the pâte à Génoise commune as usual, pour it into an 18 cm. (7 inch) moule à manqué, so as to obtain a fairly large flat cake. Bake in a moderate oven, gas mark 5 or 375° F. (190° C.) for 30–35 minutes. Unmould and allow to get perfectly cold.

Make the glace amandine. Bring the milk to boiling point, stir in the ground almonds and allow it to simmer for 10 minutes, stirring occasionally. Whilst this is taking place, work the yolks and the sugar together with a wooden spatula until light and creamy, pour on the almonds and milk and mix well. Return the mixture to the saucepan and place it over a low heat. Stir until it thickens sufficiently to coat the back of a wooden spoon. Do not allow it to reach boiling point. Strain the custard through a clean damp cloth and put it aside to allow it to become completely cold.

Pack the ice bucket with crushed ice and salt in the usual way. When the almond cream is absolutely cold, put it into the container and churn as usual. When the ice is firm remove the paddle, stir in the browned almonds, replace the lid of the container and set aside to freeze for 1–2 hours.

To Serve: Whisk the whites stiffly, fold in the sugar lightly. Pre-heat the oven to gas mark 8–9 or 450–475° F. (230–245° C.). Put the génoise on a large cold heatproof plate. Form the glace amandine into a rough dome shape on top of the cake with the aid of a spatula. Quickly mask the ice cream and cake with the meringue. Fill any remaining meringue into a forcing bag with a large rosette tube and pipe a design all over the top. Dust with icing sugar, place in the oven to brown the surface. Turn the dish whilst it is browning so as to get an even colouring all over.

Comment: Sometimes this dish is finished by inserting a scallop shell in the meringue at each end and in the centre. Just before serving fill them with hot rum, set alight to them and spoon over the surface.

The glace Amandine may be served as an ordinary ice cream with the usual accompaniment.

SORBET AU CITRON ***

*(if you have an electric bucket and freezer)
(6–8 persons)

Ingredients:
4–5 lemons
250 g. castor sugar (10 oz.)

½ egg white
liqueur to flavour

Method: Take off a few strips of lemon peel, being careful not to take any pith. Cut the lemons in half and squeeze out the juice. Measure and if necessary make up to ½ l. (1 pint) with a little water. Dissolve the sugar in this juice. Put aside to get quite cold. Assemble the ice bucket in the usual way. Mix the unbeaten white with a little of the syrup and return it to the juice. Freeze as usual. Stir a small liqueur glass of kirsch, Grand Marnier or other liqueur in to the Sorbet when it has 'taken'. Serve sprinkled with a little liqueur.

Comment: This is a basic recipe for Sorbet. If other fruit juices are used, it is usually necessary to add lemon juice to give sufficient acidity. It should be borne in mind that when anything is frozen the flavour is less pronounced.

Cakes and Pâtisserie

PÂTISSERIE

There has never been a tradition in England for pâtisserie as it has been known on the Continent.

It is perhaps then for this reason that the home made gâteau is so much appreciated and praised. Since the second world war, afternoon tea has disappeared, and now gâteaux are most suitable for the sweet course or coffee parties.

Petits-fours still have a place at any celebration, as do large gâteaux. In each case when they are carefully quick-frozen, they can be thawed out when required in perfect condition.

The art of cake making is a technical one and attention to detail must be observed. No one will ever produce a fine cake with crudely weighed quantities, inadequate beating and an unreliable oven. Once the technique is mastered, the pleasure derived from good cake making is endless. Personally, I always feel that a good cake beautifully finished brings more praise than many much more elaborate dishes made from meat, poultry or fish.

The essential rules for success are many and only constant practice produces a good cake maker. For the beginner each cake which is made should be an improvement on the last. The following points for the amateur should be useful.

THE OVEN

It is important to have an oven in which the temperature is correct. Ovens do vary and do need adjusting and both the Gas and the Electricity Authorities will always adjust correct temperatures if they are asked. Too often one hears 'Oh my oven is hopeless for cakes, it burns them before they are cooked'. Yet when tackled the owner nearly always admits that she 'hasn't had it touched for years'. It is absolutely essential to have a correct and even temperature. If cakes are put in too hot an oven, the top will form a hard crust and the cake will be unable to rise to its full capacity, thus producing a flat, brown object not worth eating. If the oven is too cool, the cake will again rise insufficiently and will be tough and doughy. Cakes generally speaking should be placed in the middle of the oven in the centre of the shelf. The oven should be pre-heated for fifteen to twenty minutes before baking is begun.

CAKE TINS

When making French gâteaux, it is useful to use a moule à manqué, which is a type of tin used universally in France. These tins are a little deeper than sandwich tins and they have sloping sides (the bottom being narrower than the top). When the cake is made, it is reversed so the top becomes the smaller surface and the sides slope gently outwards. Cakes made in these tins are easier to ice and I think they are prettier to look at. If a moule à manqué is not obtainable, a sandwich tin must be used instead.

The size of the moules à manqués used are as follows:

For a 3 egg mixture 18 centimetres across the top or 7 inches.

For a 4 egg mixture 21 centimetres across the top or 8 inches.

For the majority of cakes or gâteaux mentioned in this chapter greasing only is needed as a preliminary preparation. This should be done by *lightly* brushing the cake tin all over the surface with melted lard. A pastry brush should be used. Occasionally, for some cakes, the tin is afterwards dusted out with flour. This should be sifted into the tin, then the tin should be gently tilted in all directions to allow the flour to coat all the surfaces. Finally it should be turned upside down and given a sharp bang on the table to remove excess flour. A cake should never be baked in a flour clogged tin. When chopped nuts and chopped fruits such as glacé cherries or pineapple are included in the mixture, a round of paper cut to fit the bottom of the tin *exactly* and brushed over with lard, will prevent the nuts or fruit from sticking to the bottom of the tin and burning.

Unsalted butter may be used for greasing tins, but if salt butter is used, it must be clarified first (see page 27). In every case the cake tin should be greased before the cake is begun, so as to avoid delay after the cake is mixed.

INGREDIENTS USED IN CAKE MAKING

1. *Flour* Plain household flour should be used, not that to which a raising agent has been added. Some recipes call for the addition of potato flour, cornflour, or arrowroot. This will produce a lighter mixture, but they should always be used in conjunction with ordinary flour and never on their own. All flour *must* be sifted before being added to a mixture.

2. *Sugar* Castor sugar must be used in all the fine French gâteaux which are cooked for a reasonably short period. Granulated sugar is too coarse and does not dissolve wholly in the beating and cooking processes.

3. *Eggs* In the following recipes, it is assumed that a normal sized egg weighing approximately 60 g. (2 oz.) is used. It is a mistaken idea to think a large egg will produce a better cake. Even if the eggs are known to be

fresh, it is still important to crack each one separately into a cup before adding them to the mixing bowl as the whites are sometimes discoloured with blood and should not be used.

4. *Butter*   It is desirable to use fresh butter in cake making, but unsalted margarine is a good substitute, especially for smaller cakes which are to be eaten within a week.

5. *Flavouring*   Most French gâteaux are flavoured liberally with vanilla. Vanilla essence as sold in this country has not the true authentic French taste. Vanilla sugar can be bought at most of the large London stores. It is far more economical to buy it by the pound or half pound than in small packets of one ounce. Even if the vanilla sugar in tins tends to go hard, it can always be sifted before adding to the cake. As an alternative to buying vanilla sugar, in a small household it may be found quite sufficient to keep an airtight tin of sugar for cake-making in which are kept one or two vanilla pods. This will give the sugar a delicate, yet pronounced, vanilla flavour.

Where grated orange or lemon rind is needed, use the fine part of the grater for grating. Coarsely ground rind with a predominance of pith is unpleasant.

6. *Baking Powder*   When baking powder is to be added to a cake, it should be sifted with the flour.

WHISKED EGG MIXTURES

These are light sponge mixtures with or without the addition of butter, i.e. Biscuit Fin and Pâte à Génoise.

Whisks   The two types of whisks which I would recommend are the balloon whisk – like a large sauce whisk with a wooden handle (metal handles are too heavy to use) or the flat wire mesh whisk made like a tennis racquet and obtainable from the TANTE MARIE SCHOOL OF COOKERY. These are very light to handle and are perfectly suitable for a cake of up to four eggs.

Electric Mixers can be used, but the texture of the cake will always be closer than that made by hand and consequently not so light.

Some whisked egg mixtures are made by beating the whole eggs with the sugar and some by whisking the yolks and sugar only and then adding the stiffly beaten whites with the flour or flour and butter as the case may be. Whole eggs or yolks, and sugar, should be beaten over a pan of hot water to give a larger bulk. The partial coagulation of the eggs enables more air to be introduced and held. The sugar in the bowl too will dissolve far more readily if it is warmed, thus much time and energy are saved.

It is important not to whisk for too long over the heat. Experience will show when a mixture has been whisked sufficiently, but a fairly reliable guide is when the mixture of eggs and sugar is twice its original bulk and half as light again in colour. Another test is to press the whisk lightly on the surface of the mixture and if the mark is retained for a few seconds, the mixture is sufficiently stiff. *Eggs and sugar should never be left standing over heat without whisking*, even if only for a moment. The eggs will coagulate and hard yellow flecks appear in the mixture. *Prolonged whisking over heat produces a very tough cake.* As soon as the desired consistency has been reached, the bowl should be removed from the heat and the mixture whisked until it is perfectly cool. Test by inserting the finger into the mixture – there is no other reliable test.

Where a recipe calls for *working* the yolks and sugar together, this means that they are beaten with a wooden spoon or spatula. When the mixture lightens and becomes frothy looking, it denotes that the sugar has become dissolved and the mixture is now ready for its other additions.

When adding stiffly whisked whites to a cake, *do not begin to whisk the whites until you are ready to use them.* The sight of a bowl of unwhisked whites is a temptation to many people – who cannot resist the temptation of 'just whisking them a little'. This does not apply only to children, but to adults of all ages!

WHISKING WHITES

As for making meringues, the same principles should be noted. The bowl should be large – a copper bowl is excellent. It should be perfectly clean and dry and free from all trace of grease. The whisk should be equally spotless. Whites cannot be whisked stiffly in a wet bowl. Some cooks add a pinch of salt which lowers the temperature of the egg whites. Start by whisking slowly and as the whites stiffen and rise, increase the tempo. It is not a satisfactory test to hold the bowl upside down and say that if the whites do not fall out they are stiff enough. They should be a great deal stiffer than that. They should, if sufficiently whisked, stand up in peaks on the end of the whisk and look *perfectly dry*.

ADDING BUTTER

Butter to be added to a mixture such as Pâte à Génoise, should be melted gently before the cake is commenced and then put aside to cool. Butter which has been made too hot and has become scorched should never be added. Although many cookery books advocate adding the butter finally after the flour has been folded in, in practice I have found that it is easier to add it together with the flour and this prevents over-folding.

CREAMING MIXTURES

Where the foundation of a cake is a creamed mixture, i.e. the butter and sugar, with the eggs added afterwards, the butter should be soft before the work is begun. It is impossible to make a creamed mixture with butter freshly taken from the refrigerator. It must be of the consistency as they say in France of 'pommade' – neither hard nor oiled. A warming drawer in an electric cooker is a useful place for softening. In very cold weather a cloth may be wrung out in boiling water and the bowl containing the butter stood on that. In this way a gentle warming will be obtained. If by any chance the butter has become too hot and has 'oiled' do not attempt to make the cake whilst it is in that condition. It will never rise or be light. Put the butter in a cool place or into a fresh bowl and whisk with a whisk until it stiffens up again.

Butter and sugar should be beaten together until white, light and fluffy. Eggs to be added may be lightly whisked first and should be introduced only in small quantities with vigorous beating in between each addition. If they are added too quickly a curdle will result. Some cooks say add a spoonful of flour and the curdle will disappear – this is not a practice to be recommended as it will produce a heavier cake. A warm cloth wrapped round the bowl and prolonged beating should rectify a curdle if it is not too bad.

FOLDING IN

This is a term which is used in relation to any ingredients to be added to a mixture already whisked or creamed. As we have seen, it can be applied in cake making to flour, stiffly whisked whites or melted butter. Flour is probably the most common ingredient. Never on any account should flour be beaten into a cake mixture. This to my mind was not sufficiently stressed in old-fashioned cookery books, where frequently the vague expression 'add the flour and pour into the prepared tin' was all the guidance the amateur cook was given. To explain verbally how to fold in is not easy, but I think that in cakes where the amount of flour does not exceed 180 g. (6 oz.) it it probably best to sift the flour in two or three batches straight on top of the mixture, then taking a flexible metal spatula cut round and through the mixture in a spiral movement, lifting up as much of the mixture as possible. *Do not try to fold in the first batch of flour completely before adding the next.* This can result in over folding. A *firm* sweep must be employed, never a hesitant one. Whisked whites are usually added in two or three additions, also using the same movement, which should be rather like a capital D. More cakes are spoilt by over folding than under folding. As I have said before, melted butter is folded in more easily when done at the same time as the flour.

TESTING A CAKE WHEN DONE

Large fruit cakes should be tested by inserting a hot blade of a knife or hot skewer, but in the case of the French type of gâteau, this is not necessary.

At the completion of the cooking time, open the oven door gently and press with two fingers lightly on the surface of the cake. If it feels firm to the touch and has begun to shrink slightly from the sides of the tin, then it should be done. This test can be applied five minutes before the cake is due to come out of the oven, as for various reasons such as its position in the oven it may be cooked in a slightly shorter time.

Finally, however carefully the cake has been made, it can still be spoilt by over anxious baking. Do not open the oven door until the cake has been in for a third of the required cooking time (i.e. after ten minutes for a cake to be baked for half an hour). Never open a door quickly, always slowly and as little as possible. Do not be tempted to move it from one shelf to another. This can be done very carefully in the last third of the cooking time, but only if it is absolutely necessary. Do not bang the oven door, it must be shut as carefully as it was opened.

COOLING

When the cake is cooked, remove it carefully and turn it out at once on to a wire rack or sieve, so as to allow the air to circulate round it and the moisture to dry off. Never leave a warm cake in a draught or put it in a very cold place. It will very soon become soggy and tough. Cakes to be stored in tins should not be put away until absolutely cold.

CUTTING CAKES FOR FILLING

This is best done when the cake is still slightly warm. A nick is made vertically in the side of the cake. The blade of the knife is then introduced at an angle and with a sawing and spinning movement the blade is run right round the cake until it returns to its original place. Now still with a sawing movement, run the knife right through the cake. The two halves will now come apart. The nick made in the first place will enable the two halves, when put together again, to be placed in their original position.

PASTRY

The success of making good pastry is to introduce the maximum amount of cold air, both in mixing and in rolling. Cold hands are naturally an advantage, but not everyone is fortunate in this respect. A cold room is essential when making pastry with a high proportion of fat, e.g. Pâte Feuilletée, and it is advisable to have the windows and door open for as long as possible before beginning. A marble or old fashioned slate slab is an asset. The pastry should be handled as little as possible. Over handling will produce a heavy pastry difficult to roll out.

MIXING PASTRY

Use plain household flour and always sieve it together with the salt if it is to be used. There are two schools of thought about this – some cooks prefer always to add a pinch of salt, others assert that if the butter or margarine is already salted it is unnecessary. Use a knife with a round blade, such as a table knife for mixing. Use water as cold as possible. Except where otherwise stated, add the water a little at a time until you can judge how much water you will need. When sufficient water has been added it should be possible to gather the pastry lightly together with the hands so that it forms a rough ball and leaves the bowl clean. Never scrape off any portions of pastry which may cling to the fingers and add them to the ball. This will give you hard flakes which do not incorporate properly into the pastry when it is rolled out. All pastries should relax either in a refrigerator or in a cold larder before being rolled out. In pastries where the content of the fat is large, this is essential.

ROLLING

Use a heavy type of rolling pin, preferably one without a handle at each end. *Lightly* flour the rolling pin and slab or board. It is a great mistake to cover the board with a layer of flour before rolling. Naturally it will spoil the proportion of fat to flour as well as making the pastry dry and heavy. Roll the pastry in short sharp movements, rolling away from you and pressing evenly with both hands. Lift the rolling pin between each movement, bringing it down again lightly and firmly. Lift the pastry frequently during rolling, so as to make sure that it is not sticking to the slab or board. Do not attempt to stretch the pastry to shape – this will produce a shrunken finish when it is baked.

BAKING

The correct temperature in the oven is as important in pastry making as it is in cake making. The oven should be pre-heated for fifteen to twenty minutes before cooking is commenced. A hot oven is important to burst the starch cells in the flour, thus allowing it to absorb the fat. The degree of heat, as will be seen in the recipes, varies with the type of pastry. Pâte Feuilletée or Puff Pastry requires the greatest heat. If the pastry is cooked in too cool an oven, the fat will tend to run out before it can be absorbed into the flour. Such pastry is tough, greasy and unpleasant to eat. Sometimes in an effort to make the pastry rise to its fullest it is put in too hot an oven – this produces the effect of making a thin, hard surface on top of the crust and the air enclosed in the dough is unable to expand and thus the opposite result is achieved. The pastry will be brittle and hard – not light and flaky. The door of the oven should not be opened before the pastry is set. This is particularly important in relation to such things as flans filled with a liquid mixture where the sudden draught of cold air will stop the pastry from rising and the filling will overflow and run out.

When cooking a dish which is fruit or meat covered with a pastry crust, a hole – small in the case of fruit and larger in the case of meat – should be made in the pastry to allow the steam to escape. In some recipes, such as a Pâté de Volaille en Croûte, a small cardboard chimney is inserted before the pastry is cooked and removed afterwards. This method is also useful for making an opening sufficiently large to enable a dish to be filled up with stock or syrup.

Many recipes state that the pastry should be 'baked blind'. This applies particularly when a flan is to be filled with a fruit or cream mixture or a savoury sauce, and frequently in small tartlets or boats. The method for flans is to crumple a piece of greaseproof paper, slightly larger than the flan case, so as to soften it and lay this in the uncooked pastry case, being careful to see that it is well down at the edges. Then fill with beans, rice, macaroni, etc., again making sure that the material used is well spread over the edges and middle. It is a mistake to use too little. Bake as usual and when cooked, remove the paper and beans, etc. (the latter can be put away in a tin and used again and again). Return the pastry case to the oven and lower the heat. Allow the base of the case which has been previously covered, to dry off completely. With smaller cases such as tartlets, etc., cut a small round of paper approximately the size of the tartlet tin. It is always advisable to prick the base of the case well with a fork before lining it with the paper.

COOLING

Cooked flans should always be slid carefully on to wire racks as soon as they are removed from the oven. The flan ring should be taken off, thus allowing the air to circulate, the moisture to escape and the pastry to harden. Baking sheets without sides can be obtained, which are helpful in sliding delicate flans on to racks, or alternatively the wrong side of the baking sheet may be used. Pastry should never be taken straight from a hot oven and left in a draught – this will make the pastry heavy.

PASTRY COOKED ON BAKING SHEETS

Generally speaking, well seasoned baking sheets need not be greased when baking pastry. New baking sheets will need a light greasing – heavy greasing tends to make the pastry fry on the under side, thus producing a dark brown, unpalatable surface. Pâte Feuilletée should be baked on a *wetted* baking sheet to prevent the high percentage of fat from causing burning.

CAKES

BASIC PÂTES

PÂTE D'AMANDES or ALMOND PASTE * (Method I)

Ingredients:

240 g. ground almonds ($\frac{1}{2}$ lb.)
120 g. castor sugar (4 oz.)
120 g. icing sugar (4 oz.)

1 whole egg
1 yolk of egg
$\frac{1}{2}$ teaspoon vanilla sugar
1 teaspoon lemon juice

Method: Sieve the sugars and vanilla sugar together into a bowl and mix thoroughly with the ground almonds. Make a well in the centre. Add the egg yolk, whole egg and lemon juice. Mix in gradually using a wooden spoon or spatula, until all the mixture is smooth. Knead with the hands. It should be kneaded only sufficiently to give smoothness. Over-working will draw out the oil from the almonds, which cannot be corrected.

To store – wrap in aluminium foil or polythene and seal thoroughly.

Comment: Additional flavours of rum, sherry or brandy can be added with advantage. This also applies to Pâte d'Amandes, Method II.

PÂTE D'AMANDES or ALMOND PASTE ** (Method II)

Ingredients:

240 g. ground almonds ($\frac{1}{2}$ lb.)
120 g. castor sugar (4 oz.)
120 g. icing sugar (4 oz.)

1 whole egg
1 yolk of egg
$\frac{1}{2}$ teaspoon vanilla sugar
1 teaspoon lemon juice

Method: Sieve the sugars into a bowl, add the egg and yolk and whisk over a pan of hot water until it is thick and fluffy. Remove the bowl from the heat and continue whisking until the mixture is cool and bears the impression of the whisk when pressed on the surface.

Gradually work in the ground almonds and lemon juice, using a wooden spoon. Once the mixture is thick, knead with the hands.

Allow it to relax for ½ hour before using.

Comment. This almond paste, although requiring more work, is easier to handle and is much smoother to mould when coating a whole cake. It also stays moist longer.

MARZIPAN * (Method I. Uncooked)

Ingredients:

120 g. ground almonds (4 oz.)
120 g. icing sugar (4 oz.)
½–1 white of egg

½ teaspoon vanilla sugar
colouring as required
flavouring as desired

Method: Sieve the icing and vanilla sugar into a bowl and mix with the ground almonds. Make a well in the centre, drop in the egg white and gradually work in the ground almonds and sugar from the sides. Knead with the hands to make it smooth. Add the colouring and flavouring gradually and knead to make it even throughout.

If the mixture is too soft, add a little more ground almonds.

Comment: This marzipan is used for the moulding of fruits and leaves, etc., for decoration. It can be flavoured with rum, kirsch, brandy, lemon juice, melted chocolate, etc.

MARZIPAN *** (Method II. Cooked)

Ingredients:

180 g. ground almonds (6 oz.)
240 g. castor sugar (½ lb)
1 dl. water (½ gill)
½ teaspoon liquid glucose

½ teaspoon cream of tartar
1 white of egg
½ teaspoon vanilla sugar
½ teaspoon lemon juice
colouring if required

Method: Put the sugar and water into a clean pan and stir over a low heat until it is dissolved. Stop stirring and add the glucose and the cream of tartar. Boil it quickly to soft ball, 238° F. (115° C.). Remove from the heat. Cool the pan quickly by letting it stand for a few seconds in a bowl of cold water. Stir in the ground almonds with the unbeaten white of egg. Return to a gentle heat and cook, stirring all the time for 2–3 minutes. Add the flavourings and colouring. Pour on to a marble slab or enamel tray. Allow to cool slightly. Whilst it is still hot, work with a wooden spatula. Then when it is sufficiently cool, knead with the hands until smooth and pliable.

Put it aside to relax for $\frac{1}{2}$ hour. It must be wrapped in waxed paper or polythene.

Use as required, moulding with a little sieved icing sugar. If the marzipan is too soft, knead in sufficient ground almonds to give the desired consistency.

Comment: This type of marzipan will keep for 2–3 months, if wrapped as described and placed in an air-tight tin.

PÂTE À BISCUITS À LA CUILLÈRE **

Ingredients:
105 g. plain flour (3½ oz.)
90 g. castor sugar (3 oz.)

3 eggs
1 teaspoon vanilla sugar
icing sugar

Method: Cut some strips of greaseproof paper approximately 15 cm. (6 inches) wide and the same length as the baking sheet to be used. Cream the yolks with the sugar until thick and light in colour. Whisk the whites stiffly and fold them into the mixture lightly, alternating with the sieved flour and vanilla sugar. Fill this into a forcing bag with a plain 1 cm. (½ inch) pipe. Pipe out into finger lengths on the greaseproof paper strips. Dust over with sifted icing sugar. Turn the strips over and lightly tap to remove the excess sugar. Place the papers on the baking sheet and bake in a very moderate oven, gas mark 4 or 350° F. (180° C.) for 10–12 minutes. Remove the papers very carefully and place the biscuits on a wire rack to cool.

Comment: It is important to cream the yolks and sugar very well indeed. If they are insufficiently worked, the biscuits will be flat and tough. These biscuits can be used for Charlotte Praliné etc., or served with ices.

PÂTE À BISCUIT FIN *

Ingredients:
4 eggs
135 g. castor sugar (4½ oz.)

120 g. plain flour (4 oz.)
1 teaspoon vanilla sugar

Method: Grease a moule à manqué or cake tin with lard. Put the eggs into a large basin and whisk them with the sugar, using a wire whisk, over very hot water, until the mixture is thick and creamy. Remove from the heat and continue to whisk them until they are quite cool. Sieve the flour and vanilla sugar and fold it in, in three batches, very carefully. Pour into the prepared tin and cook in a very moderate oven, gas mark 4 or 350° F. (175° C.) for approximately 40 minutes. When the cake is done it will begin to shrink from the sides of the tin. Turn on to a wire rack to cool.

Comment: This recipe may be adapted to smaller quantities, i.e. 3 eggs, 105 g. (3½ oz.) castor sugar and 90 g. (3 oz.) plain flour. The smaller the cake the shorter the time it will take to cook, for example the 3 egg quantity will require from 30–35 minutes. The size of the tin will also depend on the quantity used (see notes on page 320).

PÂTE À BISCUIT FIN AU BEURRE **

Ingredients:
135 g. castor sugar (4½ oz.)
105 g. plain flour (3½ oz.)

60 g. butter (2 oz.)
4 eggs
1 teaspoon vanilla sugar

Method: Melt the butter until it runs. Put it aside to cool. Sift the flour and vanilla sugar together.

Separate the eggs. Work the yolks and sugar together with a wooden spoon or spatula until light and creamy. Whisk the whites stiffly and fold them into the yolks alternating with the melted butter, flour, etc. Pour into a greased and floured moule à manqué or deep sandwich tin. Bake in a moderate oven, gas mark 5 or 375° F. (190° C.) for approximately 40 minutes. Turn on to a wire rack to cool.

Comment: As in Pâte à Génoise Commune (see below) the butter should be liquid but not hot. The process of folding in should be done as swiftly as possible. Strong firm sweeps should be made. Too much folding in will undoubtedly produce a heavy, close textured cake. This recipe may be adapted to smaller quantities, i.e. 105 g. (3½ oz.) castor sugar, 75 g. (2½ oz.) plain flour, 30 g. (1 oz.) butter, 3 eggs, 1 teaspoon vanilla sugar. The smaller the cake the shorter time it will take to cook, for example, the 3 egg quantity will require from 30–35 minutes.

PÂTE À BISCUIT DE SAVOIE **

Ingredients:
135 g. castor sugar (4½ oz.)
105 g. plain flour (3½ oz.)
55 g. cornflour (2 oz.) (light weight)

4 eggs
1 teaspoon castor sugar
1 teaspoon vanilla sugar

Method: Sift the flour and the vanilla sugar together. Separate the eggs. Work the yolks and sugar well together using a wooden spoon or spatula. They must be very light and creamy. Whisk the whites very stiffly indeed. When they begin to separate slightly, whisk in the extra sugar and continue to whisk for a further 3–4 minutes. Fold the whites and flour into the yolks and sugar mixture as lightly as possible. Pour into a greased and floured moule à manqué or deep sandwich tin and bake in a very moderate oven, gas mark 3–4 or 325–350° F. (160–180° C.) for 45–50 minutes. Turn on to a wire rack to cool.

PÂTE À GÉNOISE COMMUNE **

Ingredients:
4 eggs
135 g. castor sugar (4½ oz.)

120 g. plain flour (4 oz.)
45 g. butter (1½ oz.)
1 teaspoon vanilla sugar

Method: Grease a cake tin or moule à manqué with lard. Put the eggs and sugar into a bowl. Stand it over a pan of very hot water and whisk them until they are light and creamy and thick enough to hold the impression of the whisk. Remove from the heat and whisk until cool. Have the butter already melted, but not hot. Fold in the sifted flour and vanilla sugar, together with the butter. Pour into the prepared tin and bake in a moderate oven, gas mark 4–5 or 350–375° F. (180–190° C.) for approximately 35–40 minutes, or until the cake is firm to touch and begins to shrink from the sides of the tin. Remove from the oven and place on a wire rack to cool.

Comment: This recipe may be adapted to smaller, or larger quantities, i.e. 3 eggs, 105 g. (3½ oz.) castor sugar, 90 g. (3 oz.) plain flour, 30 g. (1 oz.) butter and 1 teaspoon vanilla sugar. The smaller the cake the shorter time it will take to cook, and vice versa.

PÂTE À GÉNOISE FINE ***

Ingredients:
4 eggs
135 g. castor sugar (4½ oz.)

105 g. plain flour (3½ oz.)
105 g. unsalted butter (3½ oz.)
1 teaspoon vanilla sugar

Method: Melt the butter until it runs and put it aside to cool. Sift the flour with the vanilla sugar. Break the eggs into a large bowl, add the sugar. Stand it over a pan of boiling water and whisk until light and creamy and the mark of the whisk is retained for a few seconds when it is lightly pressed on the surface. (The mixture should be twice its original bulk and half as light again in colour.) Remove from the heat and whisk for a further 5 minutes or until it is perfectly cool. Quickly fold in the sifted flour and melted butter *with the utmost speed*. Pour at once into a greased moule à manqué or deep sandwich tin and bake in a fairly hot oven, gas mark 4 or 350° F. (180° C.) for 35–40 minutes. Remove and turn on to a wire rack to cool.

Comment: This is not an easy mixture to make. The flour should be perfectly dry and unsalted butter (not margarine) should be used.

PAIN DE GÊNES **

Ingredients:

165 g. castor sugar (5½ oz.)
135 g. butter (4½ oz.)
105 g. ground almonds (3½ oz.)

45 g. plain flour or cornflour (1½ oz.)
3 eggs
3 tablespoons of kirsch

Method: Well grease a moule à pain de gênes or alternatively a square baking tin. Place a piece of greased paper to fit exactly in the bottom of the tin.

Melt the butter and put aside to cool.

Work the almonds and half the sugar together in a bowl. (It is important not to 'oil' the almonds.) Put the butter and the rest of the sugar together in another bowl and work them very well with a spatula. When the mixture lightens and forms a 'ribbon', add the ground almonds and sugar and work the whole together. Add the eggs, one at a time and beat well in between each addition. Lastly fold in the sifted flour and the kirsch. Place it in the prepared tin and bake in a very moderate oven, gas mark 4 or 350° F. (180° C.) for 45–50 minutes. Turn out on to a wire rack to cool. Serve without icing or decoration.

PÂTE À MERINGUE SUISSE **

Ingredients:

4 whites of egg
270 g. sieved castor sugar (9 oz.)

1 teaspoon vanilla sugar
icing sugar to sift over

Method: Brush over 2 or 3 baking sheets with melted lard and lightly dust with flour. Turn them upside down and tap to remove excess flour.

See that the sugar to be used is perfectly dry. Whisk the whites as described until they stand up in peaks (see page 322). Add one tablespoon of sugar and continue to whisk for a further 3–4 minutes. Fold in the rest of the sugar sifted with the vanilla sugar in two batches. Do not over fold. Place the meringue in a cloth forcing bag with a plain 1 cm. (½ inch) pipe. Pipe out on to the baking sheet as required. *Sift over the tops of the meringues with icing sugar. Turn the tin upside down and tap it to remove the excess sugar.* Repeat this process * – *. Cook in a very cool oven, gas mark ¼ or 200° F. (90° C.) for 2–3 hours, according to their size. When they are cooked, it will be found possible to run a thin bladed knife under the meringues and they will come away from the baking sheet easily, without sticking.

PÂTE À MERINGUE ITALIENNE ***

Ingredients:
3 whites of egg
270 g. castor sugar (9 oz.)
1 dl. water (¾ gill)
1 teaspoon vanilla sugar

Method: Put the sugar and water into a perfectly clean pan and boil to 238° F. (115° C.) (soft ball). Brush down the sides of the pan with a wet pastry brush during the boiling.

Whilst the sugar is boiling, whisk the whites very stiffly indeed. Pour the sugar syrup on to the whites, continuing to whisk all the time. Add the sifted vanilla sugar. Whisk until quite cold.

Comment: This type of meringue is not cooked in the oven, but is used to decorate gâteaux and to replace Crème Chantilly.

PÂTE À MERINGUE CUITE ***

Ingredients:
4 whites of egg
270 g. icing sugar (9 oz.)
1 teaspoon vanilla sugar

Method: Sieve the icing sugar and vanilla sugar together. Put the whites and sugars into a bowl, copper for preference, and stand the bowl over a pan of boiling water. Whisk until the mixture is very thick indeed. Use for piping small 'mushrooms', etc. Cook in a fairly cool oven, gas mark 2–3 or 300–325° F. (150–160° C.).

FLAKY PASTRY **

Ingredients:
120 g. plain flour (4 oz.)
45 g. pure lard (1½ oz.)
45 g. butter or margarine (1½ oz.)
pinch of salt
cold water to mix (about 4 tablespoons)

Method: Sieve the flour and salt into a mixing bowl. Divide the lard into half and the butter into half. Rub one half of the butter into the flour with the tips of the fingers, palms upwards, thus allowing the mixture to run through the fingers like sand. When the mixture resembles fine breadcrumbs, make a well in the centre and add the water gradually, mixing it in with a round bladed knife. When sufficient water has been added, it should be possible to gather the dough up into a ball, thus leaving the sides of the bowl clean. It should not be dry or crumbly or it will be difficult to handle and will break in rolling. On the other hand it must not be a sticky dough.

Lightly flour a marble slab or pastry board and flour the rolling pin. *Roll the pastry out into an oblong strip. Take one half of the lard and place it in knobs about the size of a walnut down the top two-thirds of the pastry. (Do not put it too near the edges or it will squeeze out when the pastry is folded and rolled. In hot weather, if the lard is very soft, it can be dusted with a little *extra* flour.) Now fold up the plain piece of pastry two-thirds of the way and the top piece of pastry down on to it, thus producing a layer of pastry, fat, pastry, fat and pastry. Seal all the edges heavily with the rolling pin. Give the pastry a half turn from the left to the right, so that the last fold appears on the right hand side.* Repeat from * to * using the remaining butter and again from * to * using the remaining lard. Seal the edges firmly in between each rolling. Put it aside to relax in a refrigerator or cold place before rolling into the final shape.

Comment: It is essential to roll always in the same direction. After all the fat has been incorporated, the pastry can then be rolled in any direction.

PÂTE À CHOUX **

Ingredients:

60 g. plain flour (2 oz.)	1 egg
30 g. butter (1 oz.)	1 yolk of egg
	1½ dl. water (1 gill)

Method: Sieve the flour on to a piece of stiff paper or thin card. Put the butter and water into a small pan and bring it to the boil. Whilst it is boiling rapidly, draw it aside from the heat and slide in all the flour at once. Immediately beat the mixture with a wooden spatula or, if preferred, a wire sauce whisk. When the paste leaves the sides of the pan and forms a ball, take away from the heat. Beat in the yolk of egg and then gradually the whole egg, which has been previously whisked. It may not be necessary to add all the egg. Beat very well indeed until the mixture looks shiny. Use as required.

Bake in a hot oven, gas mark 7–8 or 425–450° F. (220–230° C.) for the first 10 minutes. Then lower the heat to gas mark 5 or 375° F. (190° C.) and continue to cook for a further 30–35 minutes.

Comment: It is necessary to have flour which is perfectly dry. It can be sifted on to a piece of paper and placed in a warming drawer of an electric cooker or on the deflector plate of a gas cooker to dry.

Sweet choux paste can be flavoured with vanilla sugar if desired. Savoury choux paste should be well seasoned with salt and pepper.

Éclairs, profiterolles, choux, etc., should be placed on a wire rack to cool on removing from the oven, and away from a draught. A slight slit should be made in the side to allow the steam to escape and the inside to dry out.

PÂTE FEUILLETÉE OR PUFF PASTRY ***

Ingredients:
270 g. plain flour (9 oz.)
240 g. butter (8 oz.)

salt
1½ dl. water, approx. (1 gill)

Method: Sieve the flour into a mound on a marble slab or pastry board. Make a well in the centre with a deep wall of flour all round the sides. It is important to have no flour in the centre and the well should be about 15 cm. (6 inches) in diameter. Put the salt in the well together with half the water and using the finger tips of one hand, gradually work the flour in from the sides, breaking down the lumps. About a third of the flour should be worked in, in this manner. At no time must the water be allowed to break through the walls. The consistency now obtained in the centre should resemble a fairly thick Sauce Béchamel.

Now using the finger tips of both hands, palms upwards, 'flake' the dry flour into the mixture in the centre. Repeat this from all sides of the well, forming the whole into a dry flaky mass. Sprinkle half the remaining water all over the top of the flakes and 'flake' again. Repeat again with the rest of the water and form the mixture into a stiff ball with one hand. Knead slightly. The dough must not be over-kneaded as this develops too much elasticity and necessitates a much longer period of relaxation before rolling. This process is known as making a 'détrempe'. Put this aside to relax, wrapped in greaseproof paper and then enclosed in a clean damp cloth in a refrigerator or very cold place for 20 minutes.

Place the butter on a lightly floured slab. Cover it with a piece of grease-proof paper and tap it gently with a rolling pin to elongate it. The butter should be the same consistency as the 'détrempe'. Re-form it to a rect-angle approximately 10 × 15 cm. (4 × 6 inches). Place it on one side.

Lightly flour the rolling pin and slab. Place the 'détrempe' on the slab and roll to the shape of a large dinner plate. Place the butter in the centre of this. Now follow these directions most carefully – fold the pastry over the two long sides of the butter, from the edge to the centre, so that it overlaps slightly down the centre. Tap gently with the rolling pin, being careful not to seal the butter in at the short, exposed ends. Fold these in a similar manner again to overlap slightly. The butter inside is actually folded over to allow these ends to overlap in the centre. This dough is now known as the 'pâton'. After the last fold give the dough a half turn from the left to the right. The two last folded edges are now on the left and right hand sides.

*Roll out the pastry as evenly as possible to make a long strip, approxi-mately 18 × 35 cm. (7 × 15 inches). In the rolling process it is *most import-ant* to keep straight parallel sides and square ends. The pastry must *not* be rolled over the ends. It is helpful to roll from each end towards the centre with even pressure of the hands on each side of the rolling pin. When the pastry at each end is approximately 1 cm. (¼ inch) thick, roll evenly along the centre of the strip to give a uniform thickness throughout. Now fold the bottom end nearest to you two-thirds of the way up and bring the top end down to overlay the first fold. Tap sharply and firmly with a rolling pin to seal all edges. Give the pastry a half turn from left to right, so that the last fold is on the right hand side.* Repeat from * – *. Wrap it in greaseproof paper and a damp cloth and put it aside in a very cold place for 20 minutes or until the pastry is firm and quite cold. The pastry has now had two turns. Before putting the pastry aside to relax, very lightly mark it with the fingers, not the finger nails, to indicate the number of turns it has had. The pastry must have six turns in all with 20 minutes relaxation in between each two turns. After the sixth turn allow it to rest at least 20 minutes before using.

PÂTE BRISÉE (Method I) *

Ingredients:
270 g. plain flour (9 oz.)
135 g. butter (4½ oz.)
15 g. castor sugar (½ oz.)
pinch of salt
1 egg

Method: Sift the flour, sugar and salt on to a board. Make a well in the centre and add the butter and egg. Work up with the finger tips, exactly as for Pâte Sucrée (see page 339), but as lightly and delicately as possible, so as not to make the pastry too elastic. Roll it into a ball, wrap in a clean cloth and put it aside to relax for 2 hours before using.

Comment: This pastry may be used for dishes usually made with the English short crust pastry. If the pastry is over-handled, it will become very tough and leathery.

PÂTE BRISÉE (Method II) *

Ingredients:
480 g. plain flour (1 lb.)
135 g. butter (4½ oz.)
1 egg
pinch of salt
cold water

Method: Sift the flour on to a board. Make a well in the centre. Put in the butter lightly crushed with a fork, the egg, salt and approximately ¼ l. (1½ gills) water. Work it up with the hands to form a firm dough. (More water may be added if needed.) Wrap it in a cloth and put aside to relax for 12 hours. Use as required.

PÂTE D'AMANDES or PÂTE FROLLE **

Ingredients:

270 g. plain flour (9 oz.)
165 g. ground almonds (5½ oz.)
165 g. castor sugar (5½ oz.)

165 g. butter (slightly softened)
(5½ oz.)
2 eggs
pinch of salt
grated rind of 1 lemon

Method: Sift the flour on to a board – mix it with the ground almonds and the sugar. Make a well in the centre and break an egg into this. Work the egg, sugar and almonds together then add the softened but not liquid butter, the salt and the grated lemon rind. Gradually draw the flour into the mixture whilst adding the second egg. Work from the sides towards the centre. Knead well and put it aside to relax for at least one hour before using.

Comment: This type of pastry is used for tartlets and petits fours secs.

PÂTE SUCRÉE **

Ingredients:

150 g. plain flour (5 oz.)
60 g. castor sugar (2 oz.)

90 g. butter (3 oz.)
2 yolks of egg

Method: Sieve the flour on to a board. Put the butter, sugar and yolks into the flour. Squeeze together with the finger tips of one hand and draw the flour in gradually with a knife held in the other hand. Mix to a pliable dough. Knead it gently to ensure that all the ingredients are well blended. Put it aside in a cold place to relax before rolling out.

PÂTE À SAVARIN ** (Method I)

Ingredients:

240 g. plain flour (½ lb.)
15 g. yeast (½ oz.)
75 g. melted butter (2½ oz.)

30 g. sugar (1 oz.)
3 eggs
1 teaspoon salt
lukewarm water

Method: Place the yeast in a small bowl. Dissolve it with 2 tablespoons of warm water mixing it well with a wooden spoon or with the tips of the fingers. Sieve the flour, sugar and salt into a large warm bowl. Make a well in the centre, pour in the dissolved yeast. Break the eggs into the yeast and beat well with a wooden spoon or with the hands making a fairly liquid dough. Care must be taken to take in a little flour all the time from the sides of the bowl. When all the flour is incorporated pour in the melted lukewarm butter. Beat again for a further 5–8 minutes. Allow to rise in a warm place for 1–2 hours, until it is double its bulk.

Break it up lightly and half fill a well greased savarin mould. Put a strip of paper round the outside securing it with a piece of the pâte and a similar piece on the inside of the funnel. Put it to rise again until the mixture reaches the top of the mould. Bake in a very hot oven, gas mark 8 or 450° F. (230° C.) for about 20–25 minutes. If the savarin becomes too brown lower the temperature to gas mark 6–7 or approximately 400–425° F. (200–220° C.).

PÂTE À SAVARIN ** (Method II)

Ingredients:

270 g. plain flour (9 oz.)
1 teaspoon salt
20 g. sugar ($\frac{3}{4}$ oz.)

15 g. yeast ($\frac{1}{2}$ oz.)
2 eggs
120 g. melted butter (4 oz.)
lukewarm water

Method: Sift the flour into a warm bowl. Make a well in the centre. Place the yeast in the well and add sufficient tepid water to make a 'little dough' (about 2 tablespoons). Cover gently with some of the flour from the sides and leave to rise in a warm temperature for approximately 20 minutes. At the end of this time drop the eggs into the middle of the mixture, and add the sugar and salt. Beat with the hand for 10–15 minutes, adding another 2–3 tablespoons of tepid water to slacken the dough. When assured that the mixture is well mixed, beat in the warm, not hot, butter. Put the mixture to rise covering with a piece of brown paper for 30 minutes or until it increases to twice its bulk. At the end of this time break it up gently with a spatula and fill into a mould as for Method I, putting it back in a warm place to rise until the mixture has filled the tin. Bake as for Method I.

PÂTE À NOUGATINE ***

Ingredients:

500 g. granulated sugar (1 lb.)   a pinch of cream of tartar
250 g. finely chopped browned almonds (8 oz.)

Method: Put the prepared nuts in a cool oven, gas mark $\frac{1}{2}$ or 250° F. (120° C.) to get thoroughly heated.

Dissolve the sugar in a little water in a strong saucepan over a low heat. Stir it occasionally and when the sugar is completely dissolved, add the cream of tartar. Increase the heat and bring the syrup to the boil. Without further stirring, boil the syrup until it turns a pale straw colour, occasionally brushing down any sugar from the sides of the pan with a pastry brush dipped in cold water. Remove the pan from the heat and quickly stir in the hot nuts. It is important that the nuts are hot, otherwise they will cool the syrup too rapidly and it will not be easily manageable.

Pour the nougatine on an oiled slab. Lift and fold it over two or three times with an oiled palette knife until it cools slightly. Using an oiled rolling pin roll or beat it out. Cut it with an oiled knife or mould to shape quickly. Any nougatine not immediately required for moulding can be kept pliable on an oiled baking sheet in a warm oven.

Leave the moulded or shaped pieces to set hard before using, i.e. as decoration, confiserie, bon-bons, etc.

CRÈME À LA BOURDALOUE ** (Method I)

Ingredients:
135 g. castor sugar (4½ oz.)
45 g. crème de riz (1½ oz.)
1 egg
2 yolks of egg

45 g. unsalted butter (1½ oz.)
¼ l. Lait d'Amandes (see page 349)
  (1½ gills)
1 vanilla pod
3 tablespoons kirsch (optional)

Method: Put the sugar, crème de riz, the egg and egg yolks into a bowl. Work well with a wooden spoon or spatula. Heat the milk with the vanilla pod. Pour it on to the eggs, etc. Stir well and return to the pan which has been rinsed out. Cook as for Crème Pâtissière (see page 344), stirring continuously until it thickens and the crème de riz is cooked. Remove it from the heat, take out the vanilla pod and beat in the butter bit by bit. Add the kirsch if it is to be used.

CRÈME À LA BOURDALOUE * (Method II)

Ingredients:
135 g. castor sugar (4½ oz.)
60 g. crème de riz (2 oz.)
1 egg
2 yolks of egg

45 g. unsalted butter (1½ oz.)
3 dl. milk (½ pint)
1 small liqueur glass of kirsch or
  other liqueur

Method: Put the sugar, the egg and the yolks into a bowl and work well with a wooden spoon or spatula. Then add the crème de riz and work again. Heat the milk to boiling point and pour on to the eggs, etc. Stir well and return to the pan which has been rinsed out. Bring slowly to simmering point, keeping well stirred. Cook for 2 minutes. Remove it from the heat, whisk in the butter bit by bit and lastly add the liqueur.

CRÈME AU BEURRE **

Ingredients:
Crème Anglaise (see page 40)

270 g. unsalted butter (9 oz.)
flavouring

Method: Make up the crème Anglaise as usual. Strain it into a bowl and allow it to cool. Soften the butter slightly. Beat in the crème Anglaise little by little. The exact quantity of crème used is determined by the type of filling required. For vanilla flavour infuse a vanilla pod in the milk before making the crème Anglaise. Grated lemon or orange rind or praline can be used the same way. For coffee flavour, add strong coffee to the milk. For chocolate, soften the chocolate until it is liquid. Beat it in with the butter.

CRÈME AU BEURRE À LA MERINGUE **

Ingredients:
2 whites of egg
135 g. icing sugar (4½ oz.)

250 g. unsalted butter (slightly softened) (8½ oz.)

Method: Place the sugar and whites of egg into a large basin. Stand over a pan of very hot water and whisk briskly until it is very stiff indeed and stands up in spikes. Remove from the heat and continue to whisk until it is perfectly cold. Then add the butter bit by bit, whisking it in well. Flavour as desired.

Comment: The mixture must be perfectly cold before the butter is added, otherwise it will not thicken correctly.

CRÈME AU BEURRE MOUSSELINE **

Ingredients:
150 g. unsalted butter (5 oz.)
75 g. castor sugar (2½ oz.)

2 yolks of egg
1 dl. water, approx. (½ gill)

Method: Put the sugar and water into a thick pan and boil until it forms a thread: 215–220° F. (102–104° C.) when tested between the finger and thumb. Pour it slowly on to the beaten yolks. Beat all the time. When cool, thick and fluffy, beat in the butter by degrees. Flavour as desired.

Comment: (1) It is important to have a bowl of cold water beside the pan. Before testing for the thread, dip the fingers into the water, shake off the surplus, tilt the pan slightly, dipping the fingers quickly in and out again. If the test is unsatisfactory, do not try again without wetting the fingers.
(2) It at any time during the beating, the mixture curdles, hold the basin over hot water for a minute or two, or alternatively add more butter.

FLAVOURINGS FOR CRÈME AU BEURRE MOUSSELINE

To a basic quantity made with 2 yolks of egg etc. allow:

VANILLE Boil 2 teaspoons vanilla sugar with the castor sugar in the initial process.

CHOCOLAT Break 120 g. (4 oz.) plain chocolate into a basin and allow it to soften slowly over a pan of hot water. When smooth and free from all lumps, beat it into the plain crème au beurre mousseline.

CAFÉ Into the plain crème au beurre mousseline, mix sufficient strong coffee extract, dissolved in a little warm water, to give a pronounced coffee flavour and colour.

NOISETTE Beat into the plain crème au beurre mousseline 120 g. (4 oz.) of browned almonds or hazel nuts, which have been very finely chopped or put through a nut mill.

PRALINÉ Pound very finely 120 g. (4 oz.) Praline (see page 348) using a pestle and mortar. Beat this into the plain crème au beurre mousseline.

ORANGE Add the finely grated rind of an orange and a little Grand Marnier or other orange flavoured liqueur to the plain crème au beurre mousseline. Alternatively mix in finely chopped candied orange peel and flavour with Grand Marnier.

CITRON Add the finely grated rind of a lemon.

CASSIS Beat in a little 'Sirop de Cassis' or blackcurrant purée. Colour with a little blue and carmine colouring.

MARRON Add 2–3 tablespoons purée de marrons to the plain crème au beurre mousseline. A little rum or kirsch may also be added.

KIRSCH Add 2 tablespoons kirsch and mix well.

RHUM Add 1–2 tablespoons rum and mix well.

PISTACHE Add 60 g. (2 oz.) finely chopped pistachio nuts, flavour with kirsch or pistachio flavouring and colour green as desired.

ANANAS Mix the plain crème au beurre mousseline with 2 tablespoons pineapple conserve and 1 tablespoon rum or kirsch.

CERISE Mix plain crème au beurre mousseline with 2 tablespoons cherry jam or 60 g. (2 oz.) chopped glacé cherries, add 1 tablespoon kirsch.

FRAISE Mix plain crème au beurre mousseline with 2 tablespoons strawberry jam and 1 tablespoon kirsch.

343

CRÈME CHANTILLY * (For Decoration, etc.)

Ingredients:
1½ dl. thick cream (1 gill)

2 tablespoons milk
1 level teaspoon vanilla sugar

Method: Whip the cream with the milk, if possible standing the bowl over ice, until it thickens. Do not over-whip it. Fold in the vanilla sugar and use as required.

CRÈME PÂTISSIÈRE *

Ingredients:
1 egg and 1 yolk of egg
30 g. plain flour (1 oz.)

60 g. castor sugar (2 oz.)
3 dl. milk (½ pint)
1 vanilla pod

Method: Put the egg and yolk with the sugar into a bowl and work well with a wooden spoon or spatula. When the mixture whitens add the sieved flour. Heat the milk with the vanilla pod. Remove the vanilla pod and add the milk by degrees to the egg, sugar and flour. Pour into a clean pan and place it over a low heat and keep well stirred until it comes to the boil. Allow to simmer for 2–3 minutes, stirring continuously until it thickens.

Comment: Provided this crème is cooked gently and slowly and stirred all the time, it should not curdle.

CRÈME SAINT-HONORÉ **

Ingredients:
3 dl. milk (½ pint)
60 g. flour (2 oz.)
60 g. castor sugar (2 oz.)

4 whites of egg
1 egg and 1 yolk of egg
1 vanilla pod

Method: Cream the egg yolk and sugar together, add the flour, work together. Boil the milk with the vanilla pod, pour half of it on to the mixture. Stir well. Take out the vanilla pod. Return this mixture to the pan with the rest of the milk. Bring gently to boiling point stirring all the time. Boil for 1–2 minutes. Remove from the heat and fold in the stiffly beaten whites whilst the mixture is still hot. Allow to cool. Use as required.

Comment: This cream should not be made any longer in advance than is absolutely necessary as it does not hold its consistency.

GLACE À L'EAU or GLACÉ ICING **

Ingredients:

240 g. icing sugar (8 oz.)
3 tablespoons water
colouring as required
flavouring appropriate to the
colouring

Method: Sieve the icing sugar and place it in a pan. Mix smoothly with the water. It is important that it should be perfectly smooth before heating.

Place the pan over a very low heat and, stirring all the time, heat gently. It should be heated so that at all times the heat of the pan can be borne on the back of the hand. The icing should coat the back of the spoon. If the icing is too thin, a little more sieved icing sugar may be added. More water may be added to correct too thick a consistency.

To flavour – strained lemon or orange juice may replace the water used in making the icing. Colouring should be added last.

Coffee – strong coffee is used instead of water. Alternatively, a better sheen and colour is obtained by using coffee extract dissolved in a little water.

Chocolate – 60–90 g. (2–3 oz.) of grated chocolate is dissolved in the required amount of water. A nut of butter is added, followed by the icing sugar.

Liqueurs and rum may also be added, in which case a little less water should be used in the beginning.

GLACE ROYALE or ROYAL ICING **

Ingredients:

240 g. icing sugar, approx. ($\frac{1}{2}$ lb.)
1 drop of blue colouring, optional
1 white of egg
1 teaspoon lemon juice

Method: Sieve the icing sugar twice through a nylon sieve. Place the lemon juice and egg white in a bowl, and mixing well with a wooden spoon or spatula, gradually add the icing sugar. The icing should be beaten thoroughly to remove lumps and give a good gloss. The amount of icing sugar added varies, according to the requirements. For piping, more icing sugar may be necessary to give a slightly stiffer consistency.

Royal icing sets firmly as a result of the hardening of the egg albumen. To store royal icing, even for a short time, cover closely with waxed or greaseproof paper and a damp cloth or polythene, so that no hard crust may form.

Comment: The blue colouring is added to counteract any slight yellow-ing effect. Only a very small amount is necessary. Confectioners often used blued sugar. The colouring is added when the required consistency has been achieved. Add only a drop at a time and beat well. Use good quality colourings only, which are highly concentrated, as these give colour without altering the consistency too much.

FONDANT ICING ***

Ingredients:

500 g. loaf or castor sugar (1 lb.)
1 dl. water (½ gill)

90 g. liquid glucose or a pinch of cream of tartar (3 oz.)

Method: Place the sugar and water together in a pan. Heat it gently, stirring all the time until the sugar has completely dissolved. Remove the spoon, increase the heat and boil rapidly. During the boiling process, the sides of the pan should be brushed down to the level of the syrup with a pastry brush dipped in cold water, so that any syrup which has been splashed up the sides, will be thoroughly dissolved. When the temperature reaches 238° F. (115° C.) or soft ball, test the syrup by dipping the thumb and first finger into cold water, then into the boiling syrup. Plunge the fingers quickly in and out of the cold water again to cool the syrup slightly. Rub the thumb over the tip of the finger in a circular manner. When the sugar has cooked sufficiently, a ball will form, which when pressed gently is soft.

Now lower the base of the pan into cold water to stop the cooking. Pour the syrup on to a marble slab or enamel topped table and allow it to cool to blood heat when a skin forms over the whole surface and it is sufficiently cool to lay the hand on top.

Using a metal sugar scraper or wooden spatula, stir the whole mixture completely, so that each part is thoroughly worked. Gradually the syrup will thicken and become opaque. Eventually it will become white and very stiff.

With the palm of the hand, press the fondant down on to the slab, working it continuously and thus changing it from a rough and rocky mixture to a smooth and shiny one. Alternatively take small pieces and knead with the fingers to make it smooth.

The fondant should be stored in a close jar or wrapped in aluminium foil or a polythene bag.

Comment: If, when the fondant has become thick and white, it is too hard to knead and break down, leave covered with a damp cloth for ½ hour. During this time the fondant will soften and be more manageable.

FLAVOURING FONDANT ICING

CHOCOLATE To each pound of fondant, allow 120–180 g. (4–6 oz.) plain chocolate. Break the chocolate into pieces and stand it in a small basin over a pan of boiling water. When it is completely melted, remove it from the heat and stir it well. Add it to the melted fondant icing. Mix it thoroughly. If it is too thick, it can be thinned with a little sugar syrup (see page 24).

COFFEE Use strong coffee essence to replace the water normally used to thin down the fondant icing.

Other flavourings such as rum, kirsch, Grand Marnier and various fruit juices can be used in the thinning process.

TO ICE WITH FONDANT

Place the fondant to be used in a saucepan. Add the colouring (this is best dripped from the point of a knife), together with the flavouring. Stand it over a very low heat or if preferred stand the saucepan in another containing hot water. Whichever method is adopted the melting process cannot be hurried. It is absolutely imperative to melt it down at as cool a temperature as possible. At all times it should be possible to bear the heat of the bottom of the pan on the wrist. Stir well all the time to ensure even mixing.

When melting fondant for icing cakes the consistency should be observed and if it is too thick, water must be added to ensure that it will run smoothly and at the same time coat the cake sufficiently.

Fondant is a comparatively cheap ingredient and it is better by far to have too much fondant than too little. For a four egg cake made in the moule à manqué type of tin $\frac{1}{2}$–$\frac{3}{4}$ kg. (1–1$\frac{1}{2}$ lb.) should be used. Stand the cake on a wire rack over a clean plate or bowl. Pour the fondant quickly on the centre of the cake tilting the rack to allow it to run evenly. Give the cake and rack a sharp bang to allow it to settle then leave it for 3–4 hours to set in a warm dry atmosphere. If the cake is lifted too soon the fondant will crack and ruckle. When the cake is set the excess fondant can be scraped up and used again. It should be kept in a cool place in a clean bowl which must be covered with a damp cloth or in a polythene bag.

SUCRE AU GRAND CASSÉ ***

Ingredients: 1 dl. water ($\frac{1}{2}$ gill)
125 g. sugar (4 oz.)

Method: Dissolve the sugar in the water in a pan, stirring thoroughly over a low heat. When the sugar is completely dissolved, remove the spoon and bring to the boil quickly. During this process, brush the sides of the pan down to the level of the syrup with a pastry brush dipped in cold water. Boil the syrup to 280° F. (138° C.). Alternatively, take a spoonful of syrup and drop it into cold water. If the syrup has reached the required degree, it should be hard and break between the teeth, but should stick slightly. Remove the pan from the heat and cool at once in cold water.

Tilt the pan and holding the cake or whatever is to be dipped, on a fork, plunge it in, remove and drain it on waxed paper or an oiled baking sheet.

Comment: Cassé sugar is used for coating sweets and small gâteaux to give a crisp and decorative sheen.

SUCRE FILÉ or SPUN SUGAR ***

Ingredients:
250 g. loaf or castor sugar (½ lb.)
pinch of cream of tartar

1 teaspoon liquid glucose
1½ dl. water (1 gill)
colouring as desired

Method: Place the sugar, water, glucose and the cream of tartar in a strong pan. Heat it gently, stirring carefully, so that the sugar dissolves completely. When the sugar has dissolved, increase the heat and allow it to boil quickly.

While the boiling process is in progress, brush the sides of the pan down to the level of the syrup with a pastry brush dipped into cold water. This helps to dissolve the sugar splashed on the sides of the pan and stops the formation of sugar crystals.

Boil the solution to hard crack or 310° F. (154° C.). (A little of the sugar solution dropped into cold water will set firm and break between the teeth crisply.) Lower the base of the pan into cold water, so as to prevent the syrup from continuing to cook.

Arrange two or three rolling pins or large wooden spoons so that they extend from the edge of a table. Weight these with a board. Spread a layer of newspaper over the floor below, to catch the drips of sugar.

Take a heated fork, dip it into the sugar syrup, drain slightly and move quickly back and forwards over the handles of the spoons or the rolling pins so that the fine threads fall and are caught on them. Do not hold the fork too rigidly and move it at some height in a bold, expansive manner, so that long fine threads result.

After frequent dipping of the fork, it will be found that it is necessary to drain more thoroughly, so that the threads do not form too thickly.

Comment: Spun sugar is used as a decoration for certain gâteaux or mounted pieces, or ice creams and bombes. It should be made no more than half an hour before serving as the sugar absorbs moisture from the atmosphere and collapses.

PRALINE **

Ingredients:
125 g. unblanched almonds (4 oz.)

125 g. sugar (4 oz.)
1 dl. water (½ gill)

Method: Rinse the almonds in cold water to remove the powdery substance clinging to the skins. Put the sugar and water into a small strong pan, place it over a low heat and stir with a wooden spoon until the sugar has dissolved. Raise the heat, add the almonds and continue to boil, brushing the sides of the pan as for caramel. When it reaches a rich brown colour, remove and pour it on to an oiled slab (or if this is not obtainable an oiled baking sheet). Allow to cool and then crush it using a pestle and mortar or a strong rolling pin. Use as required.

If the praline is to be kept, place it in an absolutely airtight tin and crush before use.

Comment: A certain amount of colour will be obtained from the nuts, which in turn colours the sugar syrup. It is important to make sure that the sugar syrup has reached the correct temperature, i.e. 380–400° F. (190–200° C.) otherwise the praline will be sticky instead of brittle and will not pound.

LAIT D'AMANDES *

Ingredients:
105 g. ground almonds (3½ oz.)   ½ l. of cold water (3 gills)

Method: Place the almonds in a large basin. Very slowly add the water a little at a time stirring increasingly. Place a clean cloth across a bowl. Put the almonds and water into the centre. Gather up the corners and squeeze the liquid into the bowl.

This can be used in the preparation of various creams, especially Crème Bourdaloue.

BOULES AU CHOCOLAT *

Ingredients:
120 g. ground almonds (4 oz.)
120 g. castor sugar (4 oz.)
1 white of egg

30 g. cocoa (1 oz.)
1 teaspoon vanilla sugar
24 (approx.) hazelnuts, grilled
    and skinned
granulated sugar

Method: Place the ground almonds and the castor and vanilla sugars in a bowl, add the sieved cocoa. Mix well. Add sufficient egg white to bind the mixture together to a fairly stiff paste. Divide it into pieces the size and shape of a walnut. Enclose a nut in the centre of each. Dip first into lightly beaten egg white and then into granulated sugar. Place on a greased baking tray and bake for 10–15 minutes in a moderately hot oven, gas mark 6 or 400° F. (200° C.). Cool on a wire rack.

Variations:

BOULES MALAGA – instead of cocoa, flavour with 1 dessertspoon rum and replace the nuts with stoned Malaga raisins. Roll in finely chopped nuts instead of sugar.

BOULES AU CAFÉ – instead of cocoa, flavour with a small amount of coffee essence or instant coffee. Finish as for the Boules au Chocolat.

BOULETTES AUX MARRONS *

Ingredients:
250 g. chestnuts (8 oz.)
90 g. castor sugar (3 oz.)
kirsch to flavour

60 g. ground almonds (2 oz.)
1 teaspoon vanilla sugar
To finish:
60 g. grated chocolate (2 oz.)

Method: Make a cut in the skin of each chestnut. Put them all in a pan of boiling water and boil for 15–20 minutes. Remove them one at a time and take off the outer and inner skins. Put the chestnuts into a clean pan and just cover with boiling water and simmer until they are tender. Drain thoroughly and pass them through a sieve or vegetable mill into a bowl. Add the castor sugar, the vanilla sugar and ground almonds, mix all well together. Moisten with sufficient kirsch to give a stiff dry paste. Using a dessertspoon, take even sized pieces of paste and roll them into balls on a board, then roll them in the grated chocolate. Serve them in paper sweet cases.

Comment: If these are not to be eaten immediately, they can be stored for a week in an airtight container.

CHOUX AU KIRSCH **

Ingredients:
Pâte à Choux made with 60 g.
    plain flour (2 oz.) etc. (see page
    336)
Crème Pâtissière made with:
    45 g. plain flour (1½ oz.)
    60 g. castor sugar (2 oz.)

3 dl. milk (½ pint)
1 egg
flavoured with 2 tablespoons
kirsch (see page 344 for method)
To finish:
kirsch flavoured white fondant
    icing, halved glacé cherries

Method: Make the pâte à choux in the usual way and using a plain 1 cm. (⅜ inch) forcing tube, pipe on to a greased baking sheet, in small balls about 2½ cm. (1 inch) in diameter. Brush these with beaten egg and bake in a hot oven, gas mark 7–8 or 425–450° F. (220–230° C.) for 10 minutes. Reduce the heat and cook for a further 15–20 minutes until crisp and firm.
    Remove the choux to a wire rack, split open and allow to cool.

Meanwhile, make the crème pâtissière, flavour it with the kirsch and allow it to cool.

Fill the crème pâtissière into the choux balls. Coat each choux with the white fondant icing and place half a cherry on each. Serve in small paper cake cases.

LES DUCHESSES *

Ingredients:

60 g. butter (2 oz.)
60 g. castor sugar (2 oz.)
135 g. plain flour (4½ oz.)
105 g. ground almonds (3½ oz.)

1 egg
To finish:
beaten egg
glacé cherries

Method: Place the butter in a warm bowl and beat it well, adding the sugar. Beat until light and fluffy. Whisk the egg and beat it into the butter and sugar a little at a time. Then mix in the flour and the ground almonds.

Turn the mixture on to a floured board and knead it gently. It must not be sticky. With floured hands roll it into small balls the size of a walnut. Using the tip of the finger, make a dent in the centre of each. Brush over with beaten egg and put a cherry in the dent. Bake on a greased and floured baking sheet in a moderately hot oven, gas mark 6 or 400° F. (200° C.) for 15–20 minutes.

PETITS-FOURS

MADELONS **

Ingredients:

Pâte à Choux made with 60 g.
(2 oz.) plain flour, 1 teaspoon
vanilla sugar, 1 teaspoon castor
sugar (see page 336 for method)

a little beaten yolk of egg
large crystal grain, or 'coffee'
sugar

Method: Make up the pâte à choux in the usual way adding the castor sugar and the vanilla sugar to sweeten and flavour.

Using a forcing bag with a rosette pipe, pipe the mixture in 'S' shapes or rings on a greased baking sheet. Brush over lightly with the yolk of egg and sprinkle with the crystal sugar.

Bake the madelons in a hot oven, gas mark 7 or 425° F. (220° C.) for 10 minutes, then reduce the heat to gas mark 5 or 375° F. (190° C.) for a further 20 minutes, until they are crisp and golden brown.

These little cakes are served plain without further decoration.

RURIK **

Ingredients:
100 g. castor sugar (3 oz.)
100 g. ground almonds (3 oz.)
rum to moisten

To finish:
rum flavoured white fondant icing
  (see page 346)
halved glacé cherries

Method: Mix the sugar and ground almonds together in a bowl. Add the rum gradually to make a stiff paste. Place the paste on a board with a little sifted icing sugar, roll it out to about 1½ cm. (½ inch) thick and using a sharp knife cut it into small squares 3½ cm. (1¼ inches) across. Leave to harden. Using a two pronged fork, dip them into the fondant icing, place a halved cherry on each and leave on a wire rack to set. Serve in paper sweet cases.

MALTAIS **

Ingredients:
As for Rurik (see above),
  but with 75 g. (2½ oz.) chopped
  candied orange peel added

To finish:
orange coloured flavoured fondant
  icing (see page 346)
strips of candied orange peel

Method: Make as for Rurik, adding the chopped orange peel. Form into little round flat galettes, approximately 3 cm. (1 inch) in diameter and 1½ cm. (½ inch) thick. Put aside to harden. Dip into the fondant icing and place a strip of candied peel on each. Place on a wire rack to set. Serve in paper sweet cases.

BOURBONNAIS **

Ingredients:
As for Rurik (see above),
  but flavour with strong
  coffee essence in place of rum

To finish:
coffee fondant icing (see page 347)
crystallised coffee beans

Method: Make up as for Rurik. With the hands dusted in icing sugar, form the paste into olive shapes. Put them aside to harden. Dip into coffee flavoured fondant icing. Place a coffee bean on each. Put on a wire rack to set and serve in paper sweet cases.

Comment: Crystallised coffee beans can be purchased at most large stores or confectioners.

TRUFFES EN SURPRISE **

Ingredients:
135 g. praline (see page 348)
  (4½ oz.)
60 g. butter (2 oz.)
135 g. plain chocolate (4½ oz.)

To finish:
120–180 g. chocolate couverture
  (4–6 oz.)
90–120 g. chocolate vermicelli
  (3–4 oz.)

Method: Make the praline as usual and pound it finely using a pestle and mortar. Soften the chocolate in a bowl over a pan of hot water. Remove from the heat and beat in the butter with the praline. Mix all well together. Put the mixture in a cool place. When it becomes firm but not too hard to handle, shape it into balls the size of a walnut and leave them in a cold place to harden.

Melt the covering chocolate in a bowl over a pan of hot water and dip each truffle into this and then into chocolate vermicelli. Put into small sweet cases and allow to harden completely.

Comment: If the mixture is difficult to handle, dust the hands with icing sugar before attempting to roll it.

CROQUANTES À LA CRÈME GANÂCHE ***

Ingredients:
1 egg
85 g. castor sugar (light weight)
  (3 oz.)
60 g. plain flour (2 oz.)

Crème Ganâche:
180 g. plain chocolate (6 oz.)
90 g. butter (3 oz.)
3 tablespoons thick cream
To finish:
chocolate vermicelli

Method: Break the egg into a bowl and work well with the castor sugar for 5 minutes until the mixture lightens in colour and thickens to form a ribbon. Sift in the flour and mix evenly. Drop teaspoonful of the mixture, spacing them well apart, on to a greased baking sheet. Spread each spoonful very thinly in rounds. Bake them in a fairly hot oven, gas mark 6–7 or 400–425° F. (200–220° C.) for 5–7 minutes, until they are just browning around the edges. Then quickly loosen them with a knife and roll each around a lightly greased wooden spoon handle, with the underside inwards. Leave them to harden on a cooling tray.

Meanwhile, make the crème ganâche. Break the chocolate into pieces and put it into a basin over a pan of hot water until it is just melted. Remove the basin from the heat and beat in the butter bit by bit and the cream. Leave this crème in a cool place to allow it to thicken, stirring it occasionally. When it is sufficiently thick fill it into a piping bag with a plain tube and force a 1 cm. (½ inch) length into either end of each croquante. Using a round ended knife, spread a 1 cm. (½ inch) collar of the crème on the outside of each end of the croquantes. Dip the coated ends into chocolate vermicelli. Serve the croquantes in paper cases.

FANCHONETTES À LA VANILLE **

Ingredients:
Pâte Brisée (Method I) made with
    1 egg, etc. (see page 338)
For the Filling:
Crème Pâtissière made with 3 dl.
    milk (½ pint) etc. (see page 344)

For the Meringue:
2 whites of egg
120 g. castor sugar (4 oz.)
To finish:
apricot jam or red currant jelly

Method: Make up the pastry in the usual way and put it aside to relax. Make up the crème pâtissière and pour into a bowl to cool thoroughly. Stir it from time to time.

Roll out the pastry on a lightly floured board. Line it into tartlet tins. Fill almost full with the crème pâtissière. Bake in a fairly hot oven, gas mark 6 or 400° F. (200° C.) until the pastry is crisp, approximately 20 minutes. Remove the tartlets from the oven and place them on a wire rack to cool.

Make the meringue (see page 334). Cover the tartlets with a layer of this and put the remaining meringue into a forcing bag with a rosette tube and decorate round the edge of each. Dust with sieved castor sugar. Return to a cool oven to brown the meringue slightly, gas mark 3–4 or 325–350° F. (160–180° C.). Melt the apricot jam or redcurrant jelly and, using a forcing bag, fill the centre of each with this. Serve cold.

FICHES *

Ingredients:
135 g. plain flour (4½ oz.)
60 g. powdered roasted nuts
    (2 oz.)
60 g. butter (2 oz.)
pinch of salt

1 teaspoon vanilla sugar
1 egg
60 g. castor sugar (2 oz.)
To finish:
Glacé Icing (see page 345)
    flavoured with rum

Method: Sieve the flour and salt together into a bowl. Rub the butter into the flour until it resembles fine breadcrumbs. Mix in the nuts, sugar and vanilla sugar. Beat the egg lightly and mix with the dry ingredients to make a moist pâte. Put this into a forcing bag with a large rosette tube. Pipe in lines on a greased baking sheet. Bake for 5–6 minutes in a fairly hot oven, gas mark 6 or 400° F. (200° C.). Remove from the oven and lift them on to a cooling tray. While they are still hot brush them over with glacé icing. When cold cut them into finger lengths.

FLORENTINES **

Ingredients:

60 g. butter (2 oz.)
60 g. castor sugar (2 oz.)
60 g. plain flour (2 oz.)
2 teaspoons honey

30 g. candied peel (1 oz.)
30 g. glacé cherries (1 oz.)
30 g. blanched almonds (1 oz.)
To finish:
60–90 g. melted chocolate (2–3 oz.)

Method: Chop the peel, cherries and the almonds. Heat the butter, sugar and honey in a saucepan. When they are hot stir in the chopped fruits and almonds. Stirring all the time, cook for a few seconds, then add the flour and mix until it is smooth. Remove quickly from the heat.

Drop teaspoonsful of the mixture on to a greased and floured baking sheet. Allow sufficient room for spreading. Spread the mixture slightly. Bake them in a moderate oven, gas mark 4–5 or 350–375° F. (180–190° C.) for 8–10 minutes, until the mixture has bubbled and spread and become a golden brown. Quickly take the biscuits from the oven, leave for a few seconds to harden. Using a palette knife remove them on to a wire rack to cool. If the biscuits are too soft to handle on removal from the oven, return them for a few minutes longer to brown and crispen.

When they are cold, coat the undersides with the melted chocolate. Leave until the chocolate becomes quite hard. Serve, or store them in an airtight tin.

LES FOURRÉS AU MIEL **

Ingredients:

Pâte Sucrée made with 150 g.
plain flour (5 oz.) etc. (see
page 339)

75 g. finely chopped crystallised
fruits (2½ oz.)
thick honey
icing sugar
vanilla sugar

Method: Make up the pâte sucrée in the usual way, but add to the mixture the very finely chopped crystallised fruits. Roll out on a lightly floured board to a thickness of ½ cm. (¼ inch). Using a plain 5 cm. (2 inch) cutter, cut into rounds. Cook on a lightly greased baking sheet in a moderately hot oven, gas mark 5–6 or 375–400° F. (190–200° C.) for 10–15 minutes until light golden brown. Remove and cool on a wire rack. Sandwich them together with a layer of honey. Dust thickly with sieved icing sugar, to which has been added a good proportion of vanilla sugar.

GALETTES À LA BADOISE *

Ingredients:

135 g. ground almonds (4½ oz.)
165 g. plain flour (5½ oz.)
135 g. castor sugar (4½ oz.)
60 g. butter (2 oz.)
3 yolks of egg

½ teaspoon vanilla sugar
a pinch of salt
To finish:
a little beaten egg
split almonds

Method: Soften the butter in a bowl, add the sugar and beat them together until creamy. Stir in the ground almonds. Mix to a paste with the yolks. Gradually work in the sieved flour, the vanilla sugar and salt, kneading lightly until the paste is firm and smooth. Roll it out to ½ cm. (¼ inch) thick. Cut into biscuits with a 10 cm. (4 inch) fluted oval cutter. Place them on a greased baking sheet. Brush them with beaten egg. Mark in a trellis design with the back of a knife. Place a split almond in the middle of each biscuit. Bake in a moderate oven, gas mark 4 or 350° F. (180° C.) for 15 minutes. Place on a wire rack to cool.

GÂTEAUX DANOIS **

Ingredients:

Pâte Sucrée made with 150 g.
    plain flour (5 oz.), etc. (see
    page 339)
2–3 crushed macaroons

240 g. stoned Morello cherries
    (½ lb.)
½ l. Crème Patissière (see page 344)
    (1 pint)
3 tablespoons melted butter
icing sugar

Method: Make up the pâte sucrée in the usual way. Put it aside to relax. Make the crème pâtissière.

Roll out the pâte sucrée and line it into tartlet tins. In the bottom of each tartlet place a teaspoonful of crushed macaroon. On the top of this put 3–4 cherries. Lastly coat the whole with a good spoonful of crème pâtissière. Bake in a fairly hot oven, gas mark 5–6 or 375–400° F. (190–200° C.) for approximately 20 minutes or until the pastry is crisp. Remove them from their tins carefully and brush lightly with melted butter. Sift generously with icing sugar. Serve hot or cold for tea or as a sweet.

MACARONS DE NANCY **

Ingredients:

120 g. ground almonds (4 oz.)
240 g. castor sugar (8 oz.)
2 whites of egg

15 g. crème de riz (½ oz.)
½ teaspoon vanilla sugar
split almonds
rice paper

Method: Put the ground almonds into a bowl with the castor sugar and the unbeaten whites, add the crème de riz and vanilla sugar and work them with a wooden spatula or spoon for 7–8 minutes. Put the mixture into a forcing bag with a 1 cm. (½ inch) plain pipe (if the mixture is very stiff, a little extra egg white may be added). Pipe rounds on to rice paper about 5 cm. (1½ inches) in diameter. Brush them gently with a little 'frothed' white, put half an almond on the top of each. Bake 15 minutes in a moderate oven, gas mark 5 or 375° F. (190° C.). Remove and cool them on a wire rack. Gently tear off any surplus rice paper.

SMALL CAKES

MARIGNANS **

Ingredients:
Pâte à Savarin, Method I, (see page 339)
Syrup made with 250 g. (½ lb.)
sugar, 3 dl. (½ pint) water, 2–3 tablespoons rum, 1 vanilla pod.
Meringue Italienne (see page 335)

Method: Make up the pâte à savarin in the usual way and put it to prove in small boat-shaped moulds. When it is well risen, bake in a hot oven, gas mark 7 or 425° F. (220° C.) for 15 minutes. Remove them from the tins and place them on a wire rack.

Meanwhile dissolve the sugar in the water. Heat to boiling point with the vanilla pod, remove from the heat and pour in the rum. Put the wire rack with the marignans over a bowl and pour the hot syrup over them, basting them again and again until all the syrup has been absorbed.

Make the meringue Italienne. Using a small, sharp knife and holding the marignans carefully, split halfway through. Pipe a rope of meringue to fill the split, using a forcing bag and rosette pipe. Place them in paper cases before serving.

MIRLITONS **

Ingredients:
Pâte Sucrée made with 150 g. (5 oz.) plain flour etc. (see page 339)
apricot jam
2 eggs
100 g. castor sugar (3½ oz.)
3–4 crisp macaroons
1 teaspoon vanilla sugar
blanched almonds
icing sugar

Method: Make up the pâte sucrée in the usual way. Put it aside to relax. Roll it out on a lightly floured board to a ½ cm. (¼ inch) thickness and line it into bouchée or deep tartlet tins. Prick well all over. Place a teaspoon of apricot jam in the bottom of each. Crush the macaroons finely. Whisk the eggs with the sugar until they are light and fluffy. Stir in the vanilla sugar and macaroons. Fill the pastry cases with this mixture. Smooth over the top. Place three split almonds on the top of each. Dust thickly with sieved icing sugar. Bake in the top of a moderately hot oven, gas mark 5–6 or 375–400° F. (190–200° C.) for 15–20 minutes or until they are golden brown. Remove from the tins carefully and place them on a wire rack to cool.

NINIS **

Ingredients:
Pâte à Choux (see page 336)
Crème Pâtissière, to which has
  been added 120 g. chopped
  crystallised fruits (4 oz.) 1 egg
  (see page 344)

To finish:
white fondant icing flavoured with
  kirsch
glacé cherries

Method: Make the pâte à choux in the usual way. Using a forcing bag with a 1 cm. (⅜ inch) plain tube, pipe it into ovals 5 × 3 cm. (2 × 1½ inches) on a greased baking sheet. Brush them with beaten egg and bake at gas mark 7 or 425° F. (220° C.) for 10 minutes, then reduce the heat to gas mark 5 or 375° F. (190° C.) for a further 20 minutes or until they are crisp and golden brown.

Meanwhile, prepare the crème pâtissière. Stir in the chopped fruits and allow it to cool.

Make a small hole in the choux ovals and fill with the crème pâtissière. Coat each Nini with a spoonful of the fondant icing and place a halved glacé cherry on top. Serve in paper cake cases.

LES PAMELAS **

Ingredients:
Pâte Sucrée made with 75 g. plain
  flour (2½ oz.) etc. (see page 339)
For the Filling:
250 g. chestnuts (½ lb.)
90 g. castor sugar (3 oz.)

60 g. butter (2 oz.)
1 teaspoon vanilla sugar
To finish:
a little white fondant icing
  flavoured with rum (see page 346)
small chocolate pastilles

Method: Make up the pâte sucrée in the usual way and put it aside to relax. Roll out evenly ½ cm. (¼ inch) thick and line it into tartlet tins. Prick them well and bake in a fairly hot oven, gas mark 6 or 400° F. (200° C.) for 15–20 minutes or until a pale golden colour.

Prepare the marron filling. Cut a small piece of skin from each chestnut. Place the chestnuts in a pan of cold water, bring to the boil and boil for 10 minutes. The skins should be easy to remove. Put the chestnuts into a pan of boiling water and simmer them gently until they are just tender. Pass them through a sieve or vegetable mill. Dissolve the sugar in 1 dl. ($\frac{1}{2}$ gill) water with the vanilla sugar. Cook the chestnuts in this syrup until a smooth purée is obtained, stirring well to prevent it from burning. Remove from the heat and allow it to cool. When it is quite cold, add the butter and beat well.

When the pastry cases are cold, place some marron purée in each smoothing over carefully. Spoon an even layer of fondant icing over each tartlet. Place a chocolate pastille in the centre of each.

Comment: If fresh chestnuts are not available, then an alternative filling may be made using crème au beurre mousseline au marrons (see page 343). This should be filled into the tartlet cases, which are then placed in the refrigerator for 2 hours, so that the crème au beurre becomes hard and will not easily melt when coated with the fondant icing.

PETITS ROLLAS **

Ingredients:
2 whites of egg
135 g. castor sugar (4$\frac{1}{2}$ oz.)
90 g. ground almonds (3 oz.)
Creme au Beurre à la Meringue au

Chocolat made with 2 whites
of egg, etc. (see page 342)
To finish:
icing sugar
120 g. chopped browned nuts (4 oz.)

Method: Sift the sugar with the ground almonds into a bowl. Whisk the whites very stiffly and fold in the almonds and sugar lightly, but thoroughly. Fill the mixture into a forcing bag with a plain round $\frac{1}{2}$ cm. ($\frac{1}{4}$ inch) tube and pipe rounds 7 cm. (3 inches) in diameter on a greased and floured baking sheet. (Start from the outside and pipe to the centre.) Dust with icing sugar and bake in a moderate oven, gas mark 5 or 375° F. (190° C.) for 15 minutes. Loosen the biscuits with a thin bladed knife and put them on a wire rack to cool.

Make the crème au beurre à la meringue au chocolat and sandwich the biscuits together with this. Spread the rest of the crème au beurre all over the top and sides and coat with finely chopped nuts. Dust lightly with icing sugar.

PETITS MARMINS **

Ingredients:
Pâte à Génoise made with:
  2 eggs
  60 g. plain flour (2 oz.)
  75 g. castor sugar (2$\frac{1}{2}$ oz.)
  60 g. butter or margarine (2 oz.)

15 g. cocoa ($\frac{1}{2}$ oz.)
To finish:
60 g. plain chocolate (2 oz.)
chocolate vermicelli
apricot marmalade
icing sugar

Method: Make the pâte à génoise adding the cocoa with the flour (see page 333 for method). Pour the mixture into greased brioche tins and bake in a moderate oven, gas mark 5 or 375° F. (190° C.) for about 15 minutes. Turn out on a wire rack until cool. Brush the tops with apricot marmalade and dip them in chocolate vermicelli. Dust lightly with sieved icing sugar and arrange three pieces of caraque chocolate on each.

Comment: To make chocolate caraque, break up the chocolate and melt it in a basin over a pan of hot water, taking care that it does not become too warm or the gloss will be spoilt. Spread it thinly with a palette knife on a marble slab. When quite cold, scrape it off with a sharp knife, held vertically, into thin 'cigarette' rolls.

PETITES RELIGIEUSES ***

9/10

Ingredients:

Pâte à Choux made with 60 g. plain flour (2 oz.), etc. (see page 336)

beaten egg

½ quantity Crème au Beurre Mousseline au Café (see page 343)

½ quantity Crème au Beurre Mousseline au Chocolat (see page 343)

Chocolate Fondant Icing (see page 346)

Coffee Fondant Icing (see page 347)

Sucre Cassé made with 120 g. sugar (4 oz.) (see page 347)

Method: Make up the pâte à choux in the usual way. Using a 1 cm. (½ inch) plain tube and forcing bag, pipe nine large balls approximately 3 cm. (1 inch) in diameter, and a similar number of small balls 1 cm. (½ inch) in diameter on to greased baking sheets. Brush them over with beaten egg and bake in a hot oven, gas mark 7 or 425° F. (220° C.) and continue to cook until they are crisp and firm. The smaller shapes will cook quicker than the large ones. Remove them all to a wire rack to cool.

Make the crème au beurre and flavour as required. Pierce the underside of the choux balls with the point of a knife and fill with either the chocolate or coffee crème au beurre. Make the sucre cassé and dip the small filled choux quickly into this, using an oiled fork. Leave them on an oiled tray to set.

Coat the larger choux with the fondant alternate to the flavouring of the filling. Leave the fondant to harden.

Using a small star tube and forcing bag, pipe the crème au beurre to form a ring of stars on the top of each large choux. Place a small choux on top. Serve in paper cases. (*See Plate 28.*)

PROVENÇAUX **

Ingredients:

105 g. ground almonds (3½ oz.)
50 g. castor sugar (1¾ oz.)
50 g. plain flour (1¾ oz.)

135 g. butter (4½ oz.)
2 eggs
1 yolk of egg
1 tablespoon rum

Method: Melt the butter and allow it to cool. Separate the eggs. Mix the three yolks with the ground almonds, then stir in the melted butter and the rum. Whisk the whites of egg very stiffly and fold them in alternately with the sieved sugar and flour. Drop spoonsful into Madeleine tins which have been greased and dusted out with a mixture of equal quantities of castor sugar and flour. Bake in a moderate oven, gas mark 5 or 375° F. (190° C.) for 7–10 minutes until golden brown. Turn out on a wire rack to cool.

ROCHERS AUX AMANDES **

Ingredients:

135 g. sieved icing sugar (4½ oz.)
2 whites of egg

120 g. almonds, dry and shredded (4 oz.)
strawberry, vanilla or coffee flavouring

Method: Whisk the whites with the icing sugar in a bowl over a saucepan half filled with boiling water, until they are white in colour and the mixture has thickened and is warm to touch. Remove the bowl from the heat and continue to beat until the meringue is cold and very stiff. Stir in the flavouring and the almonds.

Put spoonsful of the mixture into greaseproof paper cases and dry in a cool oven, gas mark ¼ or 225° F. (100° C.) for 10 minutes or until the outside is fairly crisp and the inside is soft and sticky.

ROCHERS AUX CERISES **

Proceed in the same way as for Rochers aux Amandes (see above), but use 120 g. (4 oz.) chopped glacé cherries instead of the almonds.

ROCHERS AUX FRUITS **

Proceed in the same way as for Rochers aux Amandes (see above), but use 120 g. (4 oz.) chopped glacé fruits instead of the almonds.

LES SCHENKELES **

Ingredients:

75 g. castor sugar (2½ oz.)
75 g. ground almonds (2½ oz.)
1 egg
75 g. melted butter (2½ oz.)
3 dessertspoons brandy

150 g. plain flour (5 oz.)
deep fat for frying
To finish:
castor sugar
cinnamon

Method: Mix the sugar and almonds in a bowl and stir in the egg, butter and brandy. Add the flour little by little until a thick paste is obtained. Turn it out on to a floured board and shape it into small croquettes the size and length of the index finger. Make the deep fat hot and fry the schenkeles in this, using the frying basket. (Do not attempt to cook them all at once.) Drain them well and roll them in equal quantities of castor sugar and cinnamon. Serve with tea or coffee.

TARTLETTES AUX FRAISES AU FROMAGE **

Ingredients:

Pâte Sucrée made with 75 g. plain
    flour (2½ oz.) etc. (see page 339)
For the Filling:
120 g. cream cheese (4 oz.)
30 g. fresh butter (1 oz.)

1 tablespoon castor sugar
1 teaspoon vanilla sugar
a little thin cream
To finish:
250 g. small strawberries (½ lb.)
redcurrant jelly

Method: Make the pâte sucrée in the usual way and put it aside to relax.

Meanwhile prepare the filling. Cream the butter with the sugar and the vanilla sugar. Beat in the sieved cheese, and add a little thin cream.

Roll out the pastry and line it into tartlet tins. Prick well all over and bake in a moderately hot oven, gas mark 5–6 or 375–400° F. (190–200° C.) for 15–20 minutes or until a pale golden colour.

When the tartlets are quite cold, fill with the cheese mixture. Cover all over with small strawberries and brush all over with melted redcurrant jelly.

TUILES ALGÉROISES *

Ingredients:

105 g. chopped blanched almonds
    (3½ oz.)
105 g. castor sugar (3½ oz.)

55 g. butter (2 oz.) (light weight)
20 g. plain flour (¾ oz.)
1 small orange

Method: Cream the butter in a bowl with a wooden spoon, add the sugar and work briskly until it is creamy. Grate the zest of the orange without removing the white pith, and add it together with the juice to the butter and sugar. Stir well and then stir in the chopped almonds and sieved flour.

Lightly grease 2 or 3 baking sheets and dust them with flour. Drop teaspoons of the mixture on to the baking sheets and spread them into thin rounds, approximately 7 cm. (3 inches) in diameter. Leave sufficient space between the rounds as they will spread. Bake in a moderate oven, gas mark 5 or 375° F. (190° C.) for 5–7 minutes or until they are light brown around the edge. Remove each one from the tin using a palette knife and lay them over a lightly greased rolling pin. Press them gently to take the curve of the pin. As soon as they are cool and crisp, remove them.

Store, if necessary, in an airtight container.

Comment: These are delicious served with ice cream, as an alternative to wafers or gaufrettes.

LARGE CAKES

BISCUIT AU CITRON ***

Ingredients:
165 g. castor sugar (5½ oz.)
1 teaspoon vanilla sugar
5 eggs
115 g. plain flour (4 oz.)
    (light weight)
45 g. cornflour (1½ oz.)
grated rind of 2 lemons
For the Filling:
60 g. castor sugar (2 oz.)
2 eggs

170 g. butter (6 oz.)
grated rind of 1½ lemons
juice of ½ lemon
To finish:
1 kg. (2 lbs.) Fondant Icing, approx.
    (see page 346) coloured yellow,
    to which has been added the
    juice of a lemon and grated rind
    of ½ lemon
slices of crystallised lemon

Method: Put the sugar and vanilla sugar into a bowl. Separate the eggs and work the yolks with the sugar until light in colour. Add the grated lemon rind. Whisk the egg whites stiffly. Fold them into the mixture, alternately with the sifted flours, being careful not to overfold.

Grease a 22 cm. (8 inch) cake tin. Line the bottom with a disc of greased paper. Pour in the mixture and bake in a very moderate oven, gas mark 4 or 350° F. (180° C.) for 40–45 minutes. Turn out on a wire rack to cool.

Make the filling – whisk the eggs and sugar together over a pan of hot water until they are thick and fluffy. Remove and beat in the softened butter. (It should not be hotter than the egg mixture.) Add the grated rind and the lemon juice. Continue to whisk until cool.

Cut the cake twice transversely and fill with the cream mixture. Reform and ice with the lemon fondant. Decorate with the slices of crystallised lemon, overlapping round the edge of the cake.

Comment: This cake is equally nice filled with citron, i.e. lemon curd.

CŒUR AUX FRAISES ***

Ingredients:
Pâte à Génoise Commune made
   with 3 eggs, etc. (see page 333)
grated rind of 1 lemon
For Decoration:
¼ l. thick cream (½ pint)

250 g. small strawberries or
   fraisese ds bois (½ lb.)
150 g. icing sugar (5 oz.)
1 dl. kirsch (½–¾ gill)
a few strawberry leaves
redcurrant jelly for glaze

Method: Make up the pâte à Génoise commune in the usual way, adding the grated rind of the lemon. Pour it into a greased and floured heart shaped tin and cook it in a moderate oven, gas mark 4–5 or 350–375° F. (180–190° C.) for 30–35 minutes or until it begins to shrink from the sides of the tin and is firm to touch. Turn it out on a wire rack to cool completely.

Whilst this is taking place, carefully hull the strawberries. Put them in a bowl and sprinkle them with kirsch.

Sieve the icing sugar into a bowl and moisten it with sufficient kirsch to make a stiff paste. When the cake is quite cold spread the icing all over the top.

Arrange the strawberries in the centre. Pour off any kirsch left from the strawberries and add it to the redcurrant glaze. Melt this down to a running consistency and brush the strawberries over, taking care not to drip any glaze on the icing.

Whisk the cream until it will hold its shape. Using a forcing bag with a large rosette pipe, outline the heart shape edge of the cake with stars of whipped cream. Arrange fresh, small strawberry leaves round the edge of the dish and decorate each leaf with a tiny star of cream.

FROMAGE DE BRIE **

Ingredients:
Pâte à Génoise Commune made
   with 3 eggs, etc. (see page 333)
Crème au Beurre Mousseline au
   Kirsch (see page 343)

To finish:
granulated sugar
green colouring
icing sugar

Method: Make the pâte à Génoise commune as usual. Pour it into a greased 22 cm. (8 inch) sandwich cake tin and bake in a moderate oven, gas mark 4–5 or 350–375° F. (180–190° C.) for 30–35 minutes or until the cake is firm to the touch and begins to shrink from the sides of the tin. Remove from the tin and place on a wire rack to cool.

When the cake is cold, split it across transversely and sandwich it together with a thick layer of crème au beurre mousseline.

Colour a little granulated sugar with a greeny-blue colouring and sprinkle it lightly over the cake. Dust thickly with icing sugar and sprinkle a little more green sugar on the top. With the back of a knife, make lines to represent the straw markings of a Brie cheese. Allow to harden in the refrigerator or a cold place before serving. (*See Plate 23.*)

Comment: This cake should be well flavoured with kirsch, allowing 2–3 tablespoons.

GÂTEAU ABOUKIR ***

Ingredients:
Pâte à Génoise Fine (see page 333)
For the Filling:
120 g. purée de marrons glacées
  (4 oz.)
1½ dl. thick cream (1 gill)

To finish:
coffee flavoured Fondant Icing
  (see page 347)
sieved apricot jam for glaze
30 g. finely chopped pistachio
  nuts (1 oz.)

Method: Make the pâte à Génoise fine in the usual way. Pour it into a well greased 15 cm. (6 inch) moule à charlotte or cake tin. Bake in a moderate oven, gas mark 4 or 350° F. (180° C.) for 35–40 minutes or until it is firm to touch and shrinks from the sides of the tin. Turn it out on a wire rack to cool.

    When the gâteau is cold, split in transversely into four or five slices. Whisk the cream lightly and fold in the purée de marrons. Fill the cake with this, being careful to re-form it neatly. Brush the gâteau all over with hot apricot glaze. Pour the fondant over the gâteau to cover the top and the sides. Finish with a circle of finely chopped pistachio nuts round the top edge.

GÂTEAU ALEXANDRA **

Ingredients:
135 g. castor sugar (4½ oz.)
90 g. cornflour (3 oz.)
45 g. plain flour (1½ oz.)
75 g. ground almonds (2½ oz.)
75 g. butter (2½ oz.)

105 g. plain chocolate (3½ oz.)
4 eggs
To finish:
sieved apricot jam for glaze
chocolate Fondant Icing (see
  page 346)

Method: Separate three eggs. Put the almonds, sugar, the whole egg and 3 yolks into a bowl and work very well with a wooden spoon or spatula Melt the butter and put it aside to cool. Soften the chocolate in a bowl over a pan of hot water. Add the chocolate to the eggs and sugar, etc. and work again. Sift both flours together and whisk the whites stiffly. Fold in the whites, flours and melted butter alternately, as lightly and speedily as possible. Pour into a shallow 18 cm. (7 inch) square tin which has been greased and floured. Bake in a moderate oven, gas mark 4 or 350° F. (180° C.) for 40 minutes. Remove and place on a wire rack to cool.

When the cake is cold, brush it all over with hot apricot glaze and coat it with chocolate fondant icing. Leave to set.

Comment: This cake should have no decoration but be served perfectly plain.

GÂTEAUÀ L'ANANAS TOURANGELLE ***

Ingredients:
Biscuit Fin made with 3 eggs, etc. (see page 331)
1 good wine glass of kirsch

To finish:
Pâte à Meringue Suisse made with 2 whites of egg (see page 334)
apricot glaze made from sieved apricot jam
glacé pineapple
angelica

Method: Make the biscuit fin as usual. Pour it into a well greased oval sandwich tin and bake it in a very moderate oven, gas mark 4 or 350° F. (175° C.) until it is firm to touch and begins to shrink from the sides of the tin. Remove from the tin and place it on a wire rack. Sprinkle over the kirsch so that it soaks well into the cake.

Make the pâte à meringue Suisse and using a forcing bag with a plain ½ cm. (¼ inch) tube, pipe a design to resemble a pineapple in the centre of the cake. It should be composed of a series of rounded peaks. Leave a margin of about 1 cm. (½ inch) round the top of the cake. Dust lightly with castor sugar. Place in the top of a fairly hot oven, gas mark 6 or 400° F. (200° C.) to set and lightly brown the meringue.

Paint the meringue design and the whole surface of the cake with the hot glaze. Arrange a few neat pieces of pineapple round the margin and glaze these also. Cut thick leaves from angelica and simulate leaves at the base and top of the pineapple. Brush these also with the glaze. (*See Plate 26.*)

GÂTEAU D'AUTOMNE DE SARLAT ***

Ingredients:
Pâte à Génoise Commune made with 4 eggs, etc. (see page 333)
Crème au Beurre Mousseline made with 2 yolks of egg, etc., (see page 342)
3–4 tablespoons strong caramel to flavour

To finish:
9–10 meringues made in mushroom shapes and dusted very lightly with cocoa (see page 334)
glacé cherries
strips of angelica
crushed meringue

Method: Make up the pâte à Génoise commune as usual. Pour it into a 18 cm. (7 inch) moule à manqué or deep sandwich tin and bake it in a moderate oven, gas mark 4–5 or 350–375° F. (180–190° C.) until golden brown and firm to the touch. Turn it out on a wire rack to cool.

Make up the crème au beurre mousseline in the usual way and put about a quarter of it aside. Add the caramel to the remainder and beat well.

When the cake is quite cool, split it in half transversely and sandwich it together with a good layer of crème au beurre. Spread the rest of the flavoured crème au beurre round the sides and over the top. Crush and sieve the meringue shells and coat the sides of the gâteau with the fine crumbs. Arrange three of the mushroom shaped meringues in the centre. Put the plain crème au beurre in a forcing bag with a large rosette pipe. Arrange the remaining small mushroom meringues round the top edge of the gâteau. Pipe stars of crème au beurre in between each and decorate each star with a halved glacé cherry. Round the mushrooms in the centre pipe a mass of smaller stars of crème au beurre with a spike of angelica on each to represent grass. (*See Plate 32.*)

GÂTEAU AU CHOCOLAT SAINT PHILIPPE DU ROULE
***

Ingredients:
Biscuit Fin made with 3 eggs, etc.
 (see page 331)
Crème au Beurre au Chocolat
 made with 2 yolks of egg, etc.
 (see page 341)

To finish:
75 g. plain chocolate (2–3 oz.)
chocolate vermicelli
mimosa balls

Method: Make the biscuit fin in the usual way. Pour the mixture into a greased 18 cm. (7 inch) moule à manqué or deep sandwich tin and cook in a moderately cool oven, gas mark 4 or 350° F. (180° C.) for about 30–35 minutes. When the cake is done it will begin to shrink from the sides of the tin. Turn on to a wire rack to cool. Make up the crème au beurre in the usual way.

Whilst the cake is cooling, make the chocolate medallions. Using a small boat shaped tartlet tin as a guide, trace out on greaseproof paper about 30–40 outlines. Break up the chocolate and put into a basin and stand it in a pan of boiling water to melt. When it has fully melted spread the chocolate thinly and evenly on the traced outlines. Put them aside in a cool place to harden.

When the cake is cool, cut in half transversely and spread with a layer of crème au beurre au chocolate. Sandwich together. Spread the sides and the top of the cake in crème au beurre. Coat half way up the cake with the chocolate vermicelli. Peel the chocolate medallions off the paper and insert them at an angle on the top of the cake to represent a marguerite daisy. Fill the centre with a little crème au beurre and cover with crystallised mimosa balls. (*See Plate 30.*)

GÂTEAU CORNEVILLE ***

Ingredients:

Pâte à Génoise Commune, made with 4 eggs, etc. (see page 333)
Crème au Beurre Mousseline made with 2 yolks of egg, etc. (see page 342)
Pâte à Cornets made with:
  1 white of egg
  2 tablespoons ground almonds

2 tablespoons softened butter
2 dessertspoons plain flour
2 teaspoons vanilla sugar
2 tablespoons castor sugar
white Fondant Icing (see page 346)
carmine and pistachio colouring
strawberry and pistachio flavouring
vanilla flavouring

Method: Make up the pâte à Génoise as usual. Pour it into a greased 18 cm. (7 inch) moule à manqué or deep sandwich tin and bake in a moderate oven, gas mark 4–5 or 350–375° F. (180–190° C.) for approximately 40 minutes. Remove and turn out on a wire rack to cool.

Whilst it is cooking make up the crème au beurre mousseline and divide it into three. Colour one-third with pink and flavour with strawberry. Colour the second third a pale green and flavour it with pistachio and flavour the remainder with vanilla.

Make up the pâte à Cornets as follows. Put the egg white in a bowl and add the sugar and the vanilla sugar. Beat vigorously for 1–2 minutes with a fork. Then add the ground almonds, softened butter and sifted flour. Mix all well and thoroughly. Form into small flat rounds of equal size on a lightly greased baking sheet – they should be approximately 6–7½ cm. (2½–3 inches) in diameter. Bake in a moderately hot oven, gas mark 6–7 or 400–425° F. (200–220° C.) for 4–5 minutes. Do not overcook them. Remove them and whilst they are still warm, roll them into cornet shapes. Place in small cornet moulds until they are cold and crisp.

When the cake is quite cool, cut it in half transversely and fill it with the vanilla flavoured crème au beurre mousseline. Place it on a wire rack and pour over sufficient white fondant to coat it completely and evenly.

Using a forcing bag with a rosette pipe, fill the cornets with the pink and green crème au beurre. There should be about 13 cornets, making 6 green and 7 pink. Place a pink one standing up in the centre and arrange the others in alternate colours radiating from the centre one.

At the base of the gâteau arrange the remaining cornets, with alternate fillings of pink and green.

GÂTEAU CRÉOLE **

Ingredients:

Pâte à Biscuit de Savoie made with 4 eggs, etc. (see page 332)
Crème Pâtissière made with 3 dl. milk (½ pint), etc. (see page 344)
2 tablespoons rum

3–4 bananas
1½ dl. thick cream (1 gill)
2 tablespoons chopped browned almonds
4 tablespoons sieved apricot jam for glaze

Method: Make up the pâte à biscuit de Savoie as usual and pour it into a 18 cm. (7 inch) moule à manqué or deep sandwich tin. Bake it in a moderate oven, gas mark 4 or 350° F. (180° C.) for 45–50 minutes. When it is cooked, remove it and place it on a wire rack to cool. Sprinkle it copiously with the rum.

Make up the crème pâtissière as usual. Allow it to cool. Place the gâteau on a serving dish. Cover with a thick layer of crème pâtissière. Cut the bananas into 1 cm. (½ inch) slices. Lay these all over the crème pâtissière. Cover with apricot glaze. Whisk the cream fairly stiffly and mask the bananas with this. Sprinkle over the browned nuts.

GÂTEAU CUBAIN ***

Ingredients:

Pâte à Génoise Commune (see page 333)
Crème au Beurre Mousseline au Chocolat (see page 343)

60 g. browned almonds passed through a nut mill (2 oz.)
½ quantity Pâte d'Amandes, Method I (see page 329)

Method: Make up the pâte à Génoise commune as usual. Pour it into a greased 18 cm. (7 inch) moule à manqué or deep sandwich tin and bake in a moderate oven, gas mark 4–5 or 350–375° F. (180–190° C.) for approximately 40 minutes. Remove and place it on a wire rack to cool.

Make up the crème au beurre mousseline au chocolat, adding the powdered browned almonds.

When the cake is cool, cut it in half transversely and fill it with crème au beurre au chocolat. Re-form it and spread a thin layer of the crème au beurre all over the top and sides. Put it in a refrigerator or cool place to allow the crème au beurre to harden.

Roll out the pâte d'amandes. Cut out about 4 large rose leaves and about 12 smaller ones. Cut out also about 24 small circles, approximately one-third of an inch in diameter. With the remainder of the pâte d' amandes make a rose. Finally decorate the gâteau as follows:

Place the rose in the centre and place 4 large and 4 smaller leaves round the rose. Place the 24 small circles round the edge of the cake. Arrange the remaining leaves vertically round the sides of the cake.

Comment: The pâte d'amandes must not be coloured but left natural.

GÂTEAU DAMIER ***

Ingredients:

Pâte à Génoise Commune made with 4 eggs, etc. (see page 333)

45 g. browned, powdered hazelnuts (1½ oz.)

Crème au Beurre Mousseline made with 2 yolks of egg, etc. (see page 342)

60 g. praline, powdered (2 oz.)

chocolate flavoured Fondant Icing (see page 346)

white vanilla flavoured Fondant Icing (see page 346)

sieved apricot jam for glaze

Glace Royale Icing (see page 345)

browned flaked almonds

Method: Make the pâte à Génoise commune in the usual way, adding the powdered nuts with the flour. Bake it in a 18 cm. (7 inch) moule carré or square cake tin. When it is cooked, turn it out on a wire rack to cool.

Make the crème au beurre mousseline. Take two-thirds and mix it with the powdered praline. Reserve the rest for piping.

When the cake is cool, cut it transversely and fill it with the praline flavoured crème au beurre. Reform the gâteau. Brush the top and sides with a thin even coat of hot apricot glaze. Coat the sides only with flaked almonds.

Using the royal icing and a fine writing tube, pipe lines parallel to the sides of the cake to make six squares in each direction and thirty-six squares in all.

Warm the fondant gently. Fill the chocolate fondant into a forcing bag and pipe it carefully into every alternate square, so that it finds its own level and becomes smooth. In a similar way fill the remaining squares with the white fondant.

The cake now has the appearance of a chessboard.

With the remaining crème au beurre and a rose tube, pipe a shell border round the edge of the cake.

GÂTEAU FAIDHERBE ***

Ingredients:

Pâte à Génoise Commune made with 3 eggs, etc. (see page 333)

For the Filling:

Crème au Beurre Mousseline au Rhum, made with 2 yolks of egg, etc. (see page 343)

To finish:

triangular-shaped pieces of glacé or tinned pineapple

halved glacé cherries and green glacé cherries OR rounds of angelica the same size as the red cherries

a little Chocolate Fondant Icing (see page 346)

very finely chopped nuts

7 halved almonds

Method: Make up the pâte à Génoise commune as usual. Pour it into a greased moule à manqué, 18 cm. (7 inch), or deep sandwich tin. Bake it in a moderate oven, gas mark 4–5 or 350–375° F. (180–190° C.) for about 30–35 minutes or until the cake is firm to touch and begins to shrink from the sides of the tin. Remove from the tin and place it on a wire rack to cool.

Make up the crème au beurre as usual, adding 2–3 tablespoons of rum. When the cake is cool, cut it into half transversely. Allow it to get quite cold, then sandwich it together with about half the crème au beurre. Spread the rest of the crème au beurre fairly thinly round the sides and fairly thickly over the top. Smooth over with a palette knife to make the surface perfectly even. Coat the sides of the cake with chopped nuts, which have been put through a nut mill to make them very fine. The nuts should come only half way up the sides.

For the decoration – Place a red glacé cherry in the centre of the cake, and around it arrange the 7 split almonds to represent the petals of a flower. Cut each halved green glacé cherry in half again, put one of these quarters at the tip of each almond. Arrange 7 triangles of pineapple equally round the edge of the cake, in between each put a halved red cherry. Using a fine pipe, pipe two lines of chocolate fondant from the flower to each pineapple triangle. (*See Plate 31.*)

GÂTEAU FRAGARIA ***

Ingredients:

Pâte à Génoise Commune made with 3 eggs, etc. (see page 333)
Pâte d'Amandes (Method I) made with 120 g. ground almonds (4 oz.) (see page 329)

360 g. strawberry jam, flavoured with 2–3 tablespoons kirsch (¾ lb.)
100 g. chopped browned almonds (3 oz.)
icing sugar

Method: Make up the pâte à Génoise commune as usual. Pour it into a greased 15 cm. (6 inch) moule à manqué or deep sandwich tin and bake it in a moderate oven, gas mark 4–5 or 350–375° F. (180–190° C.) for 30–35 minutes. Remove and place it on a wire rack to cool.

Roll out the pâte d'amandes and cut it to make a circle, approximately 5 cm. (2 inches) smaller in diameter than the top of the cake.

When the cake is quite cool, cut it across into three and spread with the kirsch flavoured jam. Sandwich the cake together and brush it all over with the jam.

Coat the cake with the browned almonds, leaving the centre clear to receive the circle of pâte d'amandes. Dust the pâte d'amandes thickly with icing sugar and place it in the centre of the cake. Heat a skewer until it is red hot and caramelise a lattice design on the icing sugar. (*See Plate 24.*)

GÂTEAU FRASCATI **

Ingredients:
Pâte à Génoise Commune made
  with:
  2 eggs
  60 g. castor sugar (2 oz.)
  60 g. plain flour (2 oz.)
  30 g. unsalted butter (1 oz.)
  1 tablespoon moist brown sugar

1 tablespoon honey
To finish:
pale pink Fondant Icing (see
  page 346) flavoured with kirsch
  or Grand Marnier
glacé fruits
pistachio nuts
angelica

Method: Make up the pâte à Génoise commune in the usual way, but add the honey and the brown sugar to the castor sugar and whisk them over heat. Pour the mixture into a greased 18 cm. (7 inch) ring and bake in a moderate oven, gas mark 4 or 350° F. (180° C.) for 25–30 minutes. Turn it out carefully on to a wire rack to cool completely.

Pour the fondant icing over the cake. Decorate with glacé fruits, making leaves with angelica. Arrange halved pistachio nuts in between the fruits.

GÂTEAU GIGI ***

Ingredients:
Pâte à Génoise Commune made
  with:
  6 eggs
  195 g. castor sugar (6½ oz.)
  180 g. plain flour (6 oz.)
  60 g. butter (2 oz.)
  1½ teaspoons vanilla sugar
For the Filling:
Crème au Beurre (see page 341)
1–2 tablespoons Grand Marnier
a little grated orange rind

For the Decoration:
Pâte à Choux (see page 336)
beaten egg
¼ l. thick cream (½ pint)
orange coloured Fondant Icing
  (see page 346)
  flavoured with Grand Marnier
crystallised violets
pistachio nuts
sieved apricot jam for glaze
crushed meringue shells

Method: Make up the pâte à Génoise as usual (see page 333 for method). Pour it into a prepared 25 cm. (10 inch) moule à manqué and bake at gas mark 4–5 or 350–375° F. (180–190° C.) for approximately one hour or until it is firm to the touch and golden brown. Turn it out on a wire rack to cool.

Whilst it is cooking, make up the pâte à choux and using a forcing bag and 2 cm. (¾ inch) tube, pipe it into small choux. Brush over with beaten egg and bake it in a hot oven, gas mark 7–8 or 425–450° F. (220–230°C.) for the first 10 minutes, then for a further 20–25 minutes at gas mark 5 or 375° F. (190° C.). Remove and place on a wire rack to cool.

Make up the crème au beurre, flavouring it with the grated orange rind and Grand Marnier.

When the cake is cool, cut it across twice and fill with half the crème au beurre. Fill the choux balls with the rest. Brush the side of the cake with hot apricot glaze and coat with meringue crumbs. Dip each choux ball into the fondant and arrange them decoratively on the top of the cake. Whip the cream lightly. Fill it into a forcing bag with a rosette tube and pipe stars of cream in between the choux balls. Dust the choux balls with finely chopped pistachio nuts and scatter crystallised violets over the cream.

GÂTEAU GRANDE ARMÉE ***

Ingredients:
Pâte à Génoise Commune made with 3 eggs, etc. (see page 333)
Crème au Beurre Mousseline au Kirsch (see page 343)

To finish:
½ quantity Pâte d'Amandes, coloured pink (see page 329)
a little chocolate Fondant Icing (see page 346)
sieved apricot jam for glaze

Method: Make up the pâte à Génoise in the usual way. Pour it into a greased 18 cm. (7 inch) moule à manqué or deep sandwich tin and bake in a moderate oven, gas mark 4–5 or 350–375° F. (180–190° C.) for about ½ hour or until it is firm to touch and begins to shrink from the sides of the tin. Turn it out on a wire rack to cool.

Make up the crème au beurre as usual and flavour it with kirsch. Make up the pâte d'amandes and colour it a delicate shade of pink.

When the cake is cold, cut it in half crosswise. Fill with a generous layer of crème au beurre mousseline, then brush it all over with hot apricot glaze.

Roll out the pâte d'amandes to a large circle and lay it on top of the gâteau. Smooth the top and mould it round the sides to give a perfectly smooth surface.

Using a forcing bag with a fine writing tube, pipe a lattice on two-thirds of the top of the cake, leaving one-third plain. (*See Plate 29.*)

Comment: This gâteau is a speciality of the Avenue Grand Armée in Paris

GÂTEAU ÎLE DE FRANCE **

Ingredients:
Biscuit de Savoie made with 4 eggs, etc. (see page 332)
For the Filling:
1 dl. rum or kirsch (¾ gill)
250 g. apricot jam (½ lb.)
90 g. finely chopped almonds (3 oz.)

120 g. chopped candied peel (4 oz.)
60 g. sultanas (2 oz.)
To finish:
¼ l. thick cream (½ pint)
glacé cherries
angelica
sultanas

373

Method: Make the biscuit de Savoie in the usual way. Separate the eggs and cream the yolks, sugar and vanilla sugar together until light and creamy. Whisk the whites stiffly and fold them in lightly and alternately with the sifted flour. Pour the mixture into an 15 cm. (6 inch) greased charlotte tin. Bake it in a moderately cool oven, gas mark 4 or 350° F. (180° C.) for 40–45 minutes. Unmould on to a wire rack to cool.

Macerate the candied peel and sultanas in 2 tablespoons of rum for one hour. At the end of this time, mix with the apricot jam and the chopped almonds.

Cut the cake into three slices transversely. Sprinkle each slice with the rest of the rum, then spread the bottom two copiously with the fruit, nuts and jam. Reform the cake and place it on a serving dish.

Whisk the cream until it is thick. Spread it all over the sides and the top of the cake and with a forcing bag and rose tube, pipe stars all over the top. Decorate the sides with sultanas, glacé cherries and angelica. Serve very cold from a refrigerator.

Comment: If desired, a crème Anglaise au Rhum may be poured round the cake before serving.

GÂTEAU MONTMORENCY ***

Ingredients:

105 g. castor sugar (3½ oz.)
30 g. ground almonds (1 oz.)
105 g. plain flour (3½ oz.)
2 tablespoons kirsch
4 yolks of egg
3 whites of egg
60 g. melted butter (2 oz.)
For the Filling:
500 g. cherries (1 lb.)

3 dl. red wine (½ pint)
90 g. castor sugar (3 oz.)
1 vanilla pod
135 g. unsalted butter (4½ oz.)
1 tablespoon kirsch
Meringue mixture:
4 whites of egg
270 g. castor sugar (9 oz.)
To finish:
chopped browned almonds

Method: Put 3 egg yolks into a basin with the sugar and work together with a wooden spoon or spatula for 5 minutes. Then add the ground almonds. Beat well and add the remaining yolk. Whisk the egg whites very stiffly and fold into the mixture as lightly as possible, together with the sieved flour. Lastly add the melted butter, which must be running, but not hot. Flavour with the kirsch. Pour into a greased 18 cm. (7 inch) moule à manqué or deep sandwich tin and cook in a very moderate oven, gas mark 4 or 350° F. (180° C.) for 35–40 minutes. Turn it on to a wire rack and allow to become quite cold, leaving it for at least 4–5 hours.

Stone the cherries and poach them in a syrup made of the red wine, sugar and vanilla pod. When they are cooked remove and drain on a clean cloth.

Cream the unsalted butter in a fairly large bowl. Make the meringue by beating the egg whites with the sugar over a pan of boiling water until the mixture stands up in peaks from the end of the whisk. Remove from the heat and continue to whisk until it is quite cold. Divide the mixture and pour half on to the creamed butter and beat vigorously (if it shows signs of curdling, stand the bowl over hot water for a moment). Flavour with kirsch and stir in half the cherries coarsely chopped.

Cut the cake across in three and spread each slice with the cherry cream mixture. Re-form and spread part of the plain meringue mixture over the entire surface, top and sides. Sprinkle with finely chopped browned almonds. Put the remaining meringue mixture into a forcing bag with a small ½ cm. (¼ inch) plain pipe and pipe a lattice design on the top of the cake. Into each lattice place a cherry and mass the rest of the cherries in a group in the centre. Put the cake into a moderately hot oven, gas mark 6 or 400° F. (200° C.) for 3 minutes to dry the meringue. Do not let it stay long enough to melt the cream filling.

Comment: It is easier to cut the cake into slices when it has been made the previous day and allowed to cool overnight. The flavour of this cake is dependent on the addition of the kirsch. If this is not available, another suitably flavoured liqueur should be substituted.

GÂTEAU MORTAIN ***

Ingredients:
Pâte à Génoise Commune made
  with 4 eggs, etc. (see page 333)
For the Filling:
Crème au Beurre (see page 341)
60 g. glacé pineapple (2 oz.)
2 tablespoons kirsch

To finish:
White Fondant Icing flavoured
  with kirsch (see page 346)
finely chopped browned nuts and
  crushed meringue shells
glacé cherries
angelica
pineapple jam sieved for glaze
melted redcurrant jelly

Method: Make up the pâte à Génoise in the usual way. Pour it into a greased 18 cm. (7 inch) moule à manqué or deep sandwich tin and bake in a moderate oven, gas mark 5 or 375° F. (190° C.) for 40–45 minutes. When cooked, remove and place it on a wire rack to cool.

Chop the pineapple fairly finely and macerate it in the kirsch.

Make up the crème au beurre as usual. Stir in the pineapple together with any of the liqueur which it may not have absorbed.

When the cake is cold, cut it across twice and fill it with a thick layer of the crème au beurre. Sandwich together carefully. Brush the sides of the cake with the hot pineapple glaze. Coat the sides in the nuts and meringue crumbs. Ice the top of the cake with white fondant icing. Arrange large boat shaped pieces of angelica round the edge with clusters of cherries in between each. Allow the fondant to get quite hard. Coat with a heavy glaze of pineapple. Heat the redcurrant jelly until it will run smoothly. Cool slightly, fill it into a greaseproof paper piping bag and cut the tip off to make a fine hole. Pipe 3 or 4 concentric circles of redcurrant jelly on the top of the glaze. Using the point of a sharp knife, or a hat pin, draw straight lines from the outside circle to the centre, making them about 5 cm. (2 inches) apart. Then draw similar lines from the centre to the outside, thus making a feather design. Care must be taken not to damage the fondant icing.

GÂTEAU NAPOLITAIN ***

Ingredients:

240 g. plain flour (8 oz.)
150 g. ground almonds (5 oz.)
150 g. butter (5 oz.)
150 g. castor sugar (5 oz.)
2 small eggs

pinch of salt
zest of 1 lemon or 1 orange
To finish:
apricot glaze
¼ l. Crème Chantilly (½ pint)
glacé fruits

Method: Mix the ground almonds and the sugar well together. Add one egg and work to a paste. Sift the flour on to a board, make a well in the centre, place the almond paste in this with the butter, the second egg, the salt and the grated lemon rind. Mix with the fingers and knead well until a smooth firm pâte is obtained. Leave in a cool place to relax.

Roll out the pastry on a floured board to a thickness of about ½ cm. (¼ inch). Cut eight 15 cm. (6 inch) circles, lift them on to greased baking sheets, and using a 10 cm. (4 inch) cutter remove the centre from each circle. Gather the trimmings together with the centres which have been removed and roll out as before. Cut two 18 cm. (7 inch) circles. Lift these on to a greased baking sheet. Prick all the pastry equally well. Bake in a hot oven, gas mark 7 or 425° F. (220° C.) for 7–8 minutes or until just golden. Remove the pastry carefully and cool on wire racks.

When they are cool, take one of the larger circles, brush it over with hot apricot glaze and built the rings one on top of the other, using apricot glaze to hold them together.

Whisk the cream with the vanilla sugar for the Crème Chantilly and fill the centre of the gâteau with this. Cover with the remaining circle. Brush all over the cake with apricot glaze and decorate with glacé fruits.

GÂTEAU NOISETIER ***

Ingredients:
Biscuit aux Noisettes:
135 g. castor sugar (4½ oz.)
½ teaspoon vanilla sugar
135 g. plain flour (4½ oz.)
60 g. cornflour (2 oz.)
60 g. butter (2 oz.)
45 g. browned hazelnuts (1½ oz.)
5 eggs

Marzipan, Method I (see page 330)
   coloured green
21 whole browned hazelnuts
To finish:
sieved apricot jam for glaze
white Fondant Icing (see page 346)
   flavoured with kirsch OR
white glacé icing (see page 345)
   flavoured with kirsch

Method: Melt the butter and leave it to cool. Rub off the skins of the hazelnuts and pass them through a nut mill.

Separate four of the eggs. Cream the sugars with the yolks thoroughly until they are very thick and light in colour. Add the powdered nuts and the fifth egg lightly beaten. Mix well.

Whisk the four egg whites stiffly. Fold these into the mixture alternately with the sieved flours and the melted butter. Pour the mixture into an 18 cm. (7 inch) square cake tin which has been greased and floured. Bake in a moderate oven, gas mark 4 or 350° F. (180° C.) for 40 minutes or until well risen, firm and golden brown. Remove to a wire rack to cool.

While the cake is cooking, make the marzipan. Roll the paste out thinly to a narrow strip on a board dusted with icing sugar. With a pair of scissors, cut a series of pointed teeth along one edge. Roll small sections of these round each of the 21 nuts to give the appearance of calyx. If necessary stick with a little egg white.

Put these on a sheet of oiled paper. Cook in a cool oven, gas mark 3 or 325° F. (160° C.) for 5 minutes just to set the paste.

When the cake is cool, brush it all over with a thin layer of apricot glaze and coat it with the fondant or glacé icing. Leave it to set, then decorate with a cluster of four nuts at each corner and a cluster of five nuts in the centre.

GÂTEAU AUX NOIX ***

Ingredients:
60 g. browned hazel nuts, which
   have been passed through a nut
   mill (2 oz.)
60 g. ground almonds (2 oz.)
120 g. sugar (4 oz.)
5 yolks of egg
3 whites of egg
60 g. flour (2 oz.)

For the Filling:
3 tablespoons honey
30 g. chopped nuts (1 oz.)
To finish:
coffee Fondant Icing (see page 347)
chopped nuts
halved nuts dipped in caramel
   (see page 16)
sieved apricot jam for glaze or honey

Method: Put the ground almonds, the ground nuts, yolks and sugar into a bowl and work them well with a wooden spatula until thick and light in colour. Whisk the whites stiffly and fold them lightly into the mixture alternately with the sieved flour. Grease and dust with flour a 18 cm. (7 inch) moule à manqué, or deep sandwich tin. The bottom should have a piece of greaseproof paper cut to fit as the nuts tend to stick. Pour in the mixture and bake in a moderate oven, gas mark 4 or 350° F. (180° C.) for 40–45 minutes or until firm to the touch. Turn out on a wire rack to cool.

When the cake is cold, slice it across and sandwich the two halves together with honey and chopped nuts. Brush the sides with melted apricot glaze or thin honey. Coat with chopped nuts. Ice the top of the cake with the coffee fondant icing. Dip some halved nuts into caramel. Allow them to cool on an oiled slab, and arrange them in a decoration on the top of the cake while the fondant icing is still setting.

GÂTEAU NOUGATINE ***

Ingredients:
Pâte à Génoise Commune made
with 4 eggs, etc. (see page 333)
Crème au Beurre Mousseline au
Café (see page 343)

Pâte à Nougatine made with:
240 g. sugar (8 oz.)
120 g. finely chopped browned
almonds (4 oz.)
juice ½ lemon
Glace Royale or White Fondant
Icing (see page 345 or 346)

Method: Make the pâte à Génoise commune in the normal way and put it to cook in a greased 22 cm. (8 inch) moule à manqué in a moderate oven, gas mark 4 or 350° F. (180° C.) for 40–45 minutes. When it is firm to the touch and golden brown, turn it out on a wire rack to cool.

Meanwhile, make the crème au beurre and flavour it strongly with coffee.

Make the nougat. Take half and roll it out on an oiled slab to form a circle approximately the same size as the top of the cake. Trim the edges neatly to shape and cut it into eight segments. Repeat this with the other half of the nougat. Allow the segments to harden. When the trimmings have hardened, crush them lightly in a mortar.

Split the cake and fill it with a layer of crème au beurre. Reform the cake and coat it all over with some of the remaining crème au beurre. Coat the sides with crushed nougat.

Using the icing and a fine writing tube, make a decorative pattern on the segments of nougat. Arrange these on top of the cake, radiating from the centre with a star of crème au beurre to raise one edge of each in imitation of the blades of a windmill. (*See Plate 29.*)

GÂTEAU PASCAL ***

Ingredients:

Pâte à Génoise Commune made with 4 eggs, etc. (see page 333)
Crème au Beurre Praliné (see page 341)

browned flaked almonds
Royal Icing (see page 345)
half a chocolate Easter egg about 15 cm. (6 inches) long

Method: Make the pâte à Génoise in the usual way. Pour it into a 21 cm. (8½ inch) moule carré or square cake tin and bake it for 40–45 minutes in a moderately hot oven, gas mark 4 or 350° F. (180° C.). Turn it out on a wire rack to cool.

Meanwhile, make the crème au beurre praliné.

When the cake is cool, cut it into 2 or 3 slices transversely. Sandwich them together with the crème au beurre praliné and coat the whole cake evenly with the remainder. Cover the sides with the flaked browned almonds. Place the half Easter egg in the centre of the gâteau. Fill a forcing bag with royal icing and using a fine writing tube, write the word 'Pâques' on the egg. Decorate the top edge of the cake with a decorative border of royal icing.

As an alternative to the egg, the cake may be decorated with a red or green coloured ribbon made from pâte d'amandes (see page 329).

Another decoration can be made by using several small chocolate eggs and small chocolate chickens.

GÂTEAU PATRICIEN **

Ingredients:

135 g. ground almonds (4½ oz.)
3 whites of eggs
135 g. castor sugar (4½ oz.)
15 g. cornflour OR potato flour (½ oz.)

Crème au beurre mousseline made with 4 yolks of egg, etc. and flavoured with coffee or if preferred chocolate or powdered praline (see page 343)
To finish:
icing sugar

Method: Grease one large or two smaller baking sheets and using a cake tin or saucepan lid as a guide, trace out 2 circles approximately 24 cm. (9½ inches) in diameter.

Whisk the whites very stiffly indeed, then fold in the sugar, ground almonds and cornflour very carefully. Spread this mixture evenly and carefully in the marked circles on the baking sheets, so that it is a little over 2½ cm. (1 inch) thick. Bake in a cool oven, gas mark 2 or 300° F. (150° C.) for 30–35 minutes. Cool, then remove carefully and place on a wire rack to dry off thoroughly.

Sandwich the gâteau together with a copious layer of the crème au beurre mousseline and smooth this filling with a knife all round the side, so that it is a good 1½ cm. (½ inch) thick. Dust the top lightly with sifted icing sugar.

GÂTEAU PRALINE ***

Ingredients:

Pâte à Génoise Commune au Caramel made with:
4 eggs
135 g. castor sugar (4½ oz.)
120 g. plain flour (4 oz.)
1 teaspoon vanilla sugar

45 g. butter (1½ oz.)
½ quantity Crème au Beurre (see page 341)
Praline made with 120 g. sugar (4 oz.), etc. (see page 348)
Caramel coloured Fondant Icing (see page 346)

Method: Melt the butter for the pâte à Génoise and put it aside to cool. Take 45 g. (1½ oz.) of the sugar and dissolve it in a strong pan with a little water. Boil it over a good heat until it takes on a pale gold colour and becomes slightly caramelised. Pour it quickly on to an oiled tin and allow it to cool and harden. Then pound it finely using a pestle and mortar. Put it with the rest of the sugar and make the pâte à Génoise as usual (see page 333). Pour the mixture into a greased 22 cm. (8½ inch) moule à manqué or deep sandwich tin. Bake it in a moderate oven, gas mark 4 or 350° F. (180° C.) for approximately 40 minutes.

Make a light straw coloured praline. Make the crème au beurre, and beat in ¾ of the praline.

When the gâteau is cooked, turn it out on a wire rack to cool. When it is cold, cut it into three transversely and fill it with the crème au beurre. Reform the gâteau carefully. Pour the fondant over the cake and whilst it is still soft, sprinkle over the remaining praline.

GÂTEAU REINE POMARÉ ***

Ingredients:

Pâte à Génoise Commune made with 3 eggs, etc. (see page 333)
Créme au Beurre flavoured with praline (see page 341)

Chocolate Fondant Icing (see page 346)
To Decorate:
halved blanched almonds
pistachio nuts

Method: Make the pâte à Génoise commune in the usual way. Pour it into a greased and floured charlotte mould or a 15 cm. (6 inch) cake tin. Bake for 40–45 minutes in a moderate oven, gas mark 4–5 or 350–375° F. (180–190° C.). Remove the cake from the oven and turn it on to a wire rack to cool.

Make the crème au beurre and flavour it with pounded praline. When the cake is cold, cut it into five slices transversely and sandwich them to-gether with crème au beurre. Coat the whole cake with the chocolate flavoured fondant icing and decorate the top with the halved almonds and the pistachio nuts.

GÂTEAU THÉRÉSA ***

Ingredients:
Pâte Sucrée made with 225 g. (7½ oz.) plain flour, etc. (see page 339)
For the Filling:
125 g. ground almonds (4½ oz.)
160 g. castor sugar (5½ oz.) (light weight)

4 eggs
½ teaspoon vanilla sugar
To finish:
Pâte à Meringue Cuite made with 4 whites of egg, etc. (see page 335)
2 tablespoons redcurrant jelly

Method: Make up the pâte sucrée in the usual way and allow to relax. Roll it out and line into a 23 cm. (9 inch) flan ring. Prick the base well.

Make the filling by mixing the ground almonds, sugar and vanilla sugar. Add the eggs one at a time and mix well with a whisk to obtain a moist paste. Pour it into the prepared flan case. Bake in a moderate oven, gas mark 5–6 or 375–400° F. (190–200° C.) for 25–30 minutes. Remove the flan to a wire rack to cool.

Make the pâte à meringue cuite.

Coat the top of the flan with a thin layer of meringue mixture. Fill the remainder into a forcing bag with a small rose tube. Pipe an outline of oval shaped petals radiating from the centre, and a border. Put the flan into a hot oven, gas mark 7 or 425° F. (220° C.) for a few minutes to set the meringue. Melt the redcurrant jelly and fill the centre of each petal with a thin layer. (*See Plate 27.*)

GÂTEAU TONKIN **

Ingredients:
4 eggs
135 g. castor sugar (4½ oz.)
135 g. plain flour (4½ oz.)
60 g. butter (2 oz.)
60 g. ground almonds (2 oz.)
Crème au Beurre Mousseline Praliné (see page 343)

Orange coloured Fondant Icing (see page 346) flavoured with Grand Marnier or Curaçao
flaked or chopped browned almonds
dessicated coconut

Method: Grease and flour a 22 cm. (8½ inch) moule à manqué or deep sandwich tin. Put the eggs and sugar into a large bowl and place over a pan of hot water. Whisk until the mixture is light and fluffy. Remove it from the heat and continue to whisk until the mixture holds the impression of the whisk. Fold in the sieved flour and butter, which has been melted and cooled, and the ground almonds alternately. Pour into the prepared tin and bake in a moderate oven, gas mark 4 or 350° F. (180° C.) for 40 minutes or until firm to the touch and golden brown. Remove to a wire mesh to cool.

Make up the crème au beurre mousseline and flavour it with praline.

When the cake is cool, cut it in half transversely and sandwich it with crème au beurre. Spread the side of the cake with the remaining crème au beurre and coat it with the browned almonds. Coat the top of the cake with the fondant and sprinkle with a little coconut before it is quite set.

Index

INDEX